Illustrated WordPerfect 1.0 for the Macintosh

Jordan Gold

Wordware Publishing, Inc.

Library of Congress Cataloging-in-Publication Data

Gold, Jordan.
Illustrated WordPerfect 1.0 for the Macintosh.

Includes index.
1. WordPerfect (Computer program) 2. Macintosh (Computer)—Programming. 3. Word processing. I. Title.
Z52.5.W65G62 1989 652'.5 88-33977
ISBN 1-55622-105-3

1506 Capital Ave.
Plano, Texas 75074

Printed in the United States of America

ISBN 1-55622-105-3

10 9 8 7 6 5 4 3 2 1
8901

All inquiries for volume purchases of this book should be addressed to Wordware Publishing, Inc., at the above address. Telephone inquiries may be made by calling:

(214) 423-0090

Contents

Contents (Continued)

Recommended Learning Sequence

Preface

ABOUT WORDPERFECT FOR THE MACINTOSH WordPerfect for the Macintosh is the latest version of WordPerfect Corp.'s popular word processing software package. Versions of WordPerfect work with many different types and brands of computers. Finally, a version is available for Apple's popular Macintosh computer. WordPerfect for the Macintosh includes a variety of powerful features including integrated text and graphics; styles; automatic index, list, and table of contents generation; macros; keyboard mapping; timed backup; built-in spelling checker and thesaurus; word search; and much more.

WordPerfect for the Macintosh takes word processing to the level of desktop publishing software. It is useful for letters, reports, articles, and other text-based documents. Its integrated graphics and text capabilities make it a good choice for newsletter generation, books, magazines, technical documents and more.

ABOUT ILLUSTRATED BOOKS Like all books in the Illustrated Series, this book combines the features of an alphabetic reference guide with a step-by-step tutorial. By following the Recommended Learning Sequence, you proceed in a logical fashion from the most frequently used menu selections to those occasionally needed. Each menu selection is self-contained in a single module. Every module includes numbered operational steps illustrated with exact screen replicas. After using this book as a tutorial, you can refer to it later as a handy reference guide. Modules are arranged in alphabetical order for easy lookup.

Illustrated Macintosh WordPerfect 1.0 is packed with practical examples and hundreds of screens to clarify and illustrate word processing, from basic typing to final printout. Whether you are a writer, student, or business professional, this book can help you ease the writing process.

Module 1

ABOUT THIS BOOK

INTRODUCTION

Illustrated WordPerfect 1.0 for the Macintosh describes WordPerfect Corporation's WordPerfect word processing program for the Apple Macintosh computer. It describes how the program is used in the office and home and presents detailed information about the many WordPerfect word processing functions. To help you get started right away, each description is accompanied by illustrated, recipe-like examples to help you learn, as well as to provide instant reference information.

The book is designed to meet the needs of a broad range of users. It is for users who are considering buying a word processing system for the first time and want to investigate several before making the purchase. It is also for beginning users who already have access to WordPerfect and want to learn it from scratch. Intermediate and advanced users will find *Illustrated WordPerfect 1.0 for the Macintosh* a valuable quick reference that contains many examples of WordPerfect applications and commands. And finally, it is for the classroom instructor as an instructionally designed word processing textbook.

WordPerfect is sophisticated, yet easy to learn. You will find WordPerfect's power becomes apparent within an hour of practice. You will also find word processing with WordPerfect to be fun. It's easy to create a new document and then format, type, file, and print it.

To prove to yourself how easy WordPerfect is to use, you might want to jump over to Module 3 and read through the sample session. If you already have the program, run through the sample session on your Macintosh. You will create and file a document within a matter of minutes.

Module 3 is for you if you are an adventurous person who likes to dive in. Once you have experienced a straightforward word processing session, you will have the foundation necessary to tackle the heavy stuff with relative ease.

ORGANIZATION

This book is organized into small, easy-to-read modules. These modules provide descriptions, applications, and illustrations that show you how to use WordPerfect to solve practical word processing problems. Literally hundreds of examples are presented in the Description, Applications, and Typical Operation sections of the modules within this book.

These examples can be used as models for everyday word processing tasks of your own. The working examples, based on the work of FLG Office Supply, a fictional business in Carbondale, IL, let you experiment with WordPerfect commands. This takes the mystery out of what might otherwise be a technical obscurity. In addition to conducting "hands-on" experiments, you will probably find yourself having a lot of fun.

With the exception of Modules 1 through 3, the modules in this book contain information that pertains to specific WordPerfect commands or families of commands. For experienced users, the book's alphabetical sequence provides a fast reference to WordPerfect's many capabilities. For new users, however, we also provide a Recommended Learning Sequence so you can learn WordPerfect progressively, beginning with basic concepts and later working toward the more powerful commands.

NOTE

If you are new to the Macintosh and/or computers, we suggest you preview Module 10, Cursor Movement, and Module 37, Select, before beginning the learning sequence.

The recommended sequence for learning (or teaching) WordPerfect is at the front of this book. As you work your way through the book, check off the modules you have completed. The sequence is arranged in a logical progression, with foundation information provided first and then built upon. The learning sequence can be modified to fit classroom curriculum. If you are a teacher, you may wish to use the learning sequence as a curriculum design aid.

This first module provides information about the book and gives an overview of the kind of equipment required to operate WordPerfect.

Module 2 introduces you to WordPerfect. It provides an overview of WordPerfect functions, editing commands, and control keys. Module 2 makes an excellent quick reference resource for determining the purpose of specific commands.

Module 3 walks you through a sample WordPerfect session. You will not only discover how commands are used, but you can follow the sample session using your computer.

In addition to actually using some of the basic WordPerfect system commands, you will prepare and save a sample document. By the time you have completed Module 3, WordPerfect's power and ease of use will be apparent, because you will have demonstrated how WordPerfect is used to solve common word processing problems.

Modules 4 through 41 describe and illustrate WordPerfect commands. They are arranged in alphabetical order for easy reference. You may want to use the recommended learning sequence and corresponding checklist at the front of the book as a training aid.

Appendix A contains a table of terms and definitions. Most of the entries are intended to help you better understand WordPerfect, but some of the terms include common computer jargon that creeps into any computer reference book. Do not be alarmed if the terms and definitions are not immediately clear. They will become more understandable as you use the WordPerfect program with Modules 4 through 41. The important thing is that you know where to find the terms and definitions when you need them.

Appendix B shows you how to set up WordPerfect to better work with you. It shows you how to permanently change margins, tabs, and other commands. It also shows you how to make WordPerfect automatically back up your files.

Appendix C helps you better set up WordPerfect to work in color if you have a Macintosh with a color monitor.

Appendix D explains how to work with PC WordPerfect files. It shows you how to convert PC WordPerfect files to work with your version of WordPerfect. It discusses both WordPerfect 4.2 and 5.0 for MS-DOS computers and also shows you how to convert Macintosh WordPerfect files to work with PC WordPerfect.

Appendix E explains how to work with files from other Macintosh word processing software.

Appendix F discusses using an extended keyboard with WordPerfect.

Appendix G includes troubleshooting tips to help you get over certain difficulties when using WordPerfect.

Appendix H describes importing graphics files from other Macintosh software programs.

Appendix I describes the Speller Utility. It shows you how to customize the Speller (described in Module 38) for best use with your requirements.

Appendix J shows you how to insert into your document any character your font can produce.

Appendix K is an alphabetical listing of WordPerfect commands.

Appendix L contains WordPerfect exercises. It is provided for both classroom and self-teaching situations. If you are a classroom instructor, you may wish to include these exercises in student assignments. If you are learning WordPerfect on your own, the exercises are a good way to check yourself to see what you have learned about a system or word processing function. If you can answer the questions, you are ready to move to the next module in the learning sequence.

The index helps you locate key ideas in the book.

HARDWARE AND SOFTWARE REQUIREMENTS

WordPerfect operates on a Macintosh Plus or greater (i.e., Macintosh SE, Macintosh II, etc.) with two diskette drives. A hard disk is recommended to take full advantage of WordPerfect, and this book is written largely with the assumption a hard disk is being used.

WordPerfect works with any keyboard you can connect to your Macintosh, but to take advantage of its support for Function keys, it's recommended that you use a keyboard that includes function keys, such as the Apple Extended Keyboard. The Extended Keyboard is covered in Appendix F.

A printer is not required for learning most word processing functions, but it is needed to print your documents. WordPerfect works with any printer you can connect to your Macintosh.

Before getting started, you should have three WordPerfect diskettes. The System diskette includes the latest version of the System and Finder. The WordPerfect Program diskette includes the program and related files and help files. The Speller/Thesaurus diskette includes a spell checking dictionary and a thesaurus. You also need several blank double-sided diskettes to back up each of the WordPerfect diskettes. This lets you store the original WordPerfect (master) diskettes in a safe place.

You also need to format one or two blank diskettes for data. Format one of these for a data diskette to store your documents; the other is for use as a backup of your data diskette. The data diskette is used in disk drive B (the bottom drive on a Macintosh SE, the external drive on a Macintosh Plus or Macintosh II). The working diskette containing the WordPerfect programs (called the program disk) is used in disk drive A. If you are using a hard disk and one double-sided disk drive, format one diskette as a backup for the data on the hard disk. Always put program diskettes in drive A and data diskettes in drive B. The procedure for doing this is covered in Module 2.

WHAT YOU SHOULD KNOW

You should know the parts of your computer (see the user's manuals that are available for your computer) and be familiar with the Macintosh interface and menu structure. You should also be familiar with the Finder, Desktop, MultiFinder, and other Macintosh system files. You should also know how to format diskettes and how to copy, rename, and delete files. You should also be familiar with your computer keyboard, since WordPerfect uses every key on the keyboard.

Module 2

WORDPERFECT SYSTEM OVERVIEW

INTRODUCTION

This module offers information about word processors (what they are and what they can do for you) and provides an overview of the WordPerfect system, including the word processor, speller, and thesaurus programs. It also describes how to make working copies of WordPerfect and prepare your computer for using WordPerfect.

WORD PROCESSORS A word processor is a software package that turns your personal computer into a machine that will change or "process" words. A word processor like WordPerfect lets you create and format documents (whether they be correspondence, reports, or records) and then print the text on paper. WordPerfect also lets you revise a document by simply typing over text; altering the spacing and format of part of a page or an entire document; and moving, inserting, or deleting single characters or large blocks of text. You can also copy an entire document or parts of it from one file to another and then use WordPerfect to check the spelling or count the number of words.

If you are stumped for the right word in any situation, you can use the thesaurus included with WordPerfect. When you are through with a document, you can send and receive WordPerfect files to and from other computers over phone lines. Best of all, you can create, revise, and print a document at any time.

If you have an extended keyboard, WordPerfect Corp. will send you a template that lists WordPerfect functions and keys used. This template fits over the function keys at the top of the keyboard. Functions accessible through the Cmd key are colored red, while those using the Option key are colored blue. Functions accessible through the Shift key are colored green, and those using the function keys alone are colored black on the template. The function keys can perform as many as four functions; these can be accomplished by pressing the key alone, the key and the Shift key, the key and the Cmd key, or the key and the Option key. Thus, a total of 60 functions are accessible from the 15 function keys. These functions are listed in Appendix F.

WORDPERFECT SYSTEM DESCRIPTION

WordPerfect comes on three diskettes. The WordPerfect program diskette contains the word processing program, which is used to create, file, and print documents. The program diskette also contains a help file to guide you through the execution of the program, sample learning files that guide you through much of WordPerfect's functionality, and a number of utility files for macros, document conversion, and other tasks.

The Speller/Thesaurus diskette contains WordPerfect's 115,000-word speller/dictionary program and custom dictionaries. These are used to locate and help you correct misspelled words and typographical errors within a WordPerfect document. This diskette also includes the WordPerfect thesaurus, which helps you determine the best word to use in any situation.

The System diskette includes the latest version of the System and Finder. Use it if you are using a diskette-based system. If you are using a hard disk, make sure you have the latest version of the System and Finder in your System folder.

The following paragraphs introduce you to WordPerfect. This introduction helps you become familiar with the various functions of the program so you better understand the parts of the system for different word processing tasks.

MAIN FUNCTIONS As you load WordPerfect, the WordPerfect copyright logo appears and disappears on the screen. After that, your screen displays the Menu Bar at the top, the Title Bar just beneath it, the Scroll Bar on the side, and the Status Line at the bottom. All of these functions are described in Module 35. The rest of the screen is blank. All you need to do is decide if you want to create a new document or use an old one. If you want to create a new document, just start typing and save the document periodically as you create it, as described in Module 3. If you want to use an old document, open it either by using the mouse to select Open from the File menu or by pressing Cmd-O. You can also use the File Management menu to open a file, as described in Module 14.

The word *document* is a generic name for reports, correspondence, papers, and other prepared materials that rely chiefly on words and graphics to convey a message. You can file a document, change it, and prepare the final version using WordPerfect, just as you can manually or with a typewriter. The chief difference is that WordPerfect lets you change or "modify" the document and its format without having to retype it. Rather than typing, WordPerfect lets you print the document on a printer when you are ready. Also, WordPerfect is a great place for combining text and graphics in the same document.

When you create a new document, you must give that document a name. The filename can be no more than 31 characters, including spaces. A filename can be more than one word and any character can be used in the filename except a colon (:). It should be descriptive enough so that you know what the document is without having to look at it.

Filenames are represented in the Finder as icons. WordPerfect word processing documents look like this:

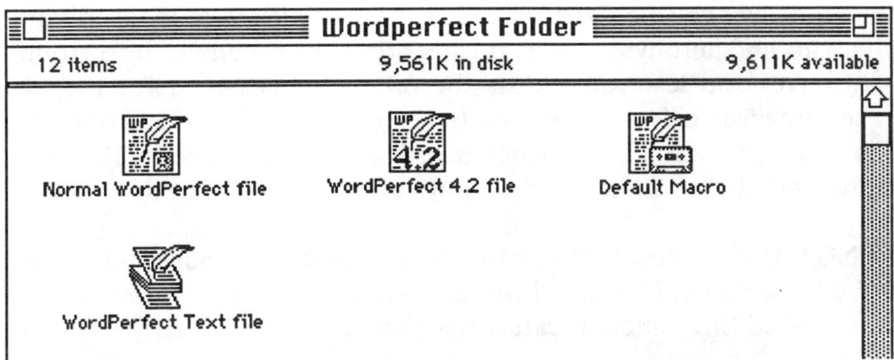

Either before, during, or after typing, WordPerfect lets you change the margins, tabs, and other formatting characteristics of a document. You can also choose the printer that you want to use, edit more than one document at at time, and copy graphics images from the Clipboard. All of these functions are described in later modules and appendixes.

TITLE BAR, STATUS LINE, AND SCROLL BAR The Title Bar tells you the filename and directory location of the file you are editing and whether you are editing document 1, 2, 3, 4, 5, or other document (as many documents as you want can be edited simultaneously). The Status Line tells you what page of the document and which line on that page the cursor is on. It is also a message area. The Scroll Bar provides a quick way to move through the document. You can drag on the scroll bar or click on the arrows to move the cursor through the document. These functions are described more fully in Module 35.

SPELL CHECKING A DOCUMENT Before you give a document to someone else to read, you can use WordPerfect's spell checking feature to make sure no embarrassing errors are in the document. Although the Speller contains 115,000 words, there will be times that WordPerfect will not recognize a word that is correctly spelled. In that case, you have the option of adding words to the supplemental dictionary at any time.

The Speller is accessed by selecting Spell from the Special menu or by pressing Cmd-E or Cmd-F2. WordPerfect compares each word in the specified dictionary with each word in your document. It notifies you of a misspelled word by highlighting that word in the text and giving you the option of replacing that word with one of its suggested correct spellings, typing a corrected spelling yourself, adding that word to the dictionary, or ignoring the word and going on to the next misspelled word.

Besides checking your spelling, WordPerfect also counts the number of words in your document, a very useful feature. The WordPerfect Spell Checker is described in Module 38.

THESAURUS WordPerfect includes a thesaurus to make sure you always have the right word in every sentence. This function is described in Module 41. Thesaurus functions are available by using the WordPerfect and Thesaurus diskettes and by selecting Thesaurus from the Special menu or by pressing Cmd-T or Cmd-F1. WordPerfect looks at your word and gives you synonyms and antonyms for it. It categorizes the synonyms into groups of nouns, verbs, and adjectives and lets you choose the proper replacement for the word in your document. The thesaurus offers a world of functionality at your fingertips. If you do not like a word, ask the thesaurus for a better one. If you do not like its initial choices, you can select more. The thesaurus can truly improve the quality of your writing.

EDITING FUNCTIONS WordPerfect offers a large number of powerful editing functions. Each is described in detail in Modules 4 through 41. The information provided below gives a brief overview of editing function categories that include:

- Standard Word Processing Functions
- Cursor/Mouse Positioning Functions
- Advanced Editing and Supporting Functions
- Advanced Functions
- Formatting and Printing Functions

Standard Word Processing Functions Standard word processing features include such functions as:

- Typeover
- Insert
- Delete
- Move
- Copy
- Search and Replace

Cursor Positioning Functions WordPerfect offers a wide variety of cursor positioning functions. Among them are:

- Arrow Up, Down, Right, and Left
- End of Screen, Page, and Document
- Top of Screen, Page, and Document
- Go to Specified Page Number
- Scroll Left and Right
- Mouse Positioning, Clicking, and Dragging

Advanced Editing and Positioning Functions WordPerfect offers a wide variety of editing and supporting functions. These include:

- Automatic Page Break, Page Numbering, and Repagination
- Automatic Alphanumeric and Text Underlining
- Decimal Tab
- Document Merge Functions
- Headers
- Footers
- On-line Help and Status Indicators

Advanced Functions There are a number of advanced functions, such as:

- Column Calculations (Horizontal and Vertical)
- Column Manipulations (Delete, Insert, and Move)
- Macros
- Automatic Generation of Indexes, Lists, and Tables of Contents
- Automatic Paragraph Numbering
- Outline Processing

Formatting and Printing Functions WordPerfect offers a number of formatting and printing options. Some of these are:

- Word and Letter Spacing
- Leading and Kerning
- Merge Print
- Variable Print Types
- Variable Print Pitch
- Support for a Wide Variety of Forms
- Print Preview

MODES OF OPERATION WordPerfect uses modes of operation to let you know what kind of activity or function is in progress. These modes are indicated on the Status Line at the bottom of the screen either in the Style Bar (P B U I O S S^1 S_1) or in the message space to the right of the Style Bar. For example, when characters are boldface, the "B" on the Style Bar is highlighted. When you have selected text either with the mouse or the Select command, a Select On message appears on the Status Line. This is described in more detail in Module 35.

WORDPERFECT LEARNING FOLDER The WordPerfect Learning folder includes sample exercises to help you get better acquainted with WordPerfect. This folder is included on the WordPerfect Program diskette. To use it, start WordPerfect and open a document in the Learn folder. Exercises using these documents are included in the Learn section in the WordPerfect manual.

WORDPERFECT INSTALLATION

You should prepare extra copies (called "working copies") of all WordPerfect diskettes. The WordPerfect diskettes can be found in the plastic pocket located in the WordPerfect user's manual. You will also need to format one or two blank diskettes (called data diskettes) for document storage. (If you are using a system with two diskette drives, format two diskettes. If you are using a hard disk, format one diskette.) Read "Using a Dual Floppy Disk System" or "Using a Hard Disk System" to learn how to format your diskettes.

If your Macintosh includes a hard disk and one or more diskette drives, it is appropriate to place the programs and data on the hard disk and to use the diskette drive to back up your hard drive, store documents, and perform other functions.

USING A DUAL FLOPPY DISK SYSTEM Label five blank diskettes as follows:

- WordPerfect System Diskette
- WordPerfect Program Diskette
- Speller/Thesaurus Diskette
- Data Diskette
- Backup Data Diskette

Complete the following steps:

1. Start your Macintosh. With the Desktop on the screen, put the original WordPerfect System diskette in drive A (internal drive in a Macintosh Plus, top diskette drive in a two-disk Macintosh SE) and the diskette you just labeled System Diskette in drive B (external drive in a Macintosh Plus, bottom drive in a two-disk Macintosh SE).
2. If the diskette has never been formatted, the following screen appears:

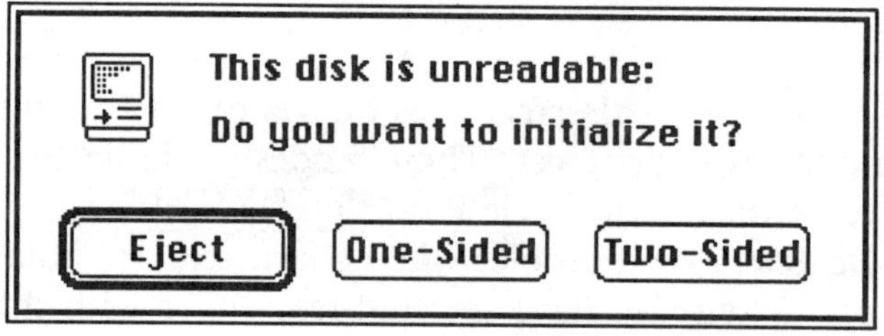

CAUTION

Do not initialize a diskette that has been used before unless you are sure you do not want the data anymore. If you initialize it, all data will be lost.

3. Click on **Two-Sided** to initialize the diskette as a two-sided diskette with 800 kilobytes of storage space.
4. If the diskette has been previously formatted and you are sure you want to erase it, use the mouse to select **Erase Disk** from the Special menu. A similar screen appears. Then click on **Two-Sided**. The Macintosh formats the diskette.
5. When formatting is complete, the Macintosh asks you to name the diskette. Type **System Diskette** and press **Return**.
6. Double click on the original System Diskette icon and press **Cmd-A** to select everything on the diskette.
7. Using the mouse, drag the files over the icon for the new system diskette and let go. Momentarily, the Macintosh copies the files to the diskette.
8. Remove the diskettes by dragging their icons to the trash can and letting go.
9. Format the other three diskettes as described in the previous procedures. Copy the contents of the original WordPerfect Program diskette to the appropriate new diskette and name it "WordPerfect Program." Copy the contents of the original Speller/Thesaurus diskette to the appropriate new diskette and name it "Speller/Thesaurus." Name the other two diskettes "WordPerfect Data" and "WordPerfect Data Backup."

Return the original diskettes in their jackets to a safe place away from extremes of temperature and dust. Use the working copies of the program diskettes whenever you use WordPerfect.

USING A HARD DISK SYSTEM Make sure your hard disk is formatted before you copy your WordPerfect programs onto the hard disk or format your backup data diskette. Use the HD Setup program in the System folder to do this.

Installing WordPerfect On Your Hard Disk The best way to store your data on the hard disk is in *folders*. A computerized folder is much the same as the traditional folder in a file cabinet. It is a place to store groups of related documents. The Macintosh uses a hierarchical file system (HFS) that lets you store folders inside of folders. To best take advantage of this, there should be three folders visible when your computer is first on — Applications (for programs like WordPerfect), Data (for data files created with programs like WordPerfect), and System (for system files). Keeping as few folders as possible at this "top level" makes your computer run faster. Therefore, the best place to put WordPerfect files is in the Applications folder.

To put WordPerfect files in the Applications folder:

1. Double click on the Applications folder. Then select **New Folder** from the File menu.

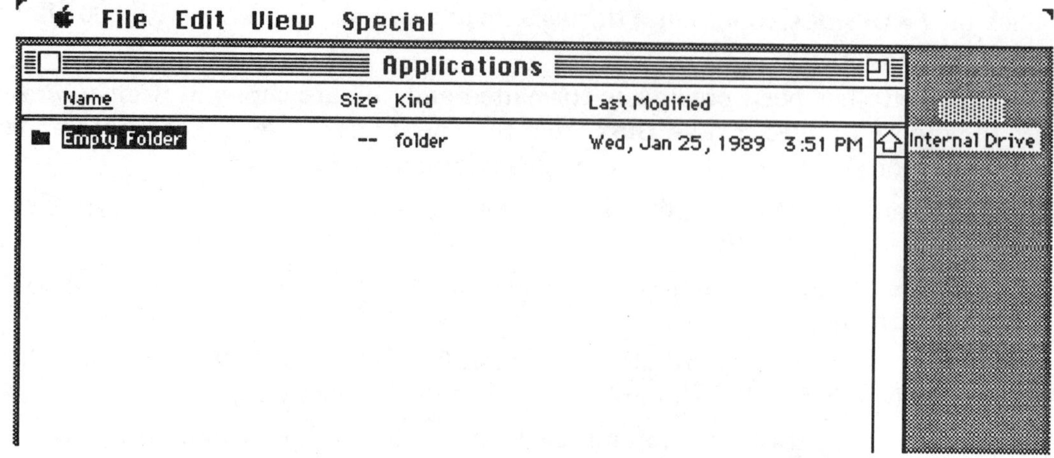

2. Type **WordPerfect** and press **Return**.
3. Put the WordPerfect Program diskette in any diskette drive and double click on its icon. Press **Cmd-A** to select all the files on the diskette.
4. Click and drag the files to the WordPerfect folder on your hard disk.
5. Remove the WordPerfect diskette by dragging its icon to the trash.
6. Insert the Speller/Thesaurus diskette in any diskette drive and double click on its icon. Press **Cmd-A** to select all the files on the diskette.
7. Click and drag the files to the WordPerfect folder on your hard disk.
8. Remove the Speller/Thesaurus diskette by dragging its icon to the trash.

Setting Up A Folder For Your Data WordPerfect data should go in the Data folder. You can put WordPerfect files in as many folders as you want. To create a data folder:

1. Double click on the Data folder, then select **New Folder** from the File menu.
2. Type **WordPerfect Data** and press **Return**.

To create a backup data diskette:

1. Put a blank data diskette into one of the diskette drives.
2. If the diskette has never been formatted, the following screen appears:

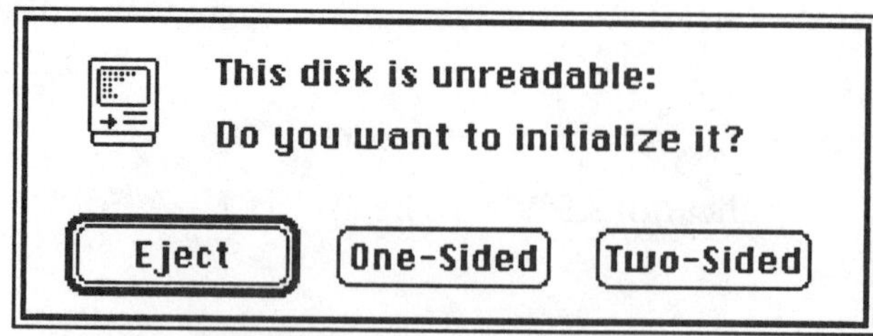

CAUTION

Do not initialize a diskette that has been used before unless you are sure you do not want the data anymore. If you initialize it, all data will be lost.

3. Click on **Two-Sided** to initialize the diskette as a two-sided diskette with 800 kilobytes of storage space.
4. If the diskette has been previously formatted, and you are sure you want to erase it, use the mouse to select **Erase Disk** from the Special menu. A similar screen appears. Then click on **Two-Sided**. The Macintosh formats the diskette.
5. When formatting is complete, the Macintosh asks you to name the diskette. Type **WordPerfect Data Backup** and press **Return**.
6. Remove the diskette from the drive by dragging its icon to the trash can and letting go.

SELECTING THE PROPER PRINTER Before WordPerfect can print your documents, you must select a printer from the Chooser. These procedures are outlined in Module 30, Printing.

Module 3

A SAMPLE SESSION WITH WORDPERFECT MACINTOSH

INTRODUCTION

This module offers information about word processors (what they are and what they can do for you) and explains how your keyboard works with WordPerfect. It then takes you through a sample session in which you create, save, and edit a document.

GETTING READY

Now that you have made working copies of your WordPerfect program diskettes, you are ready to start a sample session. Before actually starting WordPerfect, take a quick look at some of the keys you will use.

STANDARD TYPING KEYS The standard typing keys are like those on a conventional typewriter. These include letter, number, Tab, and Shift keys. Your *Shift* key is used to type uppercase letters and the symbols above the upper row of number keys, just as on a typewriter. *Special character keys* are also available on the computer keyboard, such as the vertical bar, back slash, tilde, and brace symbols. These symbols appear in the following list:

Special key	*Symbol*	*Special key*	*Symbol*
Vertical Bar	¦	Less Than	<
Back Slash	\	Open Bracket	[
Tilde	~	Close Bracket	]
Grave	`	Open Brace	{
Greater Than	>	Close Brace	}

THE RETURN KEY The *Return* key works much like the return key on a typewriter. Use it to move the cursor to the beginning of the next line. This is called a *hard return*.

NOTE

When you run out of space on a line, WordPerfect automatically moves the cursor to the next line. It does this by inserting a *soft return* at the end of the line. This process is called *word wrapping*.

The Return key is also used to complete selected commands. It is usually used when a question concerning the command is displayed in a box (called a *dialog box*) or in a *menu* on the screen. By pressing Return, you select the choice that is highlighted.

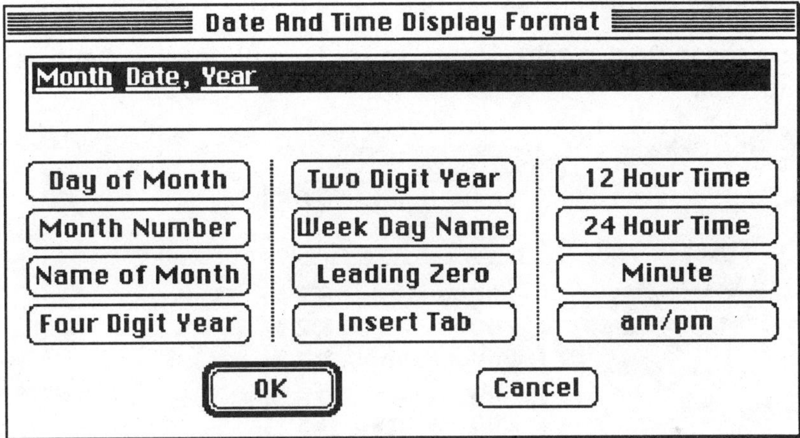

The choice with the wider circle around it is the choice *OK* in the above screen. To choose it, either click on it with the mouse or press Return. The only way to choose Cancel is to click on it.

NOTE

Choices can often be selected by pressing the Command key and the first letter of the option in the dialog box. In the above dialog box, for example, pressing Cmd-O selects OK and Cmd-C selects cancel.

COMMAND KEYS *Command keys* perform very specific tasks. They are used either with the Cmd key (designated by a cloverleaf on the key) or the Option key on your keyboard. If you have an Extended Keyboard, you can use the *Function keys* at the top of the keyboard.

Combined key sequences appear hyphenated in this book, indicating the keys to press simultaneously. If you see Cmd-P in print, for example, press the Cmd and P keys simultaneously and release them.

Commands that require a sequence of keystrokes are separated by commas. For example, if you see Enter, Enter, Up Arrow in print, press the Enter key twice, then release and press the Up Arrow key.

If you have an Extended Keyboard template, you can follow the color codes for combined key sequences. Keys that require you to press the Command key and a function key are coded red, those that require pressing the Shift key and a function key are green, and those using the Option key plus a function key are blue. Commands activated by pressing the function keys alone are colored black.

You can also use the mouse to select commands. To pull down a menu, move the cursor to the menu and click.

Format	
Show Ruler	⌘R
Copy Ruler	
Columns	⌘1 ▶
Page	⌘2 ▶
Paragraph	⌘3 ▶
Line	⌘4 ▶
Characters...	⌘5

NOTE

The cloverleaf in the above menu refers to the Command key.

If you can execute a command by pressing a Command key sequence, and therefore avoid using the mouse, that sequence is listed to the right of the menu item. If a second pull-down menu results from selecting the command, an arrow is listed to the right as well.

For example, to select the Page Format menu, press Cmd-2.

Format

Page Format

1. Page Layout...
2. Page Numbers...
3. Suppress Format...
4. Headers-Footers... ⌘⇧H
5. Conditional EOP...
6. Block Protect
7. Widow-Orphan
8. Page Break

To select the Page Format menu using a mouse, click on Page from the Format menu.

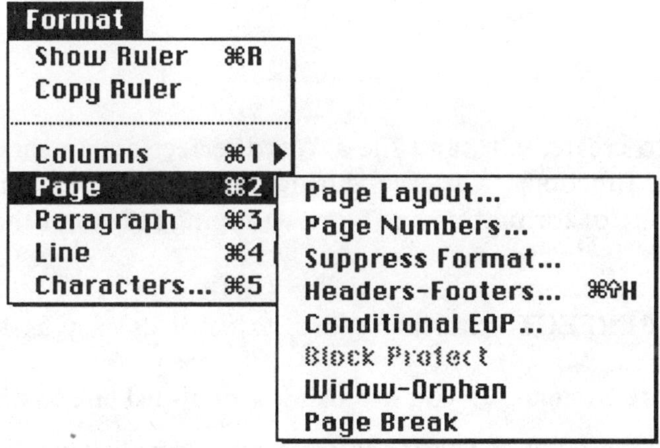

To show the second pull-down menu alone, let go of the mouse at this point.

Format

Page Format

1. Page Layout...
2. Page Numbers...
3. Suppress Format...
4. Headers-Footers... ⌘⇧H
5. Conditional EOP...
6. Block Protect
7. Widow-Orphan
8. Page Break

To select any of these options, type or click on the number next to the option.

Later modules in this book offer more detailed descriptions of each command, complete with a sample application.

SAMPLE SESSION

You are now ready to create, edit, and file a WordPerfect document and to learn several WordPerfect editing functions. Observe during the sample session how WordPerfect automatically takes care of formatting and word wrapping for you; other functions are very easy to use.

STARTING WORDPERFECT Starting WordPerfect is as easy as 1, 2, 3:

Using A Dual Diskette System If you are using a dual-diskette system:

1. Insert your working copy of the WordPerfect System diskette into drive A (internal drive on a Macintosh Plus; top drive on an SE). Insert your WordPerfect Program diskette into drive B (external drive on a Macintosh Plus; bottom drive on an SE).
2. Turn on your computer. After it has loaded, double click on the icon for the WordPerfect Program diskette.

3. Double click on the WordPerfect icon on the program diskette.

4. Observe WordPerfect load itself. Notice the WordPerfect copyright screen on the monitor. Then notice the WordPerfect Status Line at the bottom of the screen, the Title Bar at the top of the screen, and the Scroll Bar at the side.

NOTE

To save documents on the data diskette, replace the System diskette with the Data diskette after WordPerfect starts.

Using A Hard Disk System To load WordPerfect with a hard disk system:

1. Turn on your computer. After it has loaded, double click on the icon for your Applications folder. Then double click on the WordPerfect folder.
2. Double click on the WordPerfect icon.

3. Observe WordPerfect load itself. Notice the WordPerfect copyright screen on the monitor. Then notice the WordPerfect Status Line at the bottom of the screen, the Title Bar at the top of the screen, and the Scroll Bar at the side.

TYPING A DOCUMENT When you type a WordPerfect document within a paragraph, there is no need to press Return at the end of the line, because WordPerfect automatically "word wraps" for you. Use the Return key at the end of each paragraph. (The Return key is also used for other purposes, as explained in the following activity.)

Use the following key sequences to correct typographical errors.

- Cursor Movement — Press Backspace and the cursor keys, or click with the mouse.

- Correct Typos — Using the mouse, select Typeover from the Edit menu to go into Typeover mode to type over typos. Select Typeover again to leave Typeover mode. If you have an Extended keyboard, press Ins (0 on the numeric keypad at the right side of the keyboard) to turn Typeover on, and 0 again to turn it off. Press Del on an Extended Keyboard to delete characters and spaces to the right of the cursor. Use the Delete key (different key than Del) or the Backspace key on a standard keyboard to delete characters and spaces to the left of the cursor. Alternatively, highlight the text you want to delete with the mouse (by dragging the cursor over the text while holding the mouse button down and letting go at the end) and type the new text.
- Enter blank line — Press Return at the end of paragraphs and at the beginning of a blank line.
- Adjust gaps in text — Position cursor at end of gap and press the Delete (or Backspace) key. Or highlight the gaps with the mouse and press Delete.
- Add spaces in text — Press the Spacebar.

As the proprietor of FLG Office Supply, you have to write a letter to Sue, your assistant. Sue is in charge of ordering supplies for you.

NOTE

Combined key sequences are hyphenated, for example, Cmd-P. This indicates the first key is pressed and held while the second key is typed. Both keys are released simultaneously.

1. Press **Return** three times to insert three blank lines at the top of the document.
2. Type **Dear Sue:** (including the colon). Then press **Return** twice to insert a blank line between the salutation and the body of the letter.
3. Type **We are in need of the following: pencils, pens, dividers, notebooks, pads, and diskettes. Please order them immediately.** Press **Return** twice to insert a blank line.
4. Press **Cmd-Shift-C** to center the next text. Then type **Thank You,** (including the comma) and press **Return** twice.

5. Press **Cmd-Shift-C** and type **FLG** (the initials of the sender).
6. Press **Return** to end the letter. Notice the following display.

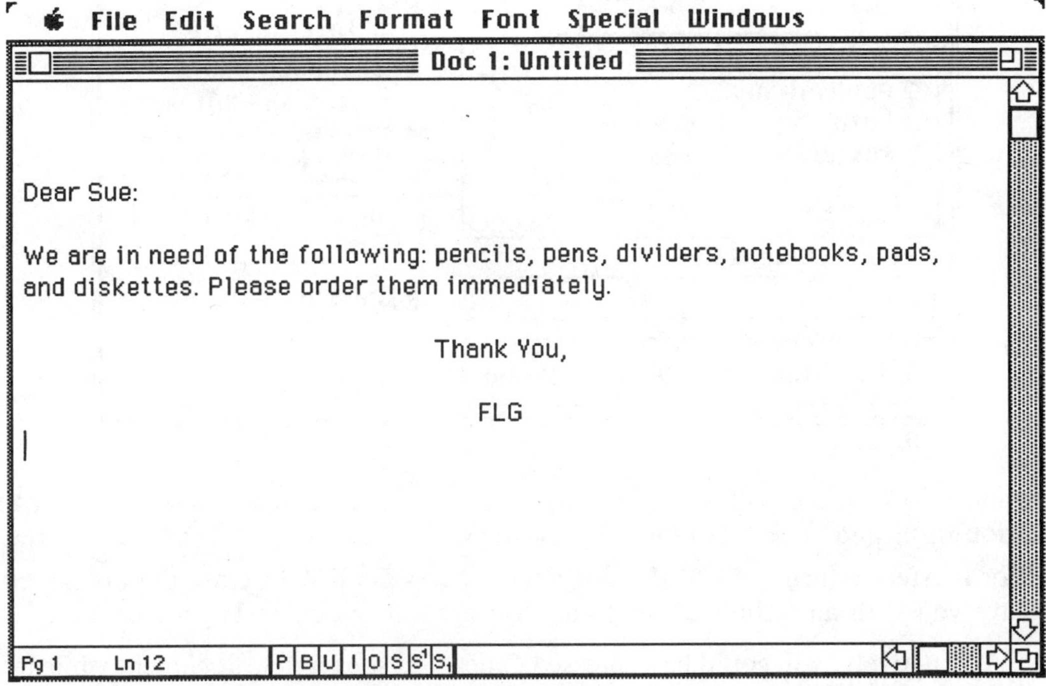

7. Press **Cmd-S** to save the document. Notice the following display:

Applications
Wordperfect
Internal Drive
Space Available
11,011,072 Bytes
Save
Eject
Cancel
Drive
Save Document As:
Password Protect
File format
Macintosh WP 1.0
IBM WP 4.2
Other...

8. Click on the (▭) icon next to the Internal Drive.

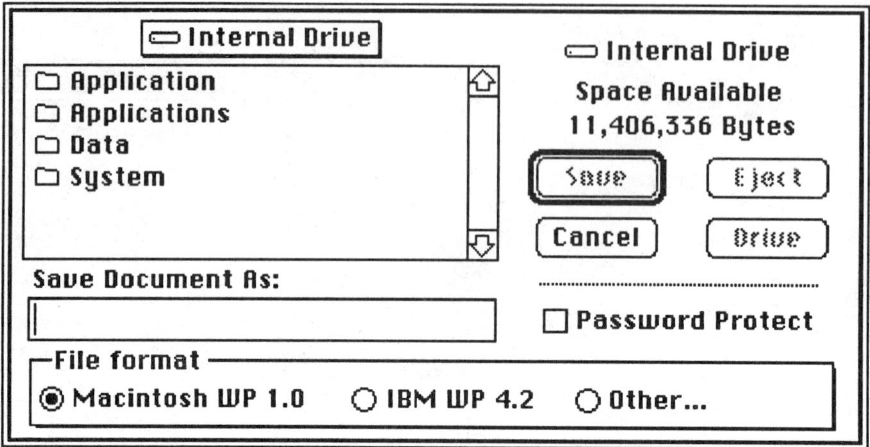

9. Double click on the Data folder and then the WordPerfect data folder. Type **Practice Document** and click **Save** or press **Return**.
10. WordPerfect returns you to the document. Press **Cmd-K** to close the document and leave you with an "Untitled" screen. You are now ready to begin something else.

TIP: Alternatively, you could have pressed Cmd-N to start a new document while leaving the Practice Document in another document window. You could then edit both documents simultaneously. WordPerfect lets you edit as many documents as your computer memory will support simultaneously.

EDITING A WORDPERFECT DOCUMENT Imagine that you have checked the inventory and realized that you did not need pencils, but you did need marking pens. You are now going to edit your letter to Sue to inform her of this occurrence.

1. Press **Cmd-O** to open the document.

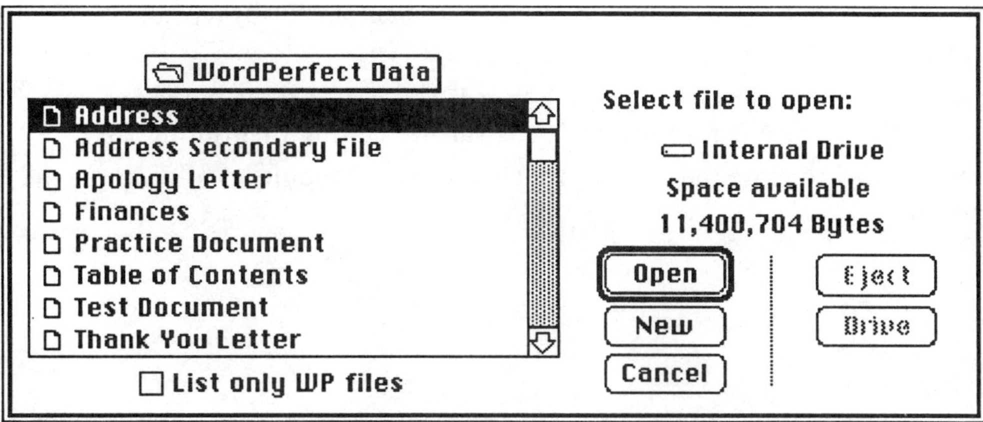

2. To open the file, click on **Practice Document** and click on **Open** or press **Return.** (Or, double click on Practice Document.) Notice the document is now on the screen as you left it. Notice also that the name of the document is displayed on the Title Bar at the top of the screen.
3. Using the cursor control keys, move the cursor to the "p" in pencils. Highlight the word and the comma following it with the mouse by clicking on the "p" and dragging the mouse to the right. Type **marking pens,** (including the comma).
4. Notice "marking pens" has replaced "pencils."

Looking at the document, you notice that it looks awkward to list "marking pens" and "pens" following each other, so you decide to change the wording a little. The cursor should be in the position where you left it.

5. Press the **Spacebar** once, and type **ballpoint.** Notice the following display:

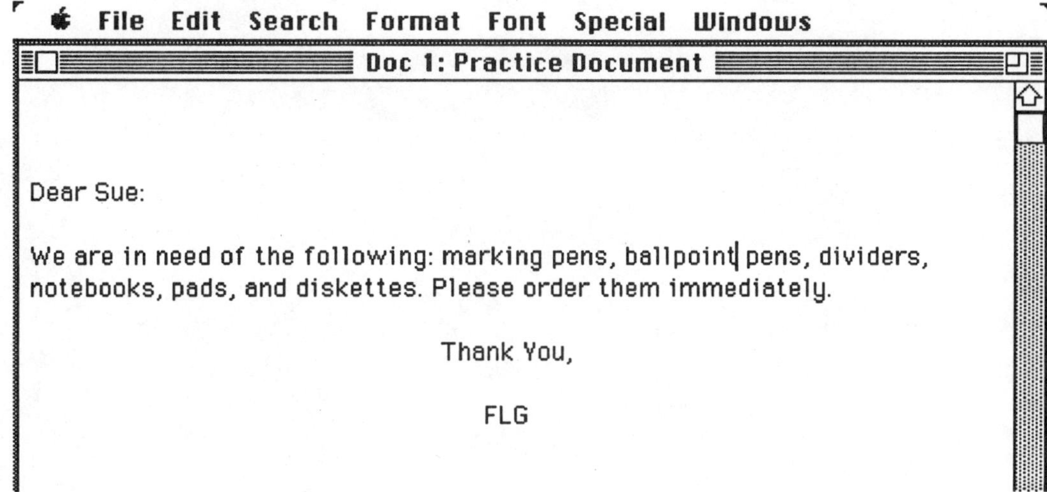

6. Press **Cmd-S** to save the document. WordPerfect automatically replaces the old document with the new one.

You have just created, edited, and saved a WordPerfect document. Your document is stored on the data disk so you can return to it for further editing or printing later.

7. Press **Cmd-K** to close the document. Then turn to Module 35 to continue the learning sequence.

Module 4

CANCEL, UNDO, UNDELETE

DESCRIPTION

WordPerfect offers three options that serve as "oops" keys to help you back out of a command or a procedure. The *Cancel* command lets you cancel any activity you decide not to complete. This can help you prevent errors while editing. The *Undo* command helps you undo the last formatting or editing task you performed. This helps you quickly restore a document to its previous margins or other format and helps you quickly restore the last text you deleted. The *Undelete* command is more versatile than Undo in that it helps you restore any of your last three deletions.

Cancel is accessed from the keyboard or as an option in many dialog boxes.

USING THE CANCEL KEY When you want to cancel any operation in WordPerfect, press Cmd-. (Cmd-period). Cancel is also an option in most menus and dialog boxes.

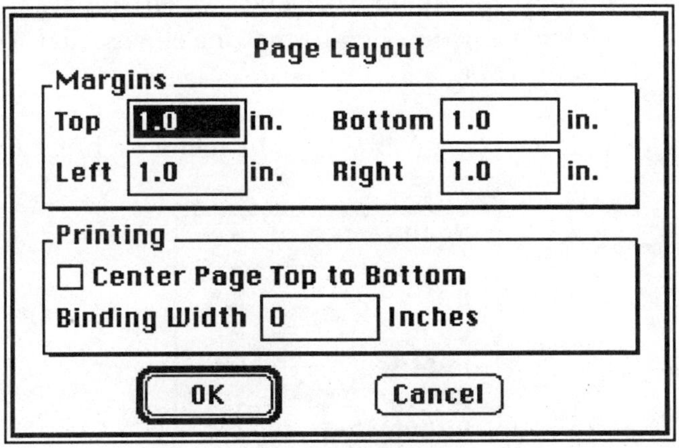

To leave this dialog box without making any changes to the document, click on Cancel.

You can also cancel commands with other keys when presented with menus in WordPerfect.

Format

Line Format

1. Center ⌘⇧C
2. Flush Right ⌘⇧F
3. Tabs...
4. Hyphenation...
5. Spacing...
6. Kerning...
7. Margin Release

Pressing any key other than the choices on the menu (1 through 7) closes the menu and returns you to the document. If you use the mouse, click on any area outside the menu to return to the document.

USING THE UNDO COMMAND The Undo command lets you nullify the last deletion or formatting change. That is, it restores the document to the same condition it was in immediately prior to the last deletion or formatting change.

CAUTION

If you delete and then enter additional text before deciding to undo your deletion, the undo command will delete all of your added text as well as restore all your deleted text. Therefore, the Undo command works best when you are undoing a deletion or a formatting change that just occurred.

To use the Undo command, access it from the Edit menu or press Cmd-Z or F1.

Edit

Undo ⌘Z

Cut ⌘X
Copy ⌘C
Paste ⌘V
Append ⌘A ▶
Undelete... ⌘U

Typeover
Case Convert ▶
Insert Literal... ⌘I

Select ⌘6 ▶

Show Codes ⌘7

The last deletion or formatting change will be restored, and any changes made since will be deleted.

UNDELETING TEXT The Undelete command lets you restore any or all of the last three deletions in memory. Thus, if you change your mind about text after you have deleted it, you can restore it. To use the Undelete command, move the cursor to the location where you would like the text to be restored. Then select Undelete from the Edit menu or press Cmd-U or Option-F13. The last text you deleted appears along with the following screen:

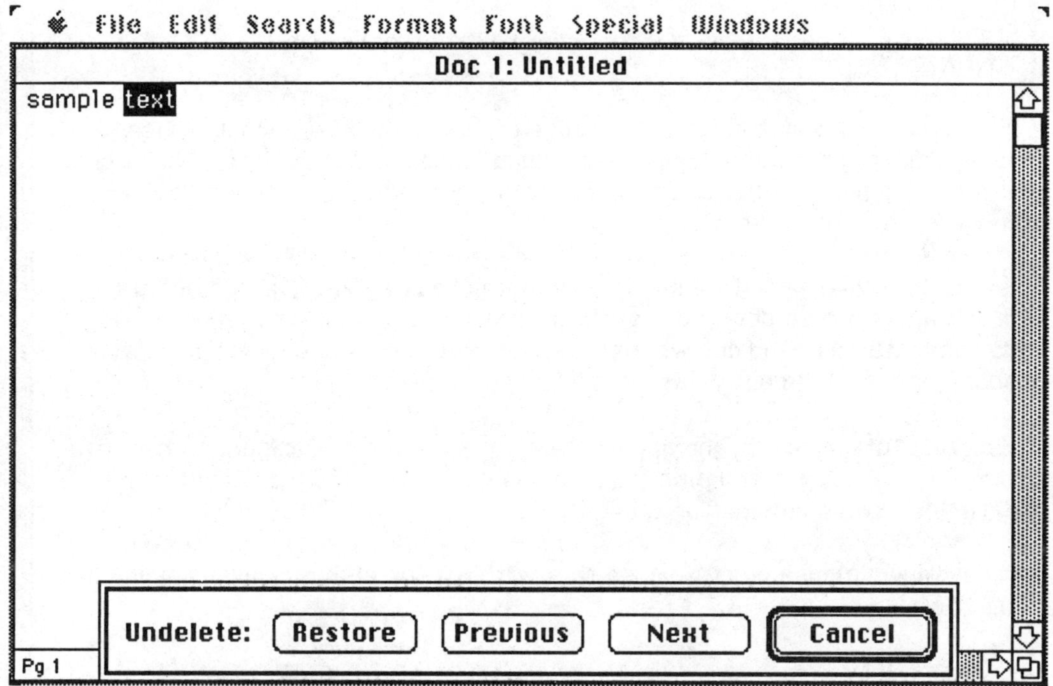

Click on Restore to restore the last deletion, Previous to look at the previous deletion, or Next to look at the next deletion. Press Return or click on Cancel to return to the document without restoring anything.

APPLICATIONS

The Cancel command is useful for leaving menus and dialog boxes, stopping printing, stopping merges or macros, or cancelling commands. The Undo command restores the last deletion or formatting change. It is most useful when you want to undo what you just did. The Undelete command restores any or all of the last three deletions. It is useful when you want to restore text you deleted earlier.

TYPICAL OPERATION

This example shows how to use the Undelete command.

1. If necessary, start WordPerfect. Then create a document similar to the following:

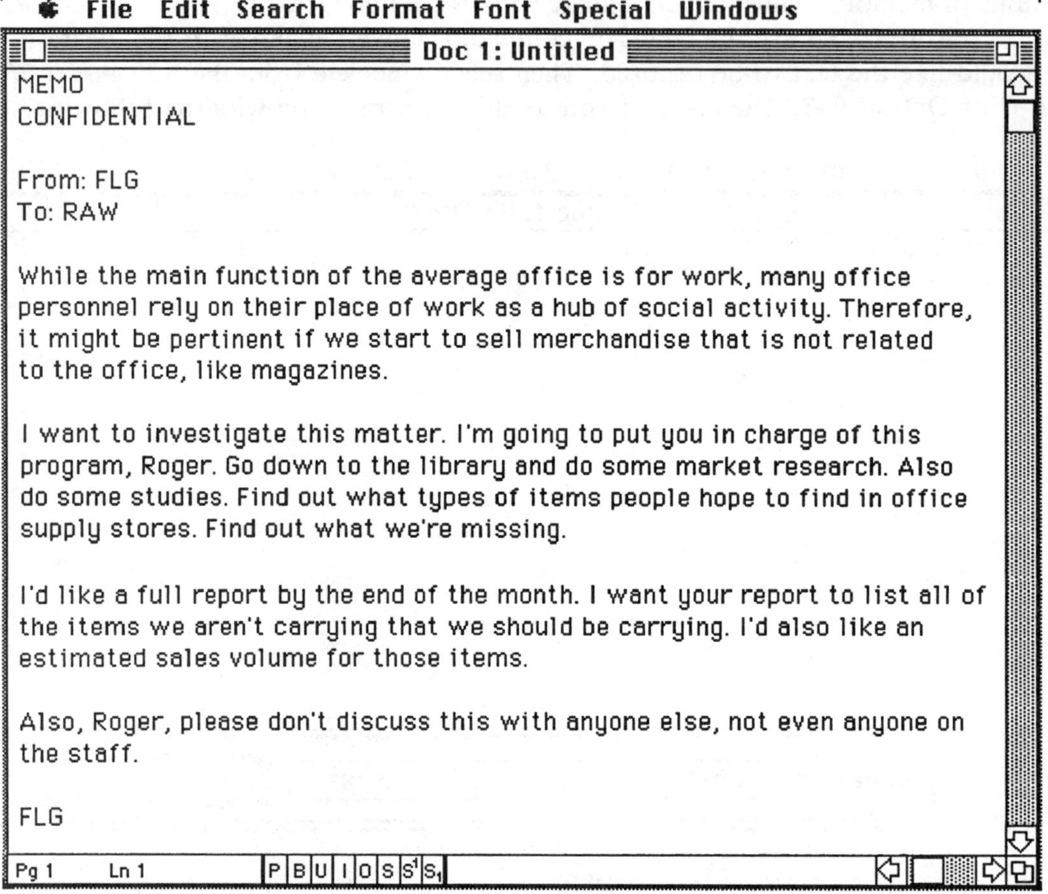
File Edit Search Format Font Special Windows

Doc 1: Untitled

MEMO
CONFIDENTIAL

From: FLG
To: RAW

While the main function of the average office is for work, many office personnel rely on their place of work as a hub of social activity. Therefore, it might be pertinent if we start to sell merchandise that is not related to the office, like magazines.

I want to investigate this matter. I'm going to put you in charge of this program, Roger. Go down to the library and do some market research. Also do some studies. Find out what types of items people hope to find in office supply stores. Find out what we're missing.

I'd like a full report by the end of the month. I want your report to list all of the items we aren't carrying that we should be carrying. I'd also like an estimated sales volume for those items.

Also, Roger, please don't discuss this with anyone else, not even anyone on the staff.

FLG

Pg 1 Ln 1

2. Move the cursor to the "A" in "Also" at the bottom of the document. Use the mouse to highlight the entire sentence and press **Delete** (or press Backspace on some keyboards). This deletes the entire sentence.
3. Move the cursor to the "f" in "for" in the first sentence.

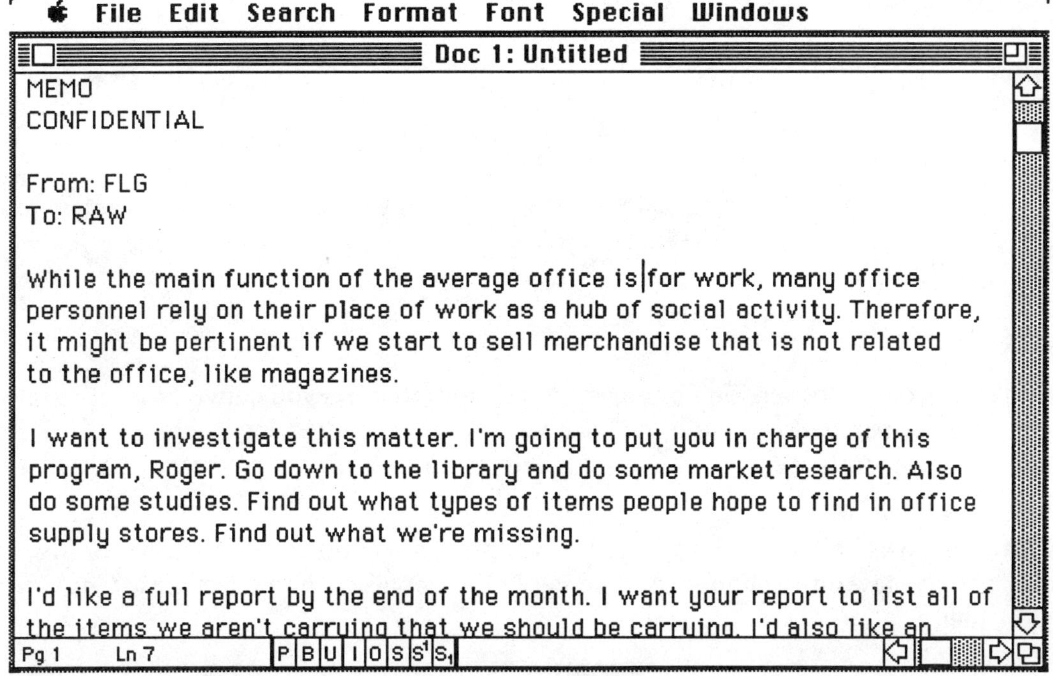

4. Select the word and the space after with the mouse and press **Delete**. This deletes the entire word.
5. Move the cursor to the next-to-last line in the document (before "FLG") and press **Cmd-U**. The Undelete dialog box comes up. Click on **Previous** to show the previous deletion.
6. Click on **Restore** to restore the text.
7. Press **Cmd-S**, type **Research Project**, and press **Return** to save the document.
8. Press **Cmd-K** to close the document. Then turn to Module 10 to continue the learning sequence.

Module 5

CASE CONVERSION

DESCRIPTION

WordPerfect's Case Conversion feature is a handy tool that lets you convert an entire selection of text from upper to lowercase and vice-versa. When converting a block to lowercase, WordPerfect leaves the first word in a sentence capitalized as well as such words as "I" and "I'm."

This feature works only with text selected. To convert a section of text to upper or lowercase, select the text you want to change to uppercase or lowercase. Then select Case Convert from the Edit menu.

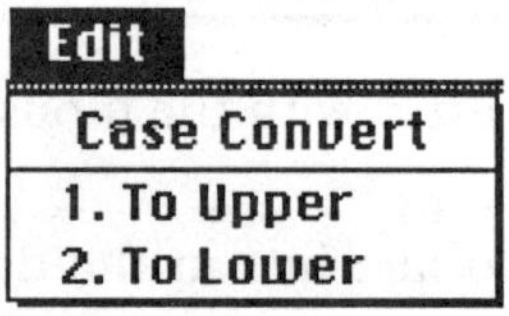

Edit
Case Convert
1. To Upper
2. To Lower

Type or click on 1 to convert the block to all uppercase. Type or click on 2 to convert the block to all lowercase. If you highlight a period to indicate that a complete sentence has been selected, WordPerfect leaves the first letter in the sentence uppercase.

APPLICATIONS

Use the Case Conversion command to convert a block of text to upper or lowercase. This command is convenient with both large and small blocks of text.

TYPICAL OPERATION

In this example, you convert various blocks of text in a memo from normal (lowercase) to uppercase and then you convert a block of text from uppercase to normal.

1. If necessary, start WordPerfect. Then create a document similar to the following:

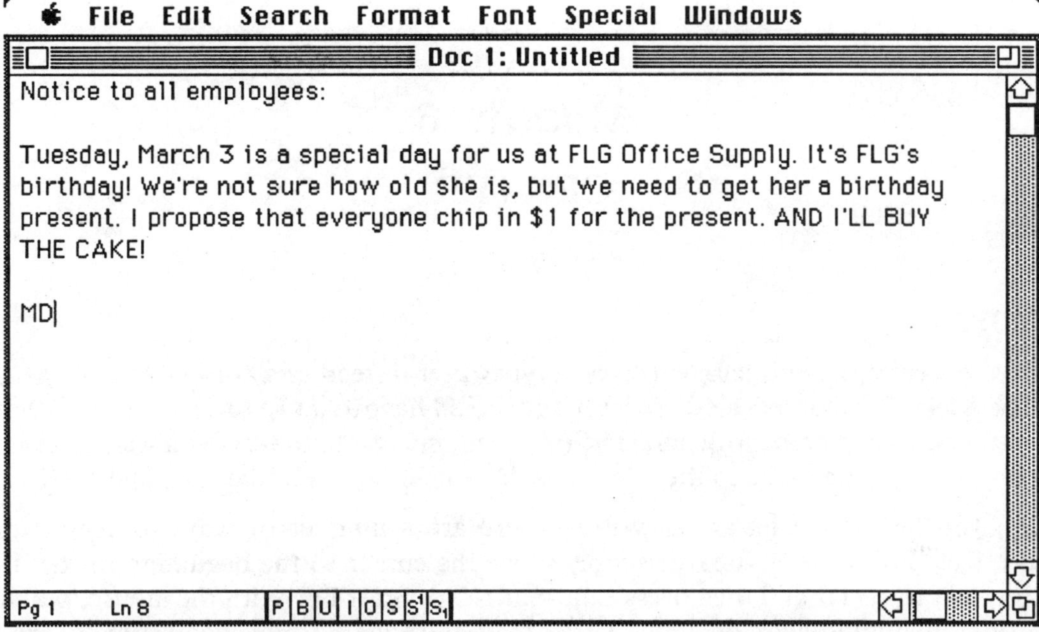

2. Select the first line of text as a block and select **Case Convert** from the Edit menu.
3. Type or click on **1** for uppercase. Then, click anywhere to deselect the block.
4. Move the cursor to the period before the "A" in "AND" in the last sentence. Select the period and the entire next sentence as a block.
5. Select **Case Convert** from the Edit menu and type or click on **2** to convert the sentence to lowercase. Click the mouse once to deselect the block.

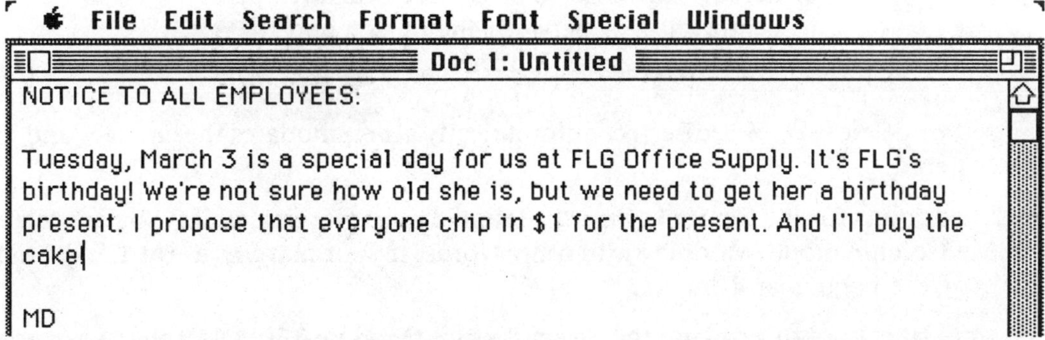

6. Press **Cmd-S**, type **FLG's Birthday**, and press **Return** to save the document.
7. Press **Cmd-K** to close the document. Then turn to Module 7 to continue the learning sequence.

Module 6
CENTER

DESCRIPTION

If you were creating your documents with a typewriter instead of a computer, centering text would be a relatively complicated process. You would have to move the carriage to the center of a page, count the number of characters (including spaces) in the text you wanted centered, move the carriage one space to the left for each two characters in the text, and finally type.

Luckily, you are not using a typewriter. There are a number of ways to center text in WordPerfect. From the keyboard, simply move the cursor to the beginning of the line of text you want to center and then press Cmd-Shift-C or Shift-F6. With the mouse, pull down the Format menu and click on Line. Then, from the Line Format menu, type or click on 1. From the Ruler (Module 33), click on the Center Text icon ([≡]).

If you have not yet typed the text you want centered, type it now and press Return when finished. (For text already typed, the Center key centers all text after the cursor on a chosen line.)

NOTE

Press Return at the end of any line you want centered. Otherwise, WordPerfect will attempt to center all text between the cursor and the next time you press Return.

If you insert or delete text, WordPerfect automatically accommodates the changes and keeps the line centered.

The reference points for the Center key are the left and right margins, unless you are centering text while in Column mode (Module 8). In other words, if your margins are at 1 and 7 inches, the center of the page is at 4 inches.

To center multiple lines of text, use the Select feature (Module 37). Select the text you want centered and press Cmd-Shift-C (or use any of the other centering methods described in this module).

To delete centered text and replace it with other text, delete the Center code ([Center>) as well. You can do this either by showing the codes (Module 7) and deleting the Center code or by changing the designation of the line on the Rulers.

APPLICATIONS

Use the Center key to center any line or number of lines of text in a document. Two of the most common uses for the center command are centering titles on documents and items on title pages.

TYPICAL OPERATION

In this example, center the lines of a memo.

1. If necessary, start WordPerfect. Then create a document similar to the following:

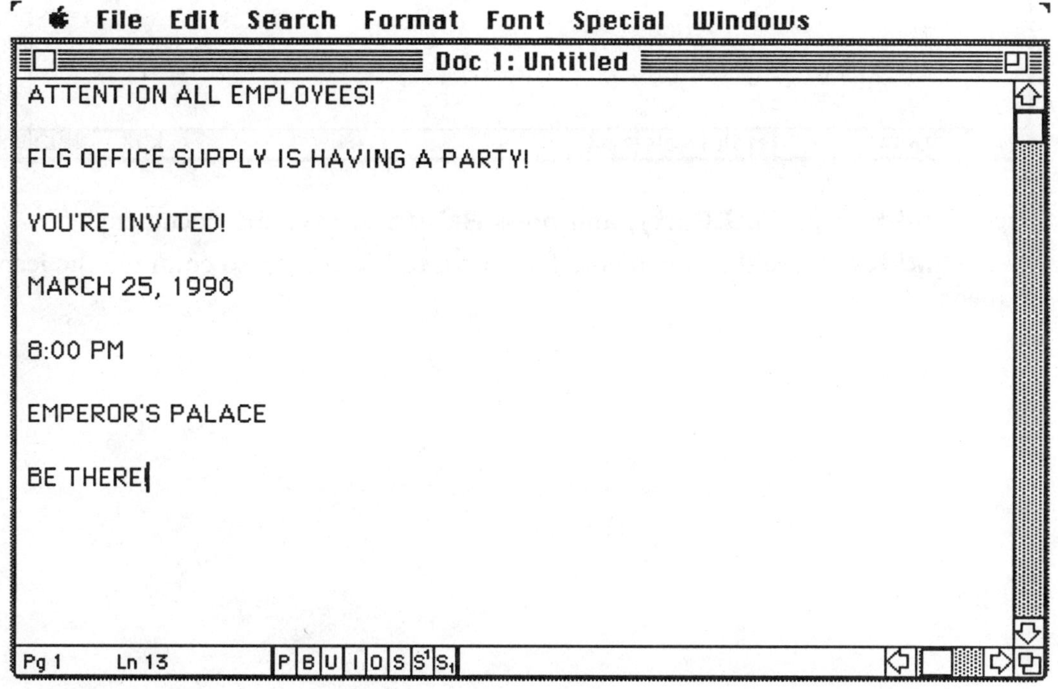

2. Press **Cmd-Shift-A** to select all the text in the document.
3. Press **Cmd-Shift-C** to center all the text. Then click the mouse once to turn highlighting off.

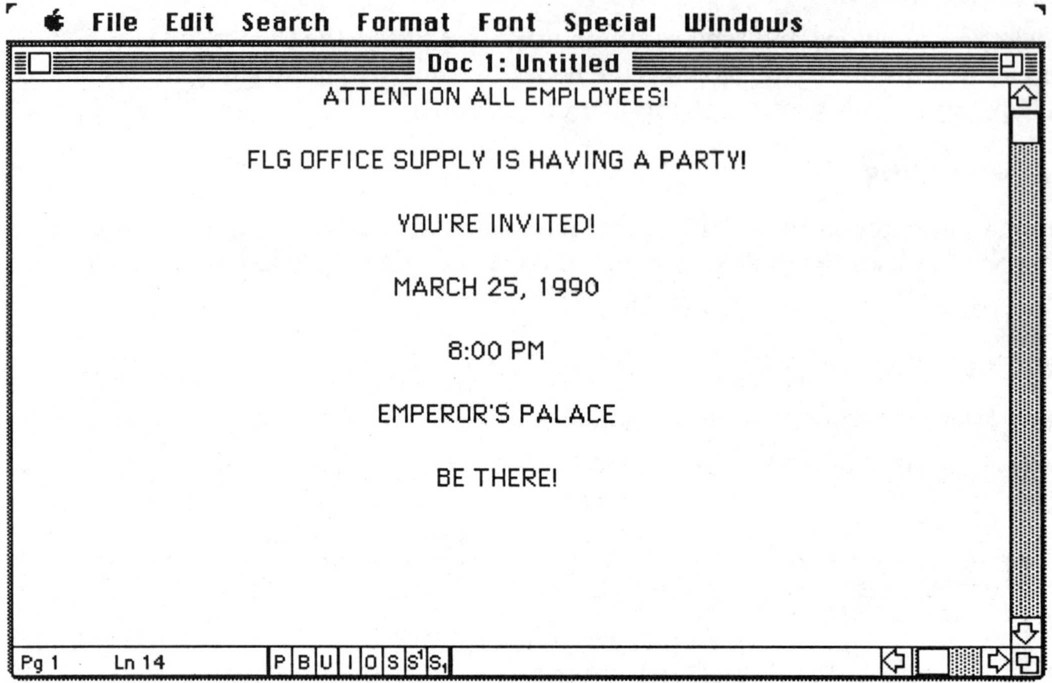

4. Press **Cmd-S**, type **FLG Party**, and press **Return** to save the document.
5. Press **Cmd-K** to close the document. Then turn to Module 15 to continue the learning sequence.

Module 7
CODES

DESCRIPTION

You use many special features in the course of creating and editing a document. You change spacing, set tabs, create new pages, and more. Whenever you use any special features, WordPerfect inserts a code into the text for the printer. Because it would be distracting to see symbols for those functions on-screen all the time, WordPerfect hides them. If you want to see where a tab is or when you changed spacing from single to double, select the Show Codes function by pressing **Cmd-7** or **Alt-F3** or by selecting the Codes option on the Edit menu.

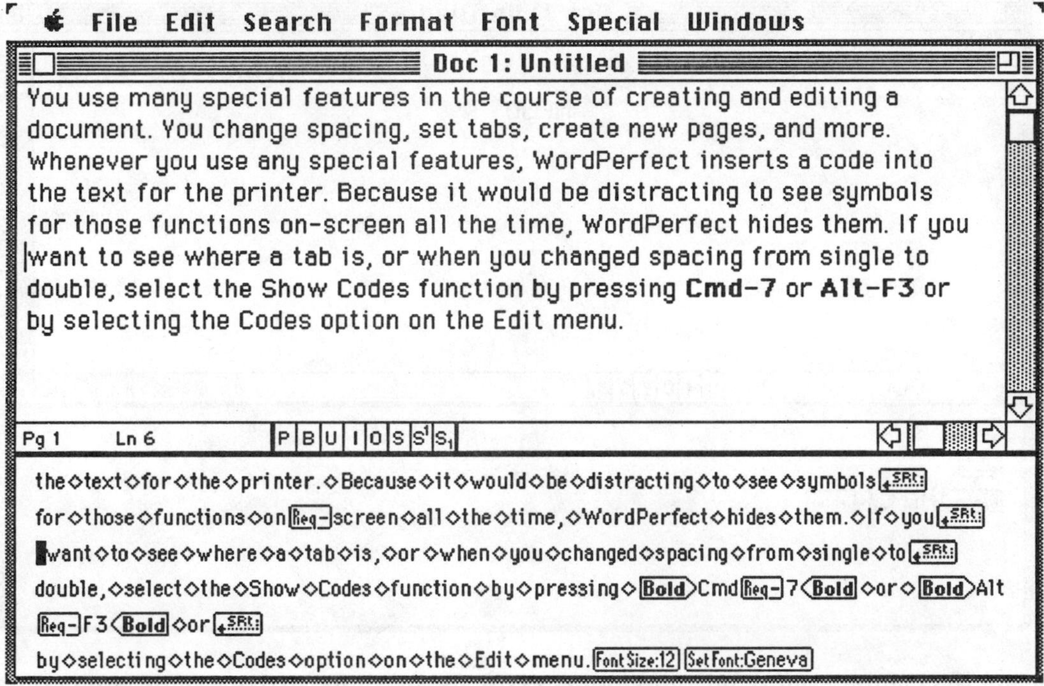

WordPerfect divides the screen in half and shows three lines above the cursor and three lines below it on each half, plus the current line. On the top half, it displays text as it would normally be seen on the screen. On the bottom, it displays text with all the codes included.

The previous illustration includes the following codes: boldface on (Bold>), boldface off (<Bold), soft return (SRt), and codes for point size and font. The cursor looks like this: (▌).

WordPerfect lets you perform any editing tasks you desire while codes are shown. You can position the cursor using any of the cursor control keys, plus the Forward Search (Cmd-F) and Backward Search (Cmd-B) keys. Use the Del and Delete (or Backspace) keys to delete any code, function, space, or character. (Del is available only on Extended Keyboards.)

To hide codes again, press Cmd-7 or Alt-F3 again or pull down the Edit menu and click on Hide Codes.

DELETING CODES You delete codes because you no longer need that function in place. For example, you might center a word and then decide later you do not want that word centered. The easiest way to delete the Center code is to use the Show Codes option to find it and then delete it with the Del or Delete key. Pressing Cmd-7 helps you find the location of the Center code.

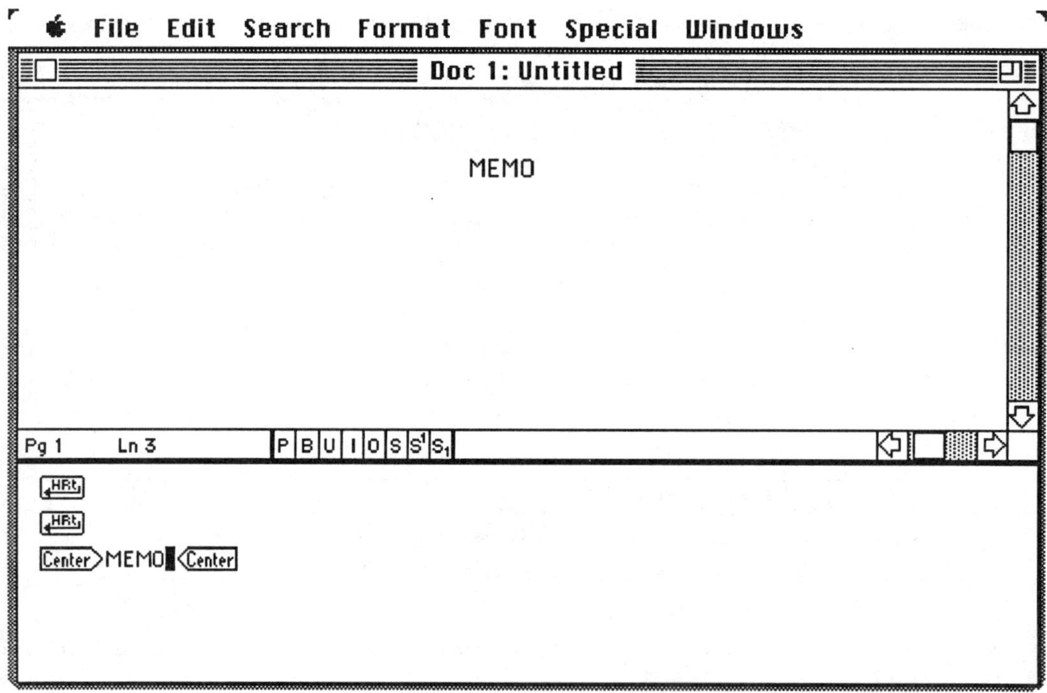

To delete the Center command, move the cursor to the right of the Center code and press Delete (or Backspace).

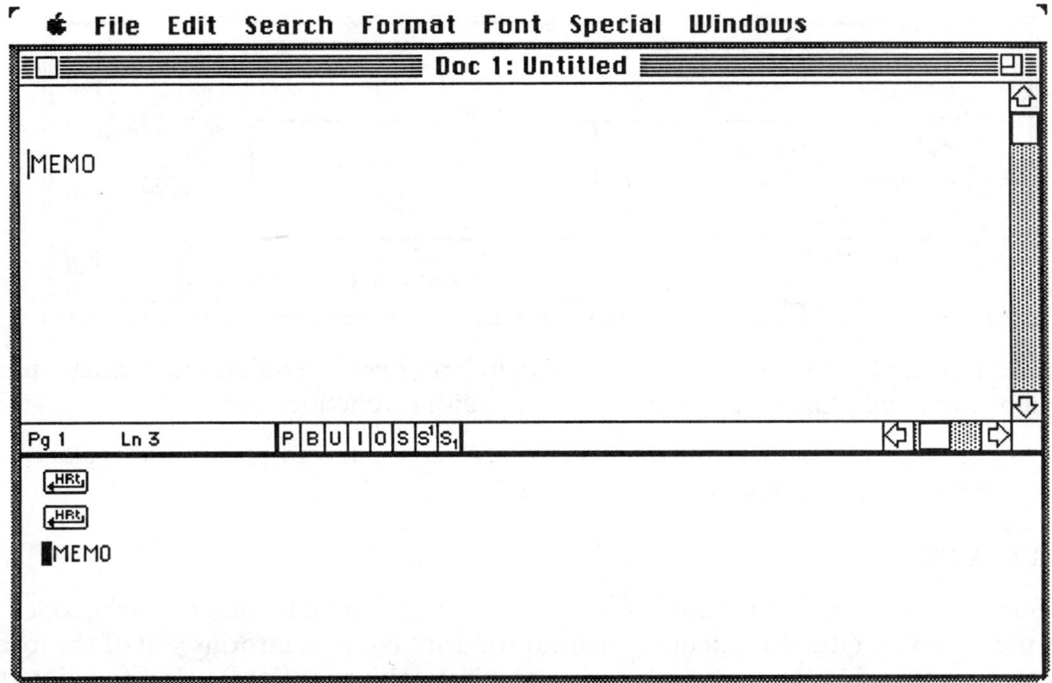

SEARCHING FOR CODES There are times, especially in long documents, when you might want to search for a code, for example, the next Underline code. To search forward for an Underline code press Cmd-F or F2 (or click on Forward Search after pulling down the Search menu).

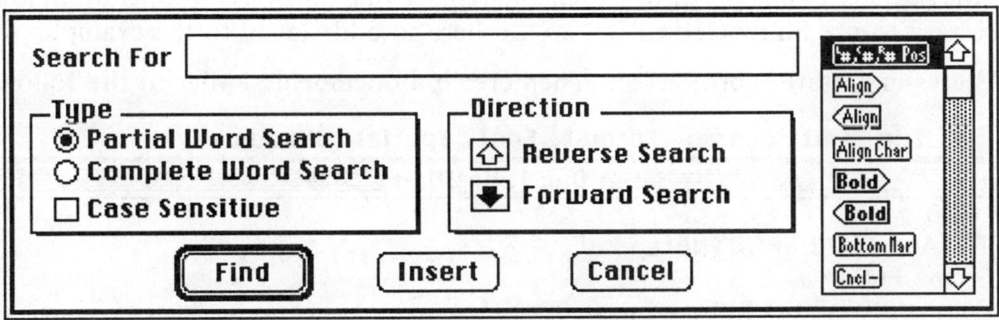

Notice the codes listed to the right. To select the Underline code, simply scroll down to it and double click on it.

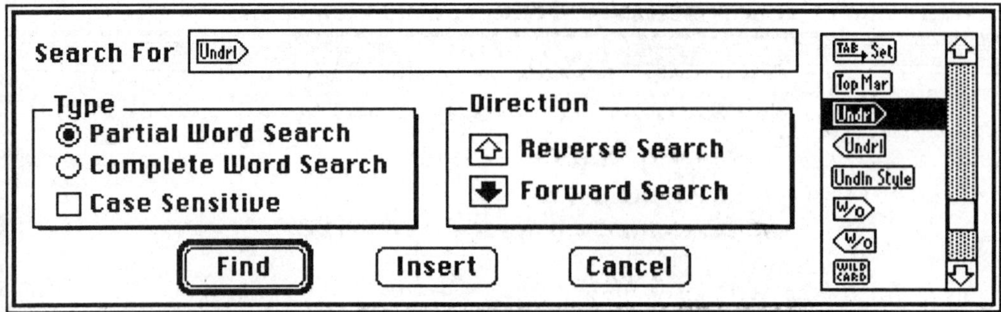

Press Return and the cursor moves to the next Underline code. You may then delete the code to remove the underline or perform any other editing functions you wish.

You can also search backward and use the Search command to search and replace (all of these functions are described in Module 36).

APPLICATIONS

Use Show Codes to delete unwanted codes from text and to make sure the right codes have been used. Show Codes is particularly helpful for printing, as it informs you of the location and message of each code. If you are having problems with any WordPerfect function, there is a good chance there is a code in the wrong place. And the only way to find that out is to use Show Codes.

TYPICAL OPERATION

Imagine you decide to delete all boldfaced text from a document. In order to do this, you will use the Search key and perform search and replace functions. In this operation, it's often not necessary to use Show Codes. But we do here to add clarity to the example.

1. If necessary, start WordPerfect. Then create a document similar to the following:

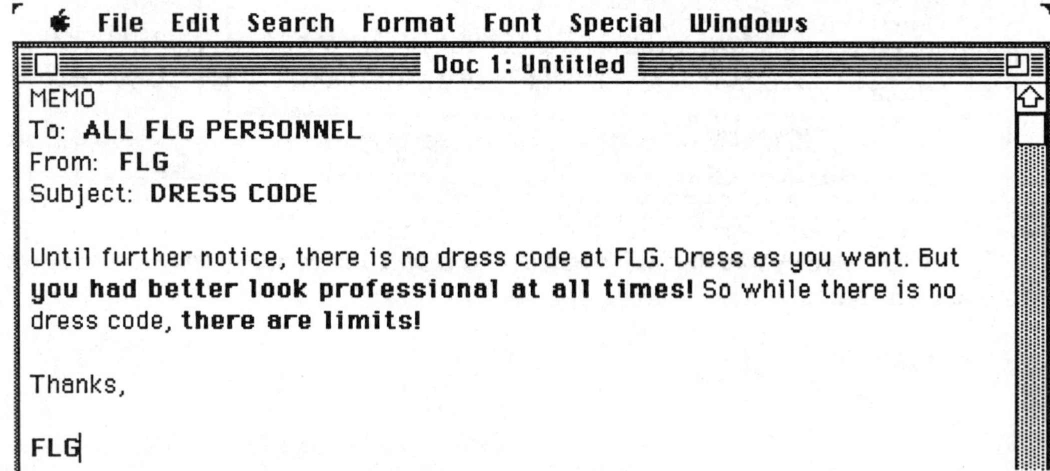

2. Press **Cmd-7**. Notice all the bold codes in the text. These codes identify where boldface starts and ends.

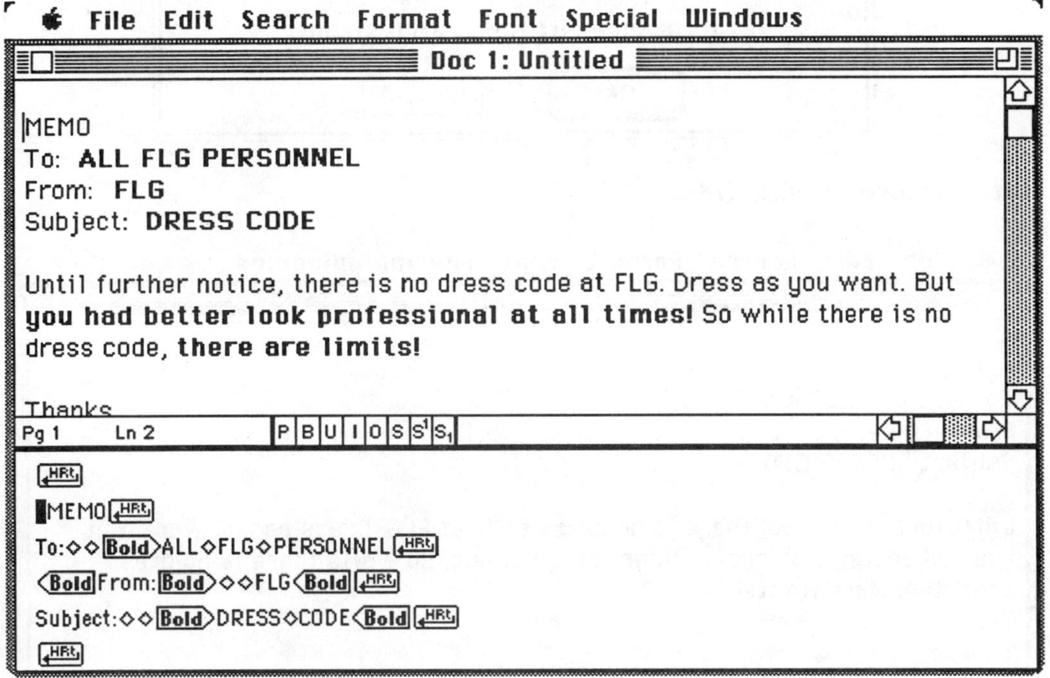

3. Press **Cmd-7** to hide the codes again.
4. Press **Cmd-H,** the Search and Replace key.
5. Double click on the Bold code (Bold>).

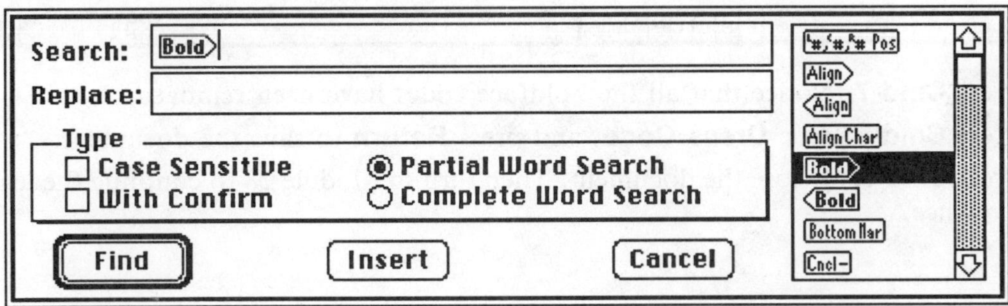

6. Press **Return**. This indicates you want to delete the boldface and replace it with nothing.

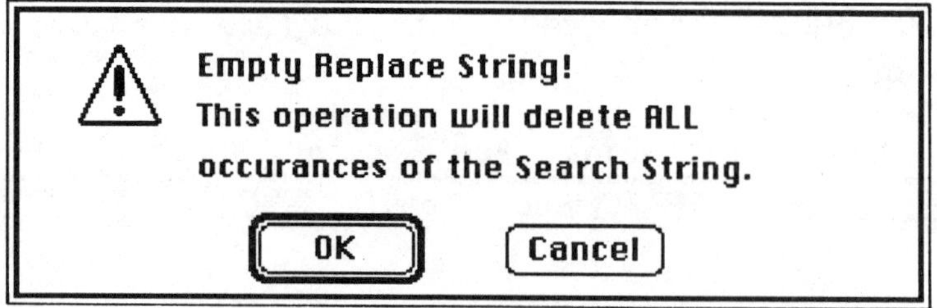

7. Press **Return** or click **OK**.

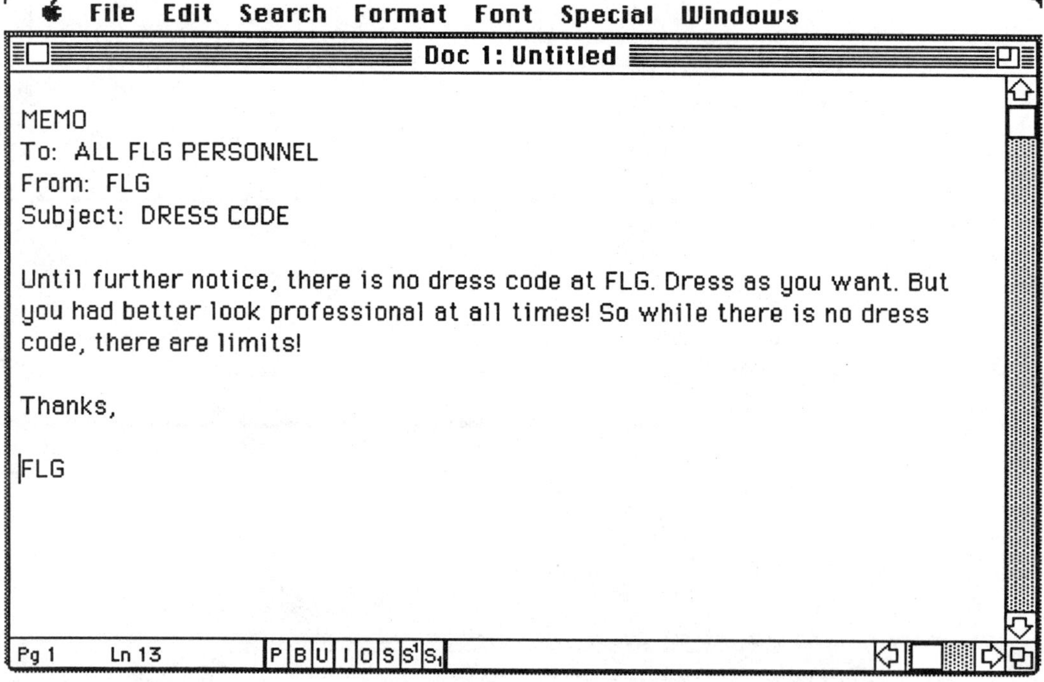

8. Press **Cmd-7**. Notice that all the boldface codes have been removed.
9. Press **Cmd-S**, type **Dress Code**, and press **Return** to save the document.
10. Press **Cmd-K** to close the document. Then turn to Module 28 to continue the learning sequence.

Module 8

COLUMNS

DESCRIPTION

If you are doing desktop publishing or would like to produce documents that are columnar in format, use WordPerfect's Column Definition command. The Column Definition command lets you put as many as 24 columns across on a page. Newspaper Style columns are the most common type of columns:

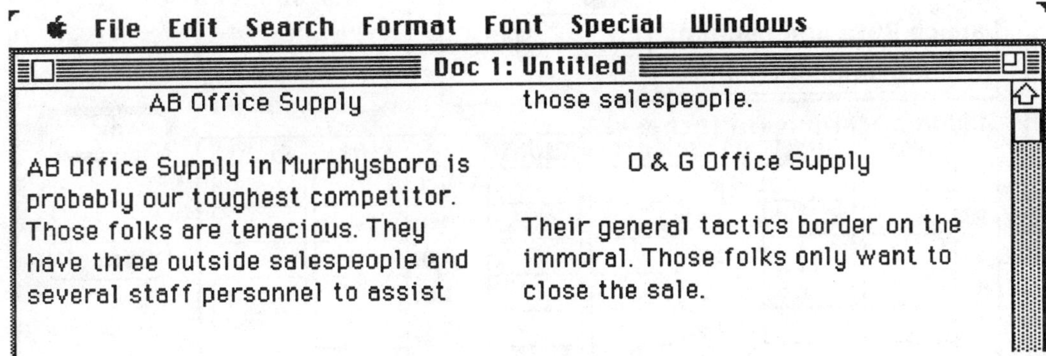

WordPerfect also lets you create Parallel columns. Parallel columns keep common groups of information together on a page. The length of the information in each column is immaterial. These are commonly used for applications like scripts, screenplays, and tables. If there is insufficient room for the entire text of both of the columns on a given page, WordPerfect moves both columns to the next page.

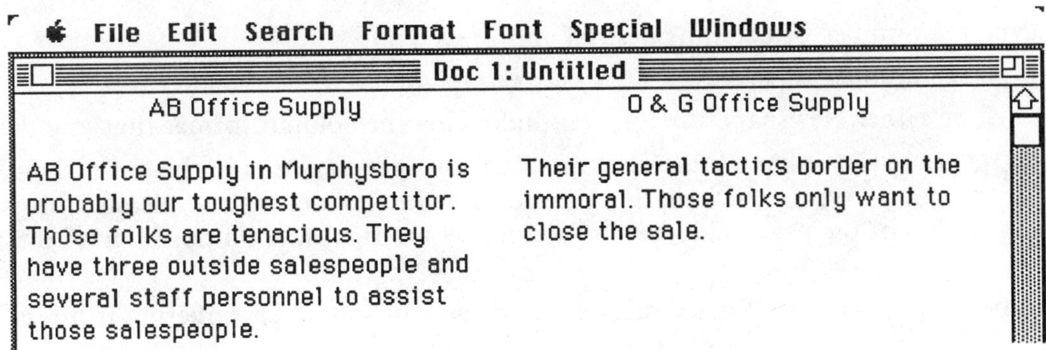

There are four steps to creating a column in WordPerfect:

1. Define the columns.
2. Turn Column mode on.
3. Type the text in the column.
4. Turn Column mode off.

DEFINE COLUMNS Before you can go into Column mode, you must first tell WordPerfect how many columns you want on a page, how you want those columns spaced, where you want the margins to be, and whether you want Newspaper or Parallel format. To define columns, press Cmd-1 or select Columns, then select Column Options from the Format menu. Alternately, you can press Alt-F7 to move directly to the Column Options menu.

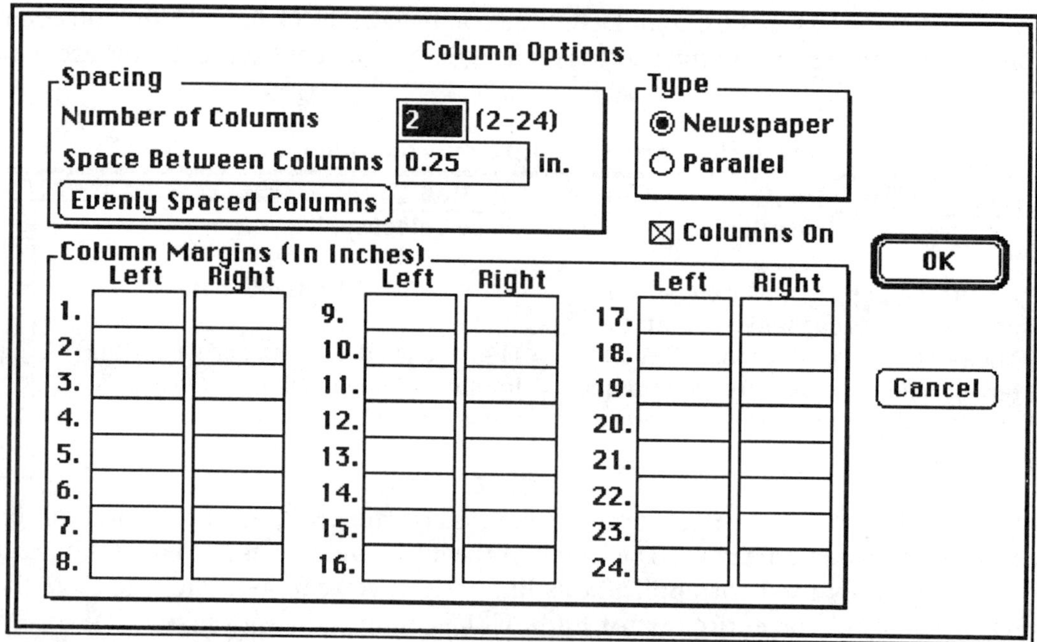

Manual Column Definition To manually define columns:

1. Type the number of columns desired and press Tab.
2. Type the number of inches desired between columns.
3. Click on either Newspaper or Parallel, indicating the column format that you desire.
4. To set your own column margins, press Tab until the cursor is in the left margin box for column 1. Type the left margin position for the first column. Typically, this is the left margin of the page. Then press Tab and set the right margin position for the first column.
5. Repeat this procedure for as many columns as you want, remembering to press Tab to move between margin settings.

6. If you would like Column mode to be on, make sure the Columns On box is checked.
7. To accept these settings and return to the document, press Return or click OK. To cancel the operation, click Cancel.

Automatic Column Definition To automatically define columns:

1. Type the number of columns desired and press Tab.
2. Type the number of inches desired between columns.
3. Click on either Newspaper or Parallel, indicating the column format that you desire.
4. Click on Evenly Spaced Columns. WordPerfect automatically calculates the margins for you. Specifically, it calculates the space between the columns and the number of columns and comes up with column margins.
5. If you would like Column mode to be on, make sure the Columns On box is checked.
6. To accept these settings and return to the document, press Return or click OK. To cancel the operation, click Cancel.

LEAVING AND EXITING COLUMN MODE Once columns have been defined, you can directly enter and exit the Column mode. Whether you are entering or leaving Column mode, the keystroke is the same — Cmd-Shift-K.

CREATING COLUMNS

The "Col" indicator on the Status Line tells you that you are in the Column mode. Type text normally. When you reach the end of the page, WordPerfect moves up to the next column. If you want to move to the next column before you reach the end of the page, press Cmd-Return.

NOTE

Most of WordPerfect's commands work normally inside columns. But margins and footnotes do not work.

CURSOR CONTROL INSIDE COLUMNS Cursor control inside columns is similar to that in any other text documents. But if you want to move the cursor between columns, use the special procedures outlined in the table below:

Keystroke	*Results*
Cmd-G, Right Arrow	Moves cursor to the next column.
Cmd-G, Left Arrow	Moves cursor to the previous column.
Cmd-G, Enter, Right Arrow	Moves cursor to the last column on the page.
Cmd-G, Enter, Left Arrow	Moves cursor to the first column on the page.

APPLICATIONS

Use Newspaper Style columns when doing desktop publishing or other types of word processing for which columns are appropriate. Use parallel columns when presenting groups of ideas that fit in columnar format.

TYPICAL OPERATION

In this example, you use parallel columns to show the approved vendor for each product in a list.

1. If necessary, start WordPerfect. Then press **Cmd-Shift-C**, the Center key.
2. Type **FLG OFFICE SUPPLY -- APPROVED VENDOR LIST** and press **Return** twice.
3. Press **Cmd-1**. Then type **2** to select Column Options.
4. Type **2** to designate the number of columns on the page. Then press **Tab** and type **1** to put one inch between columns.
5. Click on **Parallel** to create parallel-style columns. Then click on **Evenly Spaced Columns**. WordPerfect automatically determines the margins for the columns as shown on the following screen:

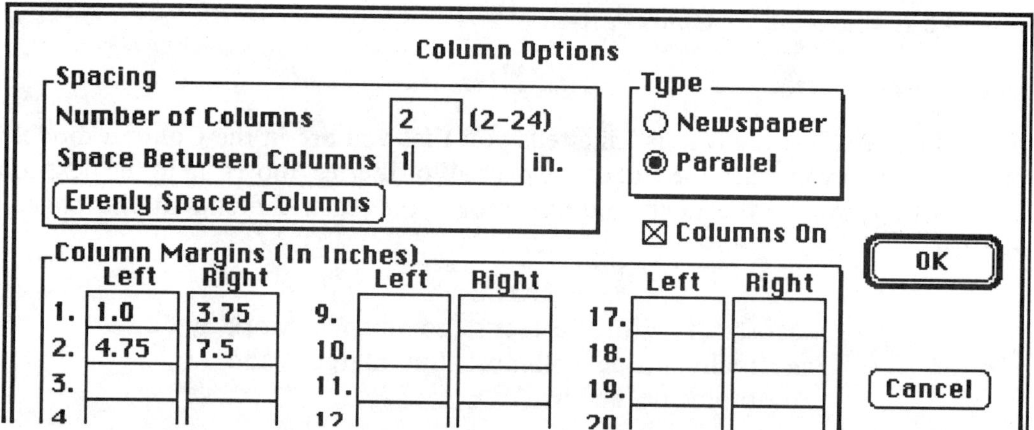

6. Press **Return** to confirm these settings and return to the document.
7. Type **Word Process Steno Books** and press **Cmd-Return** to move to the next column.
8. Type **Acme Office Products** and press **Return**. Then type **123 Lawrence Avenue** and press **Return**. Then type **Chicago, IL 60620** and press **Return**.
9. Press **Cmd-Return** to move back to the first column.
10. Type **Eye Nice Steno Books** and press **Cmd-Return** to move to the next column again.
11. Type **Warren-Johnson Products** and press **Return**. Type **158 Samuel Lane** and press **Return**. Type **Bedford, TX 76022** and press **Return**. Then press **Cmd-Return**.

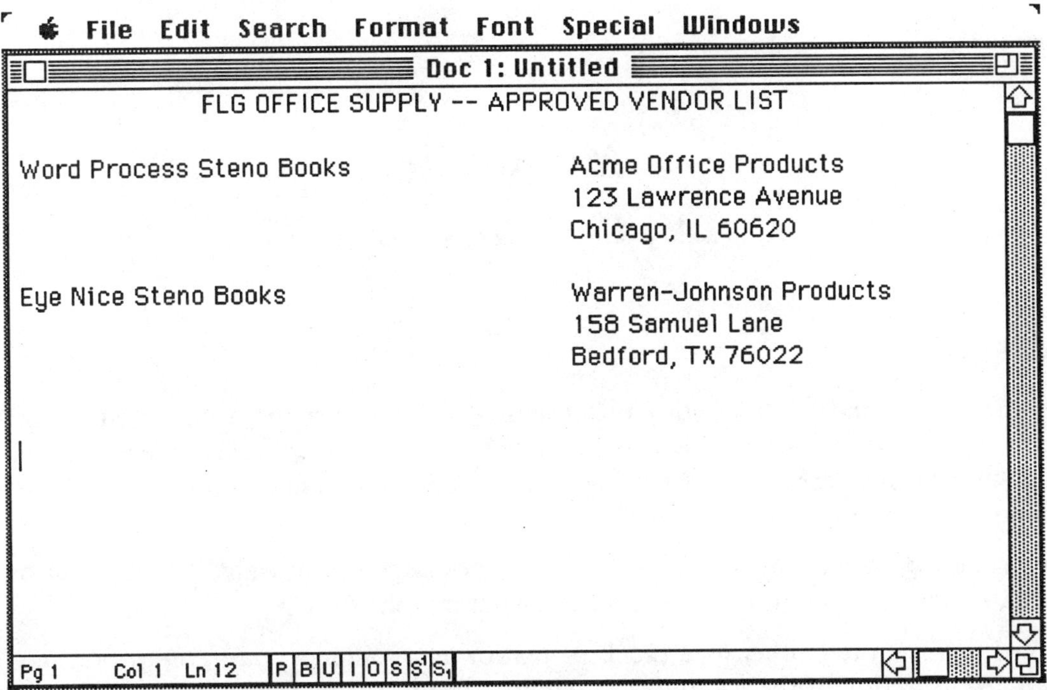

12. Press **Cmd-S**, type **Vendor List**, and press **Return** to save the document.
13. Press **Cmd-K** to close the document. Then turn to Module 24 to continue the learning sequence.

Module 9

COPY, CUT, AND PASTE

DESCRIPTION

The Copy command lets you copy text for use in other parts of a document or in other documents. The Cut command lets you cut text from a document and move it to other parts of a document or to other documents. Each command is used in conjunction with the Paste command, the mouse, and the Select command.

You can cut or copy as much or as little text or graphics as you want. You can cut or copy a block of text or graphics, or a sentence, a paragraph, or a page.

Selected text is stored either as a block of text or as a sentence, paragraph, or page in the *Clipboard*, a section of the computer's memory. Then you can move the cursor to the place where you would like to insert a copy of the text and paste it there. WordPerfect inserts the text and automatically adjusts the document. You can retrieve the same text or graphics as many times as you want, since the text stays in memory until you either define another selection of text or leave WordPerfect.

NOTE

Text selected with the mouse or the Select key and text defined as a sentence, paragraph, or page stays in the Clipboard. So if you define a block of text, for example, it will stay in the Clipboard until you either define another block or you cut or copy a sentence, paragraph, or page. To see what text has been selected, select Show Clipboard from the Windows menu.

Both the Cut and Copy commands are very useful for cutting or copying text and putting that text in other documents. The text you choose to copy stays in memory until you leave WordPerfect. One way to copy between documents is by using WordPerfect's Windows feature (Module 35), which lets you open as many documents as you have memory for simultaneously. Another way is by using the Append command, which lets you copy blocks of text from one document to another.

COPYING OR CUTTING SELECTED TEXT To copy selected text, select the text you want to copy, then select Copy from the Edit menu or press Cmd-C or F14. To cut text after you have selected it, select Cut from the Edit menu or press Cmd-X or F13.

Edit	
Undo	⌘Z
Cut	⌘X
Copy	⌘C
Paste	⌘V
Append	⌘A ▶
Undelete...	⌘U
Typeover	
Case Convert	▶
Insert Literal...	⌘I
Select	⌘6 ▶
Show Codes	⌘7

The text is then stored in the Clipboard. If you copied the text, a copy of the text is stored in the Clipboard. If you cut it, the text is cut from the document and stored in the Clipboard.

Move the cursor to the location where you want the text to be placed and select Paste from the Edit menu or press Cmd-V or F15.

Repeat the Paste procedure as many times as necessary.

COPYING OR CUTTING SENTENCES, PARAGRAPHS, PAGES, OR ALL This feature lets you cut or copy text from one location to another without having to select the text with the mouse. It is useful only if you are cutting or copying a sentence, paragraph, page, or the entire document. In order to cut or copy the text, it is only necessary to make sure that the cursor is anywhere in the sentence, paragraph, or page that you want to copy.

If the text you want to cut or copy is more complicated (i.e, two sentences, two paragraphs, two pages), manually select the text, as described in the previous section.

To copy a sentence, paragraph, page, or the entire document, make sure the cursor is anywhere in the sentence, paragraph, or page, and then press Cmd-6 or Cmd-F4 or click on Select in the Edit menu.

Edit

Select
1. Select On ⌘⇧N
2. Sentence
3. Paragraph
4. Page
5. Column
6. All ⌘⇧A

Type or click on 2 to select a sentence, 3 to select a paragraph, 4 to select a page, or 6 to select the entire document.

To copy selected text, select Copy from the Edit menu or press Cmd-C or F14. To cut selected text, select Cut from the Edit menu or press Cmd-X or F13. Then move the cursor to the location where you want the text to be placed and select Paste from the Edit menu or press Cmd-V or F15. Repeat the Paste procedure as many times as necessary.

COPYING OR CUTTING INFORMATION FROM COLUMNS If you want to copy or cut data from columns (Module 8), use the copy or cut command while in Column mode. To copy or cut columns, be sure you are in Column mode, then select the text to copy or cut.

Press Cmd-6 or click on Select from the Edit menu. Then type or click on 5 for columns.

To copy selected text, select Copy from the Edit menu or press Cmd-C or F14. To cut it, select Cut from the Edit menu or press Cmd-X or F13. Then move the cursor to the location where you want the text to be placed and select Paste from the Edit menu or press Cmd-V or F15. Repeat the Paste procedure as many times as necessary.

APPENDING TEXT FROM ONE DOCUMENT TO ANOTHER WordPerfect makes it very easy to copy or cut blocks of text from one document to another. If you have both documents available, you can cut or copy text from one document, switch to the other, and paste it there. Or you can use the Append command.

The Append command copies a block of text to the end of a file or to the Clipboard. To Append text, select the text you want to copy and click on Append from the Edit menu or press Cmd-A.

Edit

Append
1. To Clipboard
2. To File...

Type or click on 1 to append the selected text to the Clipboard or 2 to append the text to a file. If you type or click on 1, the data is copied to the Clipboard. If you type or click on 2, a screen similar to the following appears:

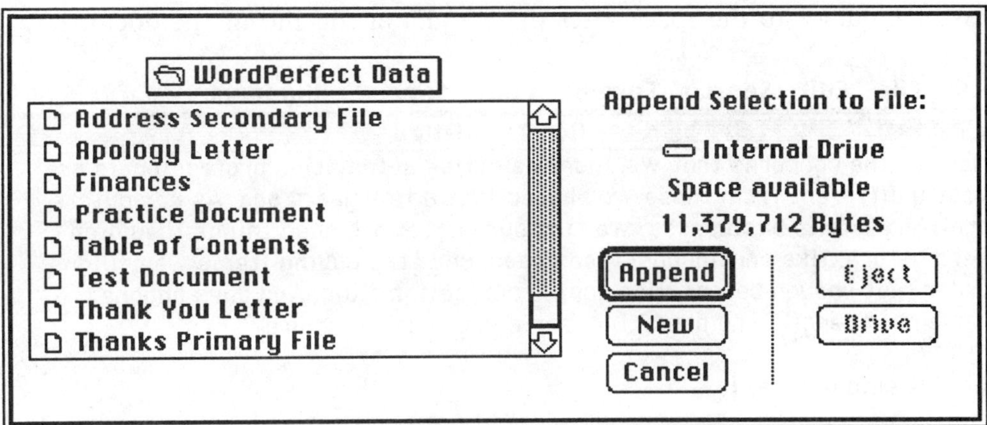

Select the file to append the data to and click on Append. The data is placed at the end of that file.

APPLICATIONS

The Copy and Cut commands, when used in conjunction with the Paste command, are useful for copying or moving text within a document or from one document to another. Each saves time and can often reduce typing errors. The Append command is useful when you need to copy text from one document to the end of another.

TYPICAL OPERATION

This example shows you how to copy a sentence from one location in a speech to another.

1. If necessary, start WordPerfect. Then create a document similar to the following:

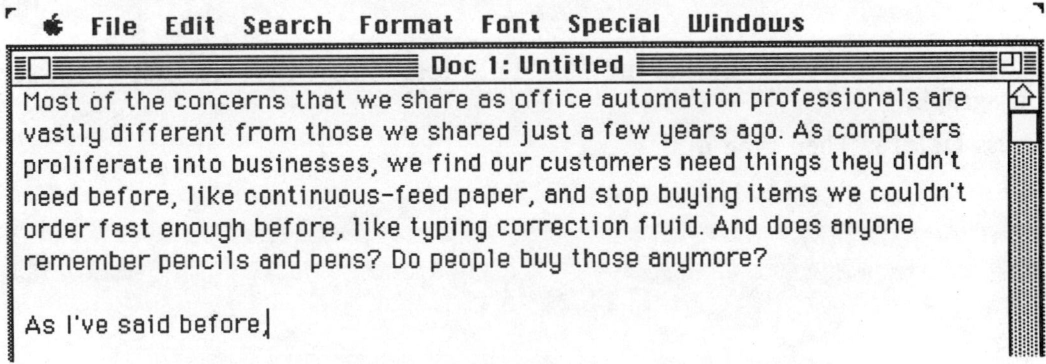

2. Place the cursor anywhere in the first sentence and press **Cmd-6** from the keyboard or click on **Select** in the Edit menu. Then type or click on **2** to select the sentence.
3. Press **Cmd-C** or click on **Copy** from the Edit menu.
4. Move the cursor to the space after the comma at the end of the document.

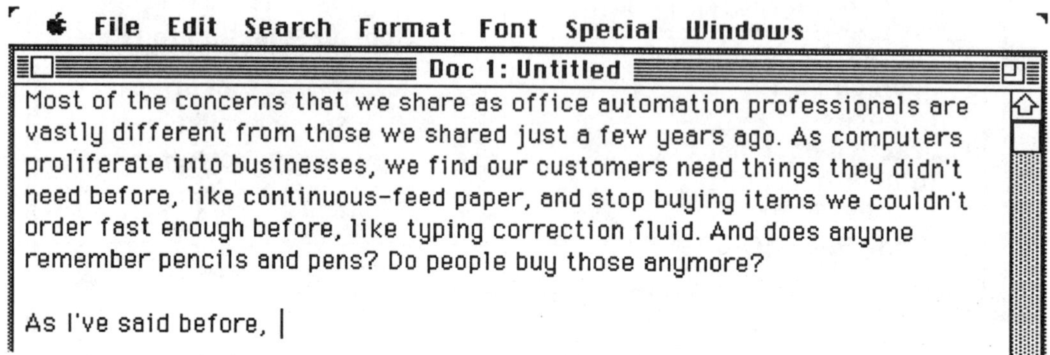

5. Press **Cmd-V** or click on **Paste** from the Edit menu.

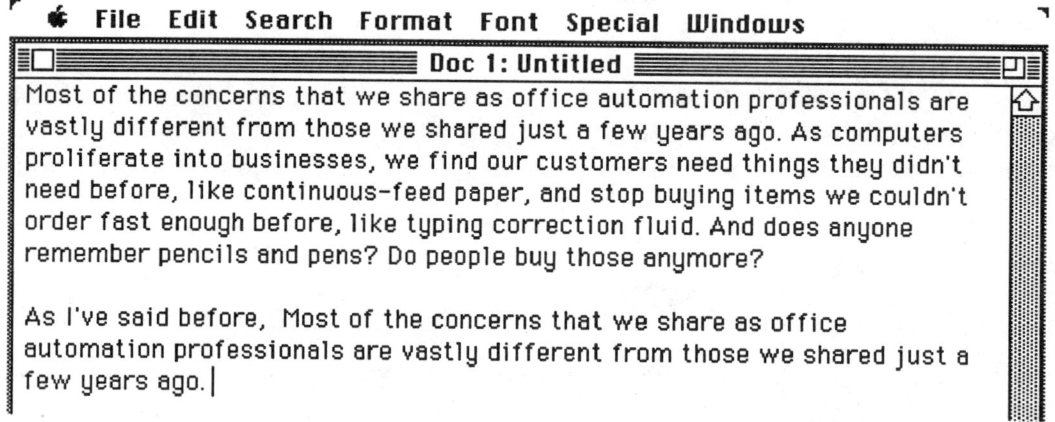

6. Move the cursor to the right of the "M" in "Most" in the first sentence of the second paragraph.
7. Press **Delete**. Then type **m**.

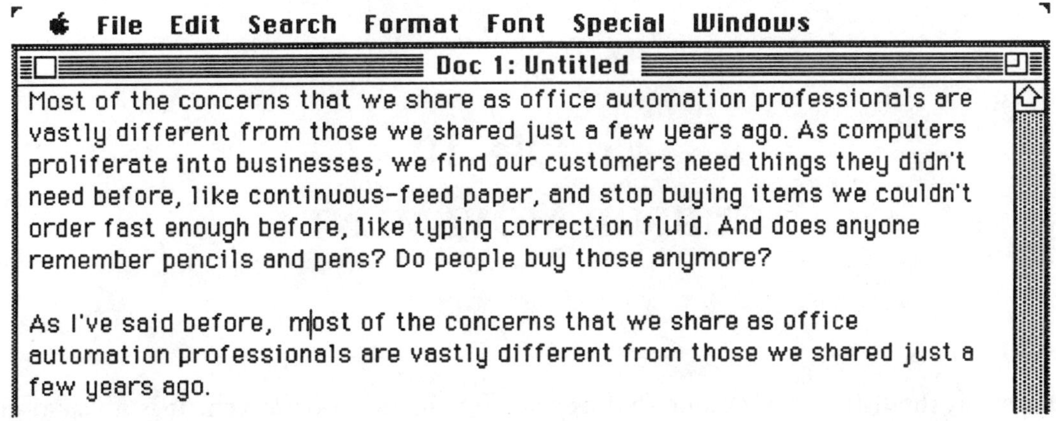

8. Press **Cmd-S**, type **Office Automation**, and press **Return** to save the document.
9. Press **Cmd-K** to close the document. Then turn to Module 39 to continue the learning sequence.

Module 10
CURSOR MOVEMENT

DESCRIPTION

The cursor is the little blinking line that appears on the monitor screen. It is a visual guide that identifies your position in the document. The cursor is your guide in all phases of word processing, from the first typed words to the final stages of editing and printing. Understanding the most efficient ways to move the cursor around a document can save editing time, thereby increasing the speed at which you process documents. Moving the cursor where you want it on the screen in the fewest keystrokes is called "cursor control." While you are creating a document, the cursor moves when you type or when you press the Spacebar. You can also move the cursor through the use of other keys on the keyboard or with the mouse.

To move the cursor with the mouse, simply point the mouse where you want to be and click. You can tell the location of the mouse by looking for the mouse pointer (I) on-screen. As you move the mouse, the pointer moves also. Or use the "elevator button" in the Scroll Bar on the right side of the screen. Drag the elevator button to move through the document. Or click on the arrows at the top or bottom of the Scroll Bar. Clicking anywhere in the Scroll Bar with the mouse moves the cursor ahead one screen at a time. Realize, however, that the cursor does not move until you click the mouse.

There is a disadvantage in using the mouse: clicking at the beginning of a line does not necessarily move the cursor to the left of all the codes on the line. In order to do this, it is necessary to move the cursor with the cursor control keys.

NOTE

The amount of control you have over cursor movement depends greatly on the type of keyboard you have. If you have an Extended Keyboard, you have more control; if you have an original Apple Keyboard, you have less. This module discusses efficient cursor movement for all Apple keyboards.

If you have a numeric keypad, the cursor keys work like this:

1	End
2	Down Arrow
3	Page Down (Pg Dn)
4	Left Arrow
5	Enter
6	Right Arrow
7	Home
8	Up Arrow
9	Page Up (PgUp)
0	Typeover
–	Screen Up
+	Screen Down
.	Delete Right

If you have an Extended Keyboard, additional Up, Down, Left, and Right Arrow keys and Home, End, PgUp, and PgDn keys are provided between the regular keys and the numeric keypad.

If you have an original Macintosh keyboard, you have fewer options:

Cmd-=	Up Arrow
Cmd-'	Down Arrow
Cmd-[	Left Arrow
Cmd-]	Right Arrow

Use the arrow keys to move the cursor by one character (letter, number, symbol, or blank space) to reposition the cursor on the screen. If you move the cursor so far to the right that it moves beyond the last character in a line, the cursor appears on the first character of the next line. This is called "wrapping around." Also, if you move the cursor too far to the left, it wraps around and appears as the last character of the previous line. The cursor always stays within the screen boundary.

While the cursor keys alone let you move the cursor by one character or line per keystroke, other keystrokes help you move the cursor farther. You can, for example, "jump" the cursor to the beginning or end of a line. Or you can move the cursor from one word to the next or to the beginning of a page or a document.

WordPerfect uses the following keystrokes for cursor control. (Cursor control with the Esc key is described in Module 13 and with the Go To command in Module 18.)

Keystroke	*Function*
Up Arrow	Moves cursor up one line. Can scroll to previous page if cursor is on line 1 of a page.
Down Arrow	Moves cursor down one line. Can scroll to next page if cursor is on the last line of a page.
Left Arrow	Moves cursor one character to the left or to the last character on the previous line if the cursor is in position 1.
Right Arrow	Moves cursor one character to the right or to the first character on the next line if the cursor is in the last position on a line.
Cmd-Left Arrow	Jumps cursor to the first character of the previous word.
Cmd-Right Arrow	Jumps cursor to the first character of the next word.
Enter, Left Arrow	Jumps cursor to the beginning of the text on the current line.
Enter, Enter, Left Arrow	Jumps cursor to the beginning of the current line (before the text, if necessary).
Enter, Enter, Enter, Left Arrow	Jumps cursor to the extreme beginning of the current line, before any codes.
Enter, Right Arrow (or End)	Jumps cursor to the end of the text on the current line.
Enter, Enter, Right Arrow	Jumps cursor to the end of the current line (after any text, if necessary).
Enter, Up Arrow	Jumps cursor to the beginning of the text on the current screen.
Enter, Enter, Up Arrow	Jumps cursor to the beginning of the current document.
Enter, Enter, Enter, Up Arrow	Jumps cursor to the beginning of the current document before any codes.
Enter, Down Arrow	Jumps cursor to the end of the current page.
Enter, Enter, Down Arrow	Jumps cursor to the end of the current document.
Screen Up	Jumps cursor to the first line of the current screen of text.
Screen Down	Jumps cursor to the last line of the current screen of text.
PgUp	Jumps cursor to the previous page.
PgDn	Jumps cursor to the next page.

USING CURSOR KEYS The Up Arrow and Down Arrow keys move the cursor up or down one line at a time. Right Arrow and Left Arrow move the cursor to the right or left one character at a time.

You can move faster through documents by using the cursor keys in conjunction with others; for example, use the Cmd key and the Left Arrow or Right Arrow keys to move the cursor one word at a time instead of one space at a time. Press these keys simultaneously to move the cursor.

Or, use the Enter key (or Home key on an Extended Keyboard) in conjunction with the Left Arrow or Right Arrow key to move the cursor to the beginning or end of any line you are on, no matter where you are on the line. Press the Enter key and let go. Then press the appropriate arrow key.

Another way to move the cursor to the end of any line is by pressing the End key.

The arrow keys help move you from one screen (approximately one-half page) of text to another. Enter, Up Arrow and Enter, Down Arrow keys move the cursor to the beginning and end of a screen of text.

Another way to move up or down a screenful of text at a time is to use the + and – keys on the numeric keypad. The – key moves the cursor up a screen, while + moves the cursor down a screen.

If you want to move faster, use the PgUp and PgDn keys to move the cursor through the document one page at a time. Or, use the Enter key in conjunction with the Up Arrow and Down Arrow keys to move the cursor to the beginning or end of a page. If you press the Enter key twice in succession and then press Up Arrow or Down Arrow, the cursor moves to the beginning or end of a document.

APPLICATIONS

Efficient cursor control is essential to word processing. You control the cursor every time you edit or create a document with WordPerfect. Learning new ways to control the cursor can help you work faster and more efficiently.

TYPICAL OPERATION

The following example shows how you use cursor control to help you edit a document more efficiently.

1. If necessary, start WordPerfect. Then create a document similar to the following. You will be using this document in other modules. Each financial statement should be on a separate page. Press **Cmd-Return** between pages. Press the **Tab** key repeatedly to position the indented lines, press the Center key (**Cmd-Shift-C**) to center text, and press **Cmd-U** to underline text. Press **Return** at the end of each paragraph, but let WordPerfect's wordwrap function break the lines within each paragraph.

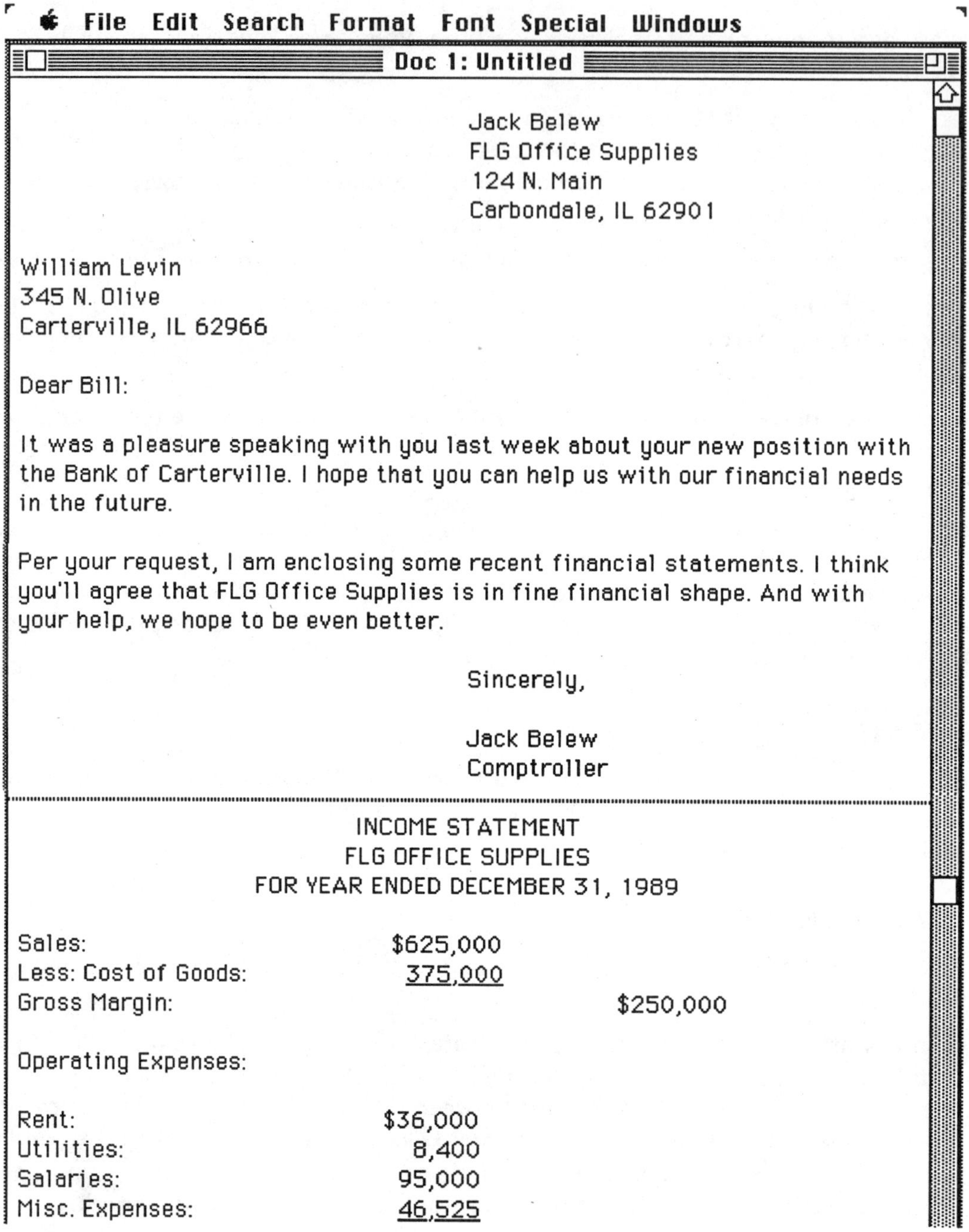

File Edit Search Format Font Special Windows

Doc 1: Untitled

Jack Belew
FLG Office Supplies
124 N. Main
Carbondale, IL 62901

William Levin
345 N. Olive
Carterville, IL 62966

Dear Bill:

It was a pleasure speaking with you last week about your new position with the Bank of Carterville. I hope that you can help us with our financial needs in the future.

Per your request, I am enclosing some recent financial statements. I think you'll agree that FLG Office Supplies is in fine financial shape. And with your help, we hope to be even better.

Sincerely,

Jack Belew
Comptroller

INCOME STATEMENT
FLG OFFICE SUPPLIES
FOR YEAR ENDED DECEMBER 31, 1989

Sales:	$625,000	
Less: Cost of Goods:	375,000	
Gross Margin:		$250,000
Operating Expenses:		
Rent:	$36,000	
Utilities:	8,400	
Salaries:	95,000	
Misc. Expenses:	46,525	

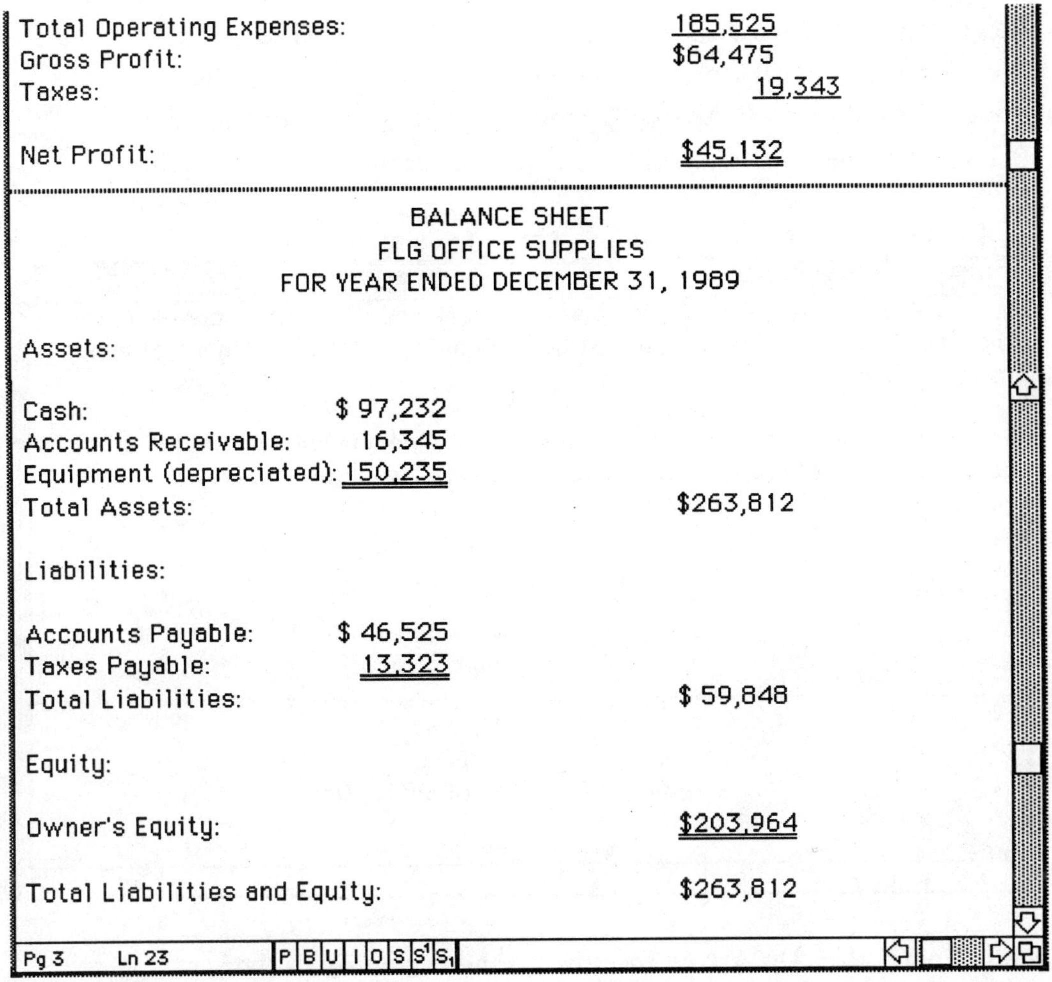

Total Operating Expenses:		185,525
Gross Profit:		$64,475
Taxes:		19,343
Net Profit:		$45,132

BALANCE SHEET
FLG OFFICE SUPPLIES
FOR YEAR ENDED DECEMBER 31, 1989

Assets:		
Cash:	$ 97,232	
Accounts Receivable:	16,345	
Equipment (depreciated):	150,235	
Total Assets:		$263,812
Liabilities:		
Accounts Payable:	$ 46,525	
Taxes Payable:	13,323	
Total Liabilities:		$ 59,848
Equity:		
Owner's Equity:		$203,964
Total Liabilities and Equity:		$263,812

Pg 3 Ln 23 P B U I O S S S

2. Press **Enter, Enter, Up Arrow** to move the cursor to the top of the document.
3. Press **PgDn** to move the cursor to the next page.
4. Press **Up Arrow** repeatedly to move the cursor to the "I" in "It" at the beginning of line 13 on page 1.
5. Press **Cmd-Right Arrow** to move to the next word.

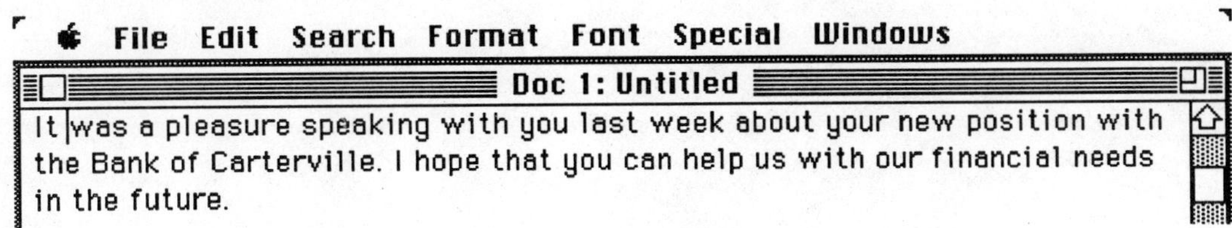

6. Press **Cmd-Left Arrow** to move back to the previous word.
7. Press **End** (key pad 1) to move the cursor to the end of the line.
8. Press **Enter**, then **Left Arrow** to move to the beginning of the line.
9. Press **Enter**, then **Down Arrow** to move to the beginning of the last line on the screen.

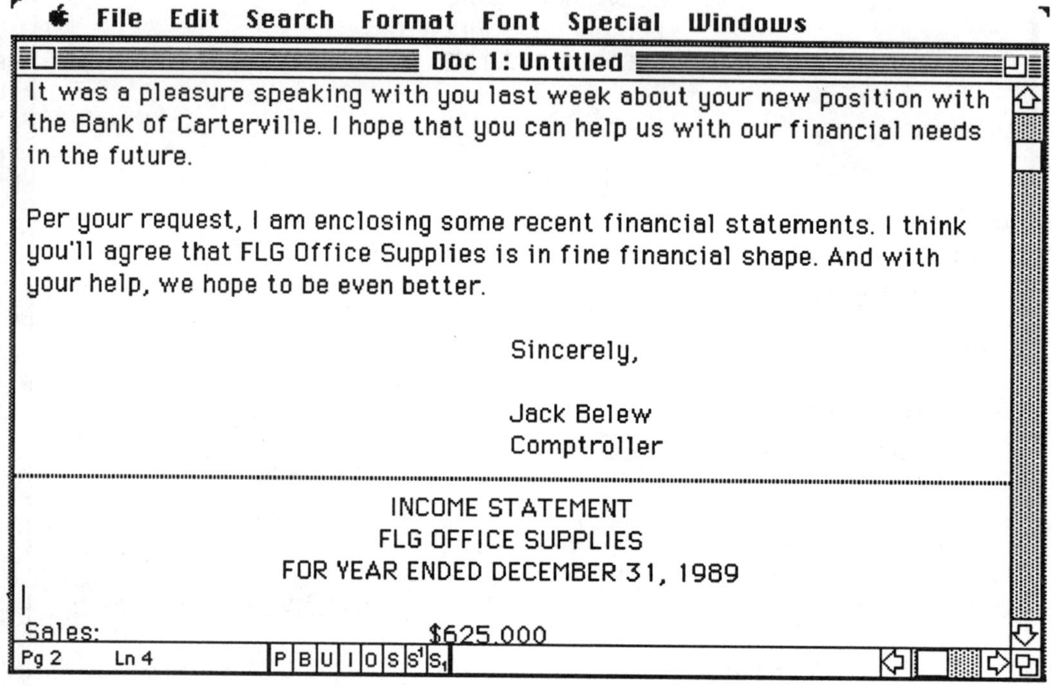

10. Press **Enter**, then **Up Arrow** to move to the beginning of the screen.
11. Press **PgDn** to move to the beginning of the next page.
12. Press **Enter** twice, then press **Down Arrow** to move the cursor to the end of the document.

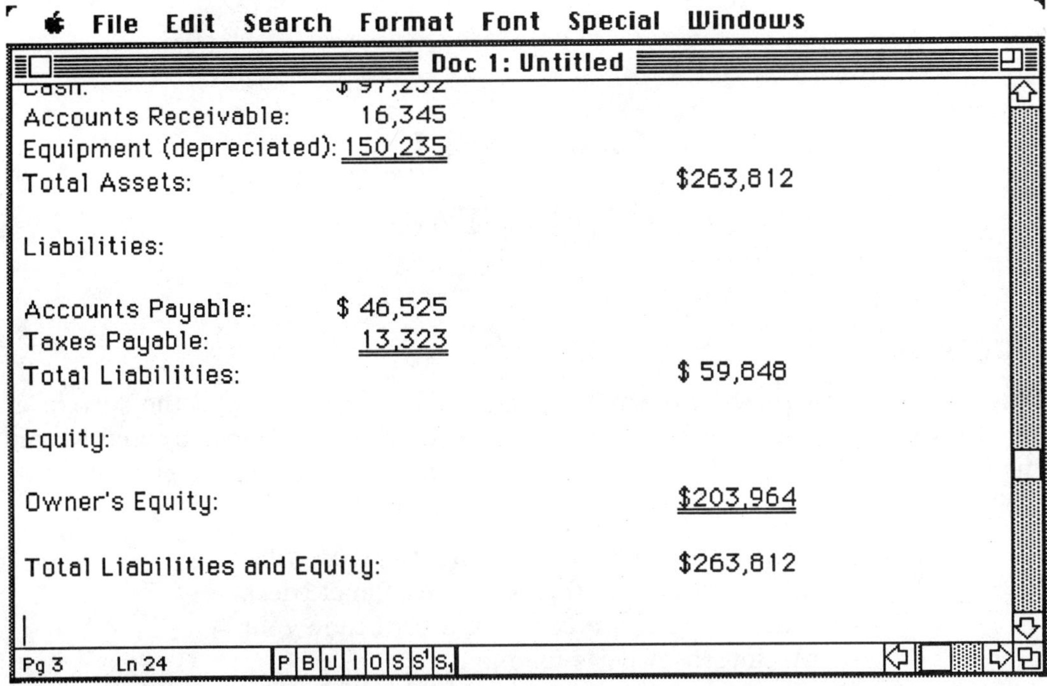

13. Press **Cmd-S**, type **Finances**, and press **Return** to save the document.
14. Turn to Module 14 to continue the learning sequence.

Module 11

DATE/TIME

DESCRIPTION

The Date command inserts the current date and/or the current time at the current cursor location. The date and time are either the current date/time (as determined by your Macintosh) or some later date/time determined when the document is retrieved or printed.

NOTE

To set the current date and time on your Macintosh, use the Control Panel desk accessory. This procedure is described in your Macintosh owner's manual.

The default date format is month, day, year (February 27, 1990). You can change this format and add the time as well. The Date command is useful for letters, legal papers, or other documents where date and time stamping is important.

USING THE DATE COMMAND Select Date from the Special menu or press Cmd-D or Shift-F5.

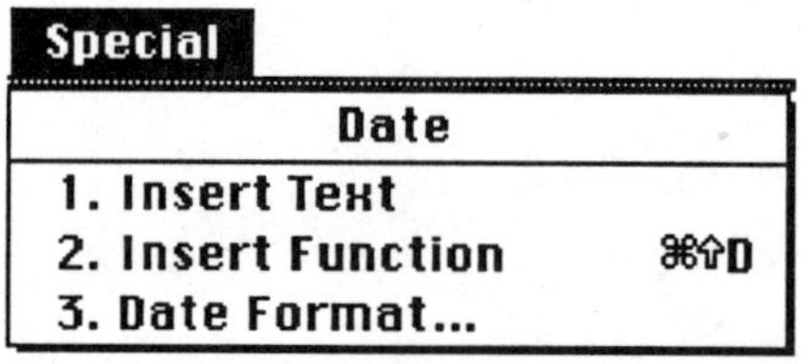

Special

Date

1. Insert Text
2. Insert Function ⌘⇧D
3. Date Format...

To insert the date, type or click on 1. The current date appears on-screen at the cursor location.

SELECTING THE CORRECT FORMAT There are several variations of the format for date and time. To select a format, type or click on 3 from the Date menu.

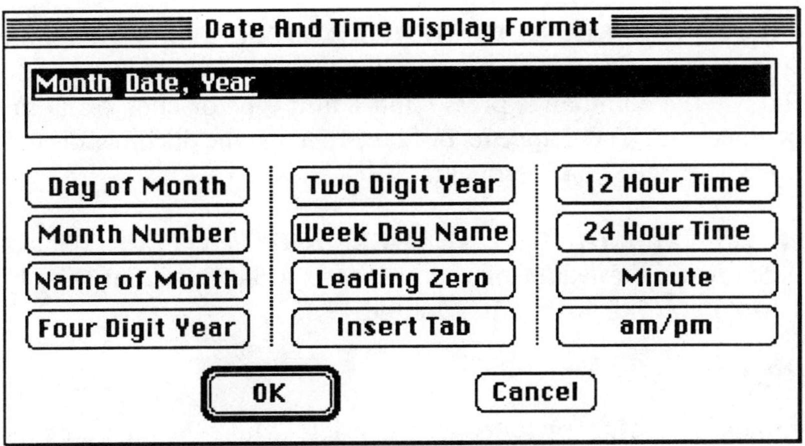

To change from the current format of month, date, year, click on the button(s) of your choice. Then click OK or press Return.

Button/Code	*Example*
Day of Month Date	23
Month Number Month#	1
Name of Month Month	January
Four Digit Year Year	1990
Two Digit Year Yr	90
Week Day Name Day,	Tuesday,
Leading Zero 0	01/09/90
Insert Tab TAB	Tuesday, January 1 9:00
12 Hour Time Hour(12)	8:13
24 Hour Time Hour(24)	20:13
Minute Minute	8:13
AM/PM am/pm	8:13 pm

You can also add parentheses, spaces, and other punctuation or text.

INSERTING A DATE FUNCTION CODE The date function code inserts the current date and/or time into your text. After the document is retrieved, the date and time are updated to the current time. When a document is printed, the code displays the date and time the document was sent to the printer. To insert a date/time function code, position the cursor where you want the code and press Cmd-Shift-D or select Insert Function from the Date menu. To avoid formatting problems, it is advisable to press Return after inserting the function code.

USING THE DATE COMMAND IN MERGED TEXT The Date command inserts the current date and time into a series of merge letters. (The Merge command is described in Module 26.) To use the command, press Cmd-8 and type or click on D in the appropriate place in the document. A " ^ D" appears on-screen. When the document is merged, the current date is inserted where the " ^ D" appears.

USING THE DATE COMMAND IN HEADERS AND FOOTERS Clicking on the Clock icon ( ) while creating a header or footer inserts a date code into the header or footer. (Headers and footers are described in Module 19.)

APPLICATIONS

The Date command is useful for letters, legal briefs, and other documents where the date and time the document was completed is critical.

The date code feature is useful for documents that need the date updated every time they are retrieved. The date code function is not intended for use in documents in which the original date is saved for future reference, because the date code changes to the current date every time the document is retrieved.

TYPICAL OPERATION

In this example, you insert a date/time code into a time-sensitive memo. The code will reflect when the memo is sent out, not when it was written.

1. If necessary, start WordPerfect. Then create a document similar to the following:

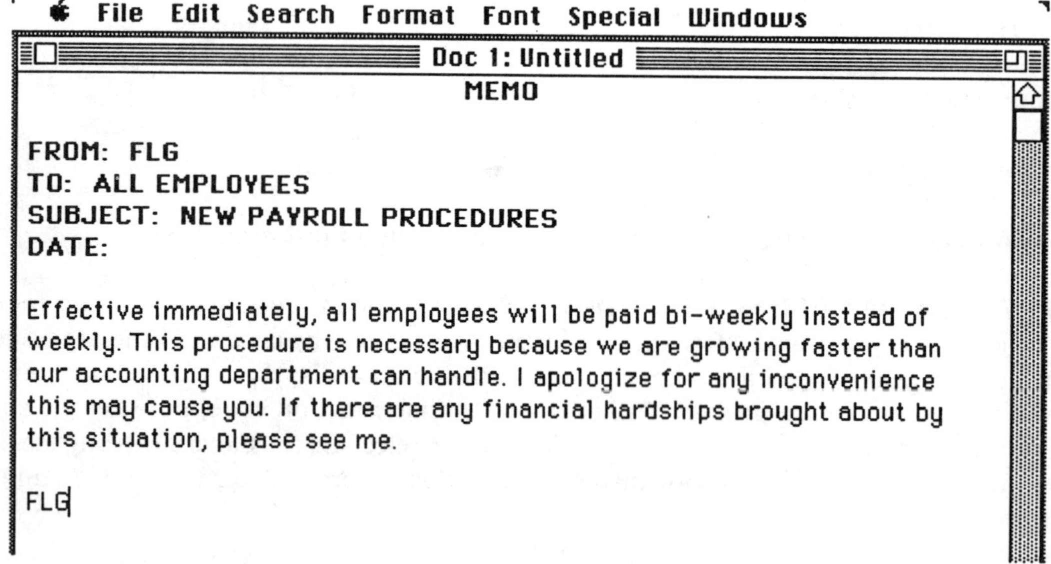

2. Move the cursor to the space after "DATE:" and press the **Spacebar**, then **Cmd-D**. Type or click on **3** to check the date format.
3. Click on **Week Day Name**, type **,** press the **Spacebar**, then click on **Name of Month** and press the **Spacebar**. Click on **Day of Month**, press the **Spacebar**, and type **- -**. Press the **Spacebar**, click **12 Hour Time**, then type **:** and click **Minute**. Press the **Spacebar** and click **am/pm**.

Date And Time Display Format

Day, Month Date -- Hour(12):Minute am/pm

Day of Month	Two Digit Year	12 Hour Time
Month Number	Week Day Name	24 Hour Time
Name of Month	Leading Zero	Minute
Four Digit Year	Insert Tab	am/pm

OK   Cancel

4. Click **OK** or press **Return**. With the cursor on the space after "Date:" press the **Spacebar** and press **Cmd-Shift-D**.

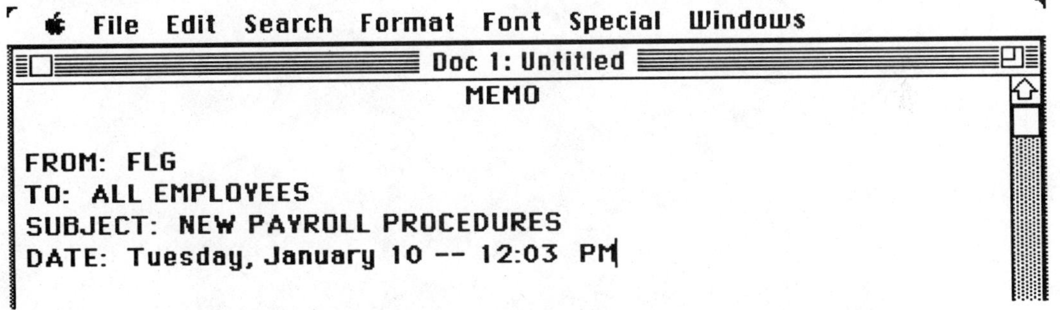

5. Press **Cmd-S**, type **Payroll Memo**, and press **Return** to save the document. Then press **Cmd-K** to close the document. Wait ten minutes.
6. Press **Cmd-O**, then move the cursor to **Payroll Memo** and press **Return**.

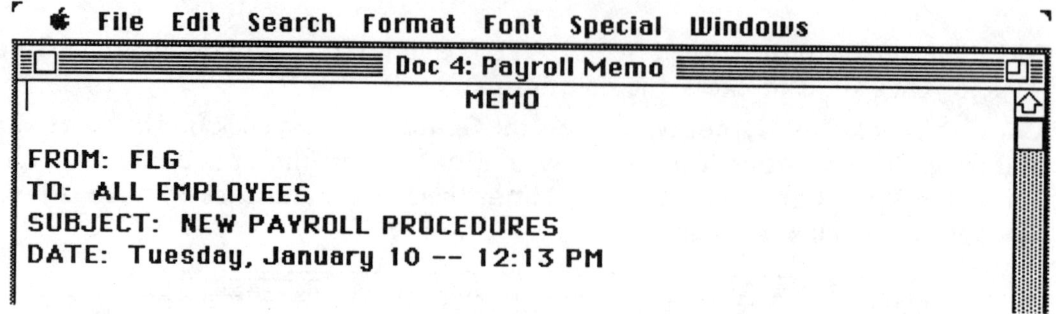

7. Press **Cmd-K** to close the document again.
8. Turn to Module 32 to continue the learning sequence.

Module 12

DELETE

DESCRIPTION

WordPerfect deletes text in many ways. The program features six types of Delete commands — Delete Left, Delete Right, Delete Word, Delete Block, Delete to End of Line, and Delete to End of Page. And, if you accidentally delete text, you can use the Undelete command to get it back. (The Undelete command is described in Module 4.)

These functions can help you remove small or large amounts of text with only a few keystrokes. They eliminate unwanted characters, words, lines, pages, or blocks of text.

You can delete as many or as few characters as you want. If you want to delete entire files or folders, use the Delete File/Folder command, referred to in Module 14. WordPerfect delete functions are listed below:

NOTE

The Delete to End of Line, Delete to End of Page, and Delete Right commands do not work on older Apple keyboards. You must have a numeric keypad for these commands to work.

Function	*Menu/Keystroke*	*Description*
Delete to End of Line	Cmd-1	Deletes text from cursor to end of line.
Delete to End of Page	Cmd-3	Deletes text from cursor to end of page.
Delete Left	Delete (Backspace)	Deletes text to left of cursor.
Delete Right	Del, decimal point	Deletes text to right of cursor.
Delete Selection	Edit, Select Cmd-6, 2, 3, or 4, or Cmd-Shift-A to select all, Delete.	Deletes selected text.
Delete Word	Cmd-Delete	Deletes word cursor is pointing to.
Undelete	Edit, Cmd-U	Negates last deletion.

DELETE RIGHT Delete Right deletes text to the right of the cursor. It is accomplished using the decimal point on the number pad or the Del key on an extended keyboard. It is most effective when deleting only a few characters. To use Delete Right, move the cursor to the character or characters you want to delete and press the decimal point key on the numeric keypad (or Del) for each character you want to delete. WordPerfect deletes characters to the right of the cursor.

DELETE LEFT Delete Left deletes text to the left of the cursor. It is accomplished using the Delete key. To use Delete Left, move the cursor to the character or characters you want to delete and press the Delete key (called the Backspace key on some keyboards) for each character you want to delete. WordPerfect deletes characters to the left of the cursor.

DELETE WORD Delete Left and Delete Right are fine for deleting one or two characters, but it is cumbersome to use those commands to delete entire words. The Delete Word Command deletes an entire word and the space after that word. It is accomplished using the Cmd-Delete key combination. To delete words, move the cursor anywhere within the word you want to delete and press Cmd-Delete for each word you want to delete. WordPerfect deletes words to the right of the cursor.

DELETE SELECTION The Delete Selection command is convenient for deleting large amounts of text. It deletes any selection you make (for further information on selecting text, see Module 37). You can quickly select large amounts of text by using the Select command or by clicking the mouse to select a block of text. To delete a block of text using the Select command, move the cursor to the beginning of the block of text you want to delete and press Cmd-6. Then type 2 to select a sentence, 3 to select a paragraph, or 4 to select an entire page. Or press Cmd-Shift-A to select the entire document. The appropriate amount of text is highlighted. Press Delete to delete the entire block.

To delete a block of text using the mouse, move the cursor to the beginning of the block of text you want to delete and click and hold the mouse button. Then point the mouse to the end of the block you want to delete and let go of the mouse button. The appropriate amount of text is highlighted. Press Backspace to delete the entire block. You can also highlight text using the Shift and arrow keys simultaneously.

DELETE TO END OF LINE The Delete to End of Line command deletes everything to the right of the cursor on the current line. It is accomplished by pressing Cmd-1 (using the 1 on the numeric keypad). To use the Delete to End of Line command, move the cursor to the beginning of the text you want to delete and press Cmd-1. To delete an entire line of text, move the cursor to the beginning of the line you want to delete and press Cmd-1 to delete the rest of the text on that line.

DELETE TO END OF PAGE The Delete to End of Page command deletes everything to the right of the cursor on the current page. It is accomplished by pressing Cmd-3 (using the 3 on the numeric keypad). To use the Delete to End of Page command, move the cursor to the beginning of the text you want to delete and press Cmd-3. To delete an entire page of text, move the cursor to the beginning of the page you want to delete. Press Cmd-3. WordPerfect asks you to confirm the Delete to End of Page command.

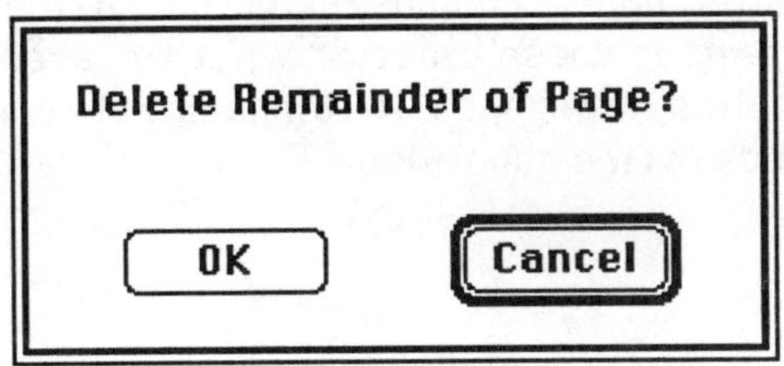

Click on OK to delete the rest of the text on that page.

APPLICATIONS

You almost always need to delete text while editing documents. WordPerfect helps you do this quickly and efficiently. To delete a small amount of text, use the Del, decimal point on the numeric keypad, or Delete keys. To delete a large amount of text, select a block or use the Delete to End of Line or Delete to End of Page commands. You can use WordPerfect's Delete commands to eliminate unwanted characters, words, lines, pages, and blocks of text. The command will delete as many or as few characters or pages of text as you wish. To delete entire files, use The Delete File command, described in Module 14.

TYPICAL OPERATION

In the following example, delete a large portion of a document by using all the Delete commands described in this module.

1. If necessary, start WordPerfect. Then create a document similar to the following:

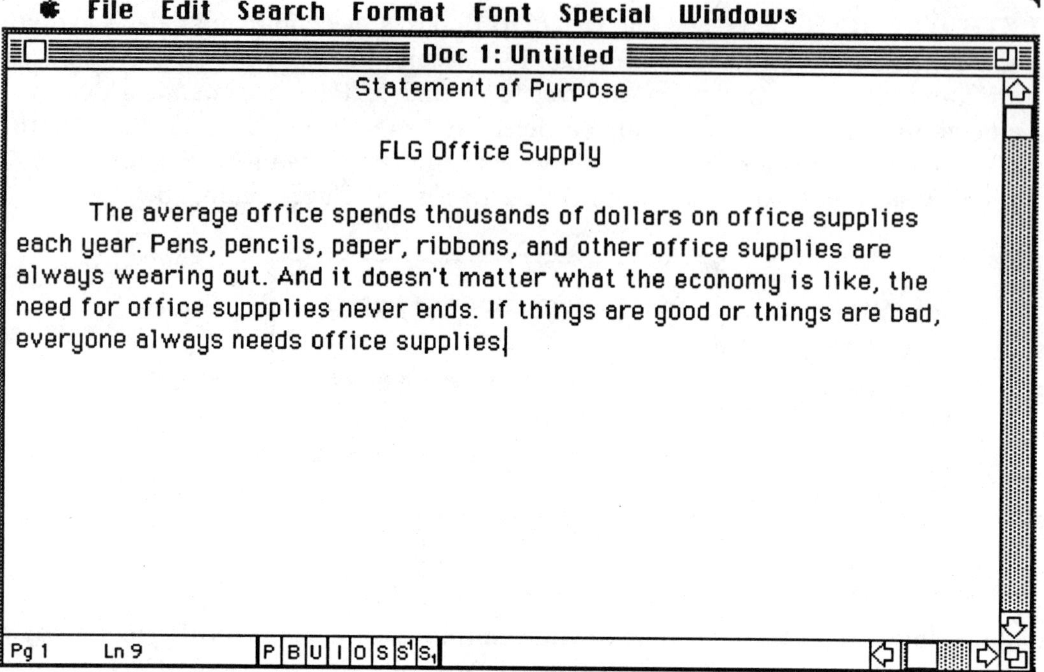

2. Position the cursor to the left of the "A" in "And." Then press **.** on the numeric keypad or the **Del** key on an Extended Keyboard four times to delete the word and the space that follows.
3. Position the cursor to the right of the "e" in the second occurrence of the word "office" in the first sentence and press **Delete** (or press **Backspace**) seven times to delete the word and the space before it.
4. Move the cursor to any character in the third occurrence of the word "office" (or in the space following the word). Press **Cmd-Delete** to delete the word.
5. Position the cursor on the "I" in "If" at the beginning of the last sentence and press **Cmd-6** (from the number keys at top of keyboard), or pull down the Edit menu and click on **Select**. Then type or click on **2** to select the entire sentence and press **Delete** to delete the block.
6. Position the cursor on the "i" in "it" and press **Cmd-1** (on the numeric keypad) to delete the rest of the text on that line.
7. Position the cursor on the "s" in "supplies" at the end of the document and press **Cmd-3** (on the numeric keypad) and click on **OK** to delete the remainder of text on the page. Your document should now look as follows:

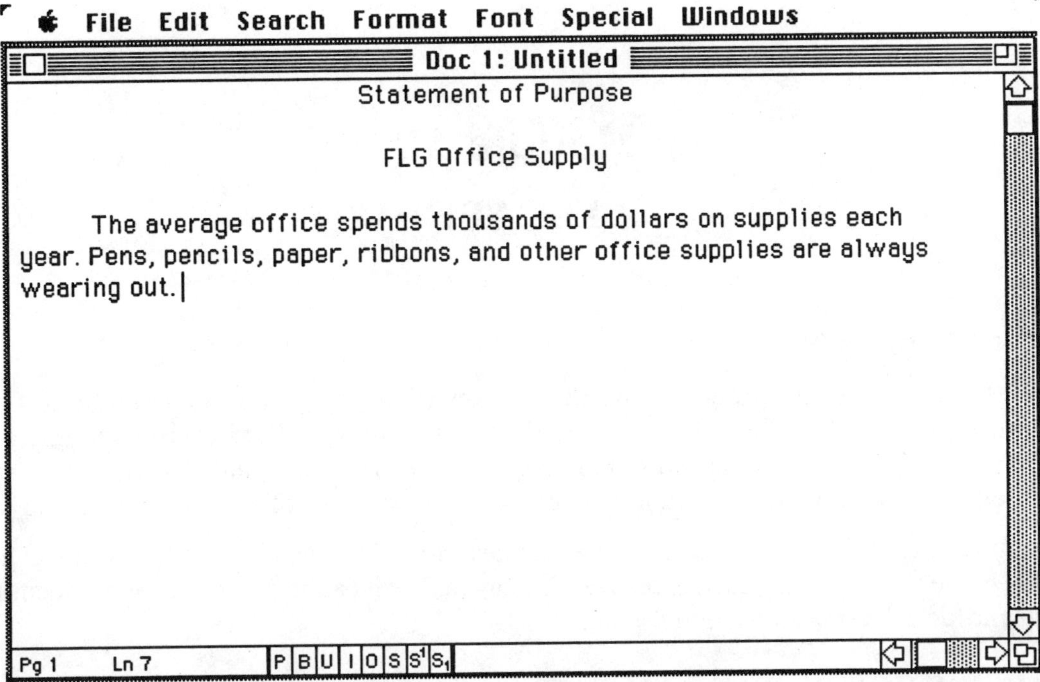

8. Press **Cmd-S**. Then type **Statement Of Purpose** and press **Return** to save the document.
9. Press **Cmd-K** to close the document, then turn to Module 37 to continue the learning sequence.

Module 13

ESCAPE

DESCRIPTION

Many MS-DOS software programs use the Esc key (Escape) to cancel a command. On the Macintosh, the Esc (or Clear) key isn't used very much. WordPerfect uses the Esc key as a repetition counter for advanced cursor control, text insertion and deletion, and macro execution. The default repeat value is 8, but you can change this to any value you want.

For example, to move the cursor eight pages ahead in a document, press Esc and PgDn and quickly move the cursor that distance. The Esc key makes it easier to move around documents, insert and delete text, and execute macros.

CHANGING THE REPEAT VALUE The repeat value can be easily changed, either temporarily or permanently. When you press the Esc key, you see:

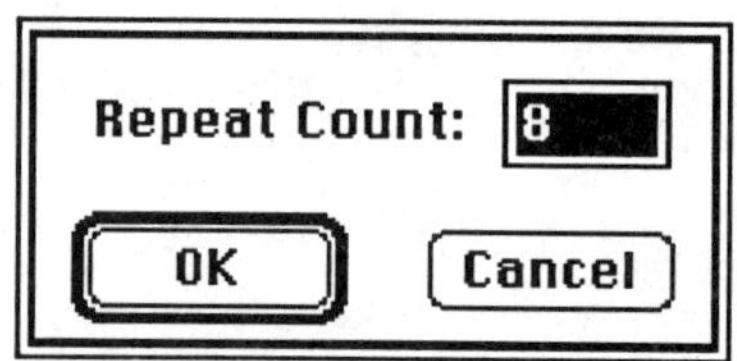

To change the repeat value, type another number. The repeat value can be any number you like. When changing the repeat value to another number, you have the option of saving that value or using it for one time only. To save a new repeat value, type the new value and press Return or click OK. To change it for one operation only, type the new value and press the appropriate key to execute the desired operation.

Clicking Cancel after you type a new value returns it to its previous value.

USING THE ESC KEY FOR CURSOR CONTROL The Esc key lets you move around a document faster than any other method. The Esc key used in conjunction with cursor control keys lets you move "n" spaces, words, lines, screens, or pages through a WordPerfect document. The options for cursor control with the Esc key are listed in the following table:

NOTE

In the keystroke sequences in this module, it is not necessary to hold down the Esc key. Simply press Esc, release it, then complete the keystroke sequence. For example, perform the sequence Esc, Cmd-End by pressing Esc, then Cmd-End.

CURSOR CONTROL USING THE ESC KEY REPEAT VALUE (n)

Keystroke	*Results*
Esc, Up Arrow	Moves the cursor n lines up.
Esc, Down Arrow	Moves the cursor n lines down.
Esc, Left Arrow	Moves the cursor n spaces to the left.
Esc, Right Arrow	Moves the cursor n spaces to the right.
Esc, Cmd-Left Arrow	Moves the cursor n words to the left.
Esc, Cmd-Right Arrow	Moves the cursor n words to the right.
Esc, PgUp	Moves the cursor n pages backward.
Esc, PgDn	Moves the cursor n pages forward.

USING THE ESC KEY TO INSERT TEXT The Esc key lets you insert the same character multiple times into a document with very few keystrokes. For example, if you want to create a dotted line at the bottom of a page in a document, move the cursor to the desired location and press Esc. Type 64, then -. You see:

File Edit Search Format Font Special Windows

Doc 1: Untitled

USING THE ESC KEY TO DELETE CHARACTERS While using the Esc key to insert characters is a relatively limited command, using the Esc key to delete characters is not. WordPerfect lets you delete "n" lines, characters, or words. It is very handy for deleting large blocks of text in a minimum of keystrokes.

The keystrokes necessary to delete text using the Esc key are listed in the following table:

TEXT DELETION USING THE ESC KEY REPEAT VALUE (n)

Keystroke	*Extend Keyboard Keystroke*	*Results*
Esc, period	Esc, Del	Deletes n characters to the right.
Esc, Cmd-Delete	Esc, Cmd-Backspace	Deletes n words to the right.
Esc, Cmd-3 (on keypad)	Esc, Cmd-End	Deletes n lines starting to the right of the cursor.

USING THE ESC KEY TO INVOKE A MACRO The Esc key can be used to perform a macro multiple times. This feature quickly gives you numerous on-screen copies of data generated by the macro.

APPLICATIONS

The Esc key can be used whenever a WordPerfect document is being edited. It allows for quick movement through a document, deletion and insertion of text, and multiple performances of a macro.

TYPICAL OPERATION

In this operation, you use the Esc key to control the cursor and move through a document very quickly.

1. If necessary, start WordPerfect. Then press **Cmd-O** and move the cursor to **Finances**, the document you created in Module 10. Then press **Return**. The first page of the document is shown here:

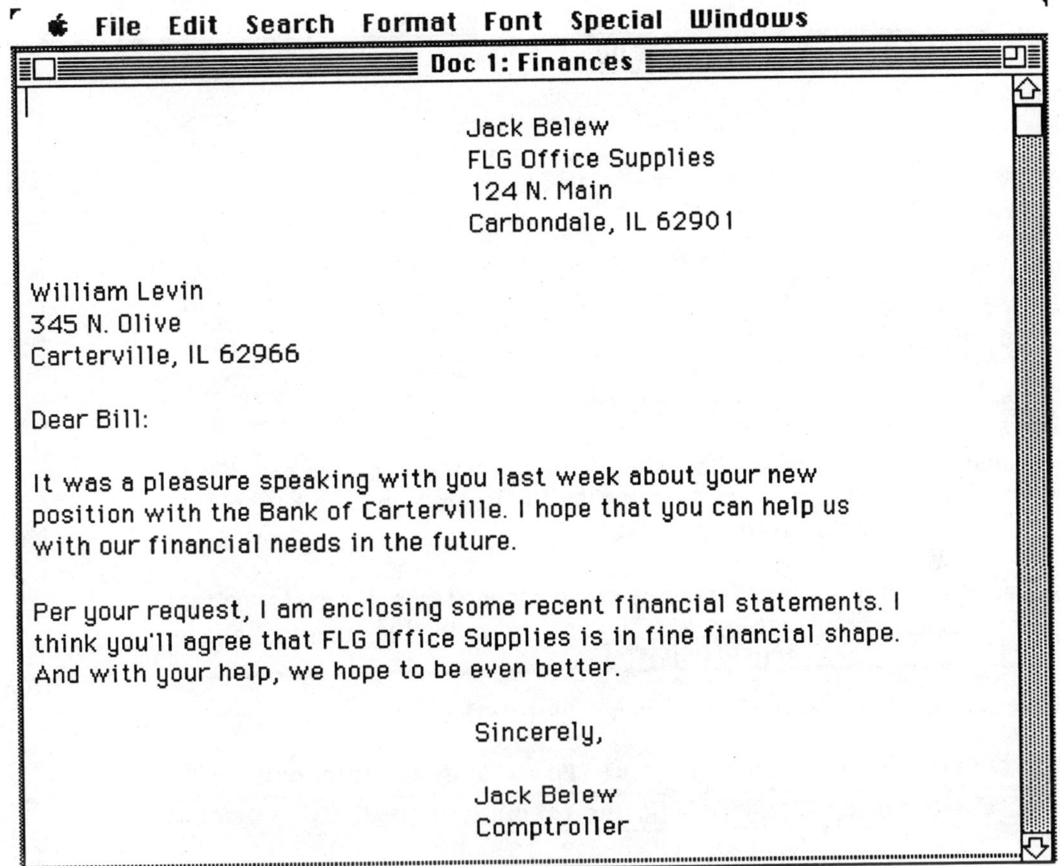

2. Press **Esc**, then **Down Arrow**. Notice the cursor move eight lines down. Press **Esc**, then **Down Arrow** again. Notice the cursor move another eight lines down.

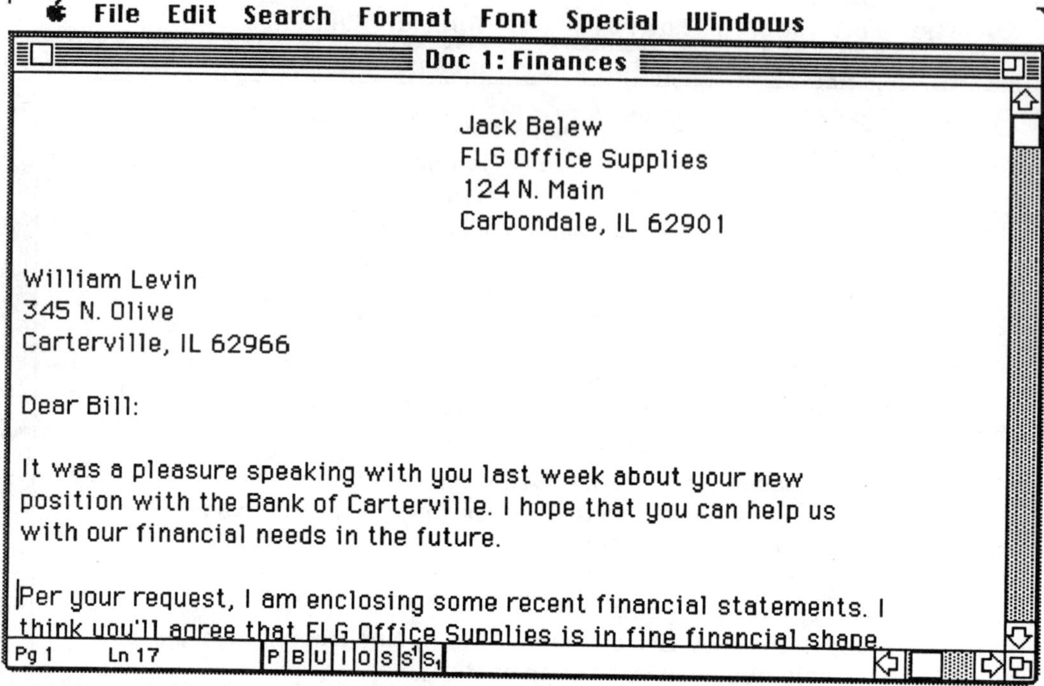

3. Press **Esc**, then **Cmd-Right Arrow**. Notice the cursor move eight words to the right.

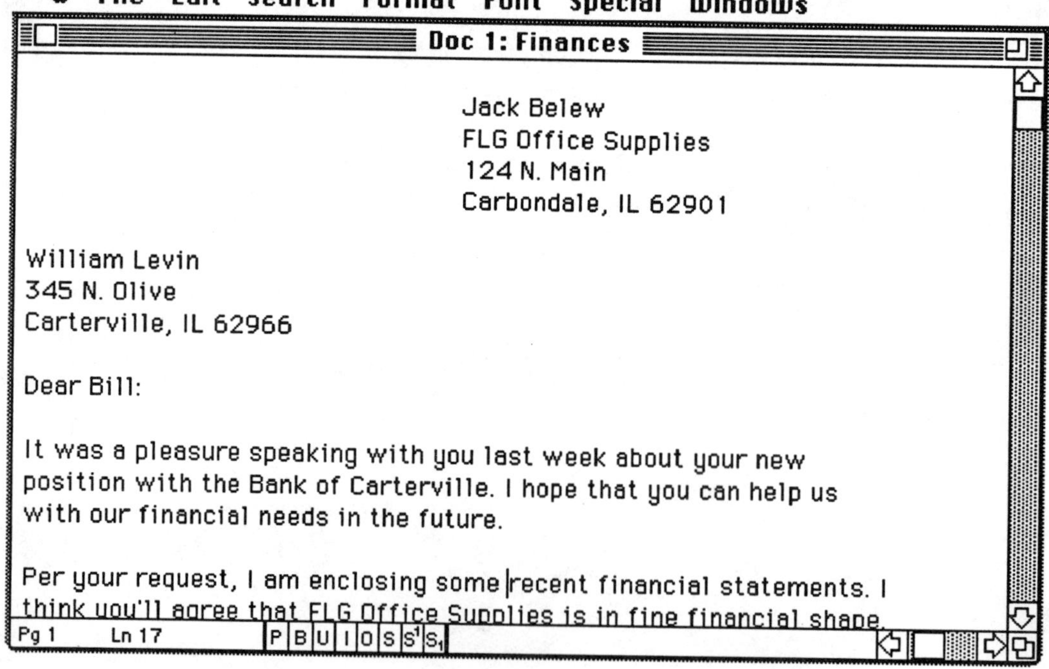

4. Press **Esc**, then **PgDn**. Since there aren't eight pages left in the document, notice the cursor move to the end of the document. Press **Esc**, then **PgUp** to move the cursor to the beginning of the document.
5. Press **Cmd-K** to close the document.
6. Turn to Module 19 to continue the learning sequence.

Module 14
FILE MANAGEMENT

DESCRIPTION

A computerized file is much the same as a file kept in a filing cabinet. It holds information. As with Macintosh filenames, WordPerfect lets you put as many as 31 letters, characters, and spaces into your filenames. Any character can be used in a filename except the colon (:). The name distinguishes the file from all the others.

Once a file is created, WordPerfect offers many options for file management. Access File Management (also called List Files) by pressing Cmd-L or F5 from the keyboard or clicking on File Management from the File menu. The File Management menu looks like this:

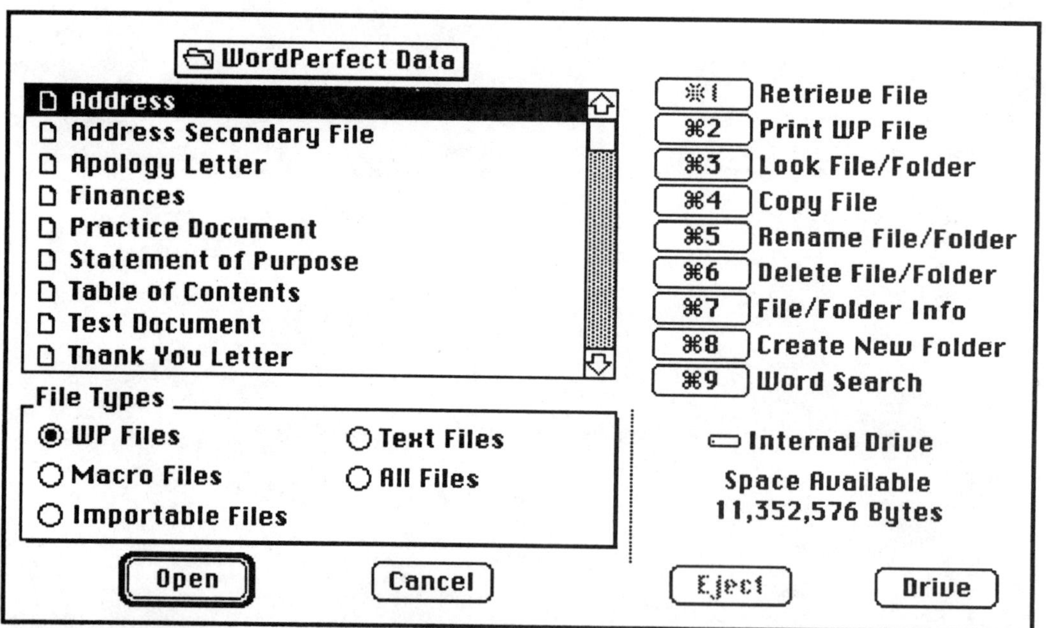

WordPerfect gives you access to the files in a particular folder or drive. It lets you open, retrieve, print, or copy files; look at, rename, or delete files or folders; create new files, or search through files for certain words or phrases. WordPerfect displays all files in a folder, or displays certain file types individually — WordPerfect files, text files, macro files, or importable files. To highlight one or more files, use the mouse or the cursor keys.

To change folders, click on the icon for the current drive (▭). To change drives, click on Drive. If you're looking at a folder on a diskette, you can click Eject to eject that diskette and look at another. To do nothing, click Cancel.

You open or retrieve files for editing purposes. The difference between retrieving and opening files is that when you *open* files they are placed into a new window. When you *retrieve* files, they are pulled into the current document at the current cursor location.

You can change the filename through the Rename feature. If you *delete* a file, you remove it from the folder, or "throw it away." If you *copy* a file, you make a "clone," or *backup copy* of the file. Backup copies protect you against the danger of accidentally losing a file due to inadvertent erasure or a damaged diskette or hard disk. WordPerfect's Look feature lets you examine the contents of a file without retrieving it. This helps you look at a number of files quickly to find the one you want to edit.

OPEN A FILE To open a file from the File Management menu, highlight the file you want to open with the mouse and either press Return, click on Open, or double click on the file.

To open a file without using the File Management menu, press Cmd-O or click on Open from the File menu.

TIP: To quickly find a file when you are searching through a large number of files, start typing the name of the file from the File Management menu. When you type the letter "F," for example, WordPerfect moves to the first file that begins with "F." If you next type "i," WordPerfect moves to the first file that begins with "Fi." You can continue this process until you get to the file you want to open or retrieve.

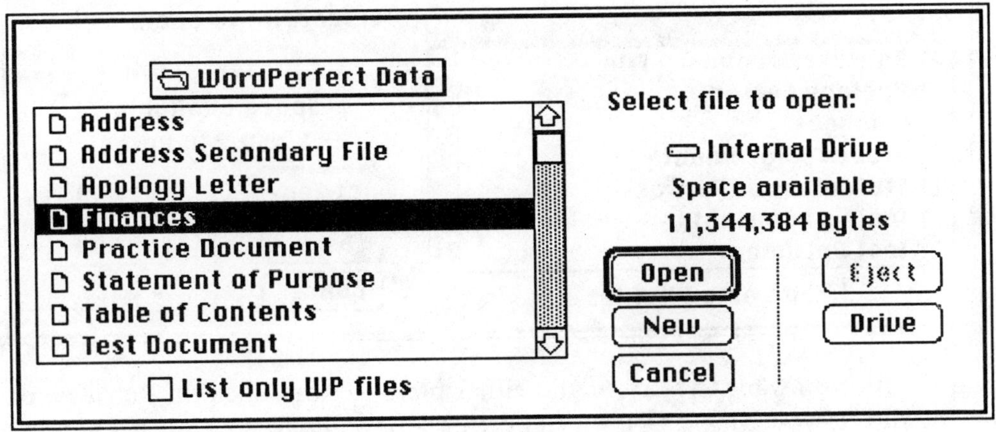

Highlight the file you want to retrieve and either press Return, click on Open, or double click on the file. If you click on New, you create a new file in an Untitled window.

If you try to open a WordPerfect 4.2 or text file, the following dialog box appears:

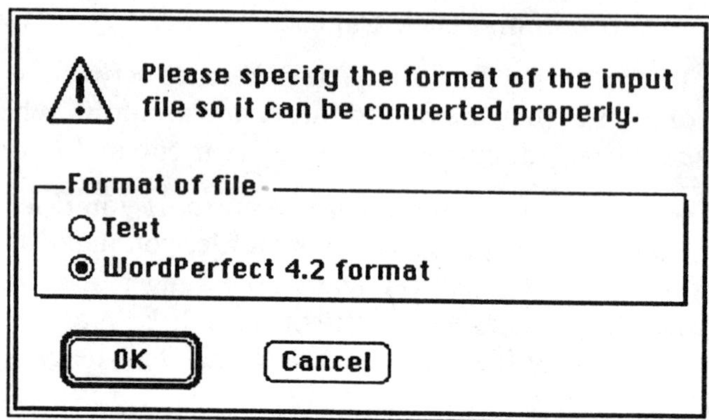

Click on the correct file format, then press Return or click OK.

RETRIEVE A FILE To retrieve a file from the File Management menu, highlight the file you want to retrieve and either press Cmd-1 or click Retrieve File.

To retrieve a file without using the File Management menu, press Shift-F10 (Extended Keyboard only). Click on List Only WP Files to list only WordPerfect files. Otherwise, this command lists all files.

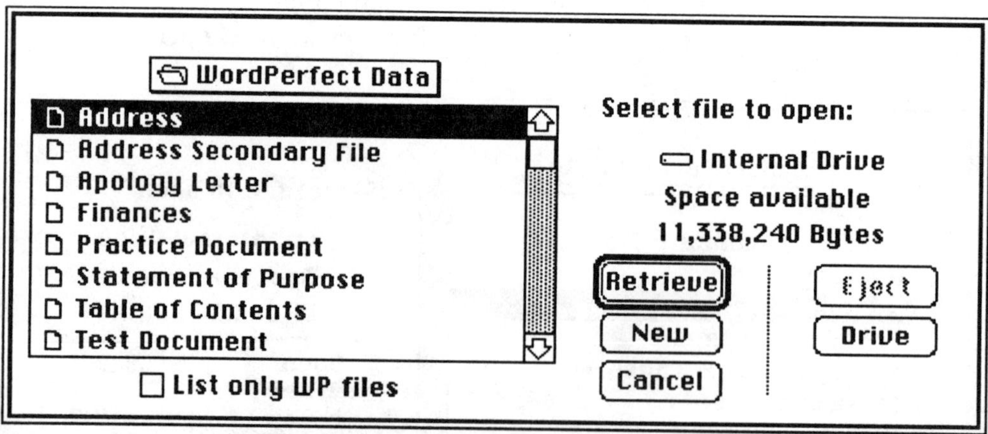

Highlight the file you want to retrieve and either press Return, click on Retrieve, or double click on the file. If you click on New, you create a new file in an Untitled window. Click on List Only WP Files to list only WordPerfect files. Otherwise, this command lists all files.

PRINT FILE To print a file from the File Management menu, move the cursor to the document you want to print and click on Print WP File or press Cmd-2. Then press Return.

NOTE

Printing is discussed in more detail in Module 30.

LOOK AT A FILE/FOLDER WordPerfect's Look command is unique among word processing software. It also is one of the most useful commands in WordPerfect. If you use WordPerfect extensively, you will find yourself creating a large number of files. Sometimes, you will not be able to remember what data is in a particular file. The Look command then becomes useful. It lets you look at a file without retrieving it and then saving it again. You can also look at the contents of a folder without opening it. To look at a file or folder, move the cursor to the file or folder you want to look at and press Cmd-3 or click Look File/Folder. If you selected a folder, WordPerfect lists the files in that folder. Click Cancel when you have completed your examination.

If you selected a file, you can look at the beginning of the file. This gives you a peek at the file, but not much else. You cannot edit the file, since you have not actually retrieved it. Pressing any key or clicking the mouse moves you back out of the file.

COPY A FILE The Copy File feature is useful for making backup copies of files or for copying files for use on other computers. To copy a file from the File Management menu, move the cursor to the file you want to copy and either press Cmd-4 or click on Copy File.

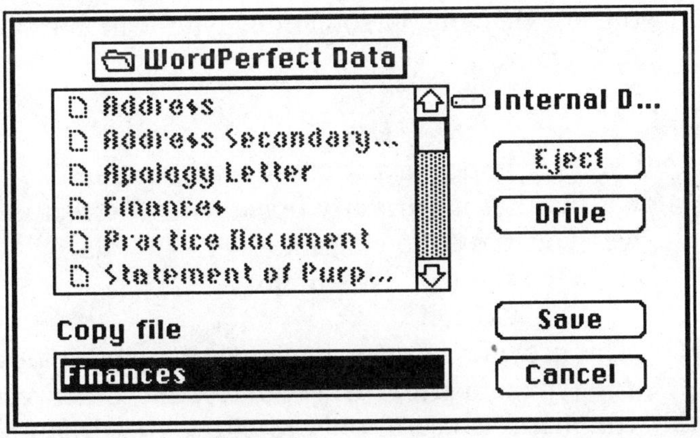

Type the new filename or click on the folder or drive location you want to copy the file to. Then click on Save. WordPerfect saves a copy of the file in the new location.

RENAME A FILE/FOLDER If you decide you do not like the filename of a file or folder, or you think the name of the file or folder fails to convey the contents of the file or folder, you can rename the file or folder. To rename a file or folder from the File Management menu, click on the file or folder you want to rename and either press Cmd-5 or click on Rename File/Folder.

Type the new name for the file or folder and either click on OK or press Return to accept the new name.

DELETE FILE/FOLDER The Delete File/Folder command often becomes necessary. Sometimes, a file has outlived its usefulness. Or, you may be running out of room on a particular diskette and decide to delete a file. You can also delete empty folders. To delete a file or folder, highlight the file or folder you want to delete and press Cmd-6 or click on Delete File/Folder. Then click OK or press Return to confirm you want to delete the highlighted file or folder.

CAUTION

Once you delete a file or folder, you cannot retrieve it again. Make sure the file or folder you are deleting is something you will not need again.

NOTE

If you try to delete a folder that is not empty or a file that is currently open, WordPerfect gives you the following message — "File Is Busy Or Directory Not Empty."

FILE/FOLDER INFO This provides information about files and folders, including creation and modification dates, file type and size, file attributes, and other technical information. For the most part, this command is useful only to check file size and creation date. The attributes in the following example identify a WordPerfect Macintosh file. Other attributes identify Microsoft Word, MacWrite, Text, and MS-DOS WordPerfect files. However, this command also lets you see the attributes for invisible, hidden, password protected, and locked files.

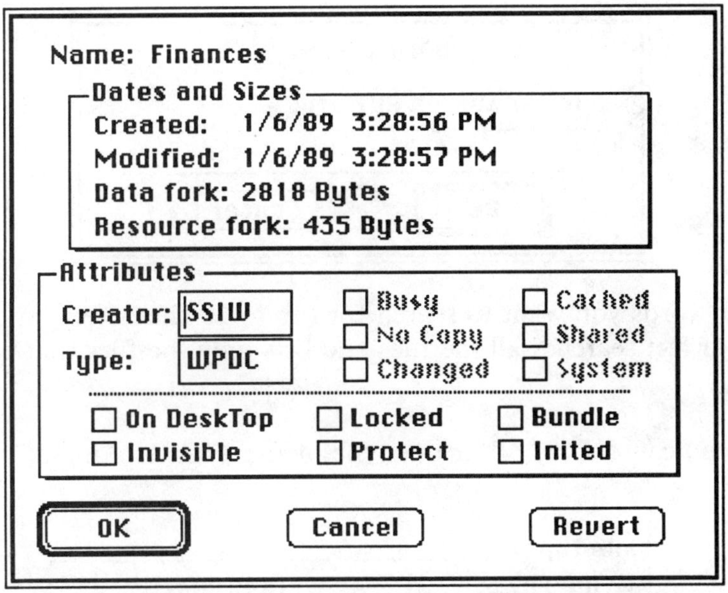

Name: Finances

Dates and Sizes
Created: 1/6/89 3:28:56 PM
Modified: 1/6/89 3:28:57 PM
Data fork: 2818 Bytes
Resource fork: 435 Bytes

Attributes
Creator: SSIW
Type: WPDC
Busy
No Copy
Changed
Cached
Shared
System
On DeskTop
Invisible
Locked
Protect
Bundle
Inited

OK
Cancel
Revert

CREATE NEW FOLDER This command is useful because it lets you create a new data folder without having to return to the Desktop. To create a new folder, press Cmd-8 or click on Create New Folder from the File Management menu.

Enter name for new folder:
Empty Folder
OK
Cancel

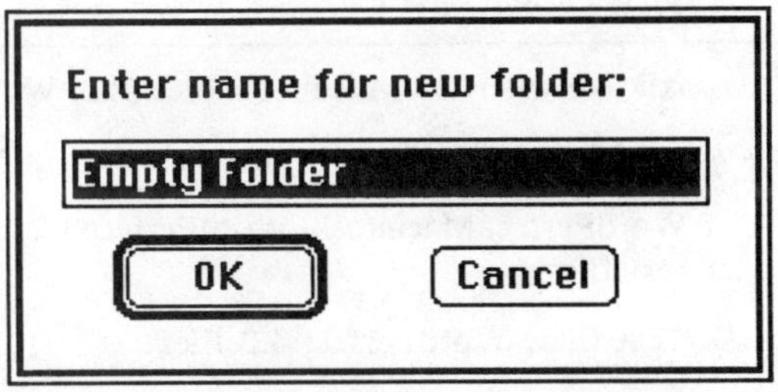

Type the name for the new folder and press Return.

WORD SEARCH WordPerfect has a feature that lets you search through all the documents on a particular disk or in a folder for a certain word or group of words. This can be very helpful when you are not sure which document or documents mention a specific subject. To use Word Search, press Cmd-9 or click on Word Search in the File Management menu.

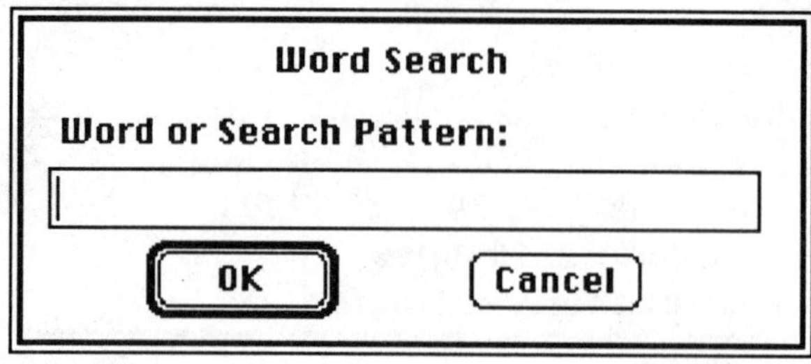

Type the word or words you want to search for (up to 20 characters) and press Return or click OK. WordPerfect searches all the files and lists only the files that contain that word or phrase.

FILE TYPES You can display all or one type of file when looking at folders. File types are listed below:

File Types
WP Files
Text Files
Macro Files
All Files
Importable Files

File Types	*Files Displayed*
WP Files	All WordPerfect Macintosh files plus WordPerfect 4.2 files
Macro Files	All Macro files (Macros are discussed in Module 24.)
Importable Files	WordPerfect Macintosh, WordPerfect 4.2, MacWrite, Microsoft Word, and text files
Text Files	Text files, WordPerfect 4.2 files
All Files	All files

APPLICATIONS

This module mentions many reasons for performing file management tasks. In order to edit a file, you must first open it. If you are not sure which file you want, use WordPerfect's Look feature to examine a file's contents before retrieving it. Use the Rename feature if you decide the name does not tell you enough about the file. Delete files that are either backed up on another diskette or of no further use to you. Copy a file to save a backup as "insurance" or to use the file on another computer.

TYPICAL OPERATION

This example demonstrates the use of WordPerfect's retrieve and open file capabilities.

1. If necessary, start WordPerfect. Then, press **Cmd-O** or pull down the File menu and click on **Open**. Click on the (▭) icon until you get to the right folder. Double click on **Research Project**. (This file was created in the Typical Operation section of Module 4.)

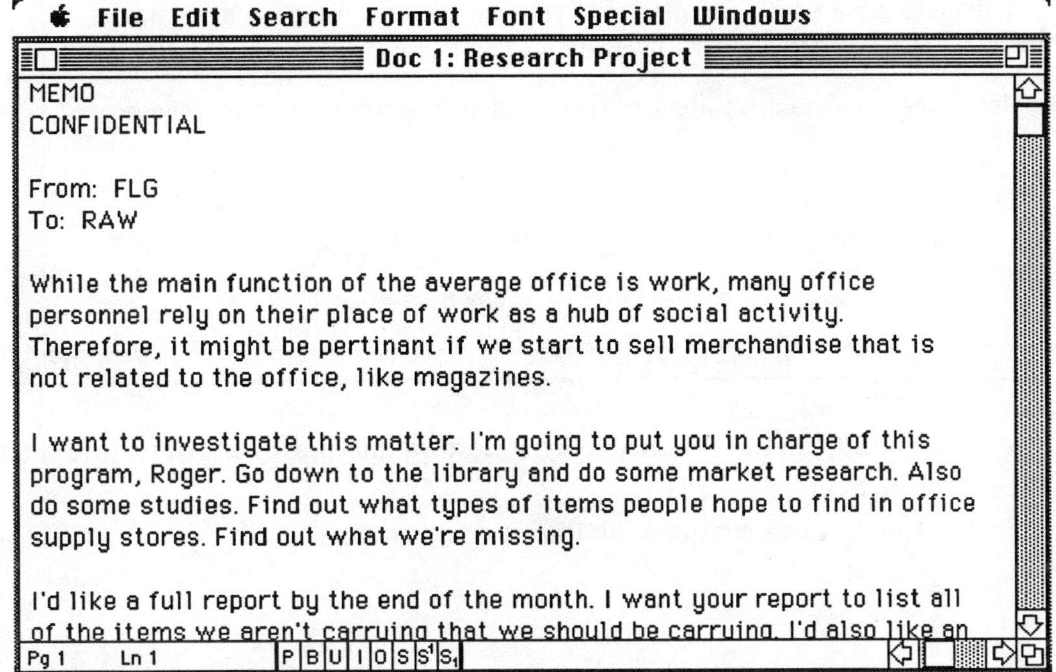

2. Press **Enter** twice. Then press **Down Arrow** to move the cursor to the bottom of the file. Press **Return** twice to add an extra space. Then, press **Shift-F10** or select **Retrieve** from the File menu. Highlight **Finances** and press **Return**. (This document was created in Module 10.)

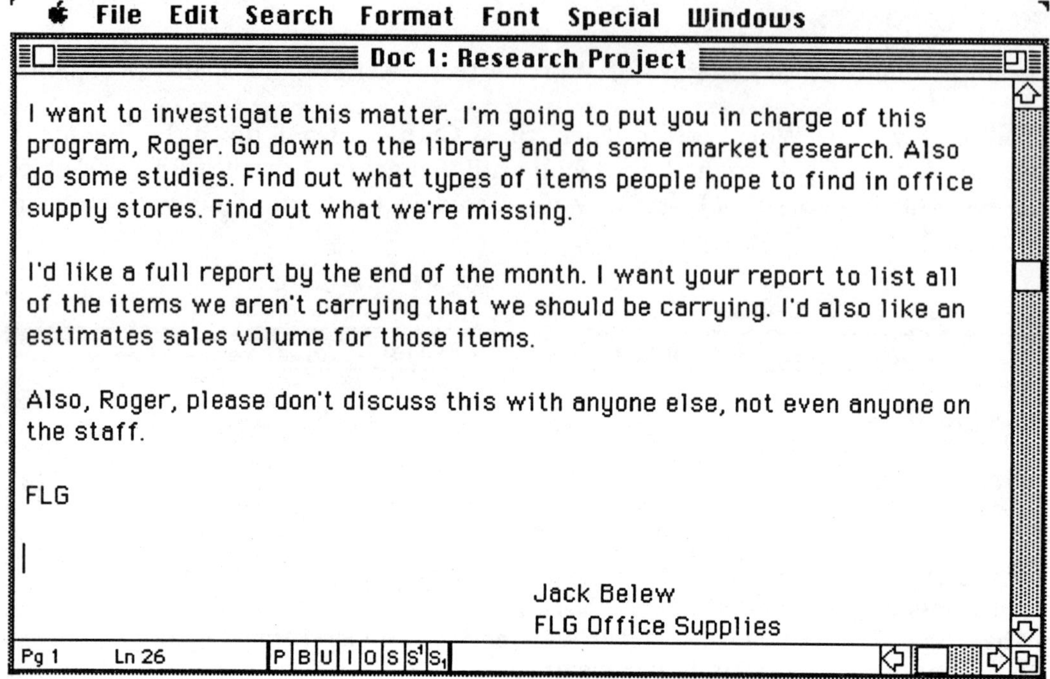
File Edit Search Format Font Special Windows

Doc 1: Research Project

I want to investigate this matter. I'm going to put you in charge of this program, Roger. Go down to the library and do some market research. Also do some studies. Find out what types of items people hope to find in office supply stores. Find out what we're missing.

I'd like a full report by the end of the month. I want your report to list all of the items we aren't carrying that we should be carrying. I'd also like an estimates sales volume for those items.

Also, Roger, please don't discuss this with anyone else, not even anyone on the staff.

FLG

Jack Belew
FLG Office Supplies

Pg 1 Ln 26

3. Select **Save As** from the File menu. Type **Letters** and press **Return** to save the file.
4. Press **Cmd-K** to close the file.
5. Turn to Module 18 to continue the learning sequence.

Module 15

FLUSH RIGHT

DESCRIPTION

Normally, typed text is flush against the left margin. There are times, however, when you want text flush against the right margin instead. The Flush Right command, accessed from the Line Format section of the Format menu (or by pressing Cmd-Shift-F or Alt-F6 from the keyboard) lets you do this.

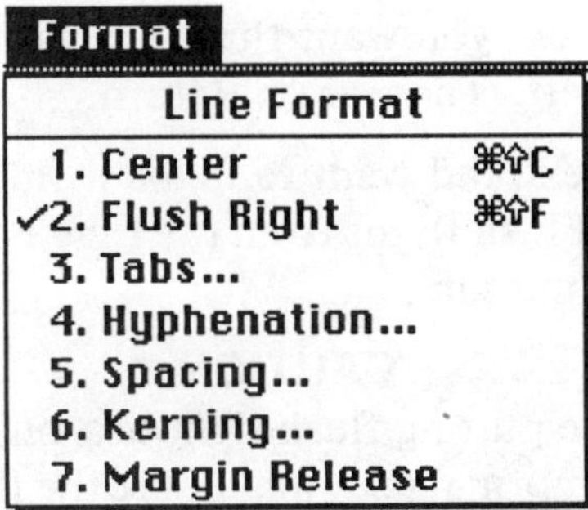

The Flush Right key is useful for a variety of applications. For example, the headers and footers on odd-numbered pages in this book are flush right. Another example is dates. This text is in the normal flush left style:

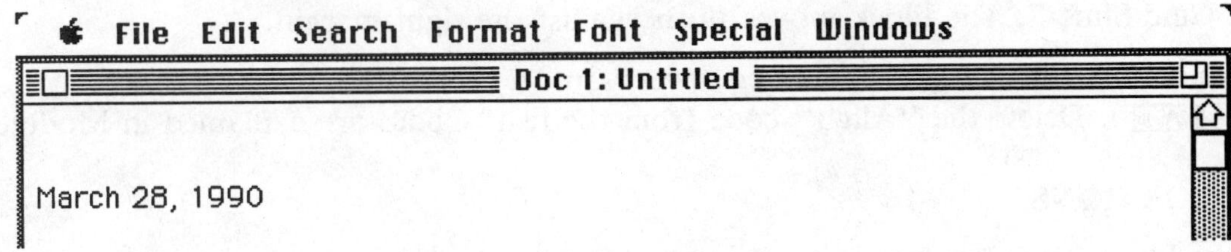

This text is flush right:

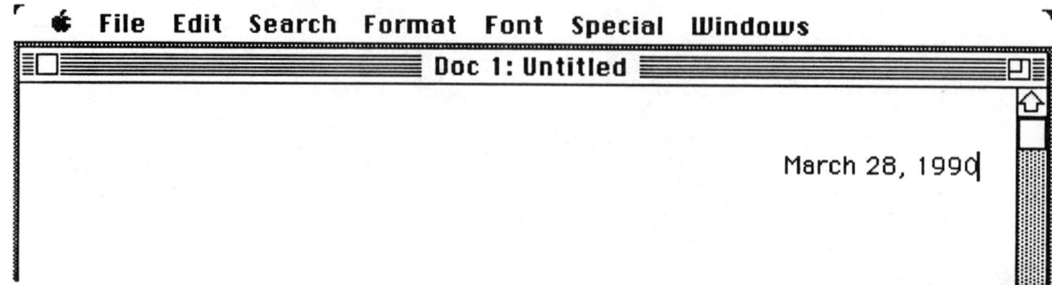

The Flush Right key works best with short lines of text (40 or fewer characters across). If you make longer lines flush right, you will either move some text down to the next line, or not notice that the text is flush right.

To use the Flush Right key, select Flush Right from the Line Format menu or press Cmd-Shift-F or Alt-F6 and type the text you want flush against the right margin. Text will look as though it is moving to the left. Then press Return.

If you have already typed the text and want to make it flush right, move the cursor to the beginning of the text and select Flush Right from the Line Format menu or press Cmd-Shift-F. Text will move to the right margin.

CAUTION

If you are putting flush right text on the same line with normal text, make sure the flush right text does not "run over" the normal text. WordPerfect deletes any normal text that gets in the way of flush right text.

If you have a block of text that you want to make flush right, select the block of text and press Cmd-Shift-F. The block moves flush against the right margin.

To cancel the Flush Right command, press Cmd-7 to see the code for flush right text (Align>▮<Align). Delete the "Align" code from the text. Codes are explained in Module 7.

APPLICATIONS

Use the Flush Right key for effect. Dates and headings often look best when they are flush against the right margin. Headers and footers also are often flush right. The Flush Right key is not a key you use often, but it is very useful when needed.

TYPICAL OPERATION

In this example, you move an address flush against the right margin. Notice this is not the way a normal address looks since the lines are not aligned with each other on the left.

1. If necessary, start WordPerfect. Then create a document similar to the following:

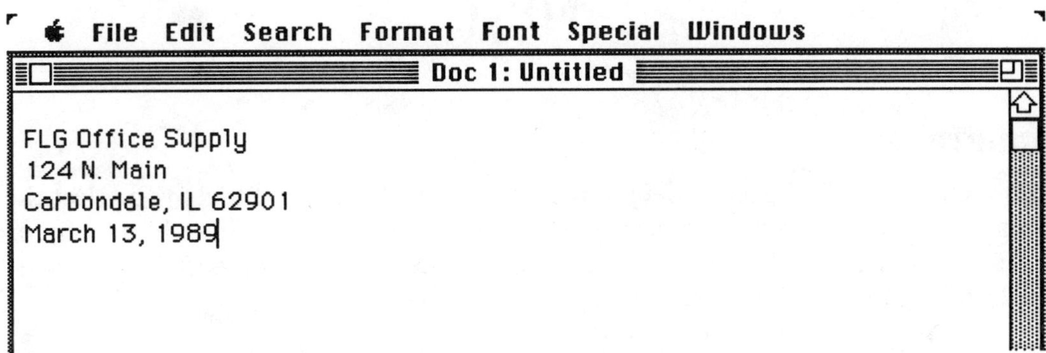

2. Press **Cmd-Shift-A** to select all the text on the page. Then press **Cmd-Shift-F**. Click the mouse once to turn highlighting off.

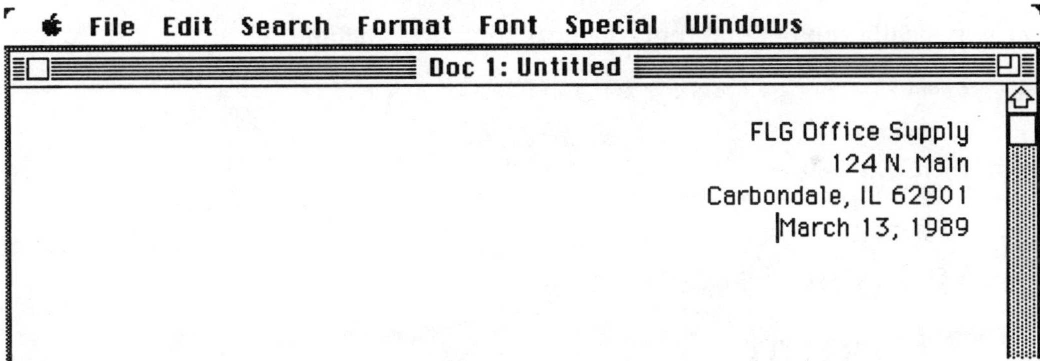

3. Press **Cmd-S**. Then type **Address** and press **Return** to save the document.
4. Press **Cmd-K** to close the document, then turn to Module 21 to continue the learning sequence.

Module 16

FONT

DESCRIPTION

Fonts are typefaces of a specific weight and point size. WordPerfect lets you select the font or fonts in which you want your document displayed on-screen. (These fonts may or may not be supported by your printer. Check your printer manual for details.) Typical fonts available on a Macintosh include:

Geneva	Helvetica
Chicago	Monaco
Courier	Times

Geneva is typically the default font. Typical font sizes include:

9 point
10 point
12 point
14 point
18 point
24 point

The 10-point font size is the familiar elite typestyle from our typewriter days. The 12-point size represents pica. The larger the point size, the larger the letter.

NOTE

Styles, such as boldface, underline, shadow, and italics, which are also font changes, are discussed in Module 39.

WordPerfect supports as many fonts as you have on your System and displays them on the Font menu, accessible only through the mouse. You can have as many fonts and font sizes in a document as you want.

There are two ways to change fonts in a document — through the Font menu or through the Characters dialog box.

CHANGING FONTS AND/OR FONT SIZES WITH THE FONT MENU To change fonts, move the cursor to the location where you want the new font to begin and pull down the Font menu.

Notice that a checkmark indicates the current font and font size. Click on the new font. To change font sizes, pull down the Font menu and click on the new font size. When you begin typing, the text appears in the new font and/or font size.

CHANGING FONTS WITH THE CHARACTERS DIALOG BOX To change fonts with the Characters dialog box, move the cursor to the location where you want the new font to begin and click on Characters from the Format menu or press Cmd-5 or Shift-F1.

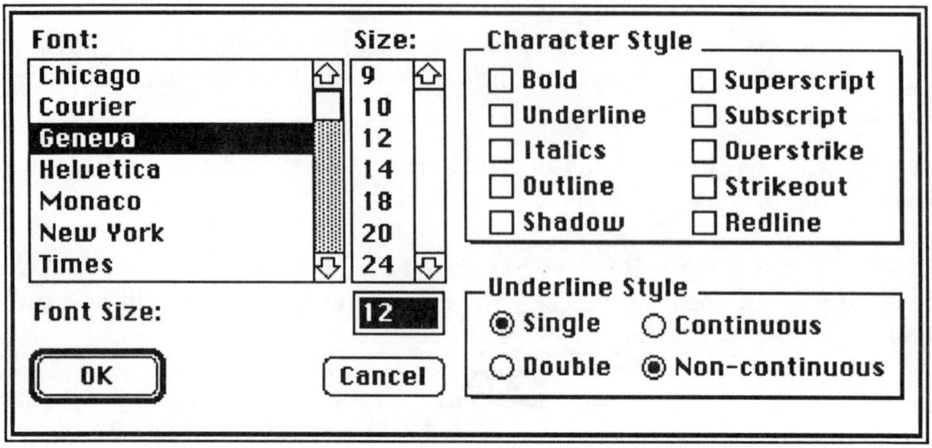

Font: Chicago, Courier, Geneva, Helvetica, Monaco, New York, Times
Size: 9, 10, 12, 14, 18, 20, 24
Font Size: 12
Character Style: Bold, Underline, Italics, Outline, Shadow, Superscript, Subscript, Overstrike, Strikeout, Redline
Underline Style: Single, Continuous, Double, Non-continuous
OK Cancel

Notice that the current font and font size is highlighted. Click on a new font and/or font size and press Return or click OK. You can also change the style of the character from this selection (described in Module 39).

CHANGING THE FONT OF EXISTING TEXT To change the font of existing text, highlight the text you want to change, using either the mouse, the Select command, or the Shift and cursor keys, and select a new font from either the Font menu or the Characters dialog box. Click anywhere in the document to turn off the selection.

APPLICATIONS

The Font feature can help you dramatically change the appearance of printed text. Use any of the fonts available in your System folder to add variety to your document. Change either the font (Geneva, Courier, Times, etc.) or the font size, depending on the application.

Smaller font sizes often elicit just as much reader attention as larger font sizes because the reader tends to notice text that is not the same size as the rest of the text on the page. Use these fonts for effect as well. Also use them for extraneous, but necessary, information.

Smaller font sizes are often used for the "fine print" portions of contracts, documents, and other publications.

Larger font sizes direct attention to the content of your text.

TYPICAL OPERATION

This typical operation illustrates the use of the Font command in sprucing up a document.

1. If necessary, start WordPerfect. Then create a document similar to the following:

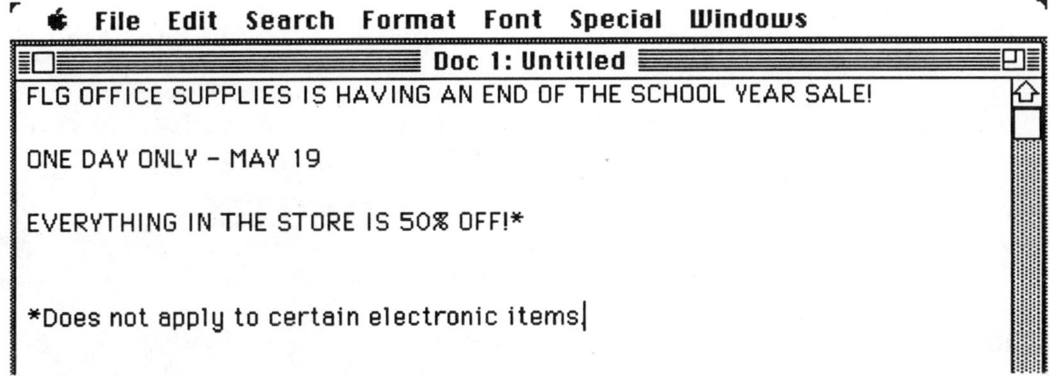

2. Move the cursor to the top of the document and highlight the first line of text. Pull down the Font menu and click on **18** to change the font size to 18 point.
3. Move the cursor to the next line and highlight the next two lines of text. Pull down the Font menu and click on **Helvetica** to change the font. Then click on **14** to change the font size.
4. Move the cursor to the last line. Define the line as a block of text by highlighting it with the mouse. Then pull down the Font menu and click on **9** to change the font size. Click the mouse once to turn highlighting off.

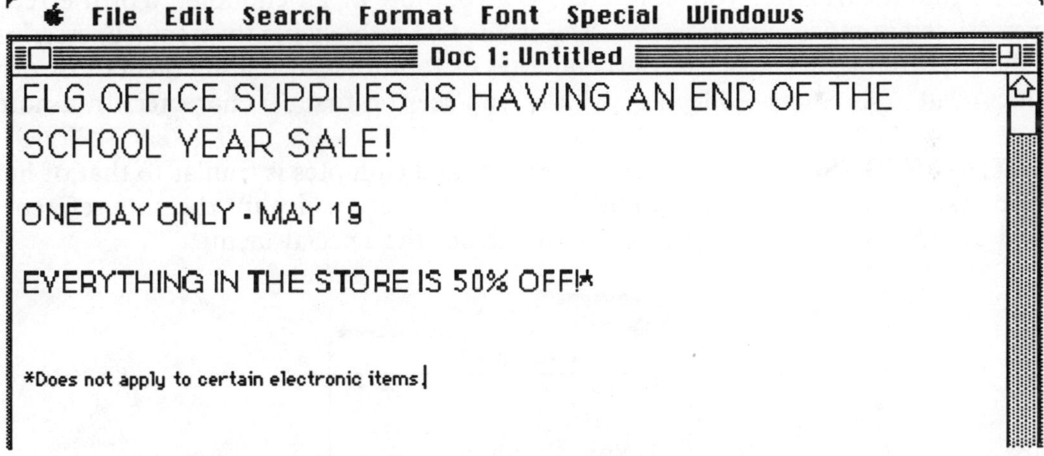

5. Press **Cmd-S**. Then type **Back To School Sale** and press **Return** to save the document.
6. Press **Cmd-K** to close the document, then turn to Module 30 to continue the learning sequence.

Module 17

FOOTNOTES AND ENDNOTES

DESCRIPTION

Footnotes and endnotes provide further information about a subject that is referenced in a document. While footnotes are reference notes placed at the end of a page, endnotes are placed at the end of a document. WordPerfect lets you create endnotes and footnotes in the same document. WordPerfect also lets you place endnotes anywhere you want in a document.

One blank line separates the end of the text from endnotes. Therefore, at the end of the document it is advisable to create a new page with a heading that introduces the endnotes. Footnotes, on the other hand, appear automatically at the bottom of a page.

WordPerfect automatically numbers endnotes and footnotes in your document. All you have to do is create them. After you have created a footnote or an endnote, WordPerfect puts a superscripted number, character, or letter in the text referencing the item (superscripts are described in Module 40). You can view endnotes or footnotes by editing them or by printing the document. The Show Codes key will let you see the first 50 characters in a note.

CREATING NOTES The creation of footnotes and endnotes is similar to that of headers and footers. To create a note, first place the cursor where you want the note referenced in the text and press Cmd-9 or select Footnotes from the Special menu.

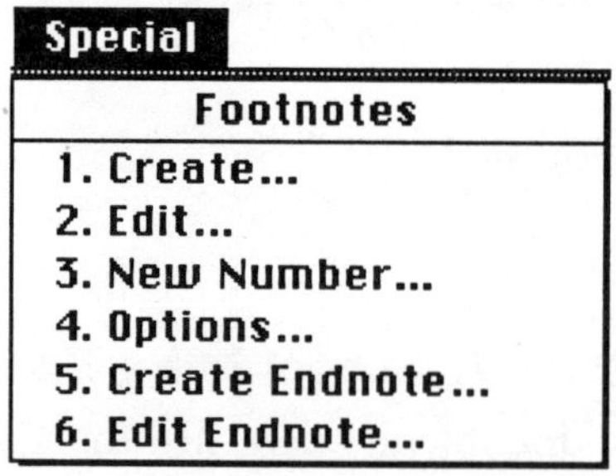

```
Special
        Footnotes
 1. Create...
 2. Edit...
 3. New Number...
 4. Options...
 5. Create Endnote...
 6. Edit Endnote...
```

Type or click on 1 to create a footnote or on 5 to create an endnote. The footnote screen is shown below, but the endnote screen is very similar.

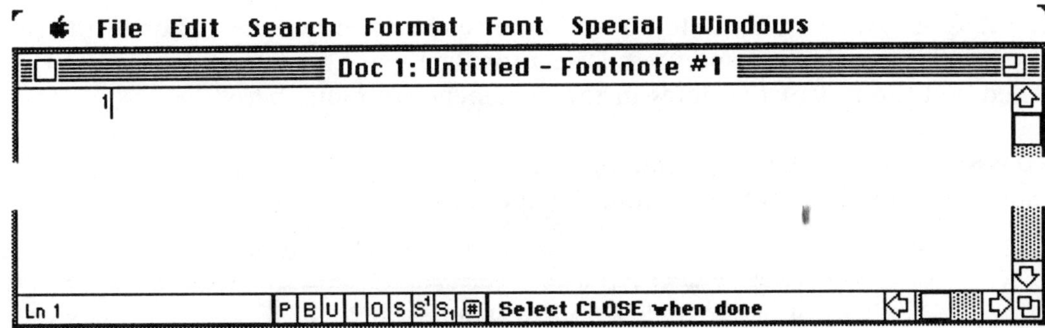

To create a note, type the information as you want it to look in the note. Use any of WordPerfect's formatting commands, such as boldface, underline, italics, or center. The "1" at the top of the screen signifies the number of the endnote. Notice the Status Line at the bottom of the screen and the note number at the top.

Press Cmd-K or select Close from the File menu when you have finished typing the note. WordPerfect puts a superscript 1 at the original cursor location in the document.

EDITING A NOTE Notes can be edited after they are created. To edit a note, place the cursor anywhere in the document and press Cmd-9 or select Footnotes from the Special menu. Type or click on 2 to edit a footnote or 6 to edit an endnote.

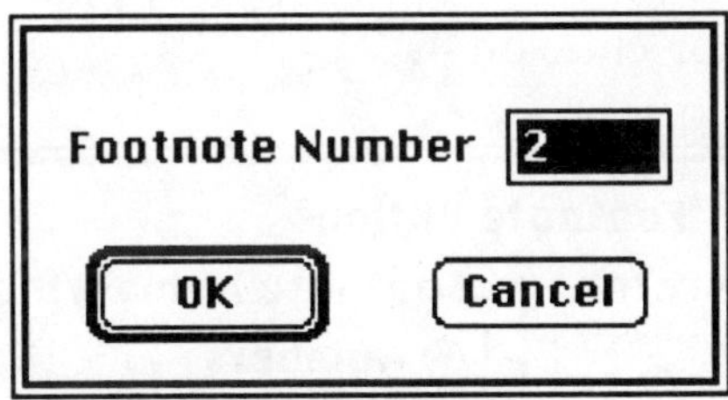

WordPerfect automatically inserts the next note number. That is, if you have created four endnotes and your cursor is located between endnotes numbered 1 and 2, the prompt will read "Endnote Number 2."

Type the number of the note you want to edit if it is not the one listed and press Return or click OK. Make your changes to the note, then press Cmd-K or click on Close from the File menu to save those changes.

NOTE

If you change the margins in your document, you must change the margins in your endnote. The easiest way to do this is to do a word count on your document. Select Spell from the Special menu, then click on Count. This procedure is discussed in further detail in Module 38.

DELETING A NOTE To delete a footnote or endnote, move the cursor to the right of the note marking in the text and press Delete (or Backspace on some keyboards). The note is deleted and the rest of the notes in the document are renumbered.

RENUMBERING NOTES To renumber a note, move the cursor before the note you want to renumber and select Footnotes from the Special menu or press Cmd-9, then click on or type 3.

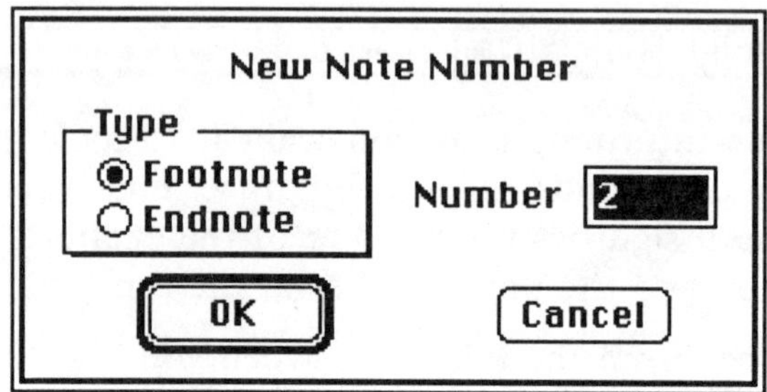

Select whether you want to renumber footnotes or endnotes. Then type the new note number and press Return or click OK. All subsequent notes are renumbered.

NOTE OPTIONS WordPerfect gives you a number of options for formatting notes. To see the options and the defaults for those options, press Cmd-9 or click on Footnotes from the Special menu. Then type or click on 4.

Footnote Options

Text-Footnote Separator
- None
- 2 inch line
- Line across page

Footnote Spacing
- From text 0.25 in.
- Between notes 0.25 in.

Footnote Position
- After text
- Bottom of page

Footnote Numbering
- Numbers
- Characters
- Letters
- Restart on each page

Endnote Numbering
- Numbers
- Characters
- Letters

Note characters *

Lines to keep together 3

OK

Styles

Cancel

TEXT-FOOTNOTE SEPARATOR Normally, a two-inch line extending from the left margin separates footnotes from the rest of the text. WordPerfect offers you the option of changing this to either no line, or a line extending across the page from the left margin to the right. Click on the separator of your choice, then click OK or press Return.

FOOTNOTE SPACING Footnotes are normally .25 inches from the rest of the text on a page. To change this, type a new value and click OK or press Return. Notes (both footnotes and endnotes) are also .25 inches apart. You can change this value as well. Type a new value and click OK or press Return.

FOOTNOTE POSITION Footnotes are typically printed at the bottom of the page. When there isn't enough text to fill a page, however, WordPerfect gives you the option of printing footnotes directly after the text. To select this, click on After Text and click OK or press Return.

NOTE NUMBERING The default numbering method for footnotes and endnotes is numbers. You can change this to either characters or letters. If you choose characters, the default is asterisks (*), but you may choose another character if you want. You can also choose up to five different characters, for example, *@#%&. When a sixth note is reached, the characters are doubled or tripled. In the above example, the sixth note would be identified as **. You can also select footnote numbering to restart on each page.

To set note numbering, click on the appropriate option for footnotes and/or endnotes. If you select Characters as an option, type the character or characters of your choice in the Note Characters box. When you have finished, click OK or press Return.

NOTE

If you change the note numbering method after you have created notes, the previous numbers will not change. So if you create two endnotes and decide to switch to letters, the endnotes will be numbered 1, 2, c, d, etc. You can fix this problem by editing the old endnotes yourself.

LINES TO KEEP TOGETHER WordPerfect keeps at least three lines of a note on a page. If there is not room for at least three lines, WordPerfect puts the entire note on the next page. To change the number of lines to keep together, type a new number and either click OK or press Return.

STYLES WordPerfect automatically superscripts (Module 40) the characters, numbers, or letters that identify footnotes and endnotes, both in the text and in the note. Footnotes are further identified by a five-space indent between the margin and the footnote number. Endnotes are identified by a number, letter, or character followed by a period. You have the option, however, of changing the style. You can underline, boldface, or place a tab before the characters, numbers, or letters, or you can have them appear as normal characters. You can also mix and match, both underlining and superscripting the identifying symbol. To change the way notes are identified in text, select Styles from the Footnote Options menu.

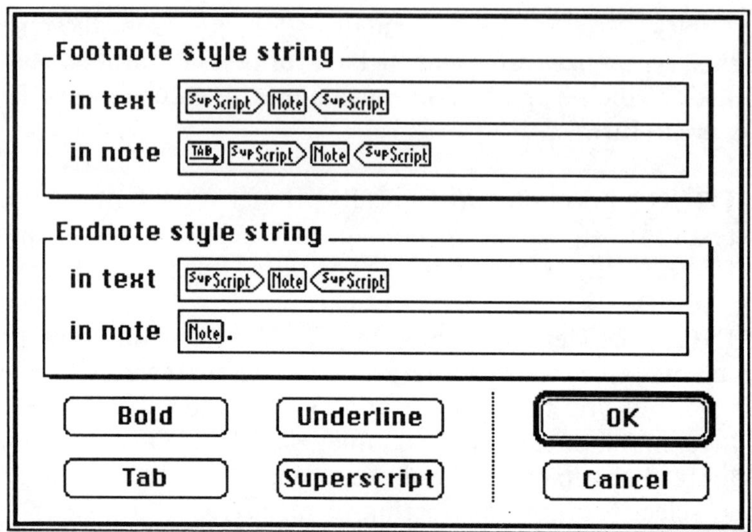

Using the mouse, place the cursor in either endnote or footnote style strings in text or notes. Then select the style of your choice. If you want the note boldfaced, click on Bold. Delete the codes you do not want. When you have finished, click OK or press Return.

APPLICATIONS

Footnotes and endnotes are most often used in formal research documents such as term papers, theses, research papers, and dissertations. They can be used in any document, however. Use them to elaborate on points made in the text when the additional information is not essential for understanding the text of the document. Or, use them to credit sources quoted in the document.

TYPICAL OPERATION

This example illustrates how to put endnotes into a document.

1. If necessary, start WordPerfect. Then create a document similar to the following:

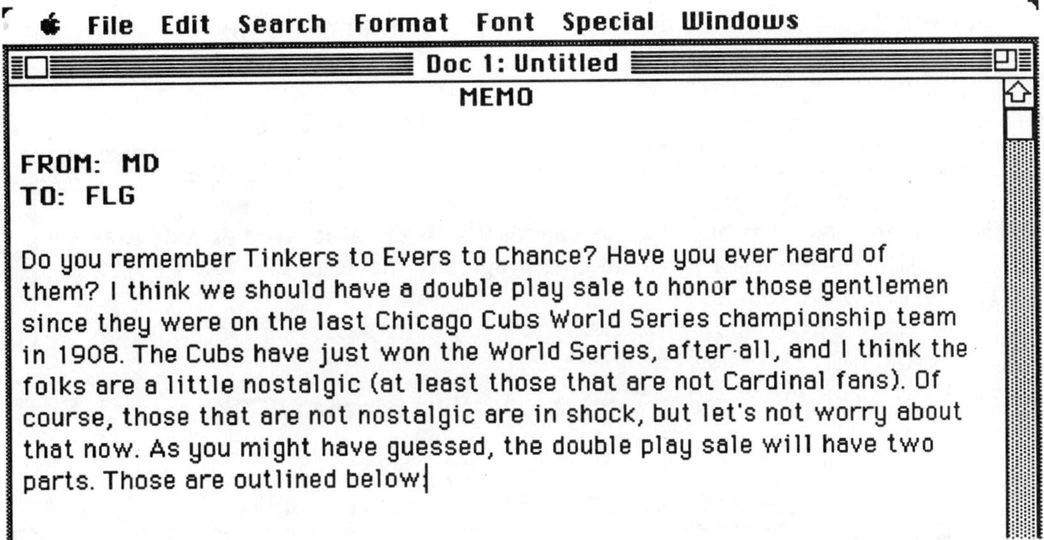

2. With the cursor to the right of the question mark next to "Chance," press **Cmd-9** or click on **Footnotes** from the Special menu. Then type or click on **5**.
3. Press the **Spacebar** and type **Joe Tinker was the shortstop, Johnny Evers the second baseman, and Frank Chance the first baseman of baseball's first celebrated double-play combination. There were other double-play combinations that were better, but none are more famous.**
4. Press **Cmd-K** or click on **Close** from the File menu to save the endnote.

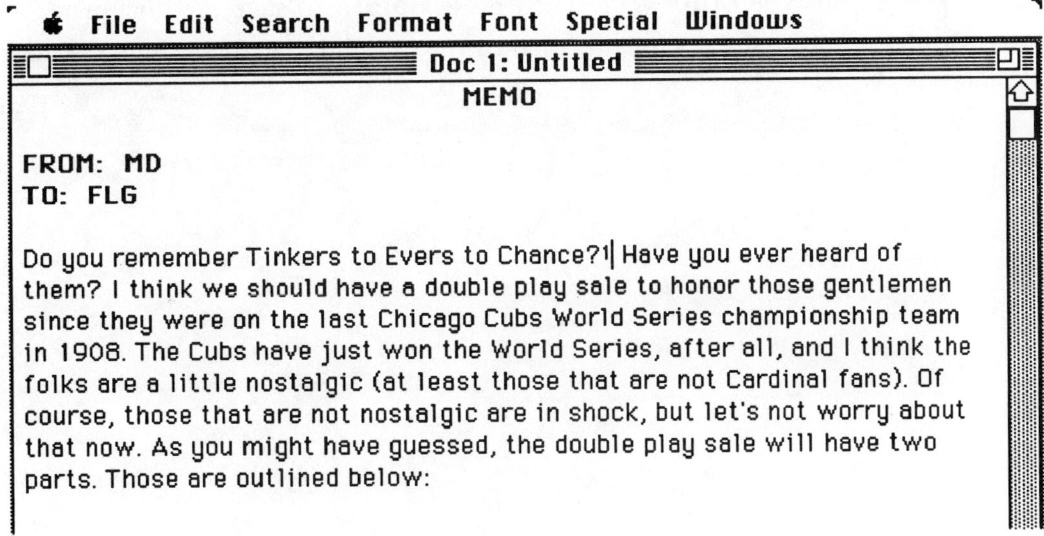

5. Press **Cmd-9** or click on **Footnotes** from the Special menu, then type or click on **6**. Type **1** to edit endnote number one and press **Return**.

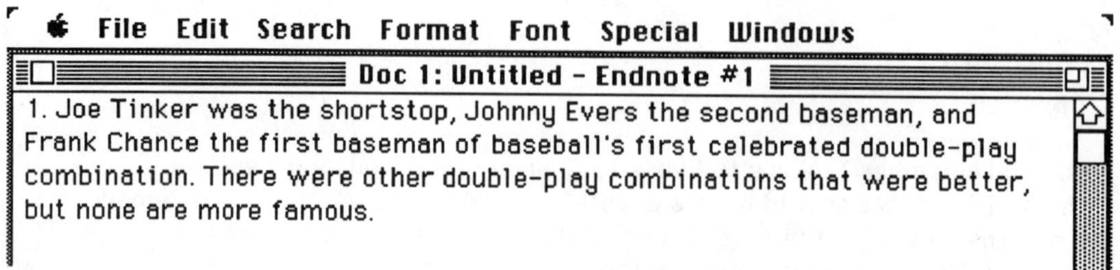

6. Move the cursor to the space after the "n" in "first baseman." Then press the **Spacebar** and type **(and manager)**. Then press the **Down Arrow** key.

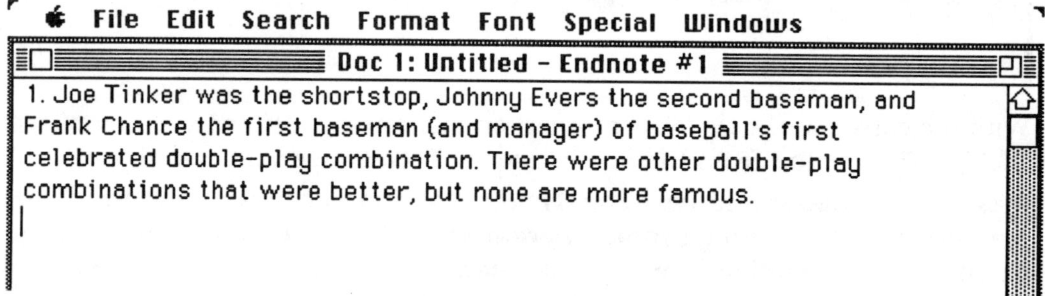

7. Press **Cmd-K** to close the endnote.
8. Press **Cmd-S** and type **Cubs Win**. Then press **Return** to save the document.
9. Press **Cmd-K** to close the document, then turn to Module 38 to continue the learning sequence.

Module 18

GO TO

DESCRIPTION

The Go To command is a specialized cursor control feature in WordPerfect that quickly moves you from one part of a document to another. (Other cursor control features are described in Module 10.) There are five major uses for the Go To command:

- Moving to a specific page number
- Moving to the next occurrence of a certain character
- Moving to the top or bottom of a specific page
- Moving back to a particular part of a document after a major motion command
- Moving through columns of text

There are five ways to access the Go To command box:

- Click on Go To from the Search menu
- Press Cmd-G
- Press Cmd-Home
- Press Cmd-Enter
- Click on the Page Number box on the Status Line

When you access the Go To command, the following box appears:

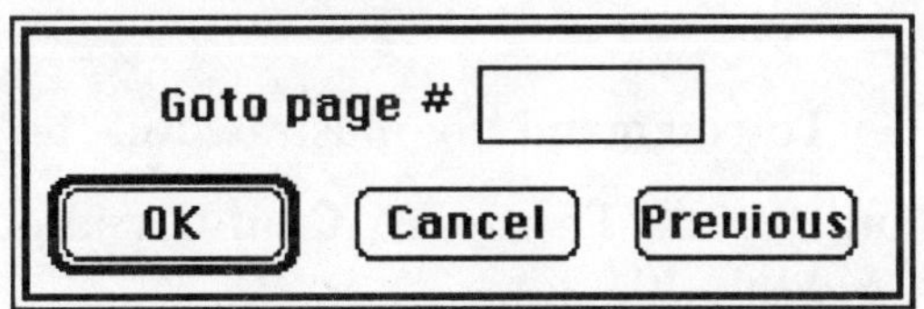

The next step is up to you. Do you want to go to a specific page or to the top or bottom of the current page? Your options are listed below:

Keystroke	*Result*
[Page Number], Return	Jumps cursor to the page of your choice.
Up Arrow	Jumps cursor to the top of the current page.
Down Arrow	Jumps cursor to the bottom of the current page.
Right Arrow	Jumps cursor to the next column. (See Module 8 for a description of the Column mode.)
Left Arrow	Jumps cursor to the previous column.
Enter, Right Arrow	Jumps cursor to the last column on the page.
Enter, Left Arrow	Jumps cursor to the first column on the page.
x	Jumps cursor to the next occurrence of the character "x," as long as that occurrence is within the next 2,000 characters (10 pages).
Click on Previous	Cursor returns to its previous position after you have either moved it with the mouse or used one of the following features: PgUp, PgDn, Screen Up, Search, Replace, Escape, any arrow key, or Go To.

APPLICATIONS

The Go To command lets you move from any page in a document to any other page very quickly. This is especially advantageous in a large document. It also lets you quickly find a specific character. This is helpful when you are moving to a seldom-used letter, like x or z, or a character like * or #. It also lets you move to the top or bottom of a page and move around in blocks or columns of text. The Go To command is a very efficient method of cursor movement.

The "Previous" option of the Go To command cancels a motion command like a PgUp or PgDn command.

TYPICAL OPERATION

Many of the uses of the Go To command are illustrated in the following example.

1. If necessary, start WordPerfect. Then press **Cmd-O** and double click on **Finances**, which was created in Module 10.

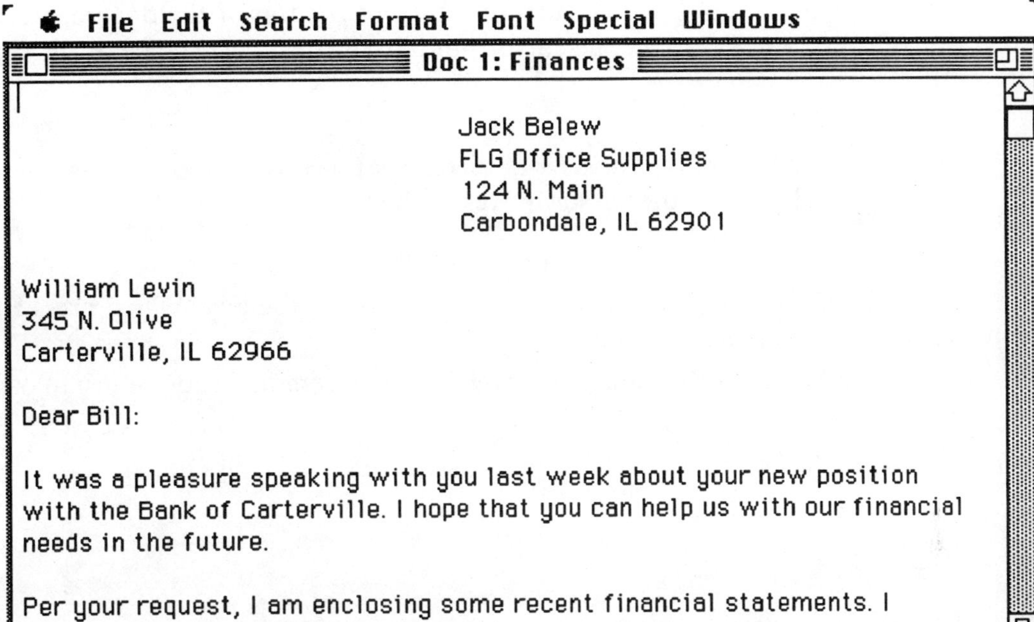

2. Press **Cmd-G**, type **3**, and press **Return** to move to page 3.

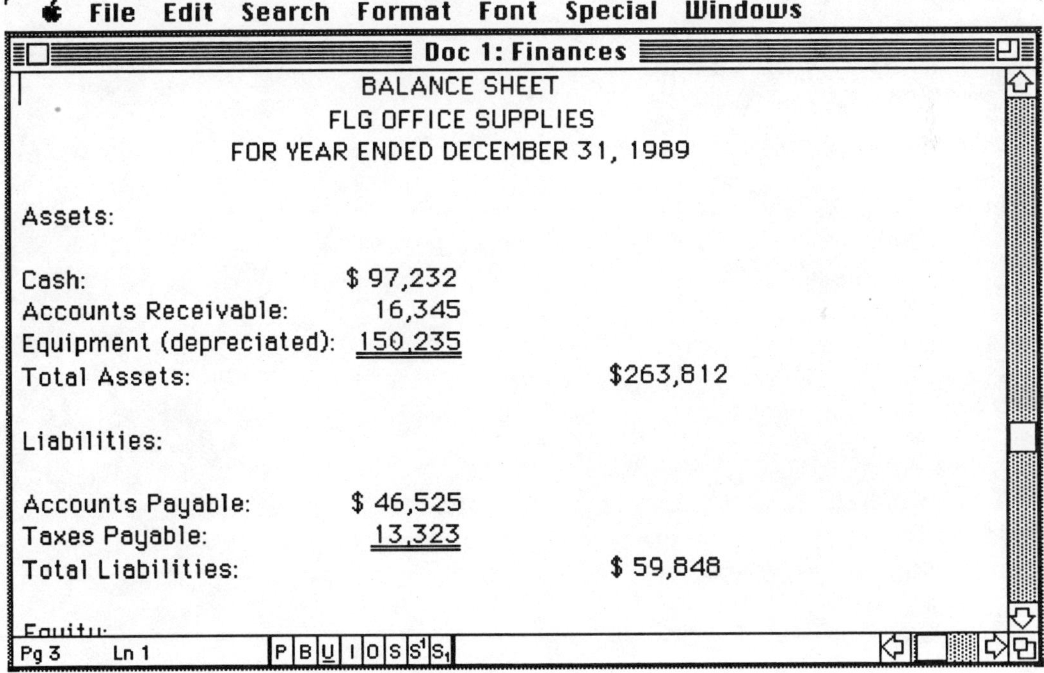

3. Press **Cmd-G**, type **1**, and press **Return** to return to the top of the document. Then press **Cmd-G** and type **R**. Notice the cursor jump to the next occurrence of the capital letter "R."

NOTE

After finding the next occurrence of a certain character, the cursor moves to the space *after* the occurrence.

4. Press **Cmd-G** and press **Up Arrow** to move to the top of the page. Then press **PgUp** to move to the top of the document.
5. Press **Cmd-G** and click on **Previous** to cancel the PgUp command and return to page 2.
6. Press **Cmd-K** to close the document.
7. Turn to Module 34 to continue the learning sequence.

Module 19

HEADERS AND FOOTERS

DESCRIPTION

The Header and Footer command lets you print information at the top or bottom of every page or on odd or even pages throughout a document. Headers are located at the top of the page, footers at the bottom. Header and footer information can be located in any horizontal part of a page. For example, information can be centered, flush against the left margin, or flush against the right margin. Header and footer information can contain text, numbers, and symbols. It can be boldfaced, underlined, italicized, or otherwise highlighted. Common headers and footers include chapter titles, page numbers, and names. This is a typical header:

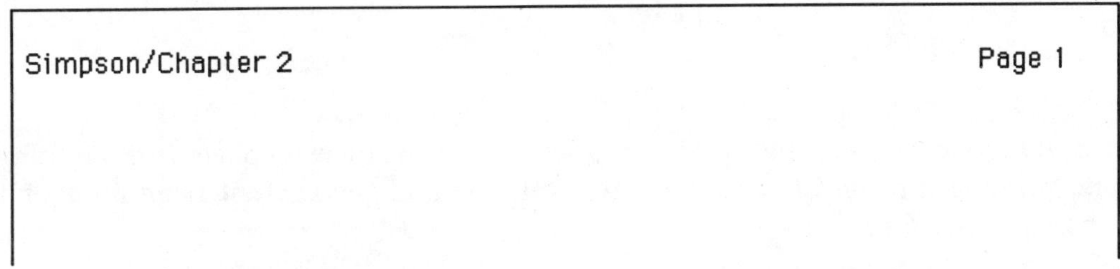

This header includes information that is repeated on the left side of every page and a page number that changes on the right. This information can be moved anywhere on a page. Page numbers, for example, could be on the next line or in the footer.

WordPerfect lets you create up to two headers and two footers at any point in a document. In reality, this lets you create an unlimited number of headers and footers. For example, if you have a 100-page document with ten chapters, WordPerfect lets you create two headers and footers for chapter one, discontinue them, create two new headers and footers for chapter two, and so on.

Headers start on the first text line on the page, footers on the last. WordPerfect allows for one blank line between the header and the start of the text. For example, if you type a header that is two lines long, WordPerfect subtracts those lines plus one more from the text lines available on a page (typically about 54). For footers, WordPerfect allows for one blank line between the document text and the footer. If your footer is more than one line long, the rest of it is printed in the bottom margin (six lines).

So, if you have one header that is three lines long and one footer that is two lines, there are 48 lines per page available for text in the document. Four lines are used in the header and two lines in the footer. Further, there is one less blank line in the bottom margin. Because headers and footers reduce the number of lines available for text, it is suggested that no more than five lines at the top and five lines at the bottom be used for headers and footers.

NOTE

If you are using two headers (or two footers) on the same page, make sure that one is either flush right or located on a different line. If you do not, one may print over another.

Headers and footers are not visible on-screen after they are created. They are visible only when a document is printed. Use the Codes command to see a header or footer on-screen (Codes are described in Module 7). The header created in the previous example looks like this in code form:

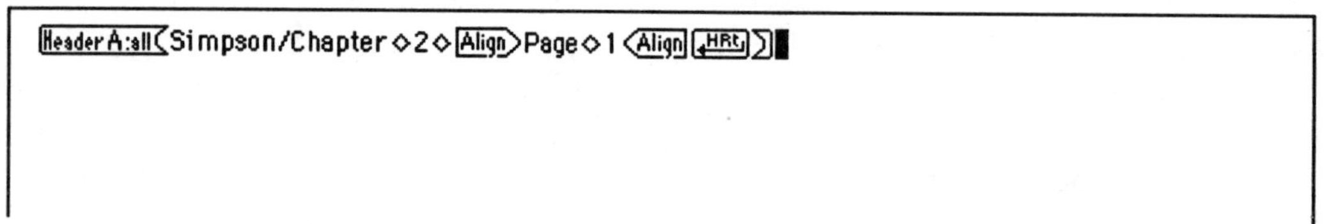

Translated, this code tells you that this is a header that occurs on even pages (see the following menu) and prints Simpson/Chapter 2 on the left side and the current page number flush against the right margin.

CREATING A HEADER OR FOOTER You create headers and footers using the Page Format command, accessed by pressing Shift-F8 or Cmd-2 or by selecting Page from the Format menu, then pressing or clicking on 4. A short cut directly to header and footer selection is accessed by pressing Cmd-Shift-H.

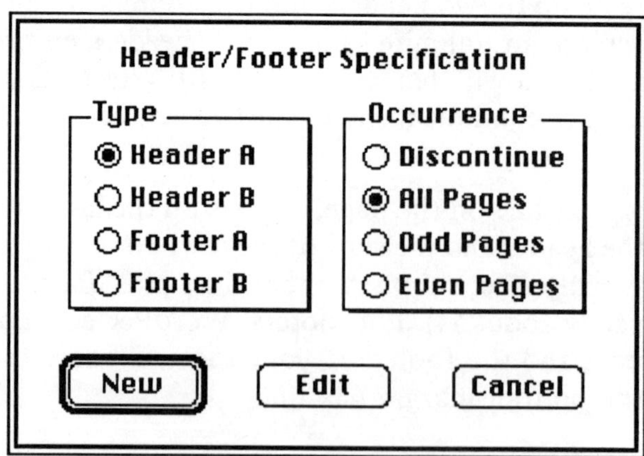

Select the header or footer that you want to create. Then select whether you want the header or footer to appear on all pages, even pages only, or odd pages only. Click on New or press Return.

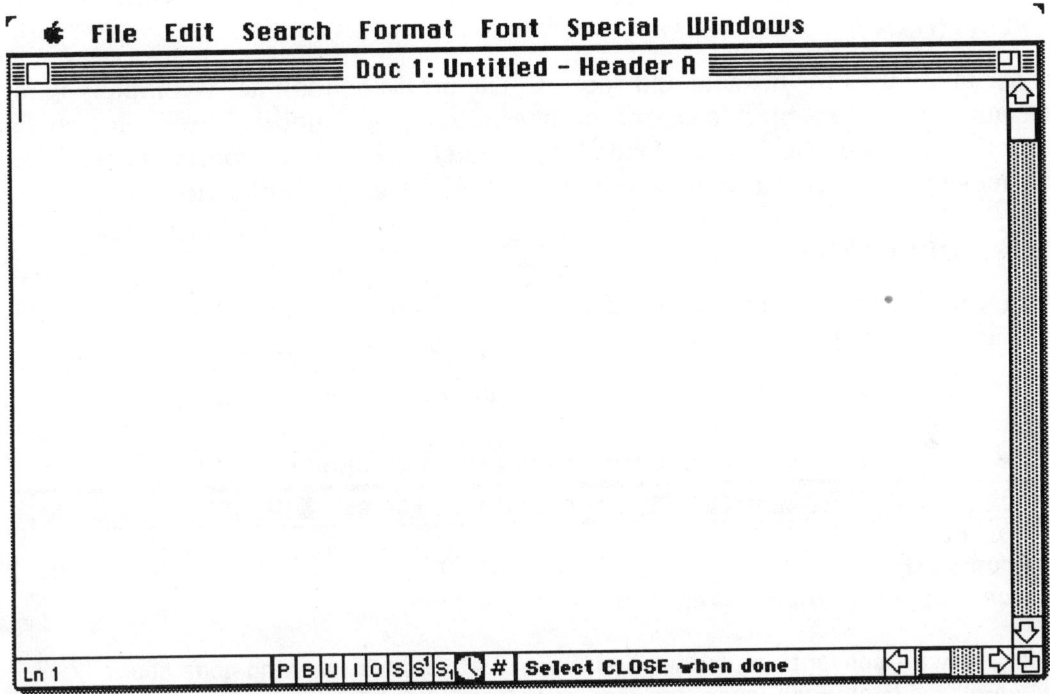

This is the area in which you create a header or footer. To create a header or footer, type the information as you want it to look at the top or bottom of the page. Use any of WordPerfect's formatting commands, such as boldface, italics, underline, or center.

Notice the Status Line at the bottom of the screen. Clicking on the Clock icon inserts the correct date and time at the cursor location. (This is according to the format set in the Date menu, as described in Module 11.) Clicking on the # icon inserts the current page number at the cursor location. When you have finished creating the header or footer, press Cmd-K or select Close from the File menu. To create other headers or footers, repeat the above steps.

EDITING A HEADER OR FOOTER You can edit headers or footers after they are created. To edit a header or footer, make sure the cursor is past the location where the header or footer was created. In other words, if you created the header or footer on page 2, do not try to edit it on page 1. To edit a header or footer, press Cmd-Shift-H, then click on the header or footer you want to edit and click on Edit. Make the desired changes to the header or footer and click on Close from the File menu or press Cmd-K.

DISCONTINUING A HEADER OR FOOTER To cancel a header or footer at any point in the document, move to the point where you want to cancel the header or footer, and press Cmd-Shift-H. Select the header or footer you want to discontinue and click on Discontinue.

APPLICATIONS

There are many uses for headers and footers. The most common are a company name, an author name, a date, a subject, a chapter number, and a page number. These items can appear in either the header or the footer. Headers and footers are used in reports, memos, articles, books, magazines, technical manuals, and a variety of other publications.

TYPICAL OPERATION

This example illustrates the use of headers and footers in a trip report. It uses all available headers and footers and alternates them on odd and even pages.

1. If necessary, start WordPerfect. Then create a document similar to the following:

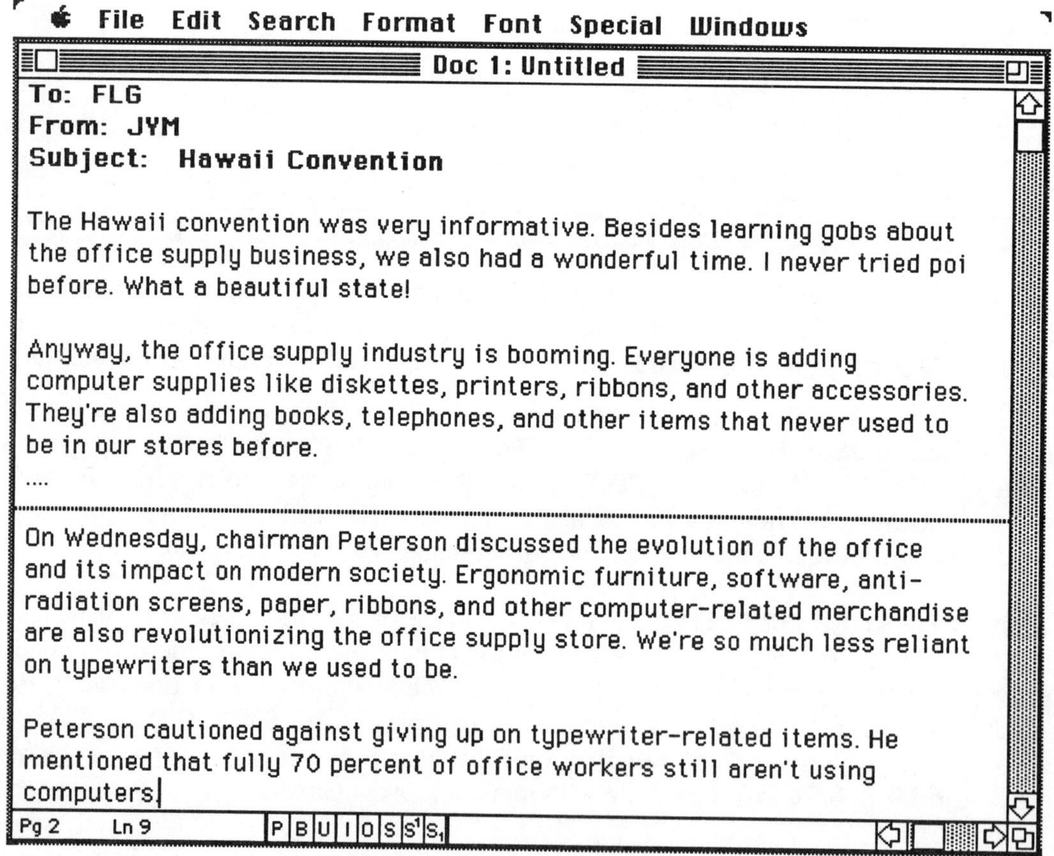

2. Move the cursor to the top of the document. Press **Cmd-Shift-H**. Click on **Header A** and then click on **Odd Pages** so that the header will only appear on odd pages. Press **Return** or click on **New**. The header screen appears.
3. Press **Cmd-Shift-F** to put all text flush against the right margin and type **Matthews/Trip Report**. Press **Cmd-K** to save the header and return to your document.
4. Press **Cmd-7** to view the header in Codes.

```
[Header A:odd[Align>Matthews/Trip◇Report<Align][HRt]]▌[HRt]
```

5. Press **Cmd-7** to hide the codes again.
6. Press **Cmd-Shift-H** to access the Header/Footer Specification menu again. Then click on **Header B** and click on **Even Pages** so that it will appear only on even pages. Press **Return** or click on **New**.
7. Type **Matthews/Hawaii** and press **Cmd-K** to save the header.
8. Press **Cmd-Shift-H**. Click on **Footer A**, then click on **Odd Pages** to select it to appear only on odd pages. Press **Return** or click on **New**. The footer screen appears.
9. Press **Cmd-Shift-F** to put all text flush against the right margin and type **Page**, press the **Spacebar**, and click on the # icon. Press **Cmd-K** to save the footer.
10. Press **Cmd-Shift-H**. Click on **Footer B**, then click on **Even Pages** to select it to appear only on even pages. Press **Return** or click on **New**. The footer screen appears.
11. Type **Page** and press the **Spacebar**. Then click on the # icon. Press **Cmd-K** to save the footer.
12. Press **Cmd-7** to view the codes for the headers and footers.

```
[Header A:odd[Align>Matthews/Trip◇Report<Align][HRt]][Header B:even[Matthews/Hawaii[HRt]][Footer A:odd[
[Align>Page◇[Page #]<Align][HRt]][Footer B:even[Page◇[Page #][HRt]]▌[HRt]
```

The headers and footers on the printed document look like this:

Odd-numbered pages:

Matthews/Trip Report

To: FLG
From: JYM
Subject: Hawaii Convention

The Hawaii convention was very informative. Besides learning gobs about the office supply business, we also had a wonderful time. I never tried poi before. What a beautiful state!

Anyway, the office supply industry is booming. Everyone is adding computer supplies like diskettes, printers, ribbons, and other accessories. They're also adding books, telephones, and other items that never used to be in our stores before.

....

Page 1

Even-numbered pages:

Matthews/Hawaii

On Wednesday, chairr
and its impact on mc
radiation screens, pap
are also revolutionizin
on typewriters than we

Peterson cautioned a
mentioned that fully
computers.

Page 2

13. Press **Cmd-7** to exit Show Codes.
14. Press **Cmd-S**, type **Hawaii Trip**, and press **Return** to save the document.
15. Press **Cmd-K** to close the document. Then turn to Module 11 to continue the learning sequence.

Module 20

HELP

DESCRIPTION

Through the Help function, WordPerfect offers you a convenient answer to questions you may have concerning any WordPerfect function, command, or keystroke. WordPerfect furnishes you a complete description of the command. This is called *on-line* help because it is available on the screen at any time while you are performing any editing function with WordPerfect. (It is not available while a menu is on-screen, however.) To use Help, press F3 or Cmd-? or select WP Help from the Apple () menu.

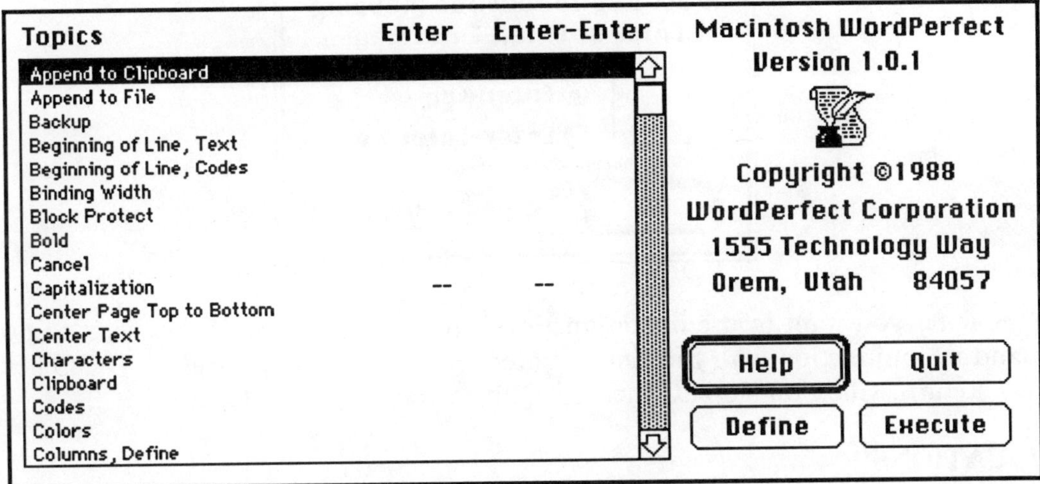

Move the cursor to the topic you want help on (or type the first letter of the topic to move quickly to it) and click Help or press Return. When you have finished reading about the topic, click on Topics to return to the above list. You then can click Quit to return to the document or you can continue looking for help.

EXECUTING FEATURES Once you get help with a topic, you may want to execute it immediately. WordPerfect lets you do this by highlighting the feature and clicking on Execute. This works with many features, such as margin settings, boldface, and other commands. Some, identified by a double dash to the right (--), cannot be executed from the Help menu.

MAPPING WITH THE ENTER KEY For convenience, Wordperfect lets you assign keystrokes to its commands. This process is called *mapping*. Mapping is accomplished in conjunction with the Help command and the Enter key. This lets you select your own keystrokes for commands. Mapping is most useful for commands not available with your keyboard, such as Delete Right, a command not available on the original Macintosh keyboard. For example, you could assign Delete Right the keystroke Enter-R or Enter-D. If two commands begin with the same letter, such as Retrieve and Required Space, you could assign one Enter-R and the other Enter-Enter-R as a keystroke. Commands with double dashes in the Enter and Enter-Enter columns cannot be mapped.

To map keystrokes, move the cursor to the command you want to map and click Define.

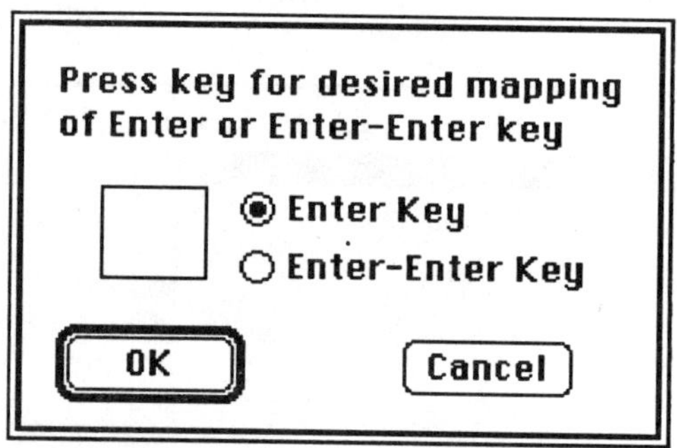

Type the letter you want to use in conjunction with the Enter key. If you want to use the command in conjunction with the Enter, Enter sequence, click on it also. Then click OK or press Return. Click on Topics, then on Quit to return to the document.

APPLICATIONS

Use Help whenever you need more information about a command or you aren't sure what the keystroke is for a certain command. Also use Help to map your keyboard for either more convenience or for creating keystrokes not otherwise available on your keyboard.

TYPICAL OPERATION

In this illustration, assume you are editing a letter. You have used the same word ("order") too many times and want a synonym to substitute for it, but you do not know how to use WordPerfect's Thesaurus (described in Module 41).

1. If necessary, start WordPerfect.
2. Create a document similar to the following. Use the **Tab** key to position the business address to the right of the page. Press **Return** at the end of each line of the addressor and addressee. Use WordPerfect's word wrapping function when typing the body of the letter. It is not necessary to press **Return,** since WordPerfect automatically wraps to the next line.

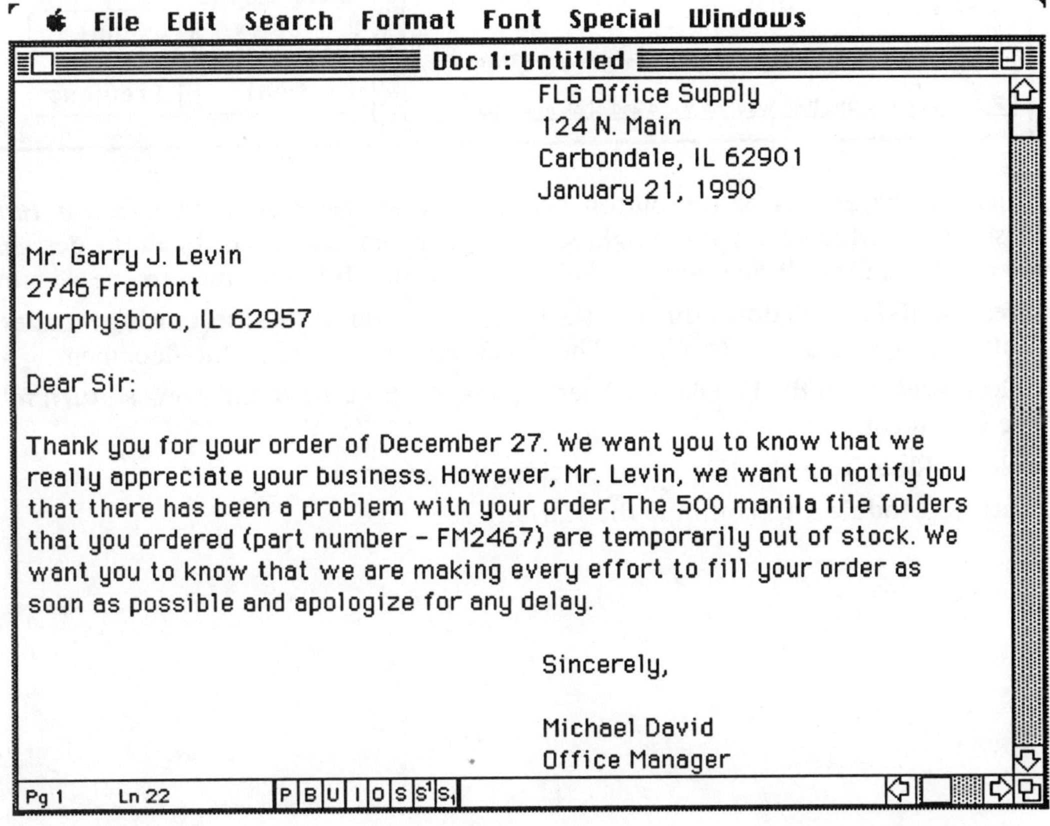

File Edit Search Format Font Special Windows

Doc 1: Untitled

FLG Office Supply
124 N. Main
Carbondale, IL 62901
January 21, 1990

Mr. Garry J. Levin
2746 Fremont
Murphysboro, IL 62957

Dear Sir:

Thank you for your order of December 27. We want you to know that we really appreciate your business. However, Mr. Levin, we want to notify you that there has been a problem with your order. The 500 manila file folders that you ordered (part number - FM2467) are temporarily out of stock. We want you to know that we are making every effort to fill your order as soon as possible and apologize for any delay.

Sincerely,

Michael David
Office Manager

Pg 1 Ln 22

3. With the cursor in the word "order" in the first line, access Help by pulling down the Apple menu and clicking on **WP Help** or by pressing **Cmd-?** or **F3**.

4. Type **T**, then move the cursor to the Thesaurus and double click on **Thesaurus**.

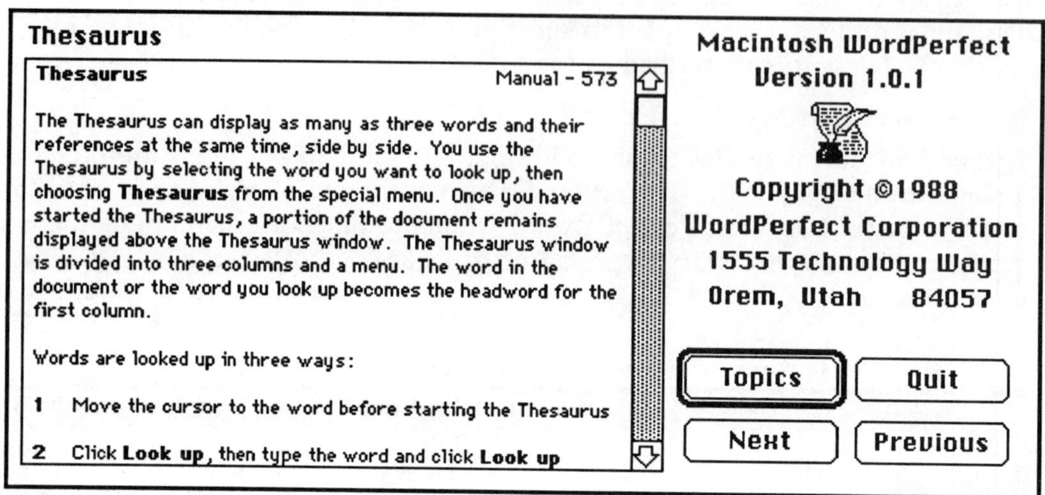

5. Click on the arrows or the button between the arrows (called an *Elevator Button*, described in Module 35) at the right side of the screen to scroll through the description of the Thesaurus. When you are finished, click on **Quit** to return to the document.
6. Press **Cmd-T**, scroll down through the list and click on **requisition** (using the Elevator Button), then click on **Replace**. Then click **Exit** to return to the document.
7. Select **Save** from the File menu. Then type **Apology Letter** and press **Return** to save the document.
8. Select **Close** from the File menu to close the document.
9. Turn to Module 4 to continue the learning sequence.

Module 21

INDENT

DESCRIPTION

The Indent key indents each line of a paragraph. In contrast, the Tab key indents only the first line. The Indent key and the Tab key share the same tab stops. The paragraph will indent one tab stop each time you press or select Indent. Once you select Indent, WordPerfect indents all lines of text from that point until you press Return. The Indent key is useful for indenting paragraphs in reports, outlines, and other documents.

To indent text you have already typed, move the cursor to the beginning of the paragraph you want to indent and either select Indent from the Paragraph Format menu or press Cmd-Shift-T or F4. Then move the cursor to the bottom of the paragraph to rewrite the screen. Or, select the entire paragraph and then press the Indent key.

TIP: You do not have to indent text at the beginning of a line. You can use the Indent key to indent text in the middle of a line, such as in lists where numbers would not be indented.

The Left-Right Indent is similar to Indent. Each time you select Left-Right Indent from the Paragraph Format menu or press Cmd-Shift-L or Shift-F4, the text is indented one tab stop from the left margin and an equal amount from the right margin. This feature is useful for centering paragraphs, for long quoted passages, or in other instances where you want text to stand out from the rest of the document. All NOTES and CAUTIONS in this book are examples of left-right indented text.

The following screen shows two normal paragraphs. Notice that the first line in each paragraph is indented to the first tab stop.

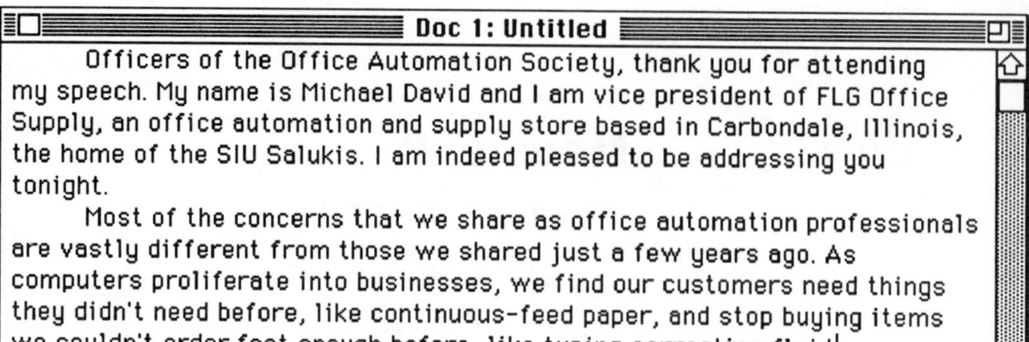

In the following example, the entire second paragraph is indented to the first tab stop.

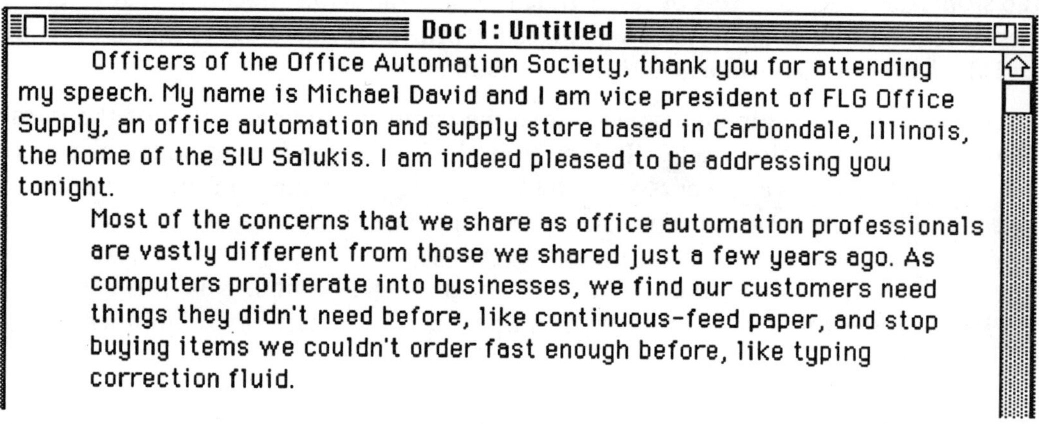

Here, the second paragraph is left-right indented.

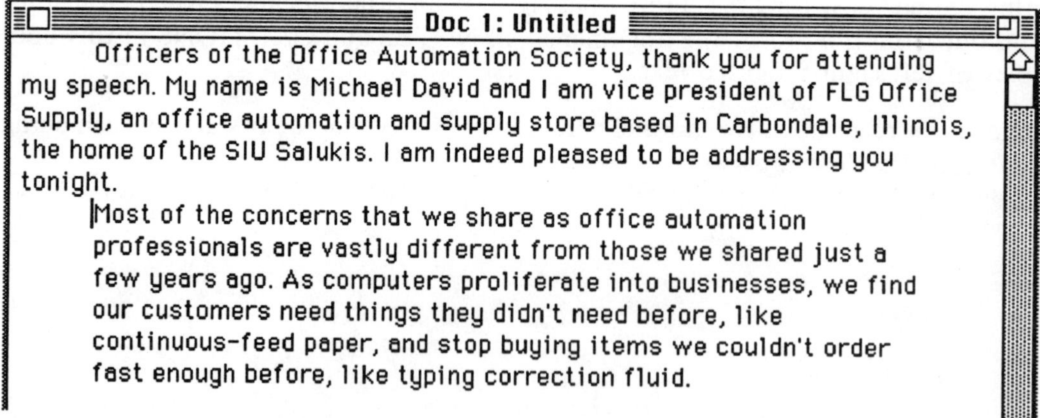

APPLICATIONS

Use the Indent key to give paragraphs a uniform left margin at a particular tab stop. This is useful in outlines, reports, tables, charts, and other documents. Use the Left-Right Indent to make certain paragraphs stand out from the rest of the document.

TYPICAL OPERATION

In this example, you use Indent, Left-Right Indent, and Tab keys to format a report. This example also demonstrates the use of tabs on the same line as indents.

1. If necessary, start WordPerfect. Then create a document similar to the following:

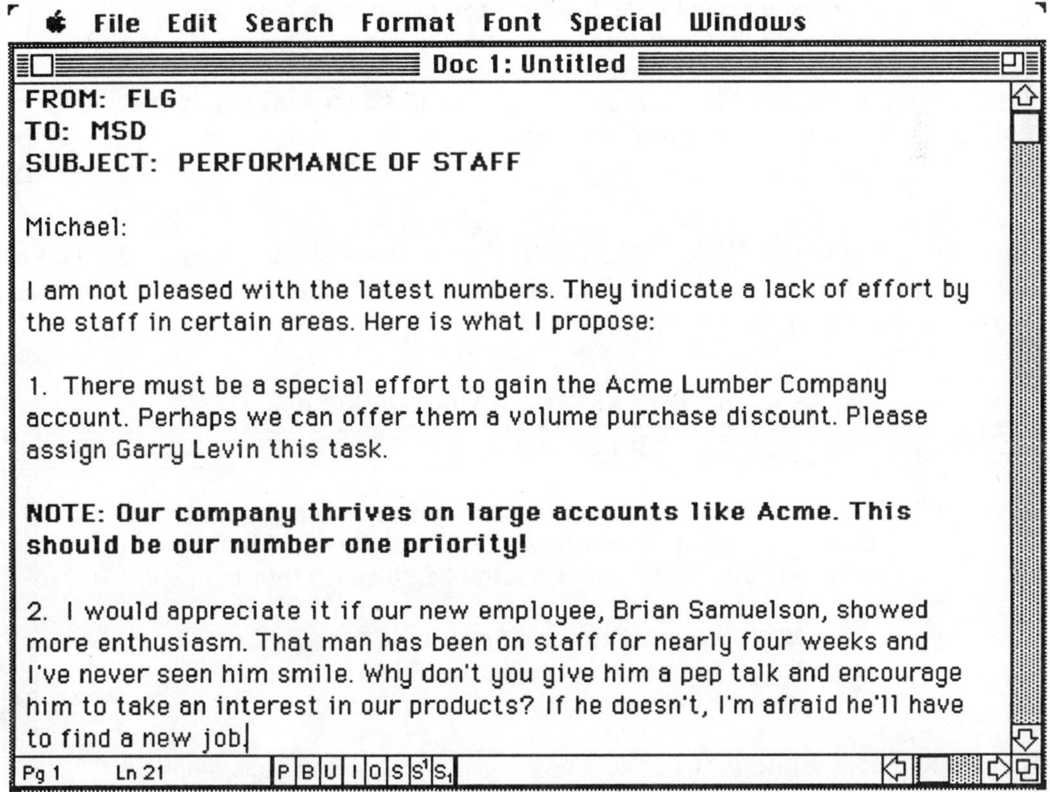

2. Move the cursor to the number "1" in the second paragraph and press **Tab**.
3. Move the cursor to the "T" in "There" and press **Cmd-Shift-T**.

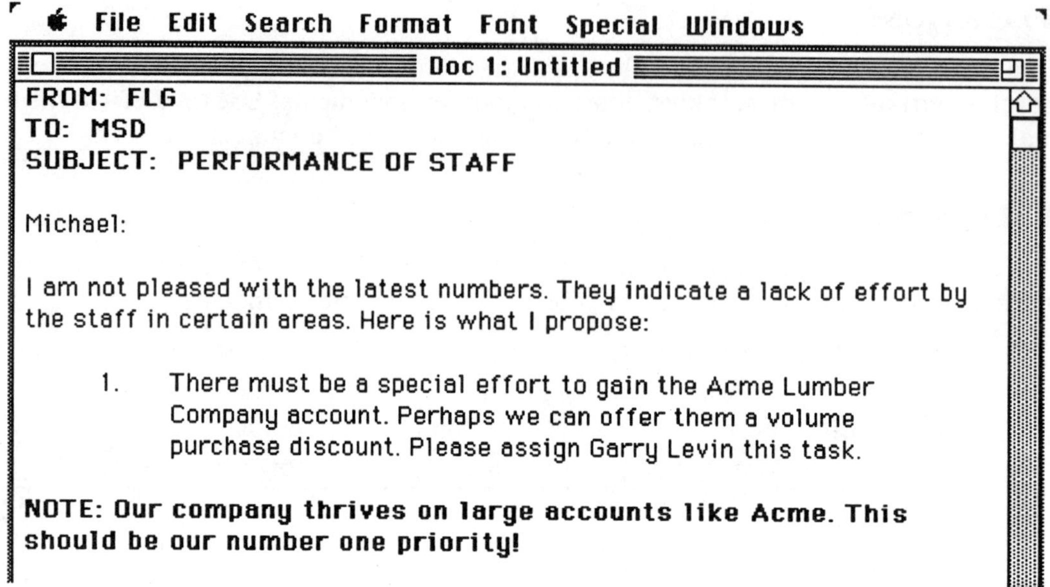

4. Move the cursor to the "N" in "NOTE" and press **Cmd-Shift-L** three times. This creates a left/right indent that is three tab stops in from both the left and the right margins. Move the cursor to the next paragraph.

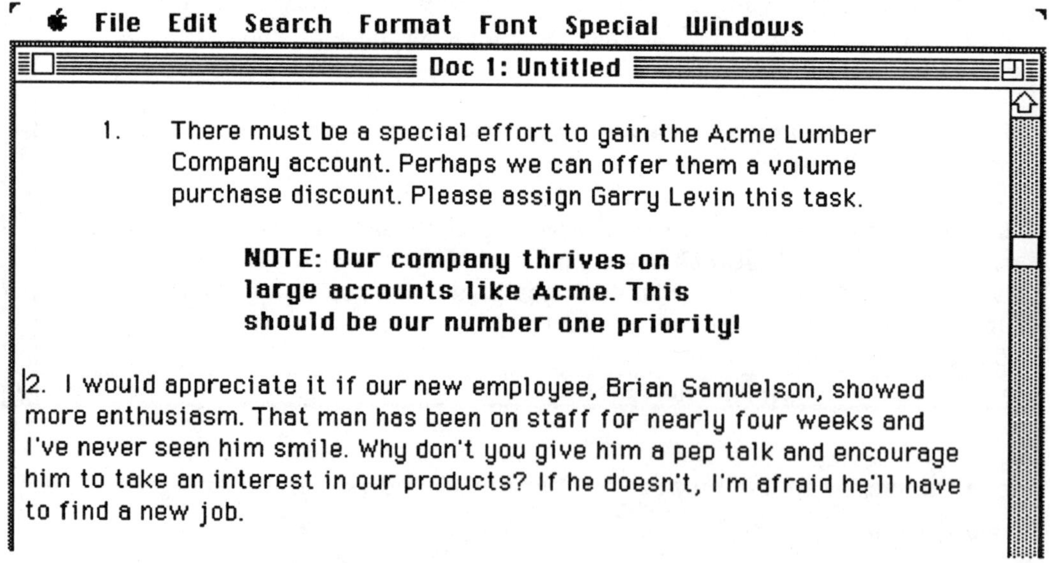

5. With the cursor on the number "2," press **Tab** twice. Move the cursor to the word "I" and press **Cmd-Shift-T**.

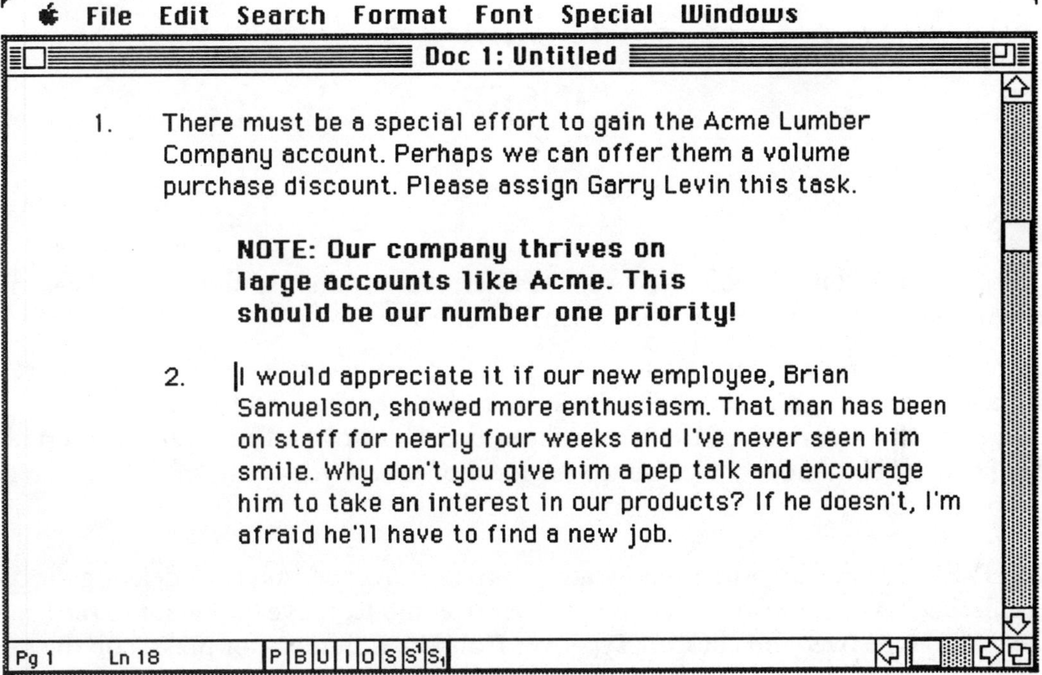

Notice the second paragraph is more indented than the first.

6. Press **Cmd-S**. Then type **Brian Samuelson Letter** and press **Return** to save the document.
7. Press **Cmd-K** to close the document. Then turn to Module 33 to continue the learning sequence.

Module 22

INSERT

DESCRIPTION

When editing a document, you often want to insert text to add information, make something more grammatically correct, or correct spelling errors.

WordPerfect lets you insert text at any time. Inserting text occurs naturally in the Insert mode, which allows you to go to any line of text in a document and add something to it. When you type, text to the right of the cursor is pushed forward and new text is inserted in its place. To insert text, move the cursor to the location where you want the new text to appear and type normally.

TYPEOVER There are other times you want to type over certain text, deleting the old text and replacing it with new words. To use the Typeover mode, move the cursor to the beginning of the text to type over and click on Typeover from the Edit menu or press 0 on the numeric keypad. A "Typeover" message appears on the Status Line at the bottom right of the screen. Any text you type now will type over other text in your document.

NOTE

The Typeover mode does not work for text that is boldfaced or underlined.

APPLICATIONS

Use the Insert mode to add text to a document without deleting anything. Use the Typeover mode to add new text and delete old text at the same time.

TYPICAL OPERATION

This example lets you use both the Typeover mode and the Insert mode to edit a letter.

1. If necessary, start WordPerfect. Then create a document similar to the following:

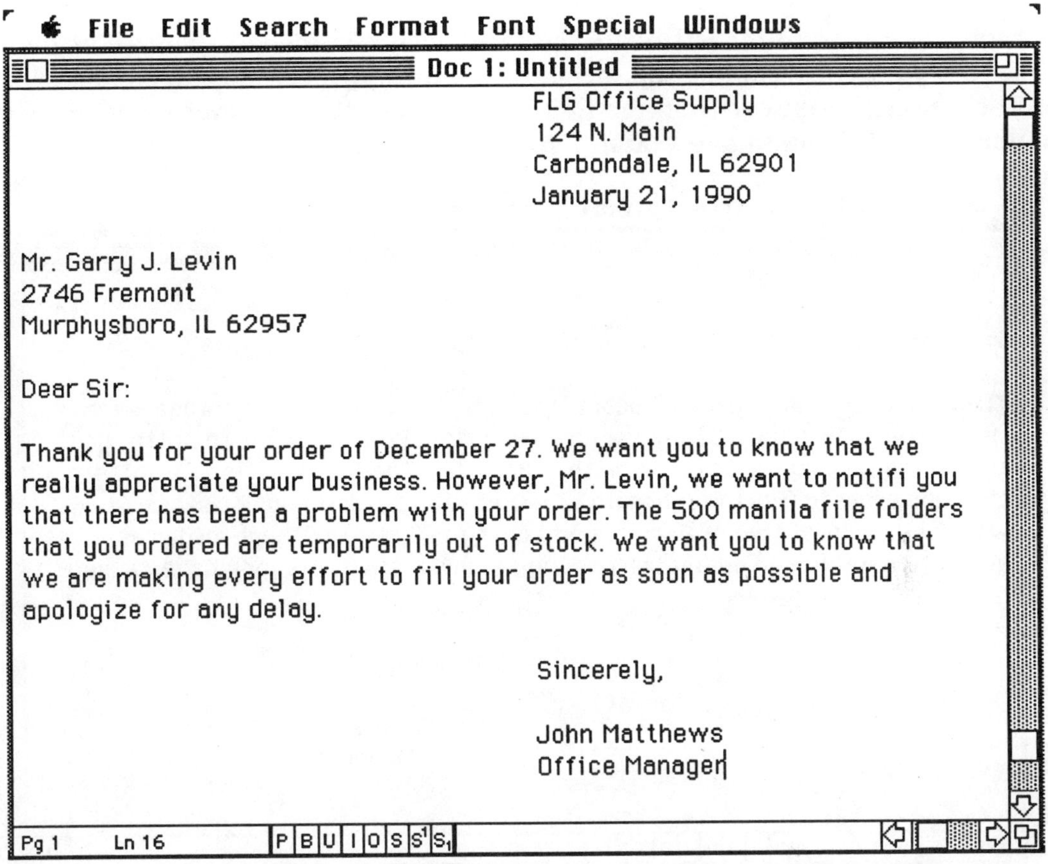

 File Edit Search Format Font Special Windows

Doc 1: Untitled

FLG Office Supply
124 N. Main
Carbondale, IL 62901
January 21, 1990

Mr. Garry J. Levin
2746 Fremont
Murphysboro, IL 62957

Dear Sir:

Thank you for your order of December 27. We want you to know that we really appreciate your business. However, Mr. Levin, we want to notifi you that there has been a problem with your order. The 500 manila file folders that you ordered are temporarily out of stock. We want you to know that we are making every effort to fill your order as soon as possible and apologize for any delay.

Sincerely,

John Matthews
Office Manager

Pg 1 Ln 16 P B U I O S S S

2. Move the cursor to the left of the last "i" in "notifi" in the third sentence and select **Typeover** from the Edit menu. Then type **y**. Notice the "y" replaces the "i."
3. Select **Typeover** from the Edit menu again to turn the Typeover mode off. Move the cursor to the space after the last "d" in "ordered" and type **(Part Number J4278W)**.

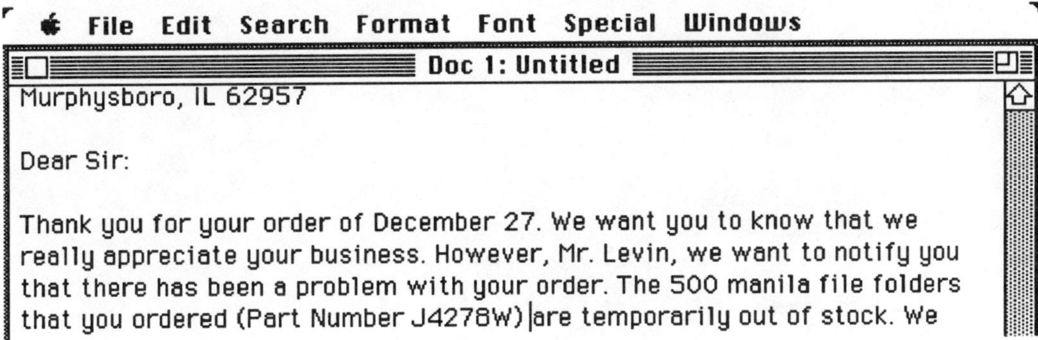

 File Edit Search Format Font Special Windows

Doc 1: Untitled

Murphysboro, IL 62957

Dear Sir:

Thank you for your order of December 27. We want you to know that we really appreciate your business. However, Mr. Levin, we want to notify you that there has been a problem with your order. The 500 manila file folders that you ordered (Part Number J4278W) are temporarily out of stock. We

4. Move the cursor to the left of the "d" in "delay" in the last sentence of the letter, select **Typeover** from the Edit menu to turn the Typeover mode on and type **incon**. Then, select **Typeover** from the Edit menu to turn the Typeover mode off and type **venience this may have caused you**.

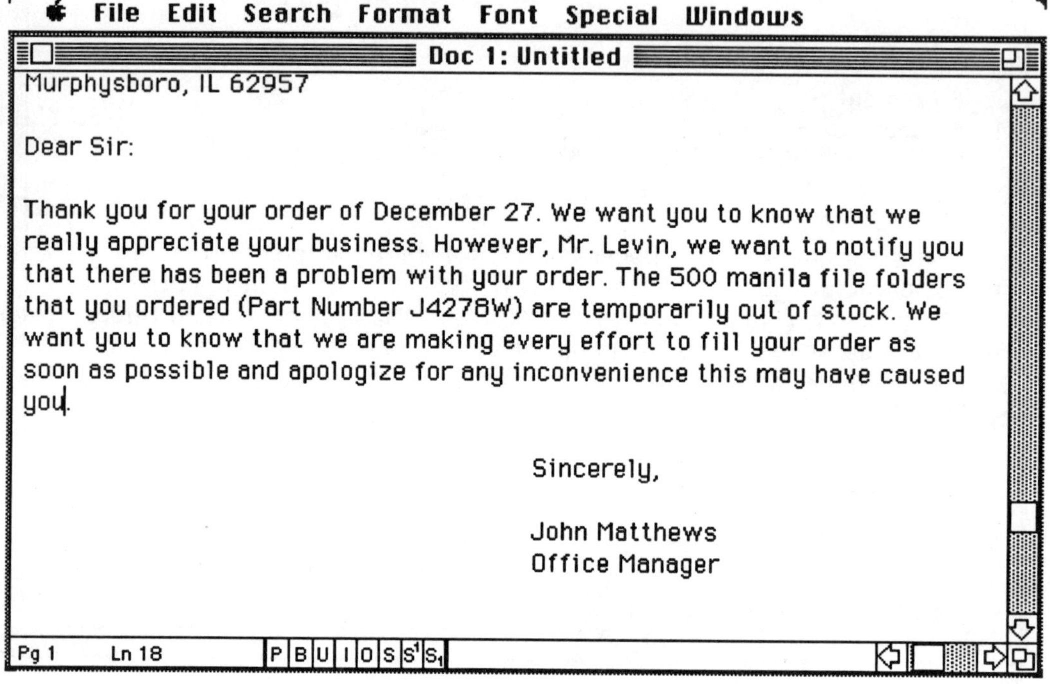

5. Press **Cmd-S**, then type **Levin Letter** and press **Return** to save the document.
6. Press **Cmd-K** to close the document. Turn to Module 12 to continue the learning sequence.

Module 23

LINE FORMAT

DESCRIPTION

The Line Format option provides a number of ways to manipulate and arrange text on a line. It helps you center text (Module 6), produce flush right text (Module 15), and set tabs, hyphenation, spacing, kerning, and margin release.

To access the Line Format menu, select Line from the Format menu or press Cmd-4 or Shift-F8.

Format

Line Format

1. Center ⌘⇧C
2. Flush Right ⌘⇧F
3. Tabs...
4. Hyphenation...
5. Spacing...
6. Kerning...
7. Margin Release

TABS Typists set tabs on their typewriters to set levels of indentation, starting points for addresses, starting points for columns within tables, and for a variety of other reasons. When tabs are set, pressing the Tab key moves the carriage or the carrier to the next tab, where the typist continues.

WordPerfect's tab settings work in a similar fashion. Instead of a carriage or a carrier, the cursor moves to the next tab setting when the Tab key is pressed. Pressing Shift-Tab moves the cursor back to the previous tab setting.

WordPerfect initially sets tabs 0.5 inches apart from the left margin to the right margin (5 spaces at the default setting of 10 characters per inch). You can reset these tabs in any manner you like. You can visually see all tab settings by showing the Ruler (Module 33).

WordPerfect offers four kinds of tabs: left justified, right justified, centered, or decimal.

- Left-justified tabs, the default setting, are the way normal tabs are set. Text appears at the leftmost portion of the tab.
- Right-justified tabs result in right-justified text. Text moves to the left as you type, with the tab setting serving as the right margin. This is similar to the flush right feature.
- Decimal tabs are decimal aligned. Text moves to the right until you type a decimal point. Decimal tabs are helpful for columns of numbers.
- Centered tabs result in centered text. The tab setting serves as the center of the text.

You can set tabs as many times in a document as you like. Realize, however, that the only text affected by a tab setting is text that occurs after that tab setting and before the next one. To set tabs, type or click on 3 from the Line Format menu.

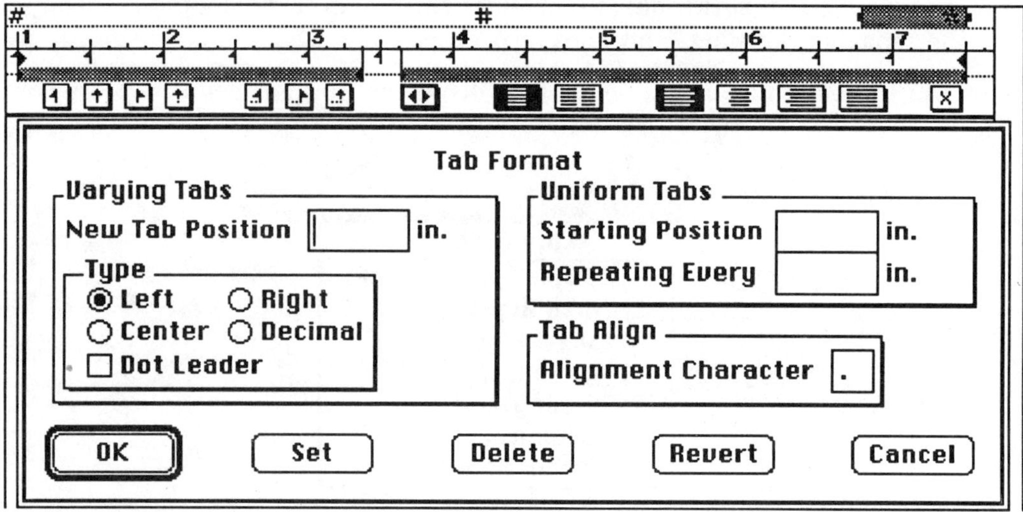

WordPerfect displays both the Ruler and the Tab Format menu to show you what the current tab settings are. Module 33 shows you how to set tabs via the Ruler. To set completely new tabs, delete all existing tabs first. Do this by either clicking on the delete box or by pressing Cmd-End. You can set either varying tabs or uniform tabs. *Varying tabs* are not a set distance apart, while *uniform tabs* are a set distance apart from the left margin to the right.

To set a varying tab, type the appropriate value for the tab position and select whether you want left, right, centered, or decimal tabs. Click the Dot Leader box if you want dot leaders between tabs. Then click Set.

To set uniform tabs, type the appropriate value for the starting position and the repeating position. For example, if you want tabs 1 inch apart starting 3 inches from the left edge of the paper, click in the Starting Position box, type 3, click in the Repeating Position box and type 1. Then click Set.

To reset tabs to their positions before you opened the tab box, click Revert. When you have finished, click OK or press Return.

Tab Align The Tab Align key makes it easy to align columns of numbers or text along a certain character. The default alignment character, as shown in the Tab Format menu, is a decimal point (.). Change the alignment character through the Tab Format menu.

This feature is most useful for aligning columns of numbers. Without the Tab Align key, you would have to count the number of spaces in each number to make sure the numbers aligned before typing them.

When you press Cmd-Tab or Cmd-F6, the cursor automatically moves to the next tab stop. All text or numbers that you type until you press the alignment character automatically move to the left. When you press the alignment character, all text or numbers after that flow normally (to the right).

CAUTION

Numbers are aligned without regard for the left margin. If you are typing a number that begins at the first tab stop, make sure it is no longer than 15 characters. Otherwise, WordPerfect will not be able to align it.

For example, here are some numbers aligned:

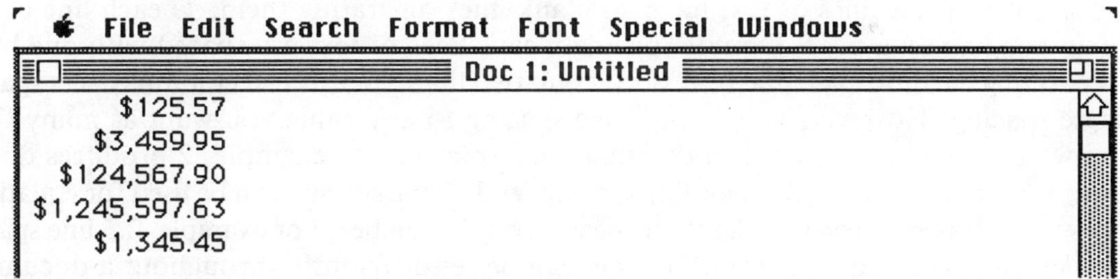

Here are the same numbers not aligned:

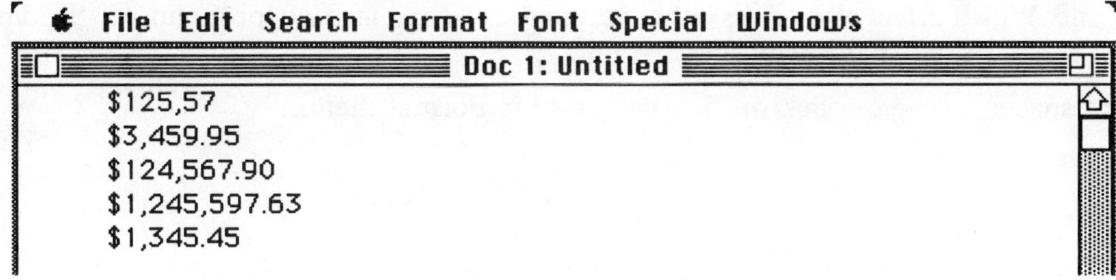

HYPHENATION Hyphenation makes your documents have more evenly spaced lines as well as a more uniform right margin. WordPerfect offers two types of hyphenation — Automatic and Auto Aided. Automatic hyphenation automatically hyphenates words according to WordPerfect's own hyphenation rules. Auto Aided asks you where you want to put the hyphens. The amount of hyphenation in a document is determined by the Hyphenation Zone, discussed in Module 33.

To set hyphenation, type or click on 4 from the Line Format menu.

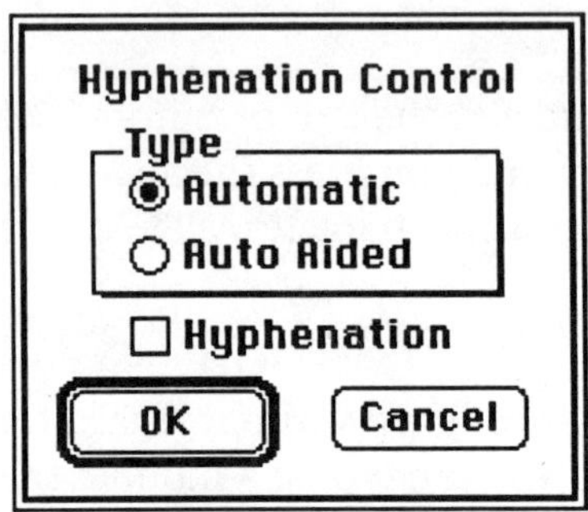

To turn hyphenation on, click in the Hyphenation box. Then click on either Automatic or Auto Aided to select the type of Hyphenation you want. Click OK or press Return.

SPACING As with a typewriter, *spacing* refers to the number of blank lines between text. Single spacing means lines of text have no blank lines separating them, so each line of text takes up one line on a page. Double spacing means lines of text are spaced with one blank line separating each, so each line of text takes up two lines. WordPerfect initially sets spacing at single spacing. However, you can change spacing to any value you want as many times as you want. Numbers are used to designate line spacing: for example, 2 produces double spacing, 1.5 produces one-and-a-half line spacing, and .5 line spacing can be used for equations. WordPerfect sets on-screen spacing to the nearest whole number. For example, 2.5 line spacing looks like triple spacing on-screen. Spacing can be set differently throughout a document, i.e., it can be single spaced in one part of a document, double spaced in another.

WordPerfect offers either automatic or fixed *line height*. Line height refers to the size of each line. WordPerfect also offers either automatic or fixed *leading* (pronounced "ledding"), which refers to the space between each line.

To set spacing, type or click on 5 from the Line Format menu.

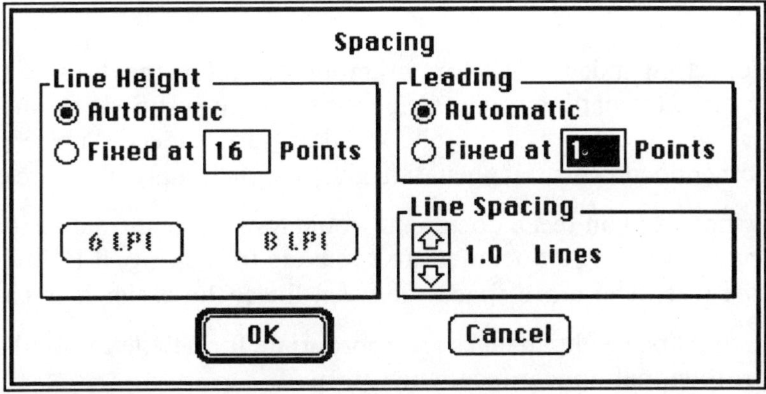

Automatic line height and leading is preset according to the font you are using. In this example, each line is 16 points high, and the space between each line is 1 point. If you want each line to be the same height no matter what font you are using, click on the Fixed button and type a new value for both line height and leading. To change line spacing, click on the arrows. The up arrow increases spacing in .5 line increments. The down arrow decreases spacing in .5 line increments. When you have finished, click OK or press Return.

KERNING *Kerning* adjusts spacing between certain letter pairs such as "l" and "t." This feature is useful for desktop publishing applications. To set kerning, move the cursor between the two characters you want to adjust the space for and type or click on 6 from the Line Format menu.

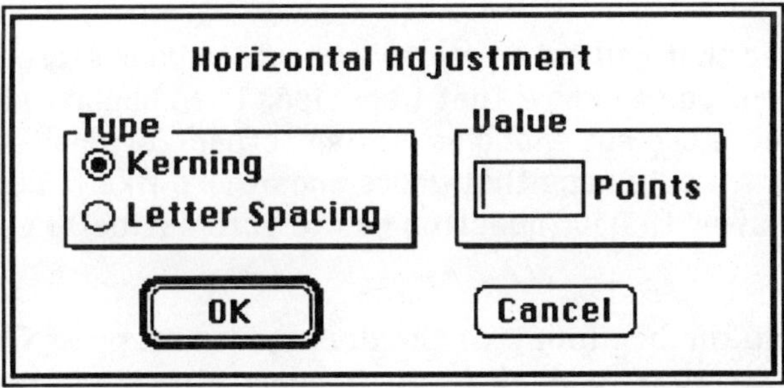

If you want to decrease the space between characters, click on Kerning. To increase the space between characters, click on Letter Spacing. Then type the number of points by which you want the spacing adjusted and click OK or press Return.

MARGIN RELEASE The Margin Release key moves the cursor one tab stop to the left each time you select it. When the cursor reaches the left edge of the page, the margin release no longer works. You can select it either by pressing Shift-Tab or by typing or clicking on 7 from the Line Format menu.

APPLICATIONS

Tabs are useful for setting indent levels for paragraphs, selecting the distance between columns in charts, and for other formatting needs. Centered and right-justified tabs are useful in tables. Decimal tabs work well in columns of numbers. Adding dot leaders is a nice touch for figures, tables, lists, and other documents. Hyphenation gives the right margin a more even appearance.

Change spacing whenever you feel a document would look more attractive if text were spaced differently. If you are sending a document to someone for editing, it is advisable to double- or triple-space the text. The more spaces between lines, the easier it is to edit.

Kerning, leading, and line height changes are appropriate for newsletters and other documents that require a professional appearance when printed.

TYPICAL OPERATION

This example illustrates the use of hyphenation in a document.

1. If necessary, start WordPerfect. Then create a document similar to the following:

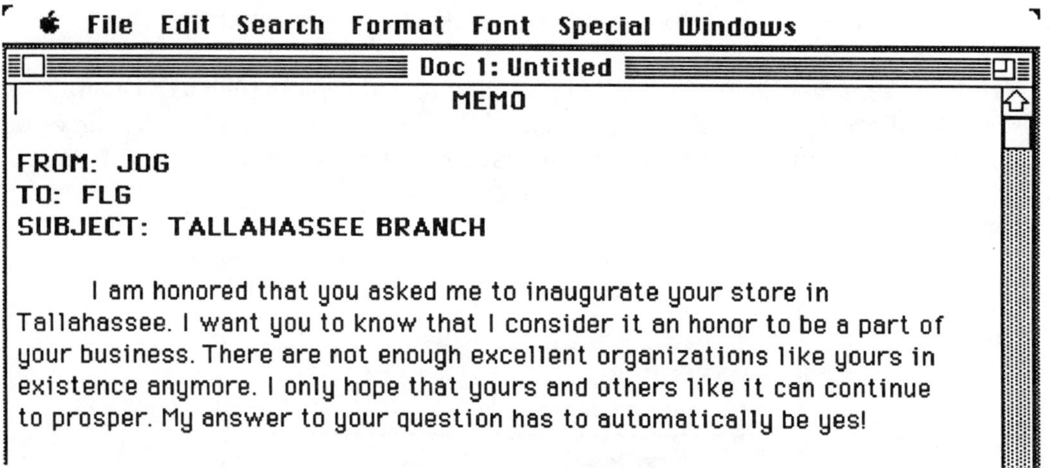

2. Move the cursor to the beginning of the document and press **Cmd-4** to open the Line Format menu. Then type or click on **4** to select Hyphenation.
3. Click on **Auto Aided**. Then click on the **Hyphenation** box, and click on **OK** or press **Return**.

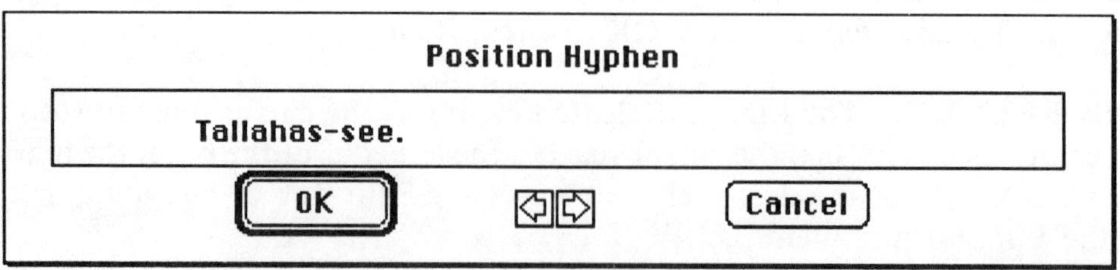

4. Using the left arrow button, move the cursor between the "a" and the "h" and click **OK** or press **Return** to position the hyphen between those two letters.

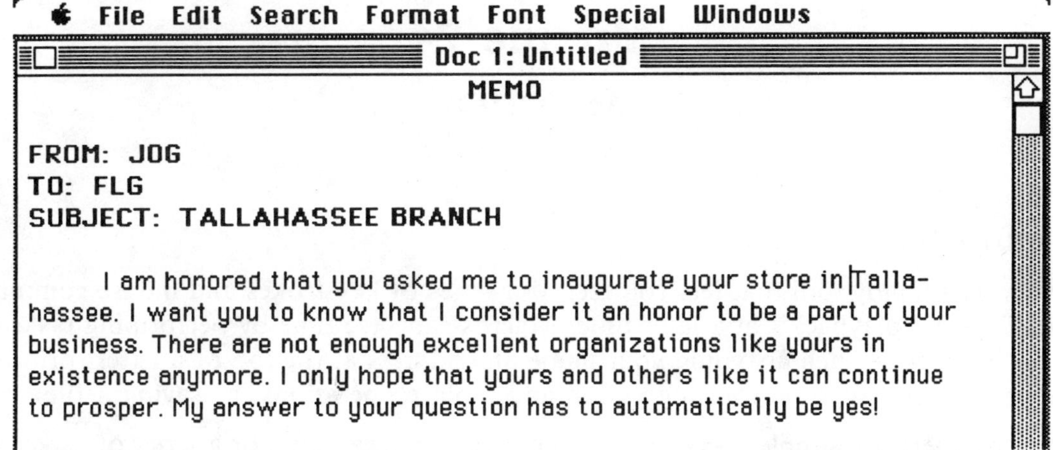

5. Press **Cmd-S** and type **JOG Says Yes!** (including the exclamation point). Then press **Return** to save the document.
6. Press **Cmd-K** to close the document. Then turn to Module 5 to continue the learning sequence.

Module 24

MACROS

DESCRIPTION

A *macro* is a handy tool that lets you record a series of keystrokes and mouse commands into a file for "playback" at a later time. Macros can save time by performing tasks that you do repeatedly, such as typing your name and address at the top of a letter, printing a number of documents, performing search and replace operations, or saving a file.

Macros can perform simple tasks, such as the preceding examples, or a series of tasks, such as searching for words, replacing them with other words, marking them in an index, saving the file, and printing it.

WordPerfect lets you chain macros together — when one macro ends, the next one begins; nest macros — execute one macro inside another; and repeat a macro through the use of the Esc key (Module 13).

Macros in WordPerfect are "invisible." In other words, you cannot see them as they are being executed. To make macros visible, assign a delay function to them when defining them.

All macro functions are accessed through the Macro menu. Access the Macro menu by selecting Macro from the Special menu, pressing Cmd-M, or pressing Option-F10.

Special

Macro

1. Define Macro... ⌘⇧M
2. Execute Macro... ⌘⇧X
3. Chain Macro...
4. Macro Delay...
5. Macro Input...
6. Pause Macro

DEFINING A MACRO Before you use a macro, you must first define, or "record" it. To define a macro, either select Define Macro from the Macro menu, press Cmd-Shift-M, or press Cmd-F10.

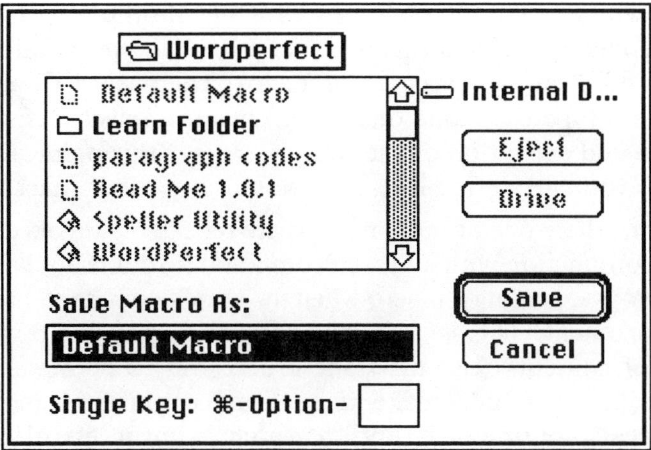

At this point, you can either type the name of the macro or assign it a key sequence that is easily accessed. This sequence is always used in conjunction with the Cmd and Option keys. Press Return or click on Save. The following message appears on the Status Line:

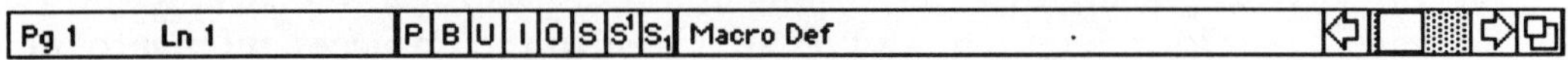

NOTE

When defining macros, move the cursor using the arrow keys instead of using mouse clicks or the Scroll Bar. This ensures that the cursor moves where you want it when you execute the macro, even if the file has been changed.

Create the macro. Everything you do at this point is included in the macro. You can place a pause in the macro (so users can insert text while invoking the macro) by selecting Pause Macro from the Macro menu.

You can even chain another macro to the macro you are defining by selecting Chain Macro from the Macro menu.

You cannot start a merge (Module 26) during macro creation. When a merge starts, macro creation automatically stops. To end macro definition, select Define Macro from the Macro menu. Many options are available during macro definition, including delays, inputs, pauses, chains, and nests.

Chaining Macros Chaining is a process where two or more macros are chained together. When one macro is completed, the next one automatically starts. There are three types of chains:

- Simple chain, where one macro is executed while another one is being defined. To create a simple chain, define a macro as described above, naming it and typing all the keystrokes necessary to execute the macro. Then select Chain Macro from the Macro menu and type the name of another macro. Select Define Macro from the Macro menu to end definition of the first macro. At this point, if the second macro is not defined, you can define it as you would any other macro.
- Repeating chain, where one or more macros are repeatedly invoked. A repeating chain only works in conjunction with a Search command (Module 36) because WordPerfect automatically stops executing a macro when the search command has finished its search through the document. This is especially useful for marking text for indexes, lists, and the table of contents. Use the same procedures to define a repeating chain as you would a simple chain, only make sure a Search command is included in the macro. The macro repeats continuously until a search is unsuccessful.
- Conditional chain, where two or more macros are chained to a macro with a Search command. This makes the macro make a decision. If the Search command finds what it is looking for, WordPerfect executes one macro; if it does not, WordPerfect invokes another. To create a conditional chain, create one macro that results in an unsuccessful search. Then define another that results in a successful search. Then define a macro intended to perform a search, and chain it first to the unsuccessful macro and then to the successful one.

Nesting Macros While a macro chain executes a second macro only after the first has been completed, a nested macro is executed as part of another macro. To nest a macro, define and name one macro and type any keystrokes necessary before executing the nested macro. Then select Execute Macro from the Macro menu and type the name of the macro you want to nest and click Execute. Then type the rest of the keystrokes for the first macro and select Define Macro from the Macro menu.

Macro Delays Macros are normally invisible when WordPerfect executes them. The Macro Delay option lets you see a macro while it is being executed. To use it, select Macro Delay from the Macro menu during macro definition.

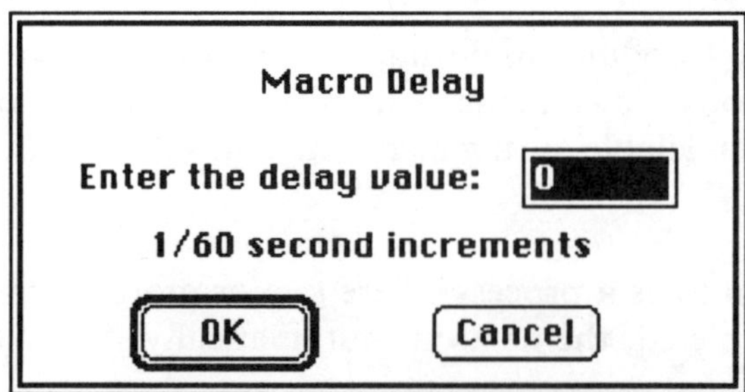

Type a delay factor up to 65,367 (about 18 minutes). Then click OK or press Return. A delay value of 1 makes the macro visible, but still operational at full speed. The delay factor postpones execution between keystrokes or mouse commands the specified amount. To make a macro invisible, select Macro Delay from the Macro menu and set it to 0.

Macro Input Some macros need text prompts to guide the user through them. For example, a macro that defines a name and address could pause long enough for users to enter today's date. A prompt that says "Enter today's date" would make this process easier. To set up a prompt, use the Macro Input feature. To do this, select Macro Input during macro definition.

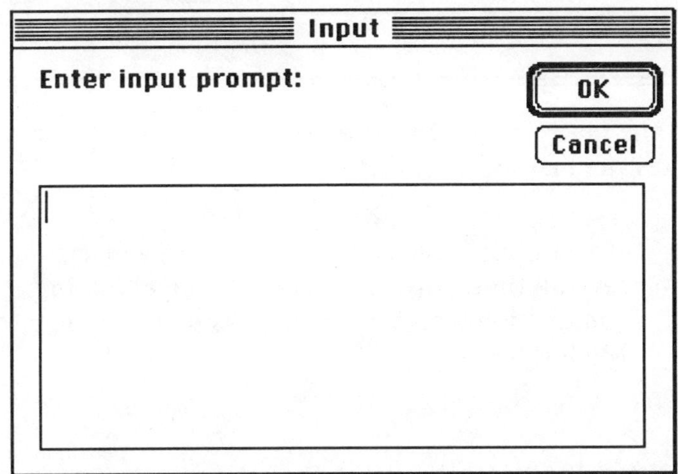

Type the text for the prompt and click OK or press Return. When the macro is being executed, WordPerfect puts the prompt on the screen and pauses for keyboard input. To make the macro resume, click Resume Macro from the Macro menu.

Pause Macro Putting a pause in a macro lets users enter text during macro execution. The above example of entering the current date is only one example of the usefulness of a pause feature. To temporarily pause macro execution, select Pause Macro during macro definition. When you are ready to resume, select Resume Macro from the Macro Definition menu.

EXECUTING A MACRO Once you define a macro, you can play it back, or execute it. If you named a macro with an Cmd-Option key sequence, press the key sequence to execute the macro. If you used an alternative method to name your macro, select Execute Macro from the Macro menu, or press Cmd-Shift-X, or press Option-F10.

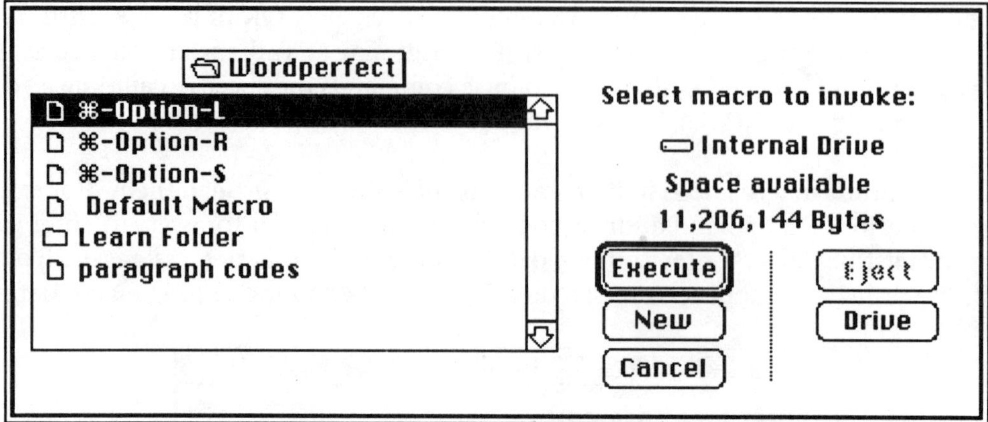

Move the cursor to the macro you want to execute and press Return or click on Execute. WordPerfect executes the macro.

NOTE

If you want to repeat the execution of a macro several times, use the Repeat Value (n) in conjunction with the Esc key, as described in Module 13.

APPLICATIONS

Any time you find yourself repeatedly typing the same keystrokes, a macro can save you time. Macros are useful for a variety of purposes. In all cases, a well-designed macro can save you much time and effort. Use macros to save keystrokes for any procedure that you perform often. For example, if you change margins frequently, you can create a macro that automatically changes the margins for you. Or if you perform the same search and replace task many times, you can create a macro that does this for you at the touch of a keystroke.

Macros can also perform more than one task at a time. For example, you can create a macro that changes boldface to italics while changing margins from 1 inch left and right to 2 inches left and right. Macros are also very useful when merging documents.

Nested and chained macros are useful for complicated search and replace operations that mark text and move it from one document to another.

TYPICAL OPERATION

In this example, you create a macro that searches for the beginning of each paragraph and inserts a tab.

1. If necessary, start WordPerfect. Then press **Cmd-Shift-M**. Type **paragraph codes** and press **Return**.

2. Press **Cmd-H** to conduct a search and replace operation. Double click on the (HRt) code twice to indicate you want to search for two Hard Returns in a row. (Hard Returns are explained in Module 2.) Then move the cursor to the Replace box and click on (HRt) two more times. Then click on the (TAB) icon. This leaves the returns in, but adds an indent at the beginning of a new paragraph.

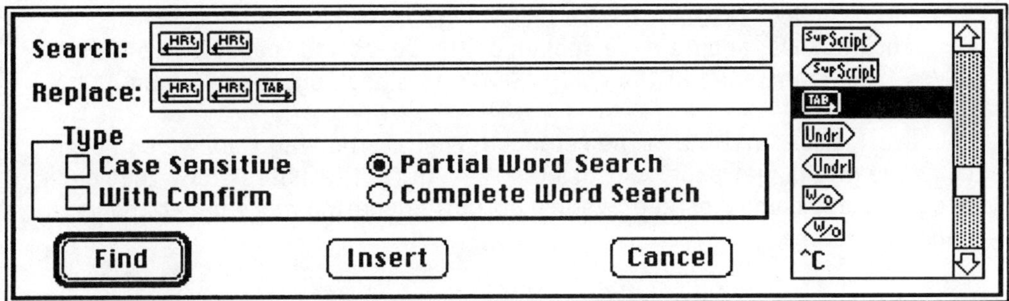

3. Click on **Find** or press **Return**. Then press **Cmd-Shift-M** to end Macro Definition.
4. Create a document similar to the following:

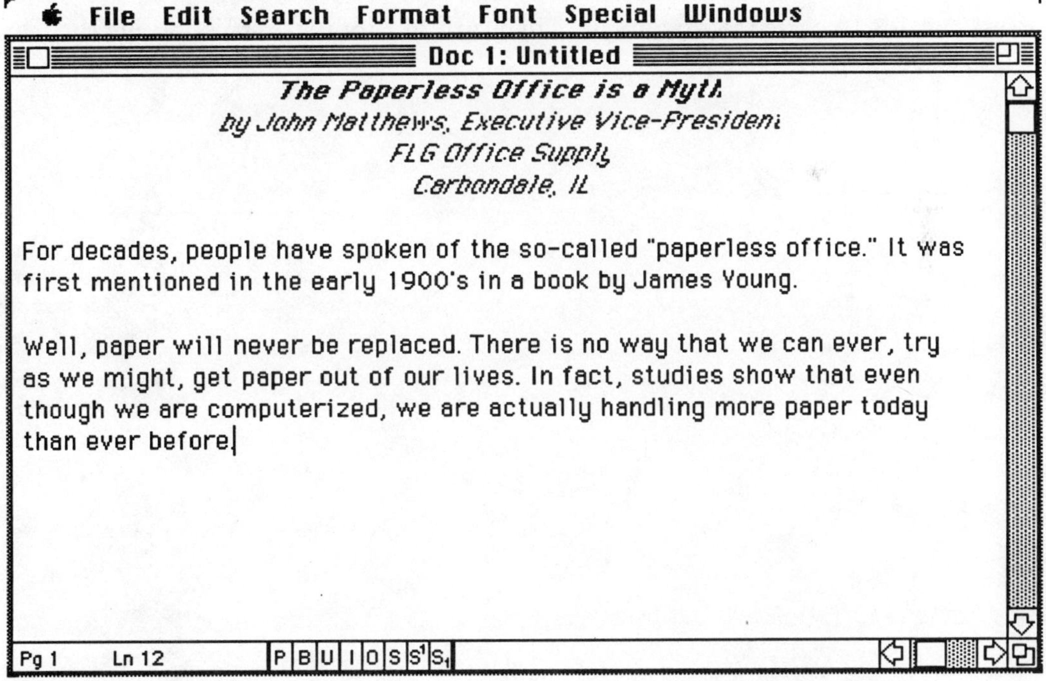

5. Move the cursor to the top of the document, press **Cmd-Shift-X**, and move the cursor to paragraph codes. Press **Enter**.

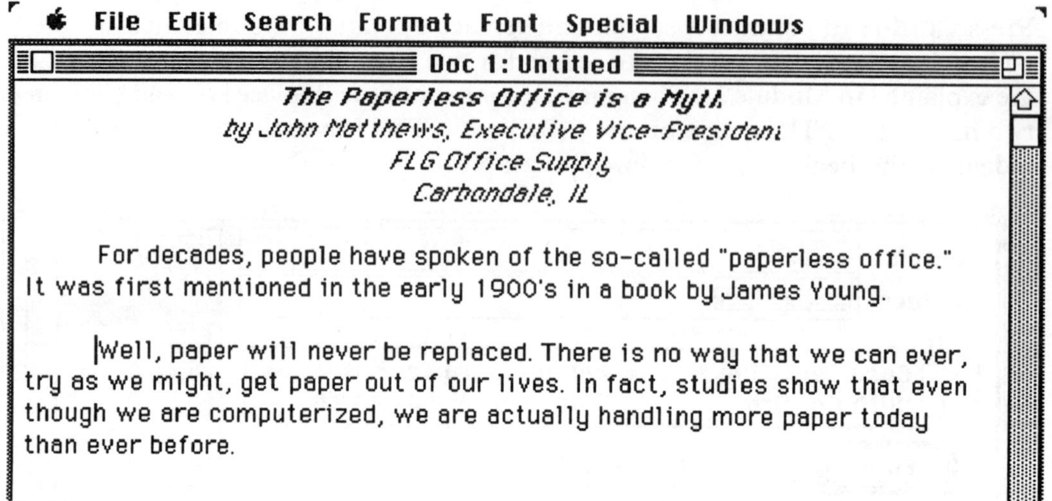

Tabs are inserted at the beginning of each paragraph. Imagine the convenience of this in a large document.

6. Press **Cmd-S**. Then type **Paperless Office** and press **Return** to save the document.
7. Press **Cmd-K** to close the document. Then turn to Module 26 to continue the learning sequence.

Module 25

MARK TEXT: INDEX, LIST, TABLE OF CONTENTS

DESCRIPTION

WordPerfect's Mark Text feature helps you generate lists, tables of contents, and indexes automatically. If you have ever created any of these documents by hand, you know what a useful feature this is. You can create an index, table of contents, or up to five lists for a document as large as this book or as small as a one-page report. It is, of course, most useful for large documents.

The Mark Text command helps you mark text for lists (of figures, illustrations, etc.), a table of contents, or an index. It also helps you generate those documents and remove redline and strikeout markings. (Redline and strikeout are discussed in Module 31.)

To access the Mark Text command, click on Mark Text from the Special menu, press Cmd-J, or press Alt-F5.

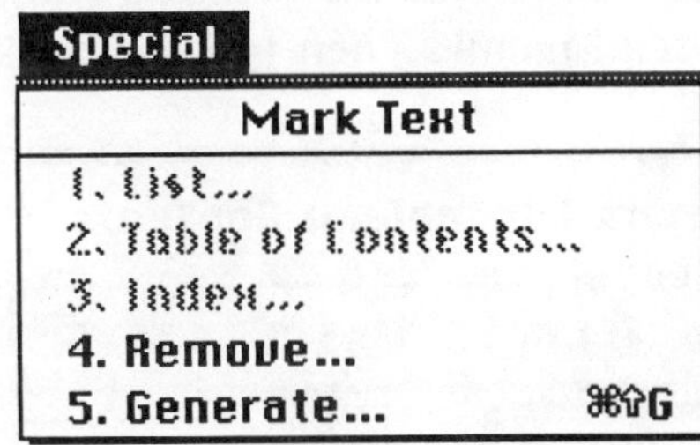

There are three steps to creating an index, list, or table of contents:

1. Mark the text to be included in the index, list, or table of contents.
2. Define the style.
3. Generate it.

The best time to mark text is as you create the document. Whenever you type a word or phrase that you feel should be included in an index, list, or table of contents, mark it. The text you mark is given a code that cannot be seen without using Cmd-7, the Codes key (Module 7). If you make a mistake while marking text, use the Codes key to show the codes. Then delete the code and re-mark the text. To mark text, highlight the text you want to mark and press Cmd-J.

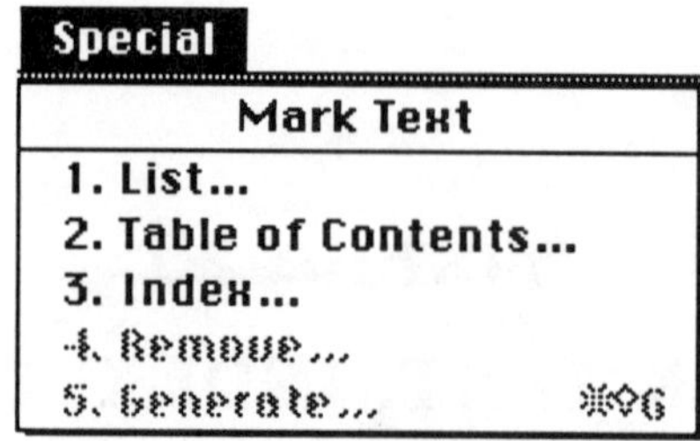

Marking Text For A List WordPerfect lets you create up to five lists per document. Type or click on 1 for list.

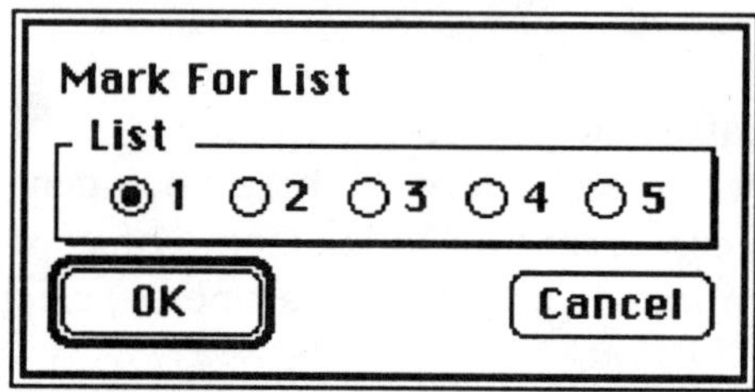

Click on the list you are marking the text for and click OK or press Return.

Marking Text For A Table Of Contents The table of contents can have up to five levels for sections such as parts of a book, sections in that part, and chapters in that section. To mark text for a table of contents, highlight the text you want to mark and press Cmd-J or select Mark Text from the Special menu. Then type or click on 2.

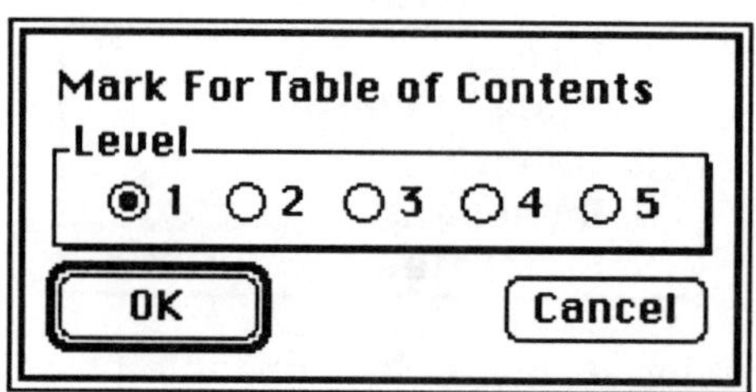

Click on the level you want the marked text to be at and click OK or press Return.

Marking Text For An Index While text for lists and tables of contents generally comes from the document itself, text for the index comes from both the document and written information. This is because indexes are created on two levels: heading and subheading. Therefore, if you have written a book about nature, for example, you can have headings for flowers, trees, and animals, and subheadings for roses, maples, and dogs, among others. While the subheadings will be in the text, the master headings may not. To mark text for an index, highlight the information you want marked and press Cmd-J or click on Mark Text from the Special menu. Then type or click on 3.

Text after the Index Heading prompt will be the text you have marked in the block. If that is what you want the heading in the index to read, press Tab. If you want the heading to read something else, type what you want and press Tab. Then fill in the information for the SubHeading. Click OK or press Return.

DEFINE THE STYLE OF AN INDEX OR LIST Before you can generate an index or list, you must define a style for it. Would you like page numbers? Where would you like them? How would you like them to look? WordPerfect gives you several choices to help you answer these questions. To define the style:

NOTE

Indexes must be generated with the cursor in a location that follows all marked text in the document.

Move the cursor to the place you want the index or list to begin. Indexes are usually at the very end of the document. Lists are usually at the beginning. Type a heading for the index or list and press Return. Then select Define Lists from the Special menu.

Special

Define Lists

1. List 1...
2. List 2...
3. List 3...
4. List 4...
5. List 5...
6. Table of Contents...
7. Index...

Select the appropriate item by clicking on it or typing it by number.

Page Number Position

Type

- (•) No Page Numbers
- ( ) Page Numbers Follow Entries
- ( ) (Page Numbers) Follow Entries
- ( ) Flush Right Page Numbers
- ( ) Flush Right Page Numbers With Leaders

OK   Cancel

Click on the page number position of your choice. Then click OK or press Return. No Page Numbers means just that. Page Numbers Follow Entries means numbers follow two spaces behind the entry. (Page Numbers) Follow Entries means numbers in parentheses follow two spaces behind the entry. Flush Right Page Numbers put entries flush against the right margin. Flush Right Page Numbers With Leaders puts page numbers flush against the right margin preceded by dot leaders (. . .).

DEFINE THE STYLE OF THE TABLE OF CONTENTS The style of the table of contents is similar to that for the index or list. Move the cursor to the place you want the table of contents to begin, usually at the very beginning of the document. Type a heading for the table of contents and press Return. Then select Define Lists from the Special menu and type or click on 6.

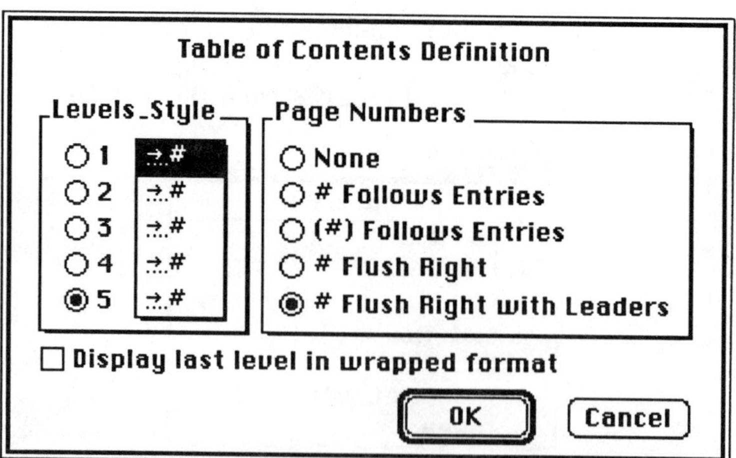

Click on the number of levels in the table of contents. Levels include items such as parts, chapters, sections, and paragraphs. You can have up to five levels. Then click on the style for each level. With the style highlighted for that level, click on the page number style (page number styles are defined in the previous section). The style for each level is defined separately. The following illustration shows the definition for a five-level table of contents with different page number styles at each level.

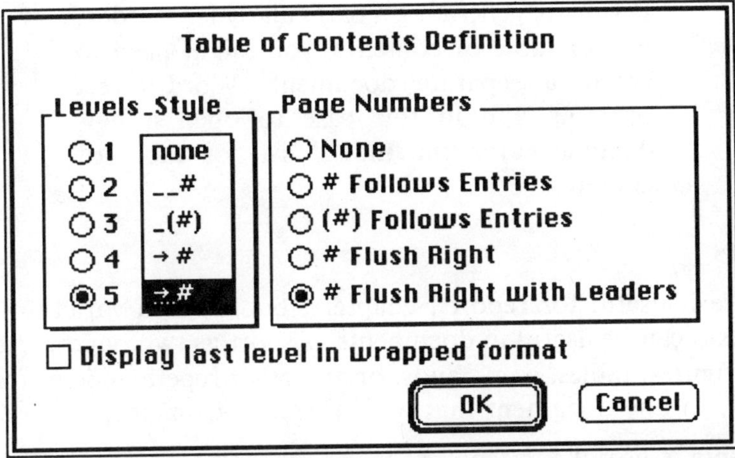

Click on the box if you want the last level displayed in wrapped format. Wrapped format is useful when you have many levels because the text introducing items on that level might be too long to fit on a line. In that case, WordPerfect wraps it to the next line, providing a neater appearance for the table of contents. Click OK or press Return.

NOTE

If you use wrapped format, the last level cannot use flush right or flush right with leader for page numbering.

GENERATE AN INDEX, LIST, OR TABLE OF CONTENTS Once you have marked the text and defined the page numbering style for your index, list, or table of contents, you are ready to generate it. To generate an index, list, or table of contents, leave the cursor where you defined the style and press Cmd-Shift-G or select Generate from the Special menu.

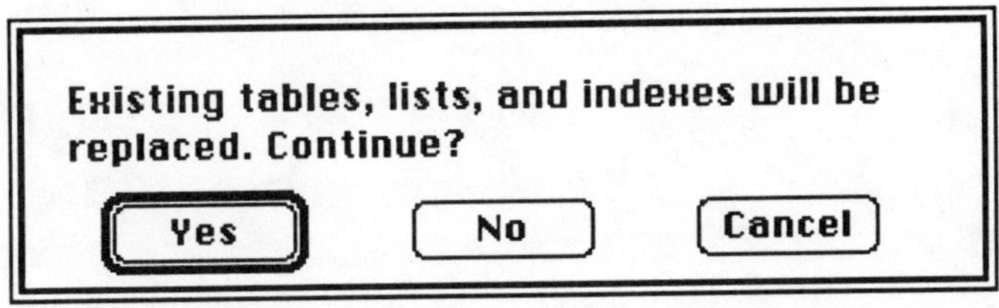

WordPerfect automatically deletes old indexes, lists, and tables of contents when you generate a new one. If you have previously created one or more of these in this document, either delete them before continuing or WordPerfect deletes them for you. If you are ready to continue, click on Yes or press Return. WordPerfect now generates the index, list, and/or the table of contents. Each soon appears on-screen.

NOTE

If you are generating a particularly large index, list, or table of contents, you might need to create a separate document. WordPerfect prompts you in this case to open a new document for the index, list, or table of contents.

APPLICATIONS

The Index feature is useful for reports, chapters, books, or a variety of large and small documents. Indexes can be useful in documents as short as two pages. Use the List feature to create lists of figures, tables, commands, or any other repetitive item for books, articles, reports, chapters, or any document that would benefit from them.

A table of contents is useful for reports, books, chapters, theses, and a variety of other documents. The Table of Contents feature helps create a table of contents quickly, efficiently, and with a minimal amount of effort.

TYPICAL OPERATION

In this example, you generate a three-level table of contents in a fictional document.

1. If necessary, start WordPerfect. Then create a document that looks similar to the following. The dotted lines signify new pages.

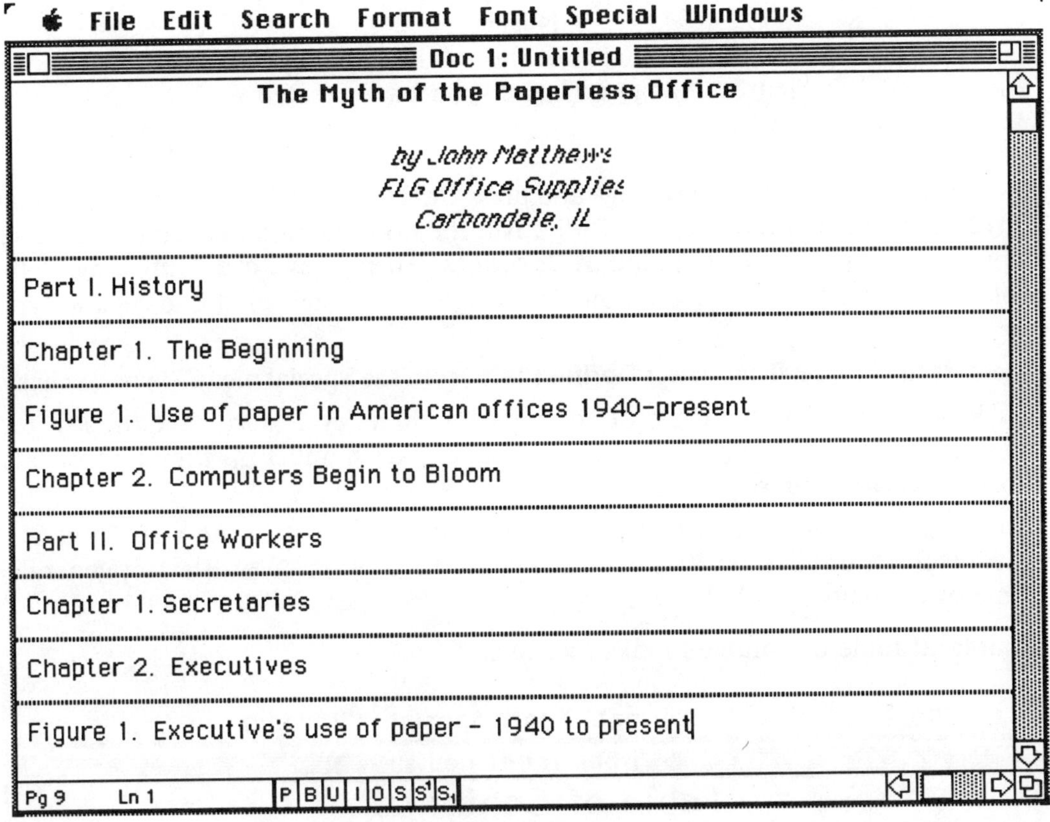

2. Move the cursor to the "P" in "Part I" (which is located on page 2) and highlight the entire title. Press **Cmd-J**, then type or click on **2**, then click on **1** and click **OK** or press **Return** to set the table of contents level at 1.
3. Move the cursor to the "C" in "Chapter 1" (located on page 3) and highlight the entire title. Press **Cmd-J**, then type or click on **2**, then click on **2** and click **OK** or press **Return** to set the table of contents level at 2.
4. Move the cursor to the "F" in "Figure 1" (located on page 4) and highlight the entire title. Press **Cmd-J**, then type or click on **2**, then click on **3** and click **OK** or press **Return** to set the table of contents level at 3.
5. Move the cursor to the "C" in "Chapter 2," (located on page 5) and highlight the entire title. Press **Cmd-J**, then type or click on **2**, then click on **2** and click **OK** or press **Return** to set the table of contents level at 2.
6. Repeat these procedures for the rest of the "Part," "Chapter," and "Figure" numbers, setting table of contents levels of 1 for the parts, 2 for the chapters, and 3 for the figures.
7. Move the cursor to the top of the document and press **Cmd-Return** to create a new page.

NOTE

The page locations of the parts, chapters, and figures change now that you have created a new page.

8. Move the cursor up to the new page and press **Cmd-Shift-C**, the Center key. Then press **Cmd-Shift-B**, the Boldface key. Pull down the Font menu and click on **18** to set the type size to 18 points. Type **Table of Contents**. Then press **Cmd-Shift-B** again to turn boldfacing off. Pull down the Font menu again and click on **12** to set the type size to 12 point.
9. Press **Return** twice. Then select **Define Lists** from the Special menu. Type or click on **6**.
10. Click on **3** to define the table of contents for three levels and leave the last level in unwrapped format. Leave flush right dot leader page number positioning for all levels. Press **Return** or click **OK**.
11. Leave the cursor in the same location where you defined the style and press **Cmd-Shift-G**. Press **Return** or click on **Yes** in response to the prompt. WordPerfect generates the table of contents.

The completed table of contents looks like this:

File Edit Search Format Font Special Windows

Doc 1: Untitled

Table of Contents

Part I. History 3
Chapter 1. The Beginning 4
Figure 1. Use of paper in American offices 1940-present . . 5
Chapter 2. Computers Begin to Bloom 6

Part II. Office Workers 7
Chapter 1. Secretaries 8
Chapter 2. Executives 9
Figure 1. Executives' use of paper - 1940 to present 10

12. Press **Cmd-S**. Then type **Table of Contents** and press **Return** to save the document.
13. Press **Cmd-K** to close the document. Then turn to Module 27 to continue the learning sequence.

Module 26
MERGE CODES

DESCRIPTION

Those form letters that you get in the mail that say you may have won a million dollars in a sweepstakes are actually two documents merged into one, creating a third. The body of the letter is sent to everyone on the mailing list. It is kept in one file, called the primary file. Since everyone on the mailing list has a different name and address, it is necessary to personalize portions of the letter. The mailing list is kept in another file, called the secondary file. The Merge command is used to combine information in those files to create a third file.

WordPerfect gives you the power to send the same document to a variety of people through the Merge command. Its most common use is in form letters, but it can actually be used for any task that involves sending the same message to a group of people.

SECONDARY FILE It is easier to understand merging files if you look at secondary files first. The secondary file is a collection of *records*. And a record is a collection of *fields*.

For example, if you are creating an address list, each person on the list has a name, address, city, state, zip code, and phone number. The information on each person, which is unique to that person, is a record. Each category of information (name, address, city, etc.), which is common to all people on the list, is a field.

While records may contain as many fields as desired, the field numbers must be consistent throughout the document. If field one in one record is a name, then field one of all records must be a name. You can leave information for a field blank, but you must be consistent when creating a secondary file.

Consistency in the sequence of fields is essential because when you create a primary file, you tell WordPerfect that you want field one, which may be the person's name, inserted in a particular place in the document. If field one in one record is a name, and in another, an address, some of those form letters are going to look pretty funny.

NOTE

Take care when selecting field numbers. It is advised that you separate city, state, and zip code into separate fields.

To create a secondary file, start WordPerfect and type the information for the first field, for example, Bob Williams. Then press Cmd-Shift-R or F9.

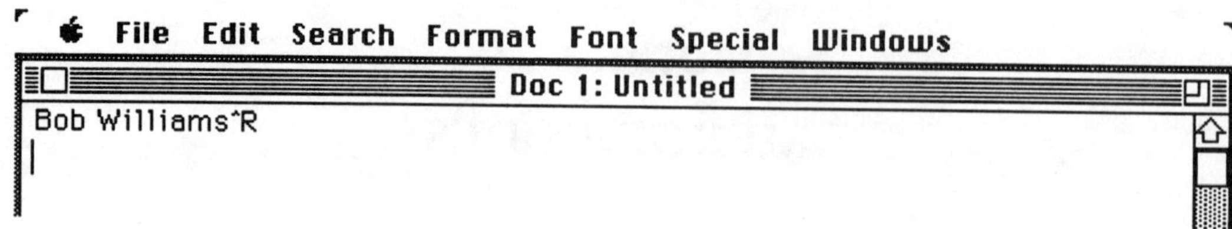

The (^ R) symbol marks the end of each field in a record and inserts a hard return into the document.

NOTE

Never add an extra hard return to a record. If you do, WordPerfect will not know which field number is which when creating the primary file.

Type the information for the next field, for example, 123 Maple Street. Then press Cmd-Shift-R. Then type the information for the next field, for example, Carbondale, and press Cmd-Shift-R. Type IL, press Cmd-Shift-R, type 62901, and press Cmd-Shift-R again. If this is the last field in the record, press Cmd-Shift-E or Shift-F9.

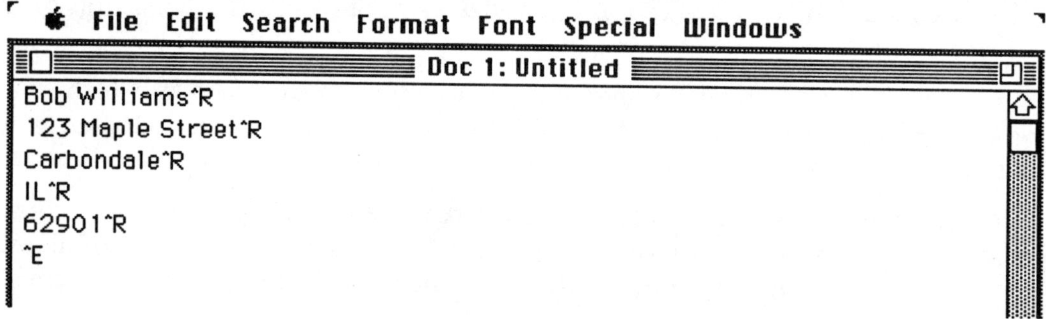

^ E is the "end of record" symbol. It tells WordPerfect you have finished the information for this record and are ready to go on to the next one. If you want to leave a field blank, press Cmd-Shift-R (or F9) and press Return.

Continue entering information in this way, making sure that fields are consistent throughout the file. Then save the file when you are finished.

PRIMARY FILE The primary file is the form letter. It includes codes that tell WordPerfect where to put the information it gets from the secondary file, as well as a variety of other commands. Most primary files will probably contain only a few Merge commands. But WordPerfect gives you a great deal of power for creating a variety of merged documents. The following table lists all the Merge commands available to you when creating a primary file.

Access Merge Codes through the Special menu or by pressing Cmd-8.

NOTE

The (^) before the letter in the following list is a symbol that indicates a merge code follows. To create a merge code, select Merge Codes from the Special menu. Then, type or click on one of the following letters.

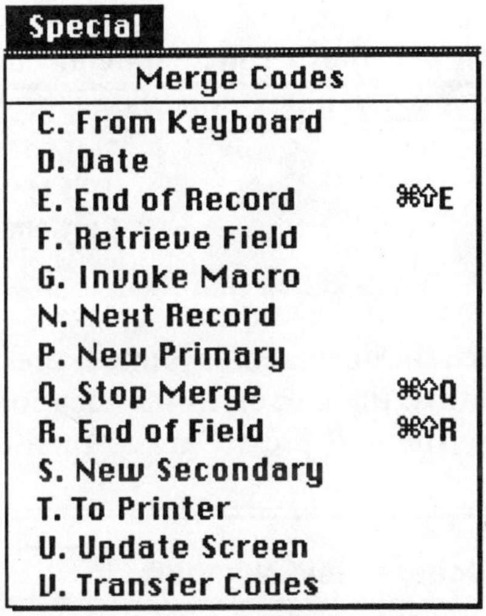

Special

Merge Codes

C. From Keyboard
D. Date
E. End of Record ⌘⇧E
F. Retrieve Field
G. Invoke Macro
N. Next Record
P. New Primary
Q. Stop Merge ⌘⇧Q
R. End of Field ⌘⇧R
S. New Secondary
T. To Printer
U. Update Screen
V. Transfer Codes

Merge Command	*Meaning*
From Keyboard (^ C)	Stops the creation of the merge document. Use this is you want to add additional information while the document is being created.
Date (^ D)	Inserts today's date at the cursor location.
End Of Record (^ E)	Marks the end of a record in a secondary file.
Retrieve Field (^ F)	Inserts the specific field number at the cursor location.
Invoke Macro (^ G)	Executes the selected macro (Module 24) at the end of the merge process.
Next Record (^ N)	Tells WordPerfect to look for the next record in the secondary file. If there are no more records, it ends the merge process.
New Primary (^ P)	If you want to change to another primary file in the middle of a merge, use this command.

Merge Command	*Meaning*
Stop Merge (^ Q)	Stops the merge process, even if there are more records in the secondary file to merge.
End of Field (^ R)	Marks the end of a field in a secondary file.
New Secondary (^ S)	If you want to change to another secondary file in the middle of a merge, use this command.
To Printer (^ T)	Tells WordPerfect to send all text that has been merged to this point to the printer.
Update Screen (^ U)	Updates the screen.
Transfer Codes (^ V)	Lets you transfer merge codes from one document to another.

To create a primary file, create the document as you normally would. If you are typing a business letter, it might start like this:

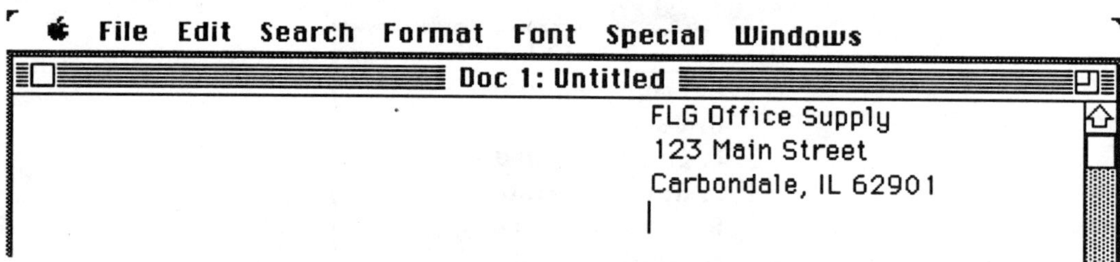

To insert today's date here when the document is printed, press Cmd-8, then type D. A " ^ D" code is inserted here. Then move the cursor to the location where you want to insert the first field from the secondary file and press Cmd-8, then type F.

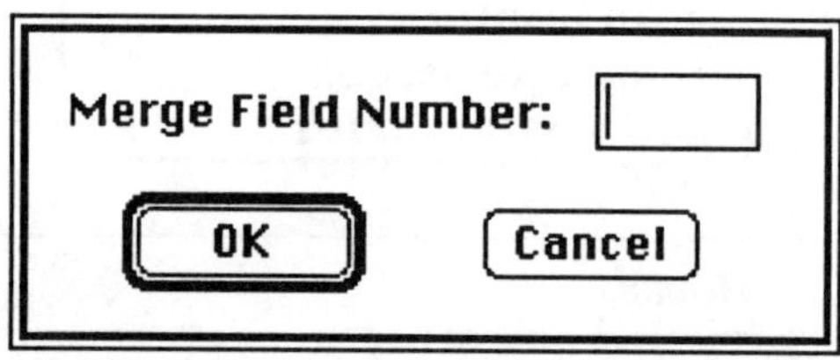

Type 1 to insert field number one at this location (field one in the prior example is name) and press Return or click OK.

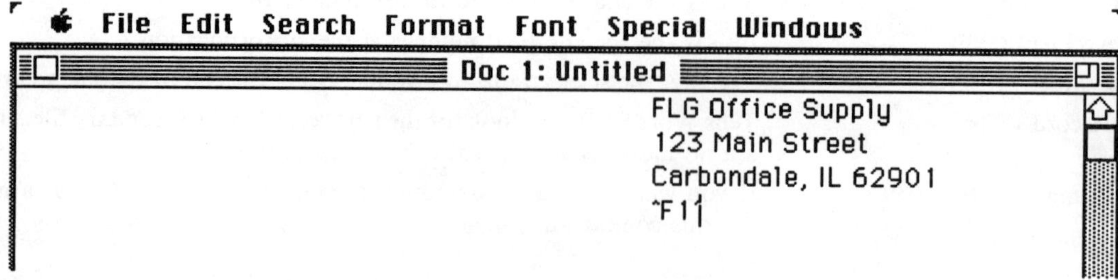

Move the cursor to the location where you want the second field inserted and press Cmd-8, type F, then 2. Press Return or click OK. Continue this process for all field numbers that you want in the merged document.

Create the rest of the primary file in much the same way you create any other file, inserting Merge commands where appropriate. Then save the file as you normally would.

MERGING A PRIMARY AND A SECONDARY FILE After you have created primary and secondary files, you can merge the files to create a number of merged documents. These documents can be saved on disk or sent directly to the printer. If you want merged documents sent directly to the printer, use the previous instructions about Merge Codes to insert a ^T command at the end of the primary file and a ^N command to tell WordPerfect to proceed to the next record. To create a merged document, select Merge from the Special menu or press Cmd-F9.

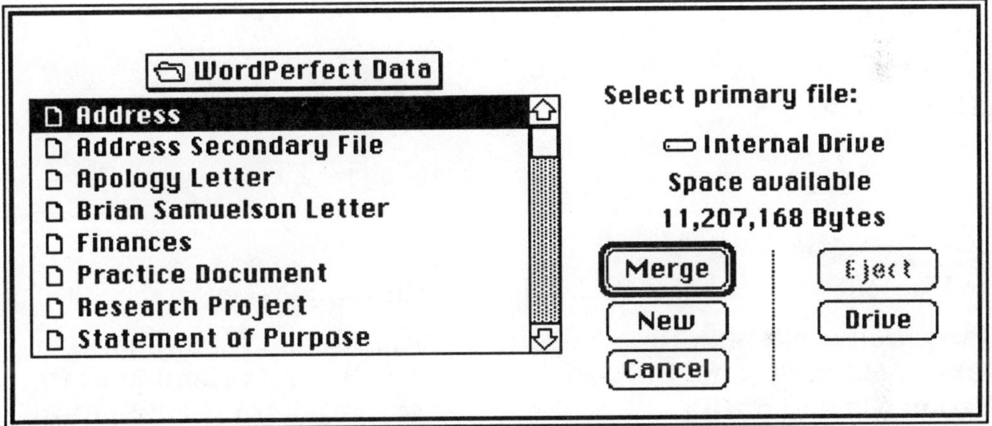

Move the cursor to the primary file and press Return or click on Merge. Then move the cursor to the secondary file and press Return or click on Merge.

After a few moments, WordPerfect creates the merged document. Each resulting merge occupies a separate page (or pages) in the same document. Save or print the document as you want.

APPLICATIONS

The variety of applications for merge documents is almost as unlimited as your imagination. Secondary files, in addition to serving in merged documents, can also be used as address lists, for mailing labels, and for addressing envelopes. Advanced merged documents can include macros, mathematical equations, and a variety of personalized information.

TYPICAL OPERATION

This example lets you create a merged document that is sent directly to the printer.

1. If necessary, start WordPerfect and turn on your printer. Then type **Roger Walton** and press **Cmd-Shift-R**.
2. Type **1720 North Brian Ave** and press **Cmd-Shift-R**. Then type **Carbondale** and press **Cmd-Shift-R**, **IL** and press **Cmd-Shift-R**, and **62901** and press **Cmd-Shift-R**.
3. Type **(618) 549-6924** and press **Cmd-Shift-R**. Then type **Roger** and press **Cmd-Shift-R**. Then press **Cmd-Shift-E**.

4. Add the following records to the list, pressing the indicated keys at the end of each line:

Harry Weil (Cmd-Shift-R)
4356 W. 53rd St.(Cmd-Shift-R)
Marion (Cmd-Shift-R)
IL (Cmd-Shift-R)
62958 (Cmd-Shift-R)
(618) 452-0851 (Cmd-Shift-R)
Harry (Cmd-Shift-R)
(Cmd-Shift-E)

Dolores Weberman (Cmd-Shift-R)
9 Summit Circle (Cmd-Shift-R)
Benton (Cmd-Shift-R)
IL (Cmd-Shift-R)
62809 (Cmd-Shift-R)
(618) 292-0596 (Cmd-Shift-R)
Delores (Cmd-Shift-R)
(Cmd-Shift-E)

A.J. Berlau (Cmd-Shift-R)
190 S. Orola (Cmd-Shift-R)
Murphysboro (Cmd-Shift-R)
IL (Cmd-Shift-R)
62904 (Cmd-Shift-R)
(618) 496-5003 (Cmd-Shift-R)
Mr. Berlau (Cmd-Shift-R)
(Cmd-Shift-E)

5. Press **Cmd-S** and type **Address Secondary File**. Then press **Return** to save the document by that filename. Press **Cmd-K** to close the document.
6. Create a document similar to the following:

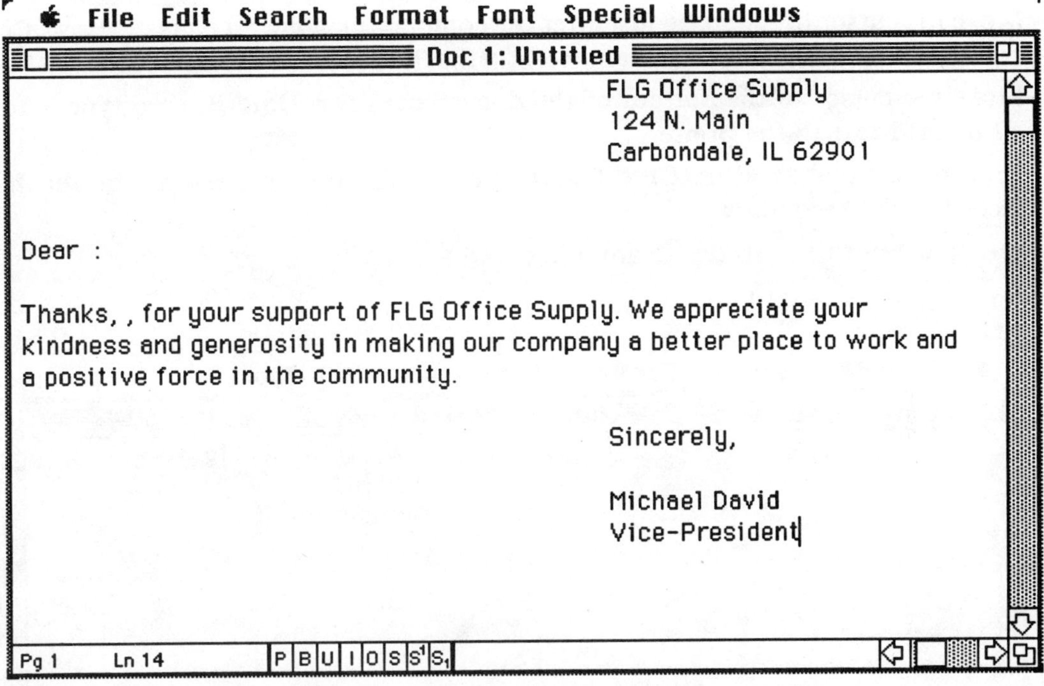

7. Make sure the cursor is on the "D" in "Dear." Press **Return** four times.
8. Move the cursor to the line under "Carbondale, IL 62901" at the top of the document. Press **Tab** repeatedly until the cursor is directly underneath the "C" in "Carbondale." Then press **Cmd-8** and type **D** to insert today's date right here. Press **Return**.
9. Press **Cmd-8**. Type **F**, then **1** to insert field number 1, the name field; then press **Return** or click **OK**. Press **Return** to move to the next line.
10. Press **Cmd-8**. Type **F**, then **2** to insert field number 2, the address field. Press **Return** or click **OK**. Then press **Return** to move to the next line.
11. Press **Cmd-8**. Type **F**, then **3** to insert field number 3, the city field. Press **Return** or click **OK**.
12. Type **,** and press the **Spacebar**. Then press **Cmd-8**, type **F**, and type **4** to insert field number 4, the state field. Press **Return** or click **OK**.
13. Press the **Spacebar**. Then press **Cmd-8**, type **F**, and type **5** to insert field number 5, the zip code field. Press **Return** or click **OK**. Then press **Return** to move to the next line.

14. Press **Delete** three times to delete some of the blank lines between the address and beginning of the letter. Then move the cursor two spaces after the word "Dear." Press **Cmd-8**, type **F**, and type **7** to insert field number 7, the first name field (in the case of A.J. Berlau, it is still a form of personal address). Press **Return** or click **OK**.
15. Move the cursor to the space just after the comma following "Thanks." Press **Cmd-8**, type **F**, and type **7** to insert field number 7 in that location also. Press **Return** or click **OK**.
16. Move the cursor to the bottom of the document. Press **Cmd-8**, then type **T** to send all merged text to the printer.
17. Press the **Spacebar**. Press **Cmd-8** and type **N** to make WordPerfect look for the next record in the secondary file.
18. Use the **Delete** key to delete any unneeded spaces.

Your primary file should look like this:

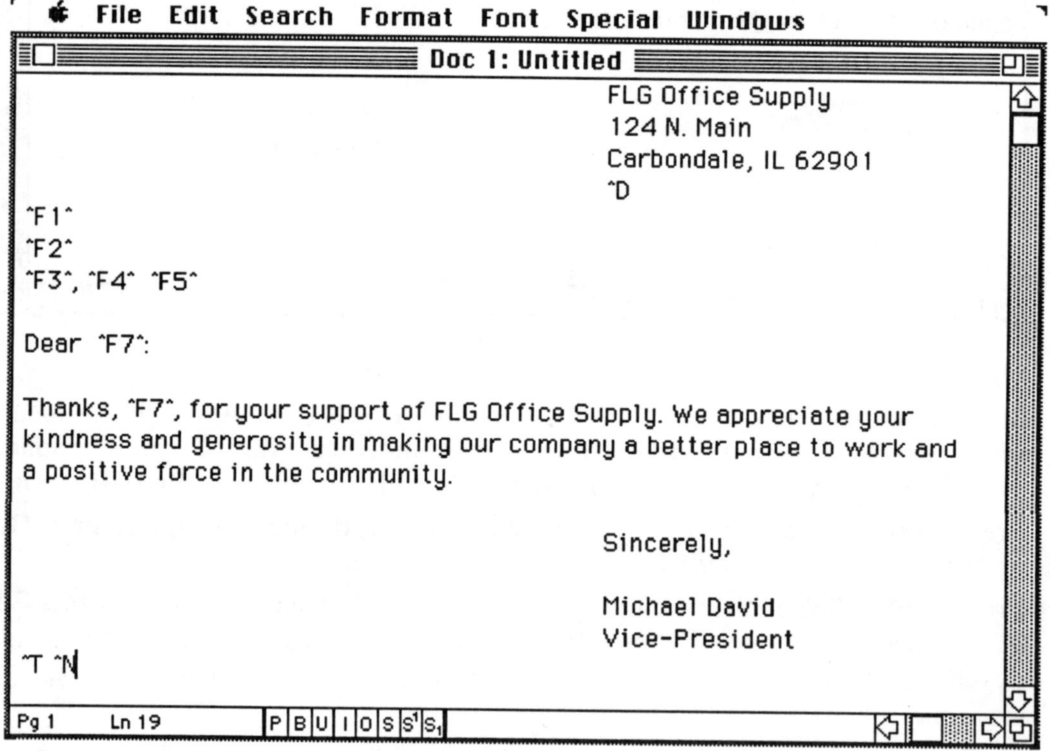

19. Press **Cmd-S** and type **Thanks Primary File**. Then press **Return** to save the document as that filename. Then press **Cmd-K** to close the document.
20. Select **New** from the File menu to open a new file. Then select **Merge** from the Special menu.
21. Move the cursor to Thanks Primary File and press **Return** to indicate the primary file. Then move the cursor to Address Secondary File and press **Return** to indicate the secondary file.

After a few moments, your document starts printing.

Your first merged document should look like this:

FLG Office Supply
124 N. Main
Carbondale, IL 62901
January 26, 1989

Roger Walton
1720 North Brian Ave.
Carbondale, IL 62901

Dear Roger:

Thanks, Roger, for your support of FLG Office Supply. We appreciate your kindness and generosity in making our company a better place to work and a positive force in the community.

Sincerely,

Michael David
Vice-President

Congratulations! This completes the learning sequence.

Module 27
OUTLINE

DESCRIPTION

You do not need an outline generator program if you have WordPerfect. WordPerfect includes an Outline feature to let you create your own outlines. Outlines are a good way to organize your thoughts. You can create better, more organized documents if you outline them first. And if you use WordPerfect instead of an outline generator program, you do not have to convert the outlined text to WordPerfect format when you use the outline to create another document.

The Outline feature automatically numbers paragraphs in outline format. Eight levels of numbering — I., A., 1., a., (1), (a), i), a), among others — are available. (See *Changing The Numbering Style* for examples.)

NOTE

Paragraph numbering, a related topic, is discussed in Module 29.

Each time you press Return in Outline mode, you create a new outline number. Each time you press Tab, you change the numbering level. When you edit an outline and add or delete numbers or levels, WordPerfect automatically renumbers the document. To outline text, press Cmd-3 or select Paragraph from the Format menu. Then type or click on 1. (Alternatively, press Cmd-Shift-Y.) Notice the Status Line.

NOTE

Do not use the Tab key when outlining text unless you want to go to the next numbering level. Use the Indent command to move the cursor to the next tab stop. Press Spacebar, then Tab to use the Tab key without changing the numbering level.

Pg 1 Ln 1 P B U I O S S¹ S₁ Outline

Press Return. Notice the Roman numeral "I" appears on-screen. Then press Cmd-Shift-T to indent the text, type your text (for example, Introduction), and press Return.

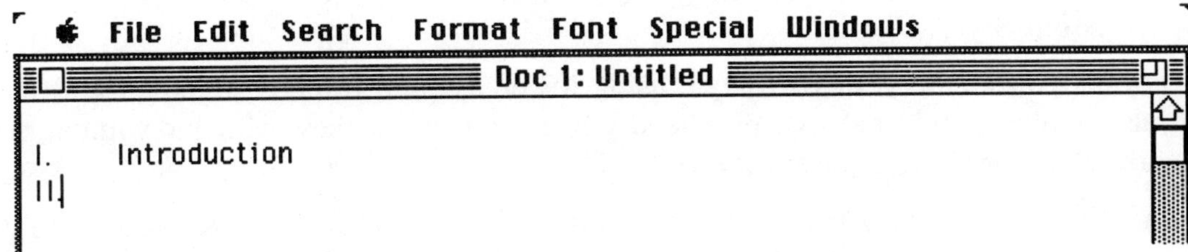

Notice the second outline number has been introduced. Press Tab to move to the next level of numbering. Notice the "II." has changed to "A."

Press Cmd-Shift-T, type the text for this level (for example, How the West was won), and press Return.

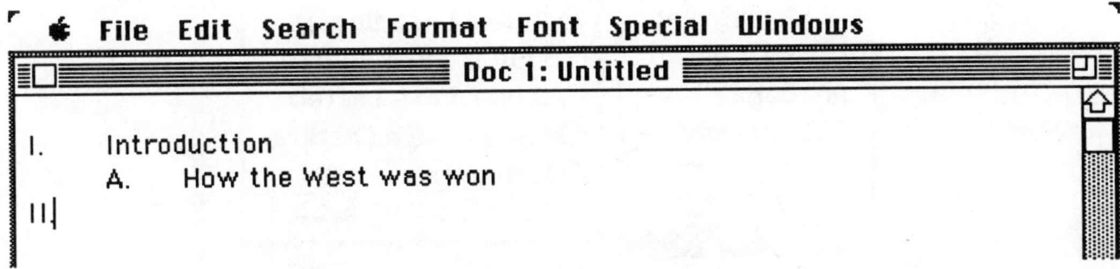

Continue creating the outline in this way until you are finished. Then press Cmd-Shift-Y to turn the Outline mode off. Notice the "Outline" message on the Status Line disappears.

The Outline key works as a toggle switch. Press Cmd-Shift-Y to turn it on and the same sequence to turn it off.

TIP: After you turn Outline mode off, edit the outline by inserting blank lines between entries and adding other editing touches.

CHANGING THE NUMBER LEVELS WordPerfect lets you change the number level (back to "II" from "A," for example). To do this, press Shift-Tab, or move the cursor to the left of the number to change and press Del. Either method automatically moves to the previous number level. The rest of the numbers are automatically updated as you move through the outline.

CHANGING THE NUMBERING STYLE WordPerfect creates a default numbering style for outlines called, appropriately enough, "outline style." If you wish to change this style, however, you may. Four styles are available:

- Paragraph Style - 1., a., i., (1), (a), (i), 1), a)
- Legal Style - 1., 1.1, 1.1.1, 1.1.1.1, etc.
- Outline Style - I., A., 1., a., (1), (a), i), a)
- Custom Style - Varies

Custom lets you create your own style using lowercase and uppercase letters and Roman numerals, numbers, and legal-style numbers. You can punctuate these with and without periods and with single or double parentheses.

You can change the numbering style of an outline either before or after you write it. To change the numbering style of the outline, move the cursor to the beginning of the outline and press Cmd-3 or select Paragraph from the Format menu. Then type or click on 3.

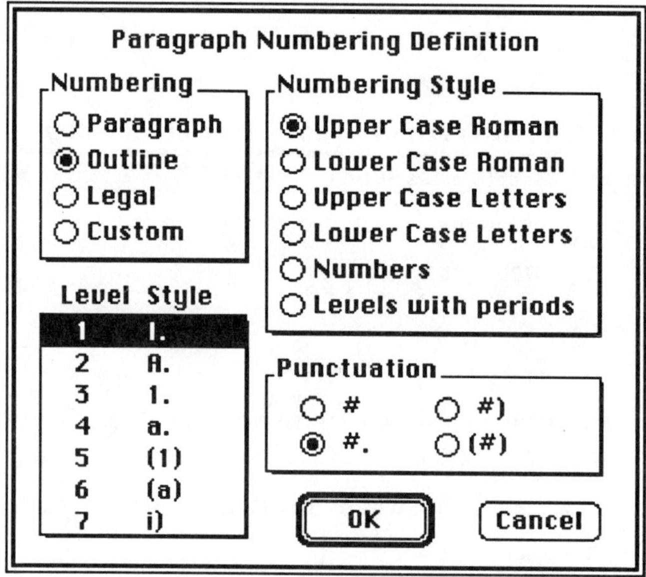

The default style for outlines is shown above. To change it, click on Outline, then click on the level you want to change. Select the numbering style you want and the punctuation you want. When you have finished, click OK or press Return.

APPLICATIONS

Use the Outline feature to organize your thoughts for time management, problem solving, planning, or writing purposes. Also use this feature when you are writing outlines for use by themselves.

TYPICAL OPERATION

In this example, you develop an outline for a hypothetical banquet.

1. If necessary, start WordPerfect. Then create a document similar to the following:

2. Press **Cmd-Shift-Y** to turn the Outline mode on. Then press **Return**.
3. Press **Cmd-Shift-T**, type **Welcoming Speech**, and press **Return**.
4. Press **Tab**, then **Cmd-Shift-T**, and type **FLG welcomes employees, associates, customers, and friends of the company.**

5. Press **Return**, then **Cmd-Shift-T**, and type **Dinner**.
6. Press **Return**, then **Tab** and **Cmd-Shift-T**. Then type **Entree - Roast Duck**.
7. Press **Return**, **Tab** twice, and **Cmd-Shift-T**. Then type **Sides - salad, potatoes, carrots, peas**.
8. Press **Return**, **Tab** twice, and **Cmd-Shift-T**. Then type **Dessert - chocolate mousse**.
9. Press **Return** and **Cmd-Shift-T**. Then type **Keynote Address - Professor Philip Feinsilver, Southern Illinois University**.
10. Press **Return**, then **Tab**, and **Cmd-Shift-T**. Then type **Topic - The Evolution of the Office**.
11. Press **Cmd-Shift-Y** to turn Outline mode off.

12. Add blank lines in the outline by pressing **Return** at the end of the two major dividing lines in the outline (after "company." and "mousse"). The final outline looks like this:

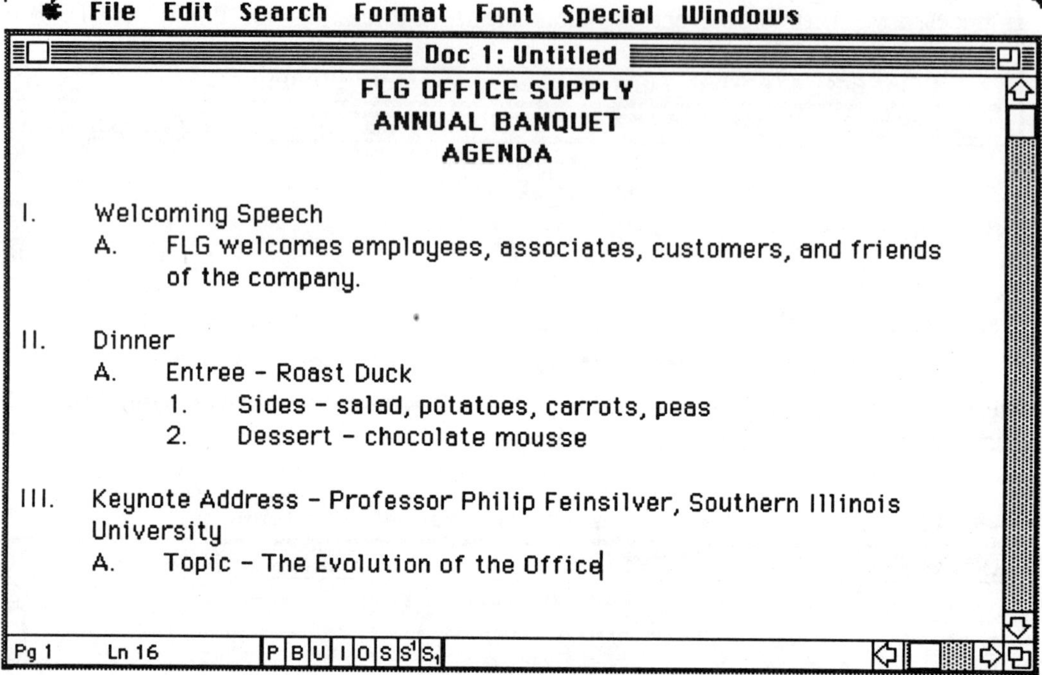

13. Press **Cmd-S** and type **Banquet Outline**. Then press **Return** to save the document.
14. Press **Cmd-K** to close the document. Then turn to Module 29 to continue the learning sequence.

Module 28
PAGE FORMAT

DESCRIPTION

Many decisions go into editing a document besides typing text. Do you want page numbers? Where do you want them to go? How many lines of text should be on the page? How much blank space should be at the top? Would you like this page centered?

The Page Format command gives you the tools to answer those questions and others. Use Page Format to number pages, select page numbers, make page numbers odd or even, position page numbers on a page, center pages, determine the paper size, set the top and bottom margins, create headers and footers, and suppress page formatting for the current page.

NOTE
The default number of text lines per page is 54. But, because many formatting options take up space on a printed page, they reduce the number of text lines available to you per page.

Select the Page Format command by pressing Cmd-2 or by selecting Page from the Format menu.

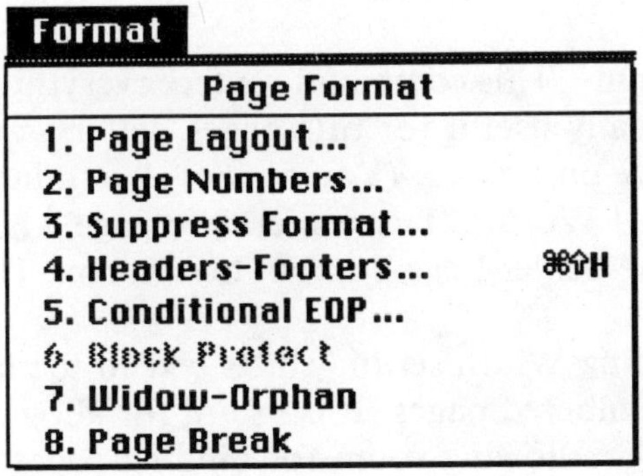

Format

Page Format

1. Page Layout...
2. Page Numbers...
3. Suppress Format...
4. Headers-Footers... ⌘⇧H
5. Conditional EOP...
6. Block Protect
7. Widow-Orphan
8. Page Break

PAGE LAYOUT The Page Layout option lets you select top, bottom, left, and right margins, set whether a page should be centered, and adjust the binding width. To access Page Layout, type or click on 1 from the Page Format menu.

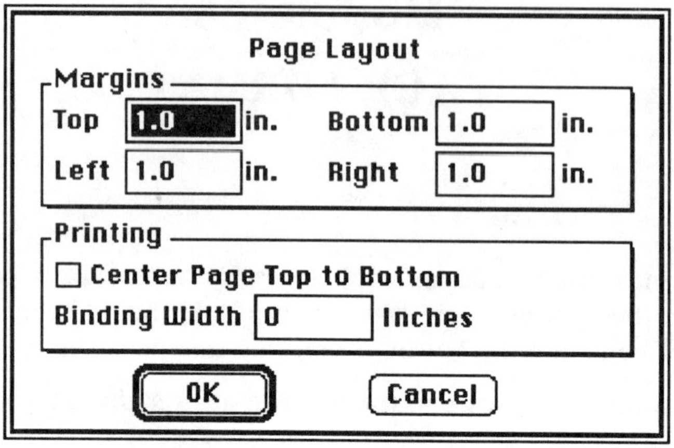

Page Layout

Margins

Top 1.0 in. Bottom 1.0 in.

Left 1.0 in. Right 1.0 in.

Printing

☐ Center Page Top to Bottom

Binding Width 0 Inches

OK Cancel

Margins WordPerfect's default setting for top and bottom margins is 1 inch at the top and 1 inch at the bottom. Left and right margins are set 1 inch at the left and 1 inch at the right.

Standard paper is 11 inches. You can typically fit 6 lines of text per inch. Thus, the largest number of lines you can fit on a page is 6 x 11 or 66. With 1 inch both at the top and bottom reserved for a margin, the maximum number of lines on a page is 9 x 6 or 54. Headers, footers, and footnotes further reduce this number. The Page Layout dialog box lets you reset the top and bottom margins to give you more or less room for text.

You can either set the left and right margins from this dialog box or from the Ruler, which is described in Module 33. To change margins, click on the box you want to change and type a new value. Then click OK or press Return.

Center Page Top To Bottom This command centers everything on a page vertically, from top to bottom. It is especially useful for title pages, letters, and other documents that do not occupy all of the space on a page. (You cannot determine whether a page is centered by looking at it on-screen.) WordPerfect centers the page when it is printed. If you want a page centered, click on the Center Page Top To Bottom box. Then click OK or press Return.

Binding Width The Binding Width setting shifts text to the left on even numbered pages and to the right on odd numbered pages. It is useful for allowing space for punching holes on two-sided copies and for allowing room for binding pages in a hard bound book. The default binding width is zero. To set a new binding width, click on the Binding Width box and type a new value. Then click OK or press Return.

PAGE NUMBERS Page numbering is normally off in WordPerfect. This option lets you turn page numbering on and off, select the proper page number for your document, and select the position of that page number in the document.

The proper page number is important if your document is a chapter in a book or other long document. For example, if the chapter begins on page 150, this option lets you change the first page of your document to 150. This is also useful for documents that include a title page and table of contents before the beginning of text. The first page after the front matter might be eight pages into the document. This option lets you number that page as page 1.

WordPerfect lets you number pages in Arabic (1,2,3) and lowercase Roman numerals (i,ii,iii). Lowercase Roman numerals are appropriate for prefaces, forewords, and other similar documents. When you change page numbers in the document, the page number on the Status Line also changes.

WordPerfect offers a variety of choices for the location of the page number on the printed page. Page numbers can also be placed in headers and footers, as described in Module 19.

WordPerfect subtracts two lines of text for the page number: one for the page number itself and the other to separate it from the text. These page numbers do not appear on-screen: you see them only when the document is printed or when you access the Print Preview command.

To set page numbers, type or click on 2 from the Page Format menu.

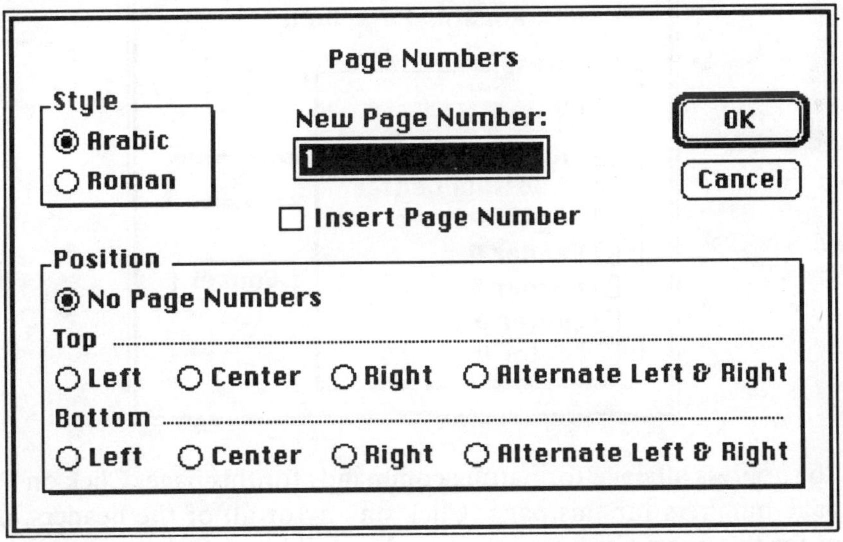

Page Numbers

Style
(•) Arabic
( ) Roman

New Page Number:
1

[OK]
[Cancel]

[ ] Insert Page Number

Position
(•) No Page Numbers
Top
( ) Left ( ) Center ( ) Right ( ) Alternate Left & Right
Bottom
( ) Left ( ) Center ( ) Right ( ) Alternate Left & Right

Click on the page number style of your choice. Then click on the New Page Number box and type the new page number. If you want to insert the page number at the current cursor location, click on the Insert Page Number box. This inserts the current page number into the text.

Then select the page number position. Page numbers can be either at the top or bottom of the page and either at the left, center, or right of the page. You can also set them to alternate between the left and right sides of the page.

When you have finished, click OK or press Return.

To turn page numbering off at any time, move the cursor to the location where you want page numbering to stop and type or click on 2 from the Page Format menu. Then click on the No Page Numbers selection and click OK or press Return.

SUPPRESS PAGE FORMATTING FOR CURRENT PAGE ONLY This command lets you suppress all or some of the headers, footers, and page numbers in your document for the current page only. This is useful when you are creating a title page somewhere in a document. This command also lets you move page numbering to the bottom center of the current page only.

To suppress page formatting, type or click on 3 from the Page Format menu.

Suppress Page Format
For This Page Only

Suppress
- ☐ All
- ☐ Place Page Number at Bottom Center
- ☐ Page Numbers
- ☐ Header A
- ☐ Header B
- ☐ Footer A
- ☐ Footer B

OK

Cancel

Click on All to suppress all page formatting commands for this page. Click on Page Numbers to turn off page numbers for this page. Click on any or all of the headers and footers to suppress them for this page. Click on Page Number at Bottom Center to put the page number at the bottom center of this page only. Click OK or press Return when you are finished.

CONDITIONAL END OF PAGE The Conditional End of Page command lets you keep a certain amount of text on the same page. This is useful when you want to make sure that text stays with an illustration or that all of the data in a table stays on the same page. WordPerfect lets you protect a set number of lines or inches after the cursor location. If all the text will not fit on the current page, WordPerfect inserts a soft page break before it and moves all the text to the next page. It automatically senses your font and point size and adjusts accordingly. If you change the font or point size, the text may no longer be protected. To set a conditional end of page, type or click on 5 from the Page Format menu.

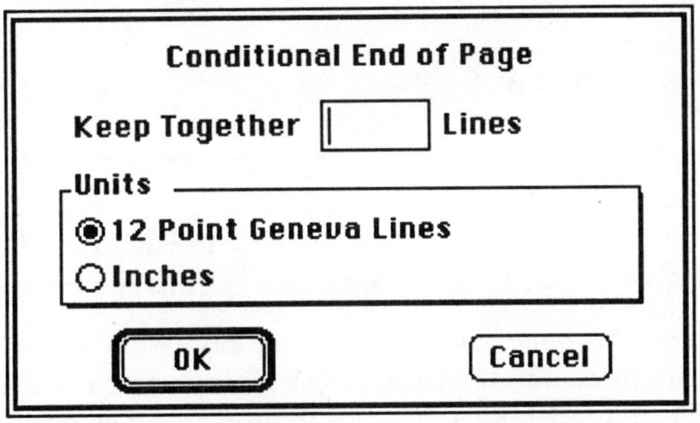

Conditional End of Page

Keep Together [ ] Lines

Units

◉ 12 Point Geneva Lines

○ Inches

OK   Cancel

To keep a certain number of lines together, type the number of lines to keep together and click OK or press Return. To keep a certain number of inches together, click on inches, then type the number of inches to keep together and click OK or press Return.

BLOCK PROTECT The Block Protect command is similar to the Conditional End of Page feature except it protects selected text regardless of font or point size. All selected text and/or graphics will be kept on the same page.

To use block protect, select a block of text using the mouse, the cursor keys, or the Select command. Then type or click on 6 from the Page Format menu. WordPerfect inserts a (Protect>) code at the beginning of the text and a (<Protect) code at the end. All text between the codes will stay on the same line.

WIDOW/ORPHAN PROTECTION *Orphans* are the first lines of paragraphs appearing alone at the end of a page. *Widows* are the last line of a paragraph appearing alone at the beginning of a page. WordPerfect typically does not prevent widows and orphans from occurring, but you can protect against them with the Widow/Orphan Protection feature. To do this, type or click on 7 from the Page Format menu. From this cursor location on, WordPerfect protects against widows and orphans.

PAGE BREAK Like typed documents, WordPerfect breaks its documents into pages. The length of these pages is determined by you. You can keep typing until you fill the number of lines on a page as determined by the size of paper you are using. WordPerfect automatically creates a new page then. This is called a *soft page break*. You can also press Ctrl-Return or select Page Break from the Page Format menu at any point to create a new page. This is called a *hard page break*.

WordPerfect shows a soft page break on-screen as a thin line:

....

A hard page break is represented as a thicker line:

....

The dotted line is considered a character and may be deleted, just like any other character. To delete a page break, move the cursor to the space before the page break and press Del.

While WordPerfect creates soft page breaks automatically, you can create a hard page break at any time. Move the cursor to the location where you want the page break to occur and press Ctrl-Return or select Page Break from the Page Format menu. A hard page break is useful for separating text or for making sure a table or chart fits on one page.

APPLICATIONS

Any time you are preparing a document for printing, you should consider changing the page formats from WordPerfect's default settings. You might want page numbering, but you might not want it to begin with page one of the document. If you are typing a short letter, you might want to center the document on a page. There are numerous reasons for formatting the pages in a document before you print it.

TYPICAL OPERATION

In this operation you create a document with a centered title page, page numbering beginning on page 3, and the page number appearing at the bottom center of every page.

1. If necessary, start WordPerfect. Then create a document similar to the following:

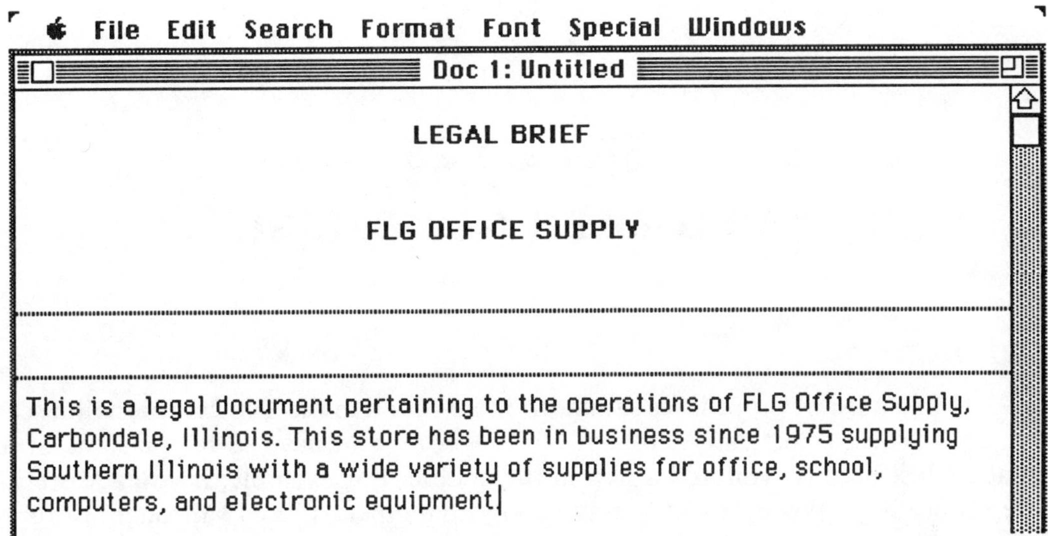

2. With the cursor at the top of the title page, press **Cmd-2**, then type or click on **1**. Click on **Center Page Top to Bottom**. Then click **OK** or press **Return**.
3. Press **Cmd-G**, the Go To key. Type **3** and press **Return**. The cursor moves to page 3.
4. Press **Cmd-2** and type or click on **2**. Type **1**, then click on **Bottom Center** and press **Return** or click **OK**. Notice the page position indicator on the Status Line.

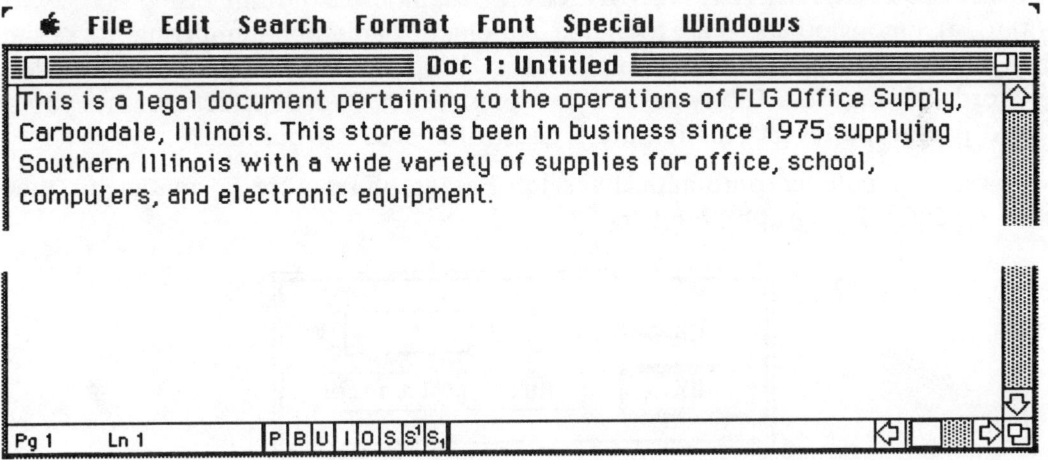

5. Press **Cmd-S** and type **Legal Document**. Then press **Return** to save the document.
6. Press **Cmd-K** to close the document. Then turn to Module 36 to continue the learning sequence.

Module 29

PARAGRAPH NUMBERING

DESCRIPTION

If you are typing a list of procedures similar to those found in the Typical Operation sections in this book, WordPerfect can help you. No longer do you have to retype some or all of the numbers just because you add a step in the middle. For example, if you add step 12 in a 30-step procedure, WordPerfect automatically renumbers steps 13 through 30 for you.

This is done with the Paragraph Number feature. Paragraph numbering is similar to the Outline feature (Module 27), but instead of adding numbers every time you press Return, WordPerfect adds them when you need them. You tell WordPerfect when you want to add a number, and it does it. If you add a step in the middle, all the other paragraphs are renumbered. There are two ways to set paragraph numbers: automatic and fixed.

AUTOMATIC PARAGRAPH NUMBERING Eight levels of numbering — I., A., 1., a., (1), (a), i), a), among others — are available. Automatic paragraph numbering works similarly to the Outline feature. Each time you press Tab, WordPerfect changes to the next level. In other words, if you press Tab twice and then press Enter, WordPerfect assumes you are on the third paragraph level. This feature is useful for creating outlines.

To set paragraph numbers automatically, select Paragraph from the Format menu, then type or click on 2 for Paragraph Numbers.

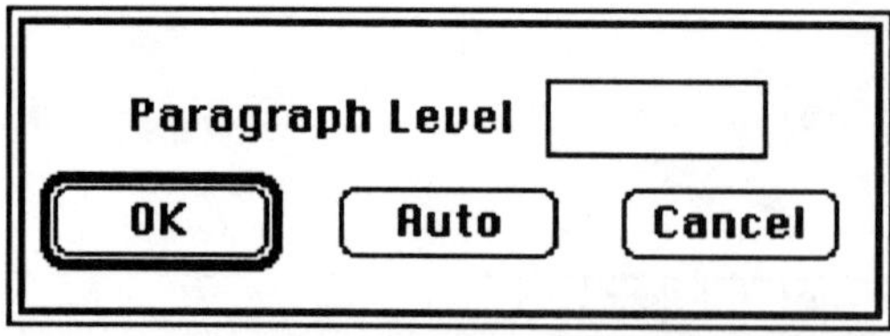

Click on Auto for automatic paragraph numbers.

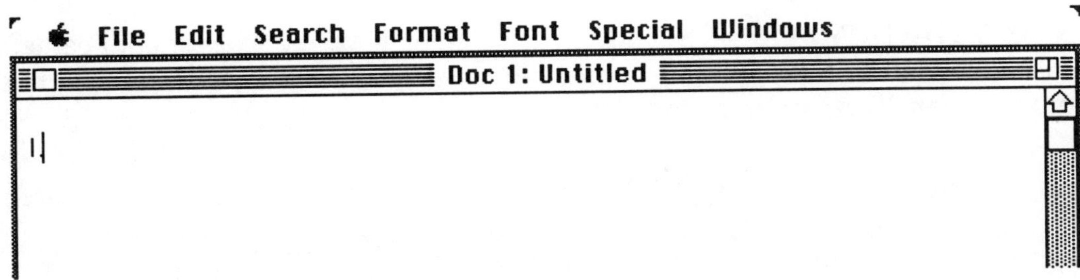

Notice the Roman numeral "I" appears on-screen. This is the first paragraph level. If you had moved the cursor to the "I" and pressed Tab six times, the screen would look as follows:

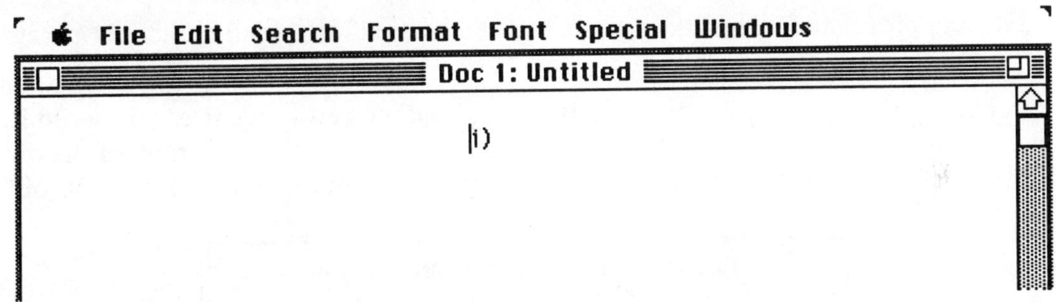

Move the cursor after the paragraph number and type whatever text you like. You do not need to create another paragraph number until you want to. When you want to add another paragraph number, repeat the above steps.

FIXED PARAGRAPH LEVEL If you always want to be on the same level, such as when you are typing a set of procedures, use the fixed paragraph level. To set a fixed paragraph level, select Paragraph from the Format menu, then type or click on 2 for Paragraph Numbers. Type the paragraph level you want and click OK or press Return. The level remains fixed until you change it.

CHANGING THE NUMBER LEVELS To change the number level back to "II" from "A," for example, move the cursor to the tab stop before the number and press Del. This lets you move up to another level. The rest of the paragraph numbers are automatically updated as you move through the document. If you want to move down to another level, press Tab. To delete a paragraph number at any level, move the cursor to the number you want to delete and press Del. The number disappears.

NOTE

If you accidentally create an extra paragraph number on a line, delete it using the procedure in this section, then continue typing.

CHANGING THE NUMBERING STYLE The default numbering style for both paragraphs and outlines is Outline Style. It is a simple matter to change this style to paragraph style or another option. Four styles are available:

- Paragraph Style - 1., a., i., (1), (a), (i), 1), a)
- Legal Style - 1., 1.1, 1.1.1, 1.1.1.1, etc.
- Outline Style - I., A., 1., a., (1), (a), i), a)
- Custom Style - Varies

Custom lets you create your own style using lowercase and uppercase letters and Roman numerals, numbers, and legal-style numbers. You can punctuate these with and without periods and with single or double parentheses.

Legal style is appropriate for legal documents and can be used with either outlines or paragraph numbers.

You can change the numbering style of a paragraph either before or after you write it. To change the numbering style of the paragraph, move the cursor to the beginning of the outline and press Cmd-3 or select Paragraph from the Format menu. Then type or click on 3.

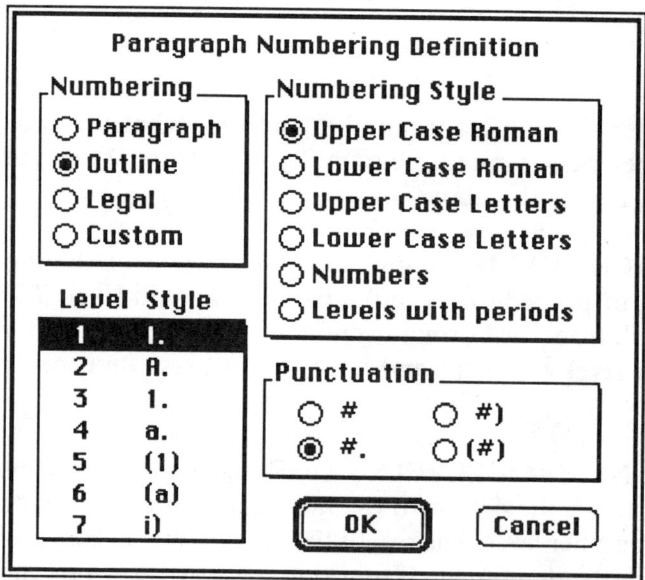

The default style for paragraphs is shown on the preceding screen. To change it, click on Paragraph, then click on the level you want to change. Select the numbering style you want and the punctuation you want. When you are finished, click OK or press Return.

APPLICATIONS

Use the Paragraph numbering feature to create long procedures more easily. You can also use it to create outlines if you are not comfortable with WordPerfect's Outline feature.

TYPICAL OPERATION

This example illustrates how to number a set of rules automatically.

1. If necessary, start WordPerfect. Then create a document similar to the following:

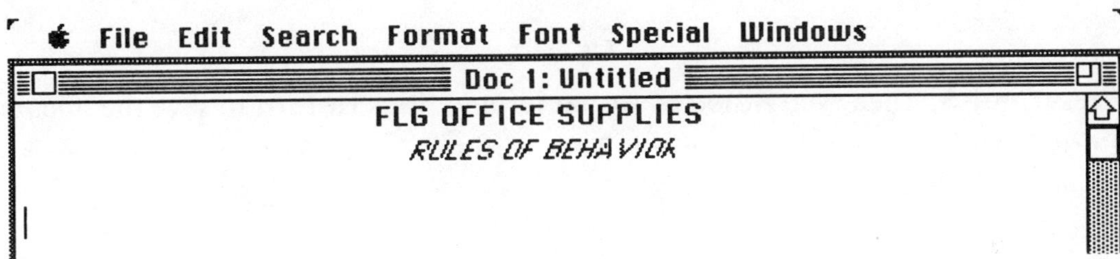

2. Press **Cmd-3** and type or click on **2**.
3. Type **1** to fix the paragraph level at 1 and press **Return** or click **OK**. Press **Cmd-Shift-T** and type **Employees are expected to be on time, all the time.** Press **Return.**
4. Press **Cmd-3** and type or click on **2**. Type **1** and press **Return** or click **OK**. Press **Cmd-Shift-T** and type **Employees are to be courteous at all times to our customers.** Press **Return.**
5. Press **Cmd-3** and type or click on **2**. Type **1** and press **Return** or click **OK**. Press **Cmd-Shift-T** and type **Employees are to wear clothing appropriate for work. No jeans, cut-offs, or other overly casual attire is allowed on the sales floor.** Press **Return.**

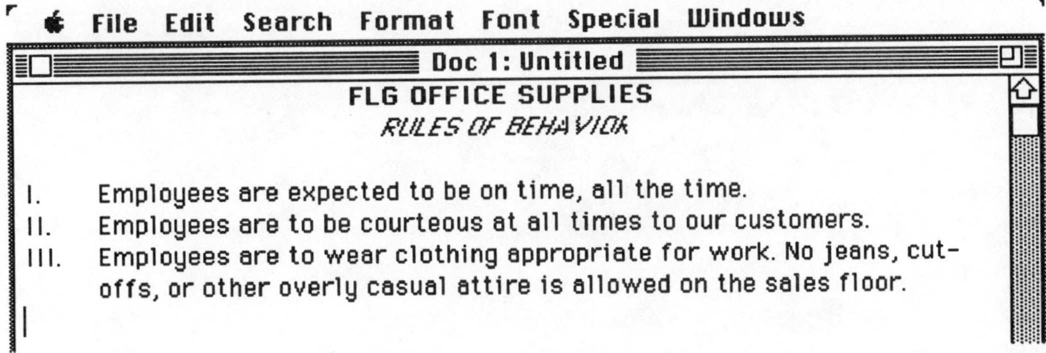

6. Move the cursor to the top of the document and press **Cmd-3**. Type or click on **3**.
7. Click on **Paragraph** then press **Return** or click **OK**.

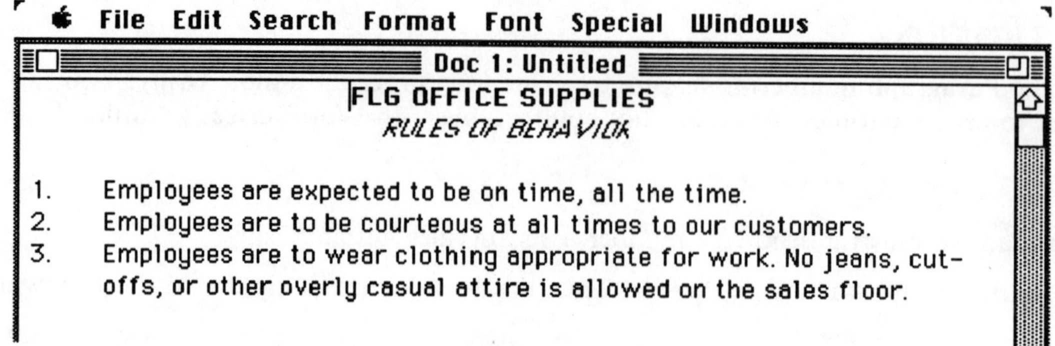

8. Press **Cmd-S**. Then type **Rules of Behavior** and press **Return** to save the document.
9. Press **Cmd-K** to close the document. Then turn to Module 31 to continue the learning sequence.

Module 30
PRINTING

DESCRIPTION

After you finish creating documents, the best way to get the information to others is by printing the documents. The Print command lets you print either the document being edited or a document on disk. You can also print WordPerfect documents from the Finder or from the File Management menu. (Printing from the File Management menu is described in Module 14.)

While editing a document, you have the following printing options:

- Print the entire document
- Print a page of the document
- Print a selection of text

When you print from the File Management menu or from the Finder, you can only print the selected document in its entirety.

Anything you print, whether it be a page, a block of text, or an entire document, is printed complete with headers, footers, footnotes, or endnotes.

PRINT OPTIONS Before printing, select your print options through the Print Options command on the File menu. Print Options lets you select what paper you want to print on, what orientation the page should be, whether smoothing should be in effect for better print quality, substitute fonts, and much more. To set print options, select Print Options from the File menu.

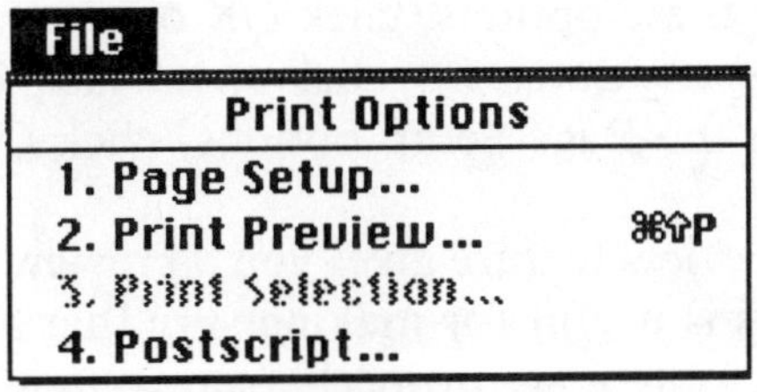

File

Print Options

1. Page Setup...
2. Print Preview... ⌘⇧P
3. Print Selection...
4. Postscript...

NOTE

This module assumes you are using an Apple LaserWriter™. Other printers offer similar options.

Page Setup Page Setup lets you tell the printer what paper you are using, what orientation you want to print on the page, and much more. To select Page Setup, type or click on 1 from the Print Options menu or press Cmd-F8.

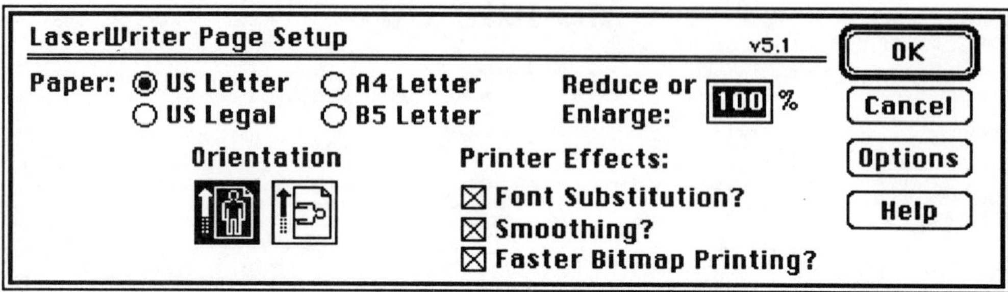

Click on the type of paper you are using. Then click on the Reduce or Enlarge box and type the amount you want to reduce or enlarge the document. Then click on the page orientation you desire. The default page orientation is up and down (portrait). You can also select sideways (landscape) printing. WordPerfect automatically selects all Printer Effects, which typically improve print quality or make the printer work faster. Then click on Options.

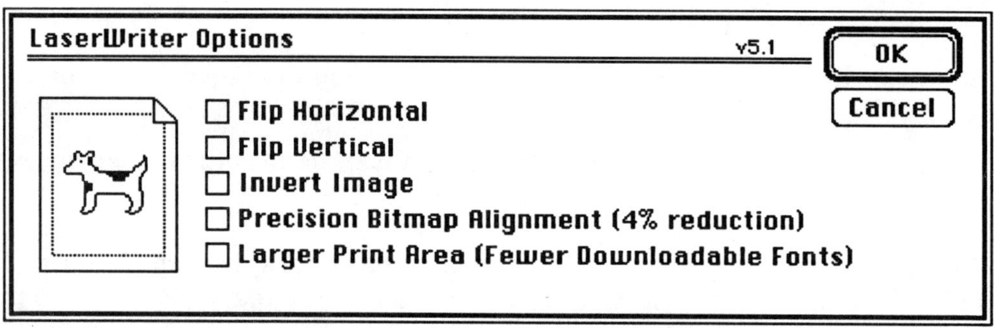

These options let you create special effects with graphics such as inverting and flipping images. They also let you provide a larger print area, use more fonts, and more. After you have made your selection(s) from these options, click OK or press Return to return to the Page Setup dialog box. (If you have any questions, click on the Help button for more information.) When you are finished with the Page Setup options, click OK or press Return.

Print Preview The Print Preview feature gives you a preview of what a document will look like before it is printed. This is useful for making sure that a document will look like you want it to, that headers and footers are properly placed, that page numbers fall where you want, and that text and graphics flow evenly. To use the Print Preview feature, click on Print Preview from the Print Options menu or press Cmd-Shift-P.

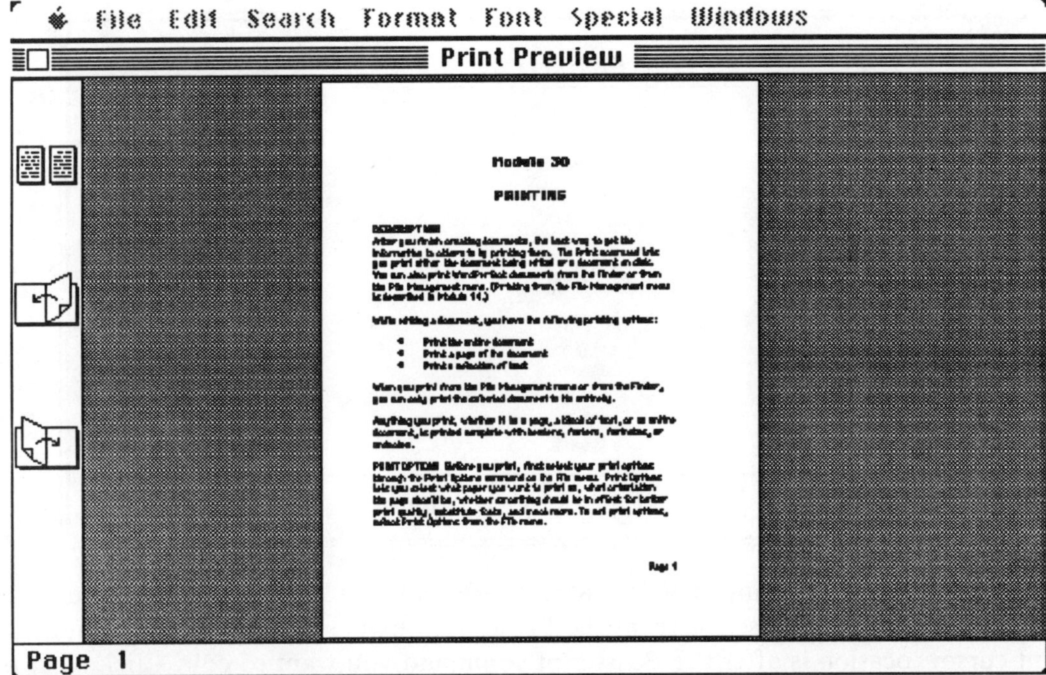

This is a long-distance look at one page of your document as it will be sent to the printer. Notice that the page or pages are listed in the lower left-hand corner. If you want to see two pages side by side, click on the top icon. If you want to see a page in real size, click anywhere on a page. To page forward through the document, click on the second icon. To move backward through the document, click on the third icon. To end Print Preview, click on the Close box at the upper left-hand corner (≣□≣).

Postscript This option lets you embed Postscript commands in your document. They will be sent to the printer when you print the document. These are useful for special effects.

CAUTION

Do not use the Postscript option if you do not know Postscript commands. This option is only for those familiar with Postscript commands.

To embed Postscript commands in a document, type or click on 4 from the Print Options menu.

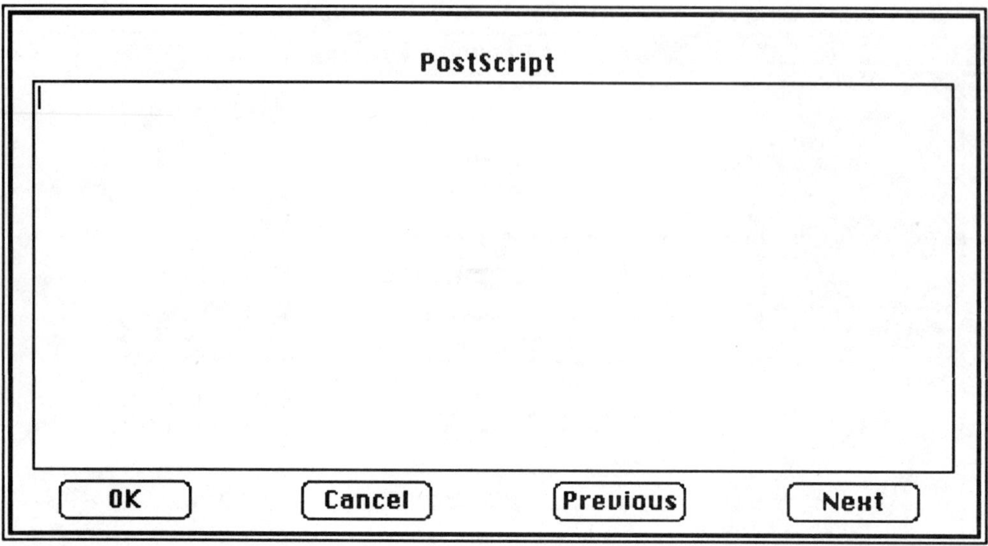

Type the commands you want to embed at this point and click OK. To edit commands you already created, select Postscript from the Print Options menu, then click Previous if the current cursor location is after the Postscript command you want to edit. Click Next if the cursor location is before the Postscript code. After editing the Postscript command, click OK.

Print Selection Print selection lets you print a portion of a document. To print a selection of text, highlight the text you want to print and select Print Selection from the Print Options menu.

PRINT You can print a document from anywhere inside that document. You can print forward, backward, or every other page. You can print multiple copies and all or part of the document. To print a document, select Print from the File menu or press Cmd-P or Shift-F7.

LaserWriter "LaserWriter Plus" 5.2
OK
Copies: 1 Pages: ◉ All ○ From: To:
Cancel
Cover Page: ◉ No ○ First Page ○ Last Page
Help
Paper Source: ◉ Paper Cassette ○ Manual Feed
☐ Every other page ☐ Print backwards

Type the number of copies to print. If you want to print part of a document, click on From, then type the pages you want to print. If there is a cover page, click whether it should be printed first or last. To print from the paper cassette connected to the LaserWriter, click on Paper Cassette. For manual feed, click on Manual Feed. To print every other page, click on that box. To print backward, click on that box. For additional Help, click on Help. When you are ready to print, click OK or press Return. The document (or part of the document, as appropriate) prints. To cancel a print job, press Cmd-period.

PRINTING FROM THE FINDER Printing from the Finder is a convenient way to print more than one file at a time. To print from the Finder, highlight the documents you want to print and select Print from the File menu. Shift-Click to select more than one document at a time. Momentarily, the WordPerfect icon appears on the screen and the Printer dialog box appears. Select the print choices as described in the Print section earlier in this module. Then click OK or press Return. After the first document prints, the second document begins printing. When all the documents have been printed, you return to the Finder.

APPLICATIONS

Before printing a document, select Print Options to tell WordPerfect how and in what manner you want a document printed. Use the Print Preview feature to make sure a document is ready for printing, that page numbers, headers, footers, footnotes, and graphics appear in the places you want them. Use the Print command to print a document or part of a document. Print from the Finder to print more than one document at a time.

TYPICAL OPERATION

In this example, you print part of a document using Print Options to set up the document and the Print command to print the document.

1. If necessary, start WordPerfect. Then press **Cmd-O** and move the cursor to Finances, a file created in Module 10. Press **Return** to open the file.

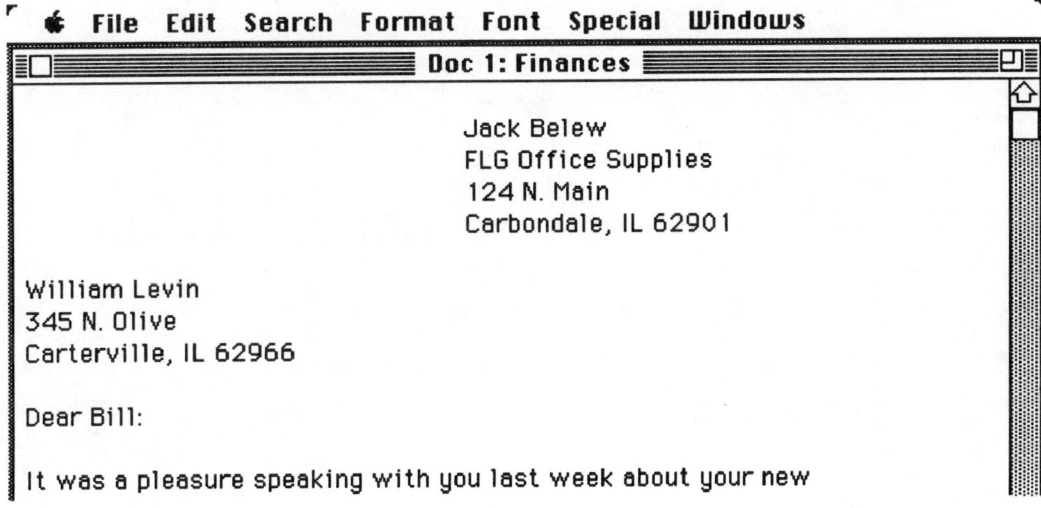

2. Choose **Print Options** from the File menu, then type or click on **1**.

NOTE

Make sure there is legal-sized paper in the cassette tray for your laser printer. If you do not have a laser printer, disregard step 3.

3. Choose **US Legal** for the paper, then click **OK** or press **Return**.
4. Press **Cmd-P**. Click **From** on the dialog box and type **2**, then press **Tab** and type **3**. Then click **OK** or press **Return**. The printer then prints pages two and three of the document.
5. Press **Cmd-K** to close the document.
6. Turn to Module 8 to continue the learning sequence.

Module 31

REDLINE AND STRIKEOUT

DESCRIPTION

Two old terms from pen and paper editing days are redline and strikeout. *Redlined* text is text that the editor recommends be added to a document. Text that is marked for *strikeout* means the editor recommends it be deleted from a document. WordPerfect lets you use both the Redline and the Strikeout feature while editing a document.

REDLINED TEXT Redlined text appears on-screen with a vertical bar at the left margin. If you have a color monitor, this can be altered using WordPerfect's Colors/Fonts/Attributes feature (Appendix C). When the document is printed, redlined text can appear in a variety of ways, including in red or with a vertical bar in the left or right margins. Your printer might even put dots under all the letters that are redlined.

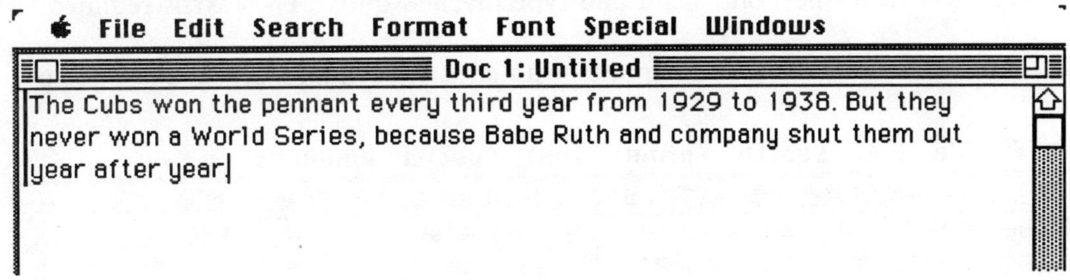

To redline text, move the cursor to the space where you want to add text and select Style from the Font menu.

Font

Style

1. Plain Text
2. Bold ⌘⇧B
3. Underline ⌘⇧U
4. Italics ⌘⇧I
5. Outline ⌘⇧O
6. Shadow ⌘⇧S

7. Superscript
8. Subscript
9. Options...

A. Overstrike ⌘⇧V
B. Strikeout
✓C. Redline

Type or click on C. Type the text you want to add and select Style from the Font menu and type or click on C to turn redlining off.

SELECTING REDLINE TEXT If you have already typed text that you want to redline, you can select it, either with the mouse or the Select key. To do this, first select the text, then select Style from the Font menu and type or click on C. The text is redlined.

STRIKEOUT TEXT Strikeout text appears with lines through it on-screen and when printed.

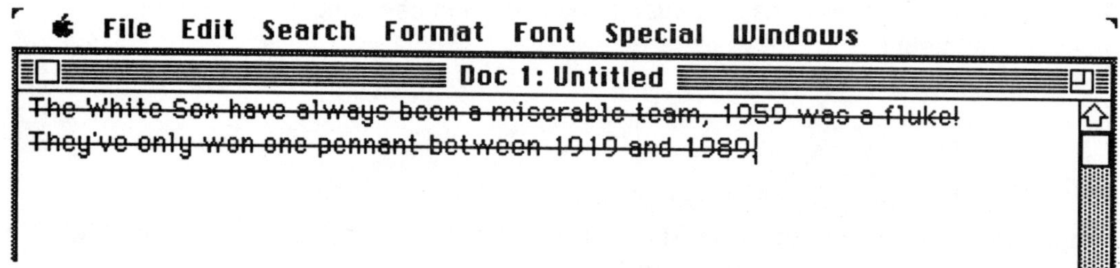

Since you are marking text for deletion, you usually use the mouse to select strikeout text. But you can type text marked for strikeout as well. To type strikeout text, move the cursor to the space where you want to add text and select Style from the Font menu. Type or click on B. Type the text you want marked for strikeout. Then select Style from the Font menu and type or click on B to turn the Strikeout mode off.

To strikeout text using the mouse or the Select key, select the text you want marked for strikeout and select Style from the Font menu. Type or click on B.

REMOVING REDLINE OR STRIKEOUT MARKINGS When you mark text for redline or strikeout, WordPerfect inserts a code marking the beginning and end of the marked text. Use Show Codes, Cmd-7, to delete these codes.

However, if you decide to accept these markings, you may remove all text marked for strikeout while adding all text marked for redline in a document. To do this, select Mark Text from the Special menu and type or click on 4.

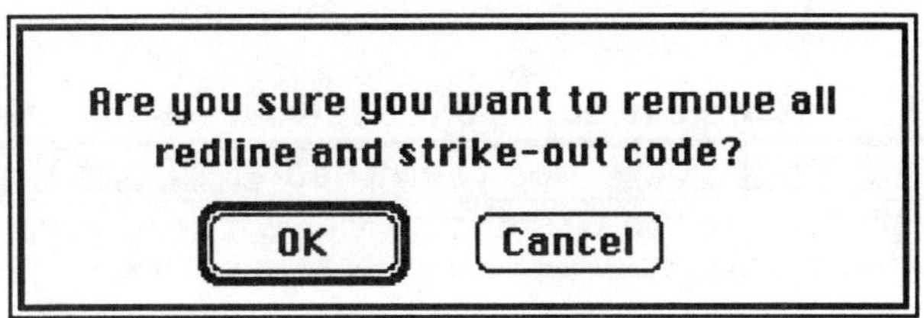

Press Return or click OK.

APPLICATIONS

Redline text that you want to add to a document. If you are editing a document for someone else, this gives that person the option of adding your redlines or deleting them. Strikeout text you want to remove from a document. Again, this gives the originator of the document the option of accepting or rejecting your changes. Once all redline and strikeout markings have been made to a document, the Remove command executes them.

TYPICAL OPERATION

Imagine you have been asked to edit a trip report. In this example, you create redlined text, strikeout other text, and use the Remove command to delete the markings from the redlined text and delete the text marked for strikeout.

1. If necessary, start WordPerfect. Then create a document similar to the following:

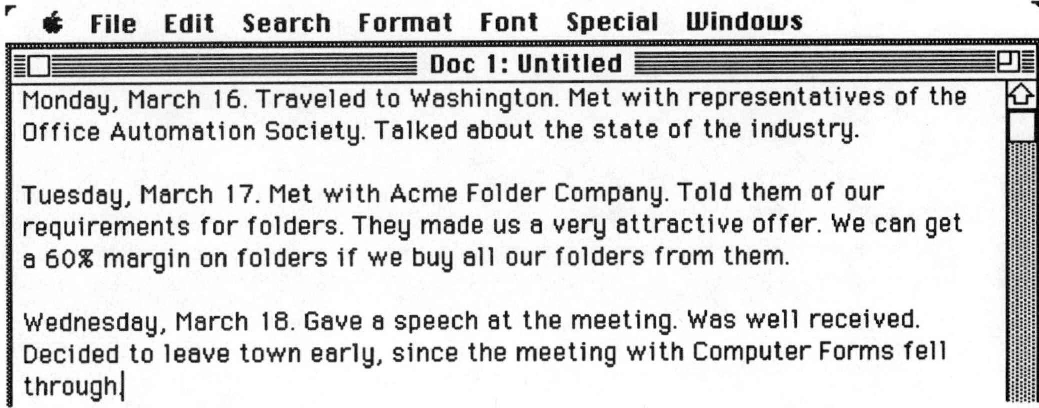

2. Move the cursor to the end of the second paragraph and press **Return** twice. Then select **Style** from the Font menu and type or click on **C**. Type **Set up meeting with Computer Forms for Thursday morning.**
3. Select **Style** from the Font menu and type or click on **C** to turn Redline off.
4. Move the cursor to the "W" in "Was" in the last paragraph and use the mouse to select the entire phrase as a block. Then select **Style** from the Font menu and type or click on **B**.

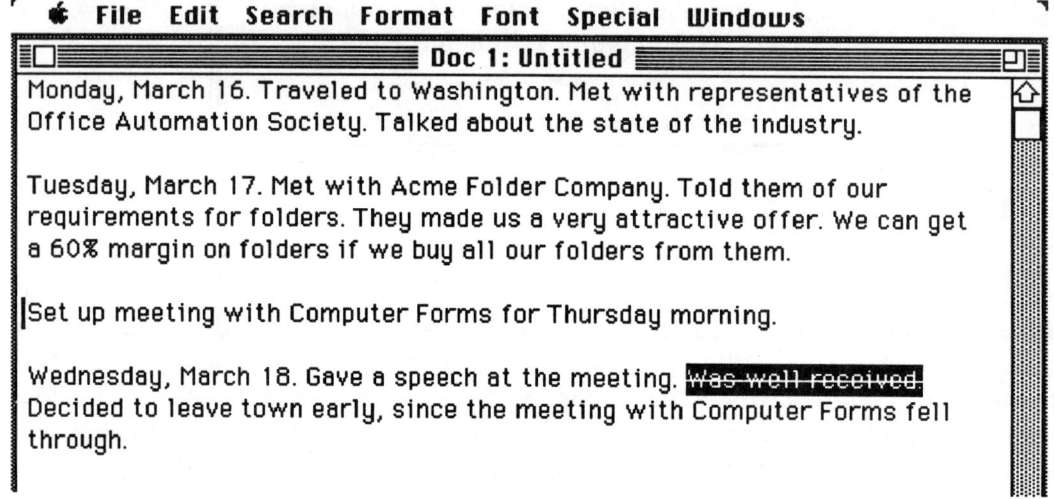

5. Click the mouse once to turn highlighting off. Select **Mark Text** from the Special menu. Type or click on **4**. Then press **Return** or click **OK** to add all redlined text and remove all text marked for strikeout from the document.
6. Move the cursor to the spaces after the period in "meeting" in the last paragraph and press **Del** to delete one of them. This is what the final document looks like:

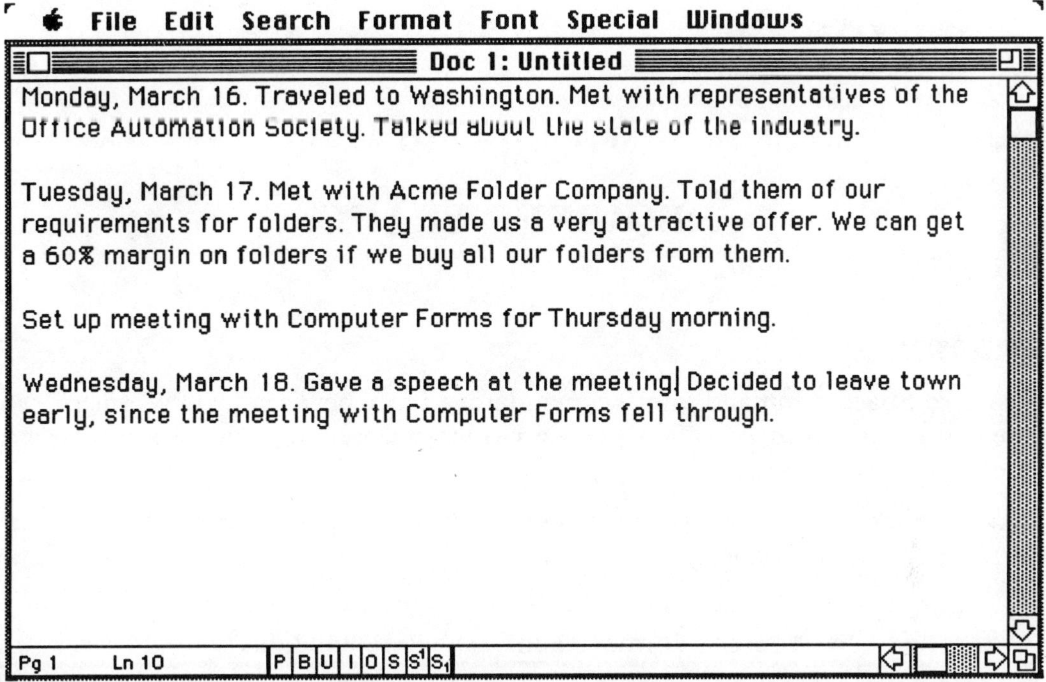

7. Press **Cmd-S**. Then type **Washington Trip** and press **Return** to save the document.
8. Press **Cmd-K** to close the document. Then turn to Module 16 to continue the learning sequence.

Module 32

REQUIRED SPACE

DESCRIPTION

The Required Space command inserts a mandatory space between text. Words or symbols separated by a *required space* will not come apart when word wrapping occurs. This is useful for dates, numbers, and names.

To introduce a required space, press Enter-Spacebar (or Home-Spacebar). Here is a passage of text without required spaces:

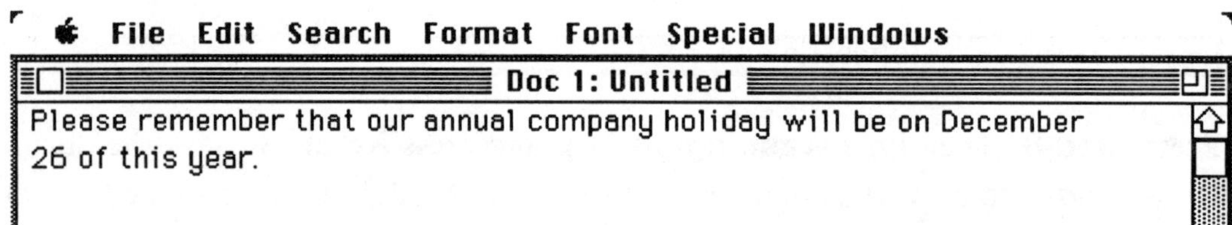

If a required space is inserted between "December" and "26," the text looks as follows:

NOTE

In order for the above example to work, you must first delete the space created by the Spacebar between "December" and "26."

To identify if a required space is in the text, use the Show Codes key (described in Module 7). The symbol for a required space is ([ReqSpce]).

APPLICATIONS

Insert a required space to keep strings of numbers, proper names, and dates together so they will not separate during word wrapping.

TYPICAL OPERATION

In this example, you insert required spaces between a series of words, numbers, and symbols.

1. If necessary, start WordPerfect. Then create a document similar to the following:

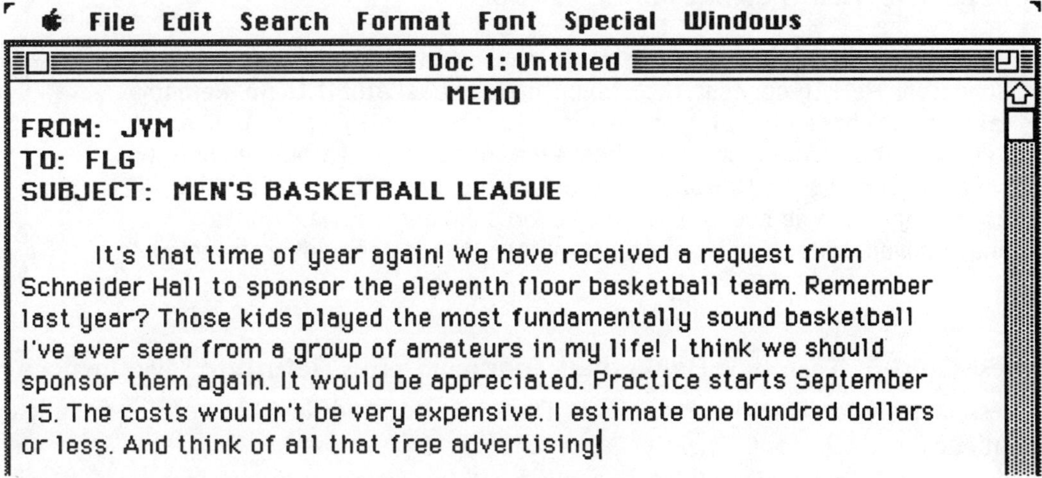

2. Move the cursor to the space between "September" and "15" and press **Delete** (or **Backspace**) to remove the space.
3. Press **Enter-Spacebar** to insert a required space.

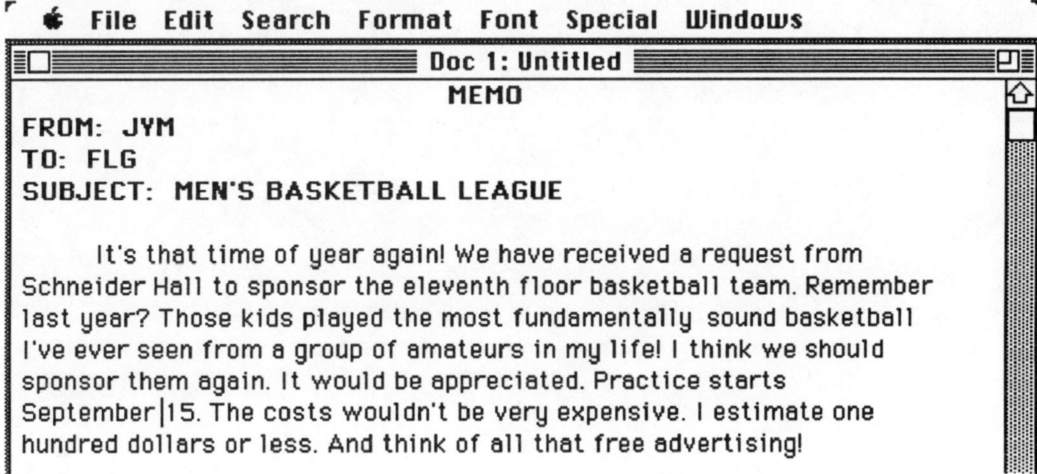

4. Move the cursor to the space between the "one" and "hundred" and press **Delete**.
5. Press **Enter-Spacebar**.

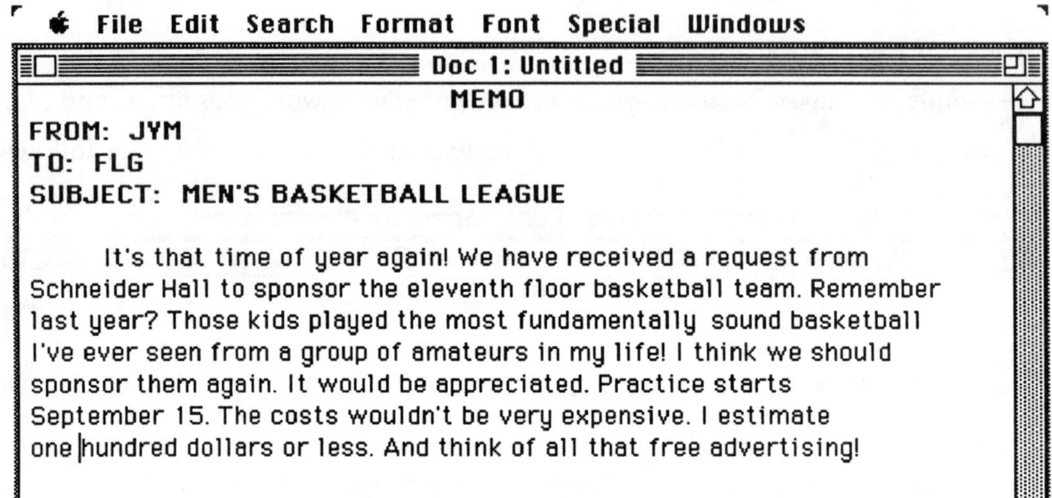

6. Press **Cmd-S**. Then type **Basketball Team** and press **Return** to save the document.
7. Press **Cmd-K** to close the document. Then turn to Module 40 to continue the learning sequence.

Module 33
RULER

DESCRIPTION

The Ruler is a handy feature that displays the current settings for margins, spacing, centering, tabs, column positions, hyphenation, and justification. You can change any or all of these settings from either the Ruler or the Line Format menu. To show the Ruler, select Show Ruler from the Format menu or press Cmd-R.

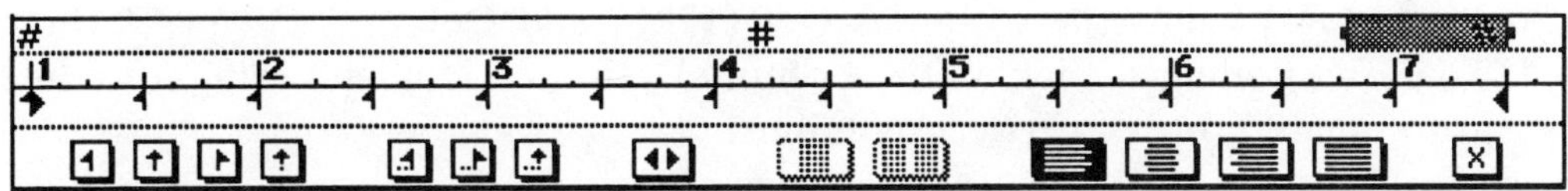

The Ruler displayed on the screen shows the settings at the current cursor position. You can change these settings throughout a document as many times as you like. That is, you can use as many Rulers as you want in a document. If you want to use the same settings throughout an entire document, make all changes at the top of the document. To change settings for a portion of the document, use the Select command to select a portion of text and change the settings for that portion only.

MARGINS Margins are indicated by the ( ) markings on the Ruler. Notice that margins are set at 1 inch and 7.5 inches from the left side of the paper, respectively. To change margins, move the cursor to the left or right margin setting and click and hold the mouse. Then drag the margin to the location where you want the new margin setting to be and let go.

You can also set margins through the Page Layout option on the Page Format menu. This method is discussed in Module 28.

TABS Tabs are the flag-like icons between the margins on the Ruler. Below the Ruler are the icons for left ( ), center ( ), right ( ), and decimal align tabs ( ), plus left ( ), right ( ), and center ( ) tabs with dot leaders. To set tabs, click on the tab icon of your choice and then click anywhere along the ruler line to insert the tab. To delete a tab, click on the tab icon and then click on the tab stop you want to delete. Click on the Tab icon again to turn the cursor back to a pointer. Tabs are also discussed in Module 23, Line Format.

PAGE NUMBER COLUMN POSITIONS When setting page number positions (as described in Module 28, Page Format), you are given a choice of left, right, or center. The page number column positions (#) are used to define left, center, and right page number positions. To change left, center, or right page number column positions, drag the appropriate icon to the position of your choice and let go.

HYPHENATION ZONE The hyphenation zone is the area that defines what words are selected for hyphenation when hyphenation is on. The larger the hyphenation zone, the less hyphenation. The smaller the hyphenation zone, the more hyphenation. If a word begins before or at the beginning of the hyphenation zone and continues beyond the end of the hyphenation zone, WordPerfect designates the word for hyphenation. The hyphenation zone is shown on the Ruler as ( ). To change the hyphenation zone, drag the appropriate edge of the zone where you want it to begin or end and let go. Hyphenation is discussed further in Module 23, Line Format.

COLUMNS You can define newspaper-style columns from the Ruler as well. The Column Definition icon ( ) plus the Columns Off ( ) and Columns On ( ) icons are included. To define columns, click on the Column Definition icon and bring it to the Ruler. Click again to create a break between columns.

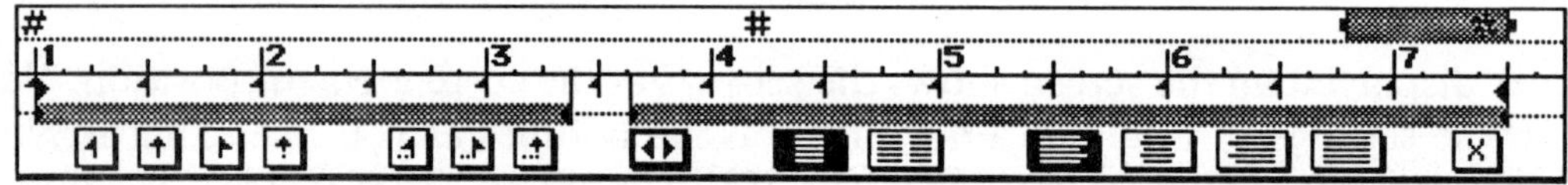

To make the break wider, drag the pointer. To make the break more narrow, click in the white space between columns. To create more columns, click anywhere on the shaded area to create another column. You can create up to 24 columns. Click the Columns On icon to turn columns on. Then click the Column Definition icon again to turn cursor back to a pointer. Columns are discussed in Module 8.

JUSTIFIED TEXT Text is normally left justified ( ), meaning each line of text is aligned at the left margin. You can also make text right justified ( ) so that it is aligned at the right margin instead of the left margin. Or you can have both left and right justified text ( ) that has smooth margins on both sides. Margin justifications are also definable from the Ruler. To change the justification, click on the icon of your choice. You can also center text ( ) with the Ruler. To center text, click on the Center icon. Center is discussed further in Module 6.

REVERT To reset all settings to their original values, click on the Revert icon ( ). When you click this icon, all settings revert to the values shown when you first displayed the Ruler.

APPLICATIONS

The Ruler provides a fast method for changing settings in a document. It lets you bypass the menu formatting commands to change margins, tabs, justification, and other settings.

TYPICAL OPERATION

In this example, you use the Ruler to change margins, justification, tabs, and other settings in a document.

1. If necessary, start WordPerfect. Then create a document similar to the following:

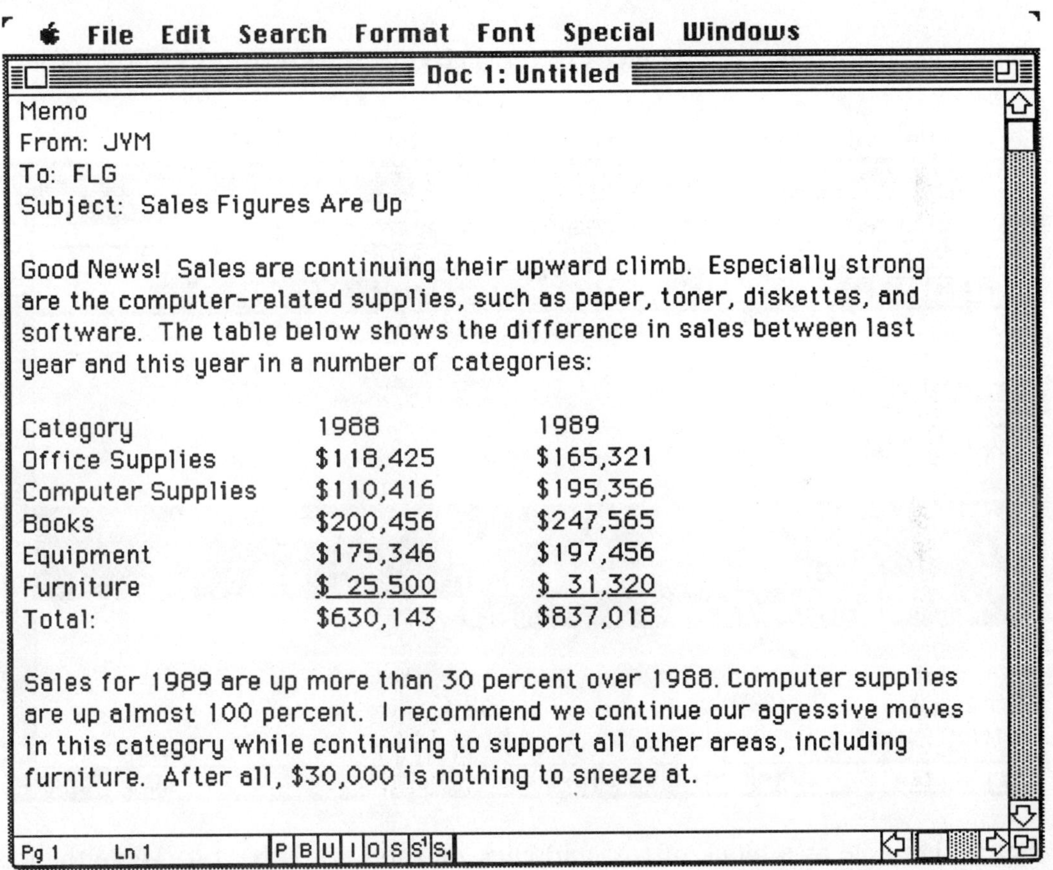

2. Make sure the cursor is at the top of the document. Press **Cmd-R** to show the Ruler.
3. Select the first word, "Memo," as a block of text and click the **Center** icon.

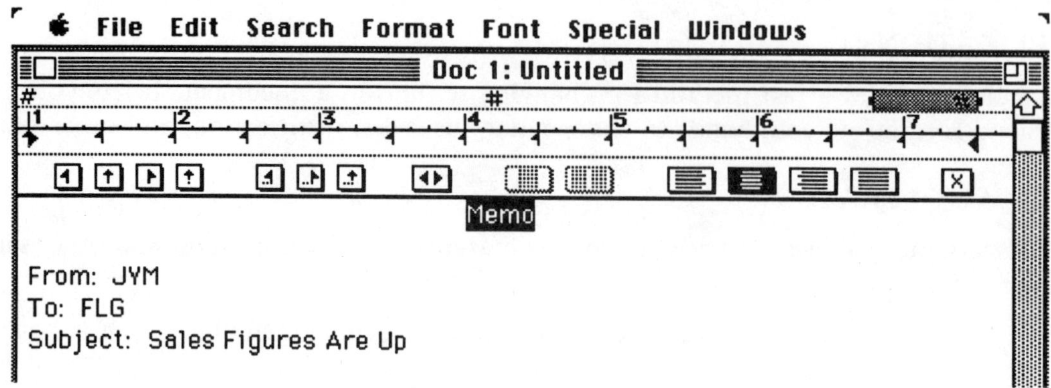

4. Select the first paragraph as a block of text and click the **Left and Right Justify** icon.

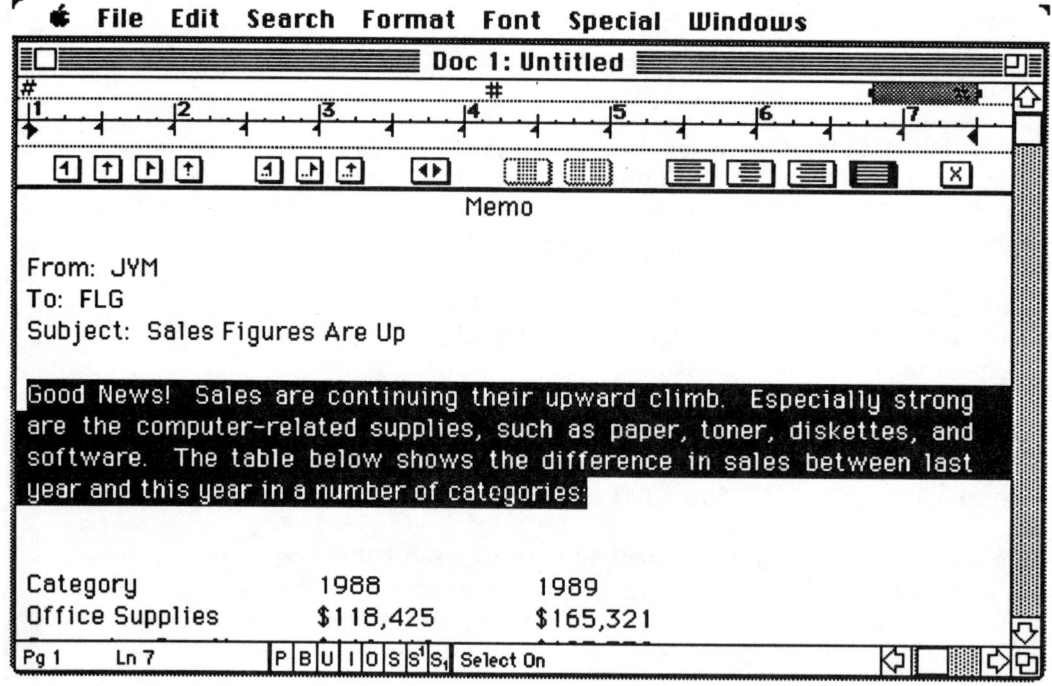

5. Select the table as a block of text and click on the **Left Tab** icon. Move the icon to the tab at the 4-inch mark on the Ruler and click to delete the tab. Repeat the procedure at the 4.5-inch mark.

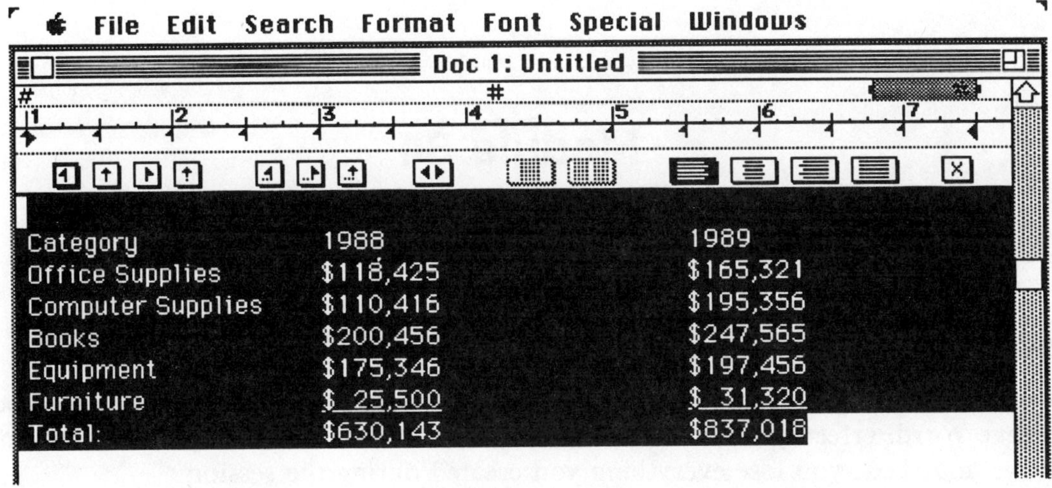

6. Click on the **Left Tab** icon to return the cursor back to a pointer.
7. Press **Cmd-S**. Then type **Sales Results** and press **Return** to save the document.
8. Press **Cmd-K** to close the document. Then turn to Module 23 to continue the learning sequence.

Module 34

SAVE, CLOSE, AND QUIT

DESCRIPTION

Before you turn off your computer, you must leave WordPerfect. More importantly, before you leave WordPerfect, you should save the text you created during the session. If you do not save your text, you lose everything you created during the session.

Three commands are related to this procedure — Save, Close, and Quit. Use the Close command to close one document when you are finished with it but are not ready to end the session. Use the Quit command to save a document or documents when you have finished all editing. Also use the Quit command to leave WordPerfect. (When you use the Quit command, you do not have to save the documents you are editing in a separate step.) If you use the Save key, you are telling WordPerfect you want to save the document and then continue editing it. Pull down the File menu to access the Save command:

File	
New	⌘N
Open...	⌘O
Retrieve...	
Close	⌘K
Save	⌘S
Save As...	
Save Copy As...	
File Management...	⌘L
Print Options	▶
Print...	⌘P
WP Defaults	▶
Transfer...	
Quit	⌘Q

USING THE SAVE COMMAND WordPerfect lets you save data through the use of the Save command. To save a document, either select Save from the File menu or press Cmd-S or F10. If you have not saved the document before, the following dialog box appears:

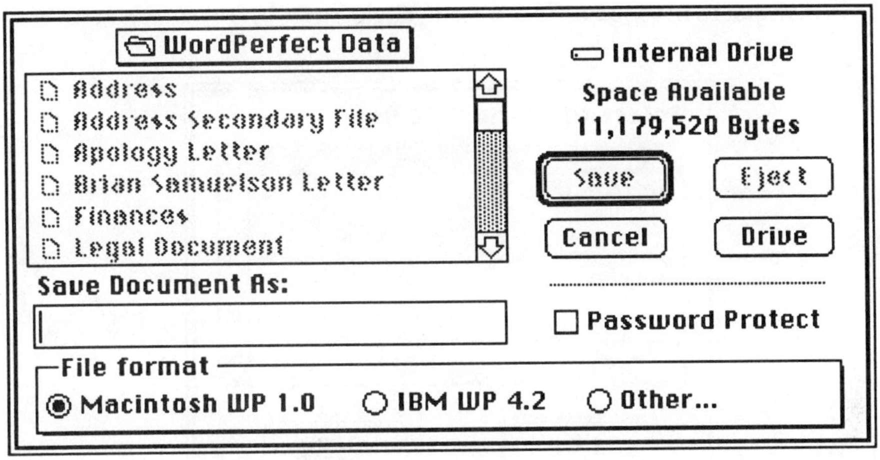

WordPerfect Data
Address
Address Secondary File
Apology Letter
Brian Samuelson Letter
Finances
Legal Document
Save Document As:
Internal Drive
Space Available
11,179,520 Bytes
Save
Eject
Cancel
Drive
Password Protect
File format
Macintosh WP 1.0
IBM WP 4.2
Other...

To save a new document, select the file format in which you want to save the file (most likely Macintosh WordPerfect), then type the filename you want to use and click on Save or press Return. To add password protection to a file, click on the Password Protect box.

If you already saved the document you are working with, WordPerfect automatically saves the file when you select Save or press Cmd-S or F10.

WordPerfect returns you to the document when it has finished saving it.

Save As To save a previously saved file under another name, use the Save As feature. To do this, select Save As from the File menu and type a new filename. Then click Save or press Return. The new file becomes the current file on-screen (the new filename appears in the Title Bar at the top of the screen).

Save Copy As To save a previously saved file under another name without making it the current file on screen, use the Save Copy As feature. To do this, click Save Copy As from the File menu and type a new filename. Then click Save or press Return. A copy of the file is saved on disk, but the current file is still the one you started with.

Save Selection As To save a portion of a document as a separate file, use the Save Selection As feature. To do this, use the mouse to highlight the text you want to save (by dragging the mouse over the text while holding down the mouse button) and select Save Selection As from the File menu and type a new filename. Then click Save or press Return. The selected text is saved on disk, but the current file is still the one you started with.

File Formats When you save a file in WordPerfect, you have the option of saving the file as a WordPerfect Macintosh file, a WordPerfect MS-DOS file (Version 4.2 of MS-DOS WordPerfect), a text file, or a Microsoft Word 3.0 file. To select a file format, click on the appropriate button in the File Formats box when saving a file. If you click on the Other button, the following screen appears after you click Save or press Return.

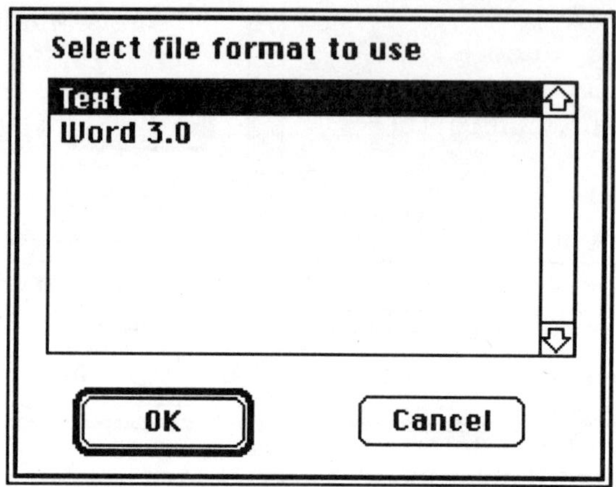

Select the appropriate file format and click OK or press Return.

Password Protection For security purposes, WordPerfect lets you add password protection to a file. This means that no one can open or print the file without knowing the password. If you do not know the password, you cannot open the file.

CAUTION

When you add password protection to a file, remember the password. If you do not, there is no way to open the file.

To add password protection, click on the Password Protect box while saving a file. Click Save or press Return.

Type the password and click OK or press Return. The letters do not appear on-screen; rather little apples appear in each letter's place. You are then prompted to reenter the password to make sure you entered it right the first time. Reenter the password, then click OK or press Return.

When you save the document again, you are asked for the password. At that time, type the password again to protect the file. If you click OK or press Return without entering the password, the file will not be protected.

To open a protected document, click on Open from the File menu or press Cmd-O. Then type the password and click OK or press Return. The file opens. If you do not remember the password, there is no way to open the file.

USING THE QUIT COMMAND Use the Quit command to end the current session. To quit, either select Quit from the File menu or press Cmd-Q or F7. If there are no documents to save, WordPerfect closes all files and returns to the Finder. If there are documents to save, a dialog box appears asking if you want to save them.

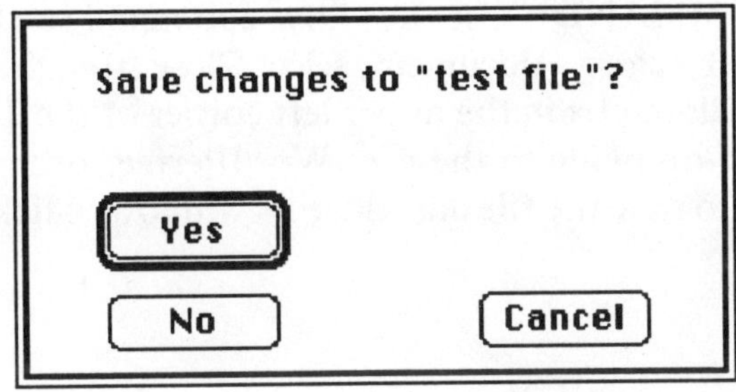

Click Yes or press Return to save the file and end the session. Click No to end the session without saving the file.

Transfer To quit WordPerfect without returning to the Finder, use the Transfer command. This lets you quickly move from WordPerfect to another application. To transfer from WordPerfect to another application, select Transfer from the File menu or press Cmd-F1.

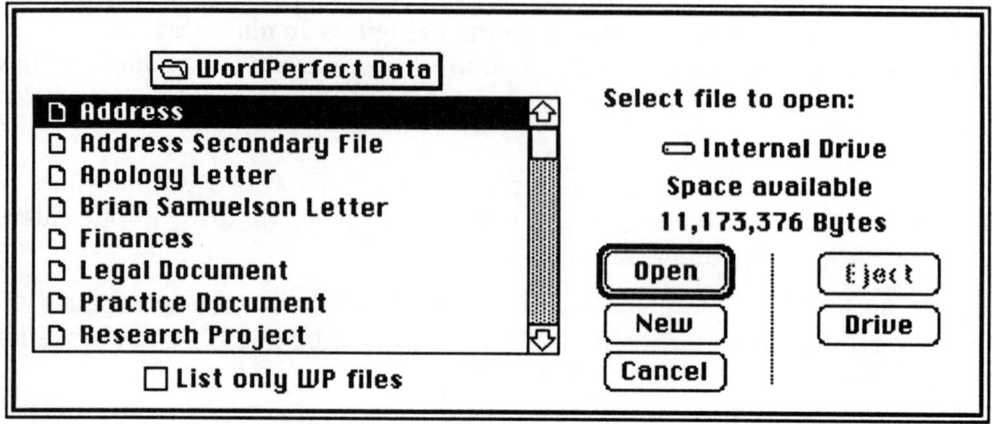

Open the necessary folders, and click on the application you want to transfer to. Then click on Transfer or press Return. WordPerfect asks you to save the documents you have been using, then transfers you to the selected application.

USING THE CLOSE COMMAND Use the Close command to close a document without ending the current session. To close a document, select Close from the File menu, press Cmd-K or Cmd-F11, or click the Close box in the upper left corner of the Text window. If you have not saved all the changes you made to the file, WordPerfect prompts you to save the file. Click Yes or press Return to save the file and close its window. Click No to close the window without saving the file.

APPLICATIONS

Saving, quitting, and closing are three of the most important features in WordPerfect. If you do not save a document, you will lose it. After you have finished using a document, close the window that it is in if you want to edit other files or quit WordPerfect, either to use other applications or to get ready to turn off your computer.

If you are working with a document for a long period of time, remember to save it periodically. (Every fifteen minutes is a good idea.) This is true especially if you are not using WordPerfect's Automatic Backup feature (Appendix B). If something catastrophic happens, such as a power failure or a lightning strike, periodic saving ensures you do not lose extensive data.

TYPICAL OPERATION

In this example, you save a document that has never been saved before and close the window that it is in.

1. Start WordPerfect and create a document similar to the following:

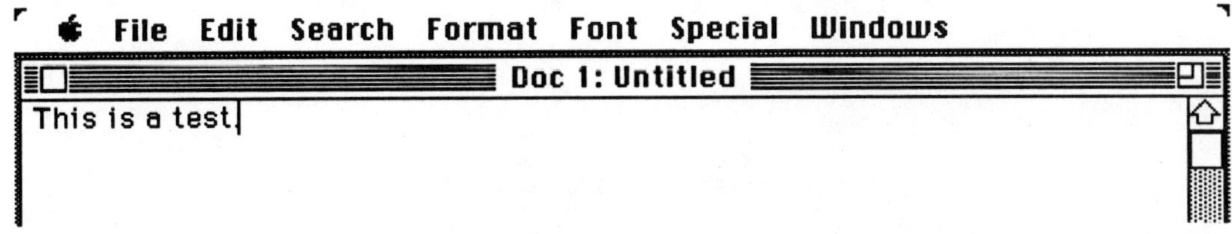

2. Press **Cmd-S**.
3. Type **Test Document** and click **Save** or press **Return**.
4. Press **Cmd-K** to close the window that the document is in.
5. Turn to Module 22 to continue the learning sequence.

Module 35

SCREEN/WINDOWS

DESCRIPTION

WordPerfect always includes a significant amount of information on-screen, including the name of the file, the cursor position, and the style of text currently in use. Three major features in WordPerfect control what you see on the screen and how you see it:

- Windows
- The Status Line
- The Screen command

WINDOWS Each WordPerfect file is displayed in a *window*. Each window includes a *Title Bar* along the top of the screen. The Title Bar includes the name of the file you are currently editing and the document number of that file.

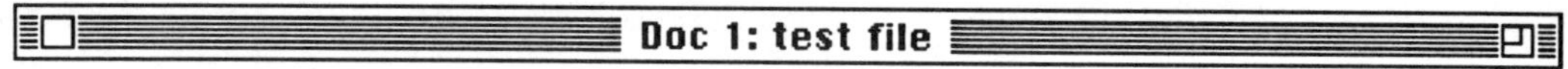

If you have not saved the document, the document is shown as ''Untitled.'' This feature serves as a gentle reminder to you to save the file.

You can have as many documents open as you want, the only limitation being the amount of RAM in your computer. If you have too many documents open, WordPerfect will tell you it is running low on memory and you ought to save and close some documents.

The box at the left side of the Title Bar is the *Close Box*. Click on it to close the document you are currently editing. This is equivalent to closing a document by pressing Cmd-K or by clicking on close from the File menu.

The box at the right side of the Title Bar is the *Zoom Box*. Use it in conjunction with the *Size Box* at the lower right corner of the screen. Click and drag the Size Box to make the window smaller or larger. Click on the Zoom Box to toggle between the last two document sizes.

Along the right side of the screen is the *Scroll Bar*. In the Scroll Bar are the *Scroll Box* and *Scroll Arrows*. Click on the top arrow to move gradually up to the beginning of a document.

Click on the bottom arrow to move gradually to the end of a document. Or, click and drag the Scroll Box to move more quickly through a document. There is also a Scroll Bar at the bottom right of the screen. Use it to move from the left margin to the right when the margin is wider than the screen.

Status Line Along the bottom of the screen is the Status Line.

The Status Line tells you the cursor position (by page and line number) and the style of text you are using (plain, boldface, underline, italic, outline, shadow, superscript, or subscript). To switch to a different style, click on the style of your choice.

WordPerfect also uses the Status Line to tell you if Select is on, if Columns are on, and for a variety of other messages from the system.

To see a more detailed view of exactly where the cursor is in the document, select Screen from the Special menu.

Special

Screen

1. Full Window ⌘⇧Z
2. Show Position
✓3. Display Justification ⌘⇧J
4. Fractional Widths
5. Colors...

Type or click on 2 for Show Position.

Pg 1 Ln 1 P B U I O S v=1.25 in. h=1.0 in.

This shows you exactly where the cursor is in relation to the top (v) and left (h) margins.

Adjusting Windows When you edit many documents at a time, the last document opened has much less room on the screen than the first document opened.

Doc 1: Screen/Windows
Doc 2: James Caron Letter
Doc 3: Untitled
Doc 4: Untitled

WordPerfect shows the Title Bars of all opened documents in numerical order. To make the document you are currently editing fill the screen, double click in the Title Bar. By clicking or typing 1 from the Screen menu or pressing Cmd-Shift-Z, you cause the Title Bar, Scroll Bar, and the menus to disappear completely to give you more room on-screen. You can make the menu appear again by moving the mouse up toward the Menu Bar. Pressing Cmd-Shift-Z again restores the screen to its normal appearance, with the menus, Title Bar, and Scroll Bar restored.

Selecting Documents It's easy to switch among documents when you have many documents open at once. Simply click on the visible Title Bar to make that document the current one. You can also select a document from the Windows menu.

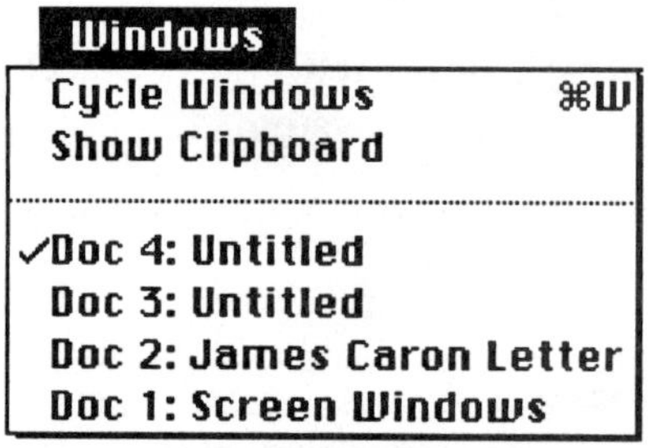

Windows
Cycle Windows ⌘W
Show Clipboard
✓Doc 4: Untitled
Doc 3: Untitled
Doc 2: James Caron Letter
Doc 1: Screen Windows

Click on the document you want to edit to make it the current one. Or select Cycle Windows or press Cmd-W to switch among documents. Pressing Cmd-W repeatedly cycles among the documents.

Display Justification WordPerfect typically displays left and right justification on-screen. To make the program work faster, turn display justification off. To do this, press Cmd-Shift-J or type or click on 3 from the Screen menu. You can turn display justification back on by repeating these procedures.

Fractional Widths To make justification more precise, choose the Fractional Widths feature. This gives documents a more professional appearance, especially if you print them on a laser printer such as the Apple LaserWriter II. Unfortunately, this feature also makes the program run more slowly. If you use fractional widths, it's advisable to first completely create and edit a document and then to activate the Fractional Widths feature just before you are ready to print the document. To use Fractional Widths, type or click on 4 from the Screen menu.

APPLICATIONS

The Windows and Screen features in WordPerfect help you edit documents by giving you control over how text is displayed on-screen. The Fractional Widths feature lets you create a more professional looking document.

The ability to edit more than one document at a time helps you be more productive. You can quickly switch from document to document, referring between documents for information and using Cut, Copy, and Paste commands to exchange information between documents.

The Title Bar tells you what document you are editing and which document number it is. It also includes a Close Box to quickly close documents and a Zoom Box to quickly change document size.

The Status Line gives you important information about the document being edited and can help you work more efficiently. It is the place for messages, cursor position, and current style.

TYPICAL OPERATION

In this illustration, observe how the Status Line keeps you informed, especially when the Show Position option is selected.

1. If necessary, start WordPerfect. Select **New** from the File menu, then select **Screen** from the Special menu. Type or click on **2**. Then create the following document:

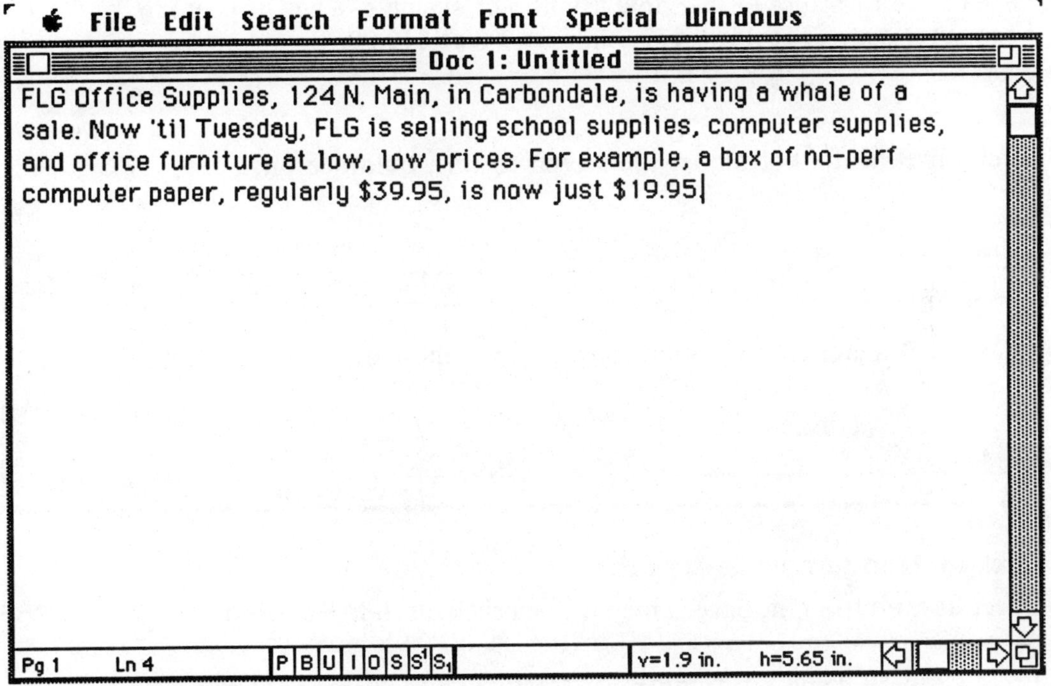

2. Press **Cmd-Return** to create a new page.

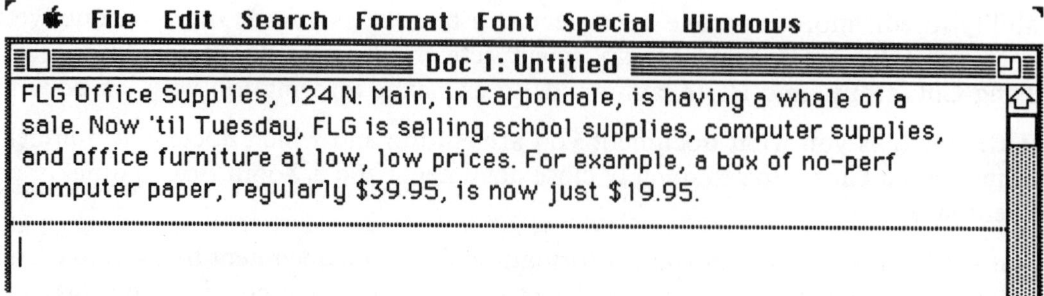

3. Press **PgUp** or type **9** on the number pad.
4. Press **Right Arrow** three times.

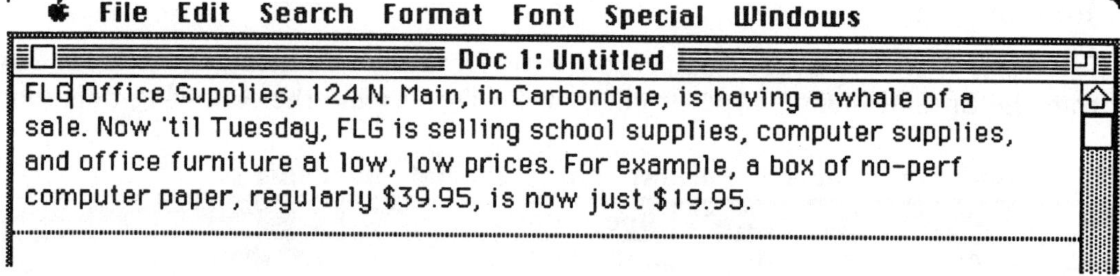

5. Click on **B** at the bottom of the screen to turn boldface on.

6. Click on **B** again to turn boldface off. Then click on **U** to turn underline on.

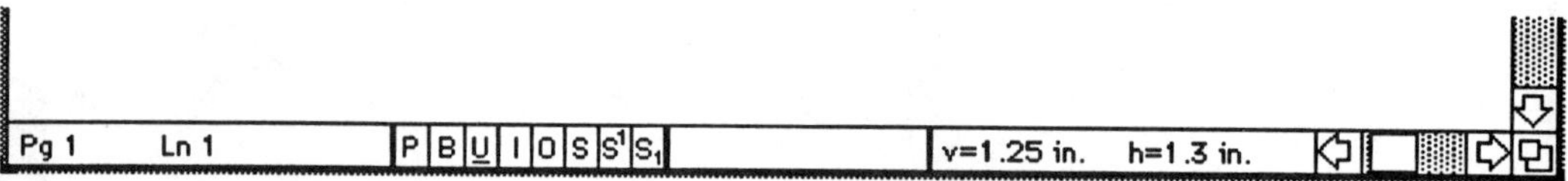

7. Click on **U** to turn underline off.
8. Select **Screen** from the Special menu. Then click on **Hide Position** to turn Show Position off.
9. Press **Cmd-S**. Type **Sale** and press **Return** to save the document.
10. Press **Cmd-K** to close the document. Then turn to Module 20 to continue the learning sequence.

Module 36

SEARCH AND REPLACE

DESCRIPTION

One of the nice things about word processing is being able to search through a document to find a word. If you have a twenty-page document, for example, and are not sure where you mentioned Dr. Jones, WordPerfect's Search feature will find the good doctor for you in a flash. If you are on the last page in that document, use the Backward Search feature to search back to page 1. If you are on page 1, use the Forward Search feature.

WordPerfect also includes a Word Search feature that lets you search through a number of documents for a specific word. This is useful if you are trying to find a document that mentions aspirin, for example, but are not sure which of the fifty documents on your hard disk is the right one. This procedure is described in Module 14.

A related feature to Search is Replace. The Replace feature lets you move through a document and change every occurrence of a word or words to something else — Mac to Macintosh, for example. WordPerfect even includes a Confirm option that gives you a chance to verify each Replace before it happens.

NOTE

The Replace feature works forward only, while the Search feature works both forward and backward. Replace also does not work in conjunction with Word Search.

WordPerfect searches for characters, strings of characters, or codes in a document or a block of text. If you search for "with," for example, WordPerfect finds "with," "without," and "within." This is called *partial word search*. You can set WordPerfect to find whole words only by selecting Complete Word Search.

Generally, WordPerfect finds all occurrences of a string of characters, whether they are uppercase or lowercase. However, you can select case sensitive searches to look for exactly the same case you typed.

There are two exceptions to this: WordPerfect always capitalizes the first letter of every sentence and it always capitalizes the proper I in words like I and I'm.

If WordPerfect does not find the string of characters you typed, it displays a "*Not Found*" message.

FORWARD SEARCH WordPerfect can search forward from the cursor position for any character, phrase, or code. To search forward, select Forward from the Search menu or press Cmd-F or F2.

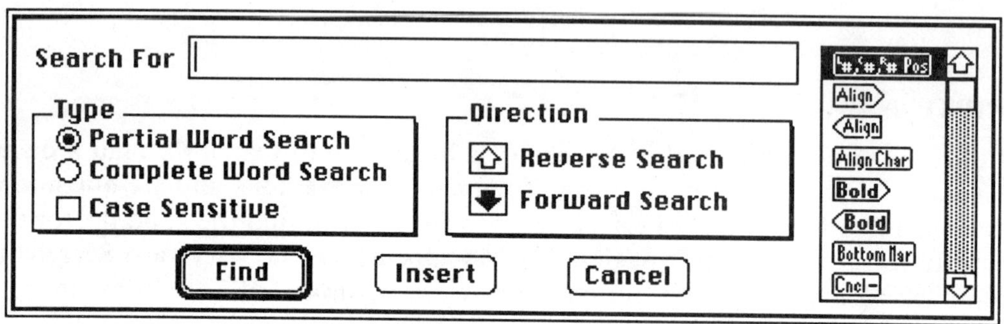

Notice the Forward Search arrow is highlighted. Type the word or phrase you are looking for. To select codes to search for, find the code you want to search for and either double click on it, or click on it once and click on Insert. Click on Complete Word Search if you want to search for complete words only. Click on Case Sensitive if you want to search for the word or phrase of exactly the same case. Then click on Find or press Return. The cursor moves to the first occurrence of the text you were searching for. To search for that same string again, press Cmd-F twice.

BACKWARD SEARCH WordPerfect can search backward from the cursor position for any character, phrase, or code. To search backward, select Backward from the Search menu or press Cmd-B or Shift-F2. Notice the Backward Search arrow is highlighted. Type the word or phrase you are looking for. To select codes to search for, find the code you want to search for and either double click on it, or click on it once and click on Insert. Click on Complete Word Search if you want to search for complete words only. Click on Case Sensitive if you want to search for the word or phrase of exactly the same case. Then click on Find or press Return. The cursor moves to the first occurrence of the text you were searching for. To search for that same string again, press Cmd-B twice. You can also search forward for that same string by pressing Cmd-F twice.

REPLACE This is one of the most useful features in WordPerfect. It lets you search through a document and replace the characters you do not want with those you do. And it works very quickly. You can search through a fairly lengthy document and replace occurrences in just a few seconds. To use Replace, select Replace from the Search menu or press Cmd-H or Option-F2.

Search:
Replace:
Type
Case Sensitive
With Confirm
Partial Word Search
Complete Word Search
Find
Insert
Cancel
Align>
<Align
Align Char
Bold>
<Bold
Bottom Mar
Cncl-

Type the word or phrase you want to search for. Or select the code or codes you want to search for from the code listing. Press Tab. Type the word or phrase you want to replace the above selection with, or select the codes you want to replace the above selection with.

Click on Complete Word Search if you want to search for complete words only. Click on Case Sensitive if you want to search for the word or phrase of exactly the same case. Click on Confirm if you want to replace a word, phrase, or code only in certain instances. Then click on Find or press Return. If you clicked Confirm, WordPerfect stops at each occurrence and asks if you want to replace the word, phrase, or code, with the new word, phrase, or code. If you want to, click on Replace or press Return. If you want to search for the next without replacing, click on Skip.

If you did not click confirm, WordPerfect quickly replaces all words, phrases, or codes, with the new character string. This is called *global search and replace*.

TIP: To delete the same word, phrase, or code multiple times, type the word or phrase or select the code in the Search box and leave the Replace box blank. Then click on Find or press Return.

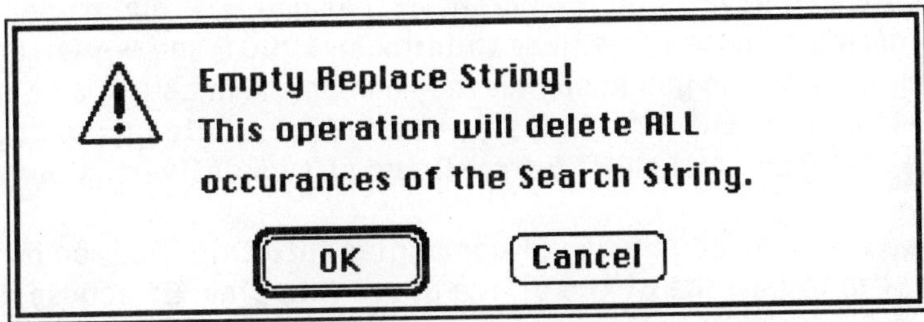

Click OK or press Return. WordPerfect deletes all occurrences.

APPLICATIONS

The Search feature helps you quickly locate words, phrases, or codes in a document. Replace quickly updates changes or revisions in a document. It is useful for form letters, business documents, reports, and other text.

TYPICAL OPERATION

Assume you have written a form letter to a person and find that the person you intended sending the letter to is not the right person after all. Replace can help you make these last minute changes very quickly.

1. If necessary, start WordPerfect. Then create a document similar to the following:

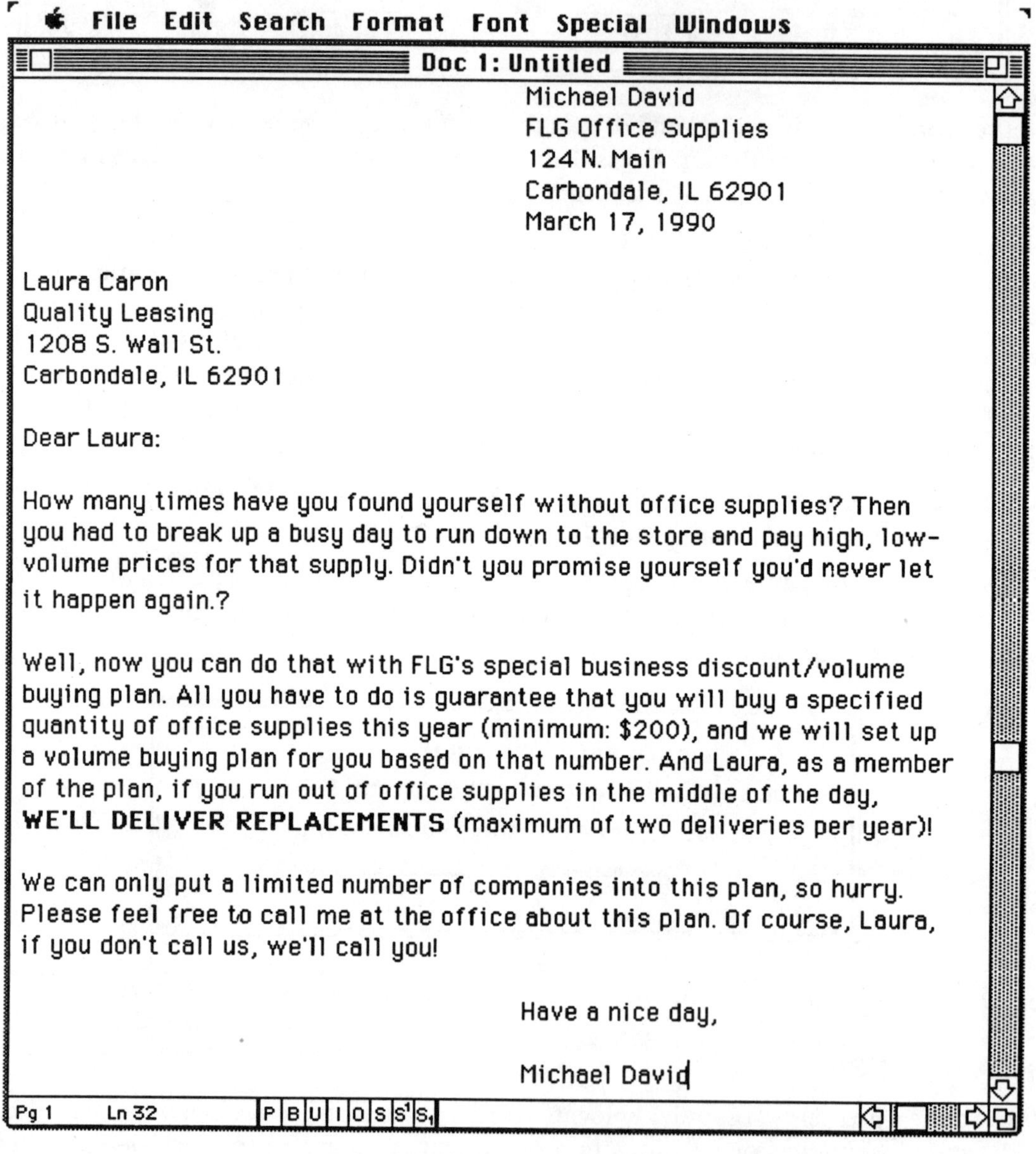

2. Move the cursor to the top of the document and press **Cmd-H**.

3. Type **Laura** and press **Tab**. Then type **James**. Select **Complete Word Search** and click on **Find** or press **Return**. WordPerfect makes the specified changes.
4. Move the cursor to the top of the document. Then press **Cmd-H**.
5. Double click on the **Begin Bold** icon, type **WE'LL DELIVER REPLACEMENTS**, double click on the **End Bold** icon, and press **Tab**. Then double click on **Begin Bold**, type **we'll deliver replacements**, and double click on **End Bold**. Click on **Complete Word Search** and **Case Sensitive** and click on **Find** or press **Return**. WordPerfect makes the changes.

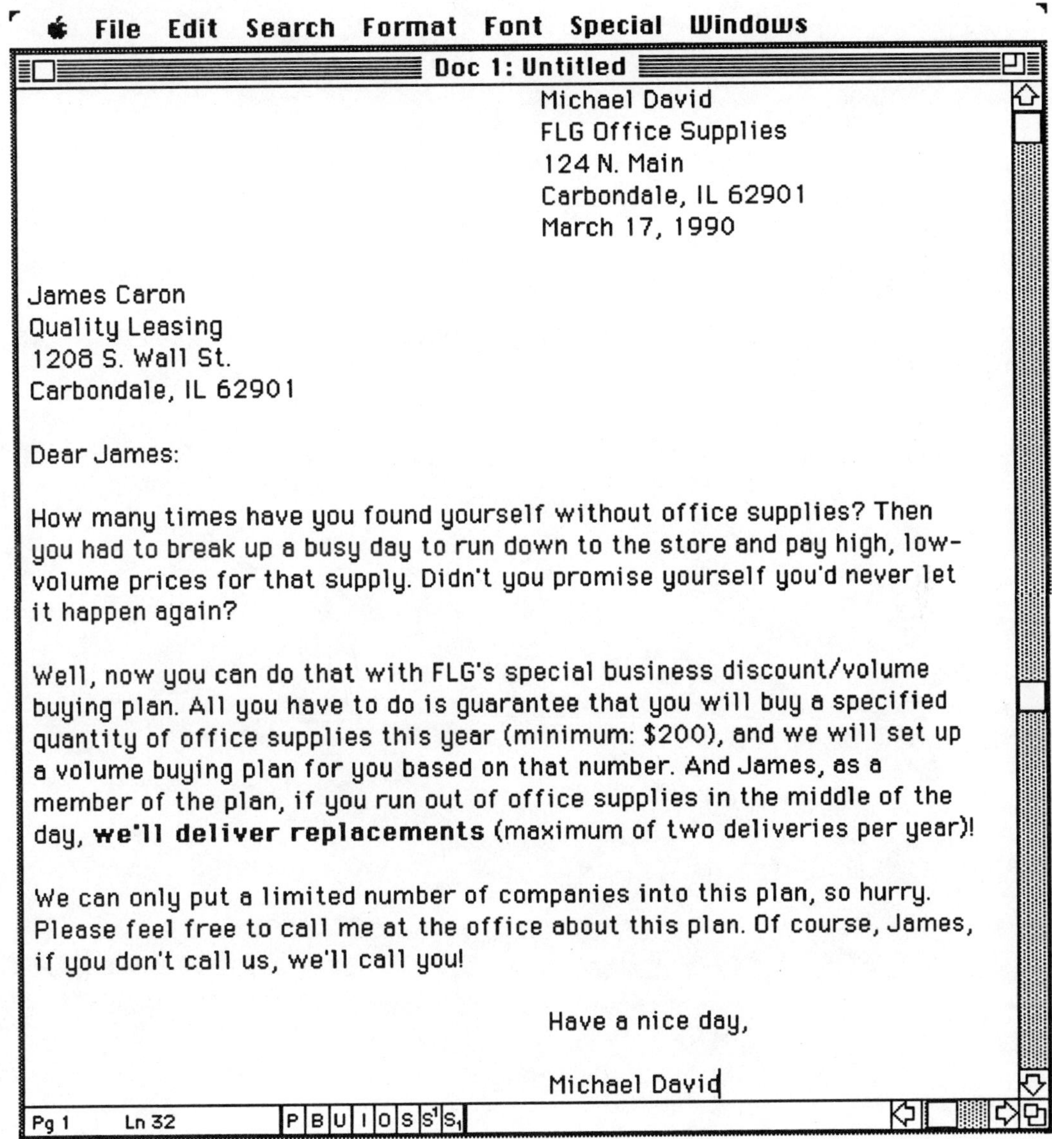

6. Press **Cmd-S**. Then type **James Caron Letter** and press **Return** to save the document.
7. Press **Cmd-K** to close the document. Then turn to Module 13 to continue the learning sequence.

Module 37
SELECT

DESCRIPTION

The Select command lets you break text into blocks for use with other editing features. The block can be as long or as short as you want it to be. You define how large the block is by either moving the cursor or clicking and holding down the mouse button.

Select is very useful for performing one or more operations to a block of text. A list of functions available to be performed on selected text is at the end of this module.

There are three ways to select text:

- With the mouse
- With the cursor keys
- With the Select command

SELECTING TEXT WITH THE MOUSE The easiest and most convenient way to select text is with the mouse. To do this, move the cursor to the beginning of the text you want to select and click and hold the mouse button. Then, while holding the mouse button, move the cursor to the end of the text and let go. As you move the mouse through the text, the text becomes highlighted. You can move the cursor either backward or forward to define any text you choose as a block. The highlighted text below is part of a block, while the unhighlighted text is not.

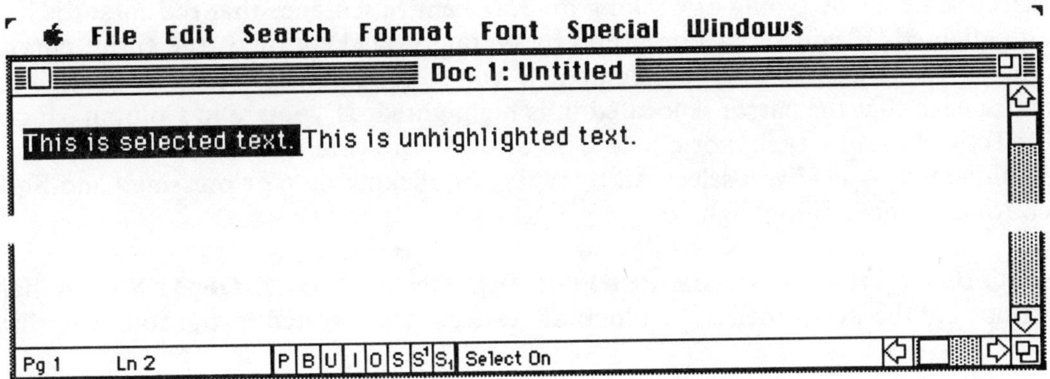

Notice the text is highlighted and the Select On message appears on the Status Line. After the text has been highlighted, you can perform other operations on it, such as cutting it, copying it, or deleting it. You can also perform more than one operation, such as boldfacing and centering the same block of text.

If you type anything while text is highlighted, the selected text is deleted and automatically replaced with the new text. If you accidentally type something, use the Undo command to retrieve it. When you have finished, click the mouse again to turn Select off.

SELECTING TEXT WITH THE CURSOR KEYS Selecting text with the cursor keys is similar to selecting text with the mouse, except instead of clicking and holding the mouse button while moving the mouse through the text, you hold the Shift key while moving the cursor through the text with the arrow keys. Hold down the Shift key and press either the Down Arrow, Up Arrow, Left Arrow, or Right Arrow key. The text becomes highlighted, and the Select On message appears on the Status Line.

USING THE SELECT KEY The Select key highlights either a sentence, paragraph, page, column, or an entire document. To use the Select key, either choose Select from the Edit menu or press Cmd-6 (from the keyboard).

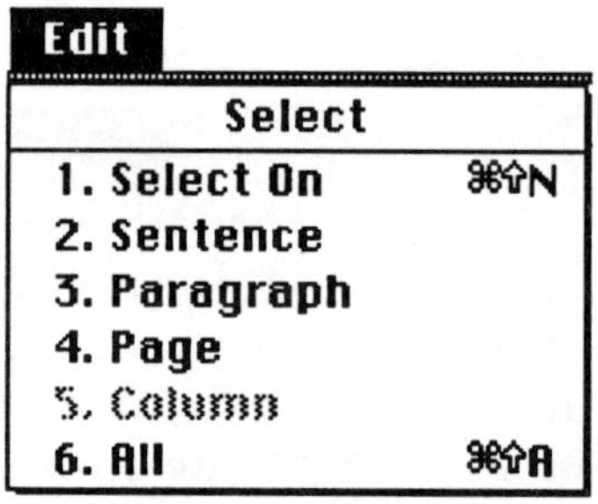

Edit

Select

1. Select On ⌘⇧N
2. Sentence
3. Paragraph
4. Page
5. Column
6. All ⌘⇧A

If you choose Select On either by typing or clicking on 1 from the above menu or by pressing Option-F4, you can select text with the cursor keys as explained in the previous section. If you select Sentence by typing or clicking on 2, the entire sentence that the cursor is located in is highlighted. If you select Paragraph by typing or clicking on 3, the entire paragraph that the cursor is located in is highlighted. If you select Page by typing or clicking on 4, the entire page that the cursor is located in is highlighted. If you are in Column Mode and then select Column by typing or clicking on 5, the entire column that the cursor is located in is highlighted. And if you select All by typing or clicking on 6 or pressing Cmd-Shift-A, the entire document is highlighted.

OPERATIONS THAT CAN BE PERFORMED ON A BLOCK OF TEXT A host of operations can be performed on a block of text, as is illustrated in the following list:

Append block to another file (Module 9)
Boldface block (Module 39)
Center block (Module 6)
Copy block (Module 9)
Cut block from text (Module 9)
Cut column from text (Module 8)
Delete block (Module 12)
Make block flush right (Module 15)
Mark block for indexing (Module 25)
Italicize block (Module 39)
Mark block for list (Module 25)
Make all text in block lowercase (Module 5)
Make all text in block outlined (Module 39)
Make all text in block plain (Module 39)
Print block (Module 30)
Protect text in block from being separated by a page break (Module 28)
Redline text in block for insertion (Module 31)
Replace text in block with new text (Module 36)
Save block as a file (Module 34)
Make all text in block shadowed (Module 39)
Check the spelling on the text in the block (Module 38)
Strikeout text for deletion (Module 31)
Subscript all text in block (Module 40)
Superscript all text in block (Module 40)
Mark block for table of contents (Module 25)
Look up selected block in Thesaurus (Module 41)
Underline block (Module 39)
Make all text in block uppercase (Module 5)

APPLICATIONS

The Select key helps you perform many editing operations. It is useful in a variety of editing applications. You will probably use it most often in moving and copying text.

TYPICAL OPERATION

In this example, define and redefine a block of text until it is exactly what you want. Assume you are going to boldface that block.

1. If necessary, start WordPerfect. Then create a document similar to the following. When typing the steps, press **F4** or **Cmd-Shift-T** after the step number. This indents procedural information.

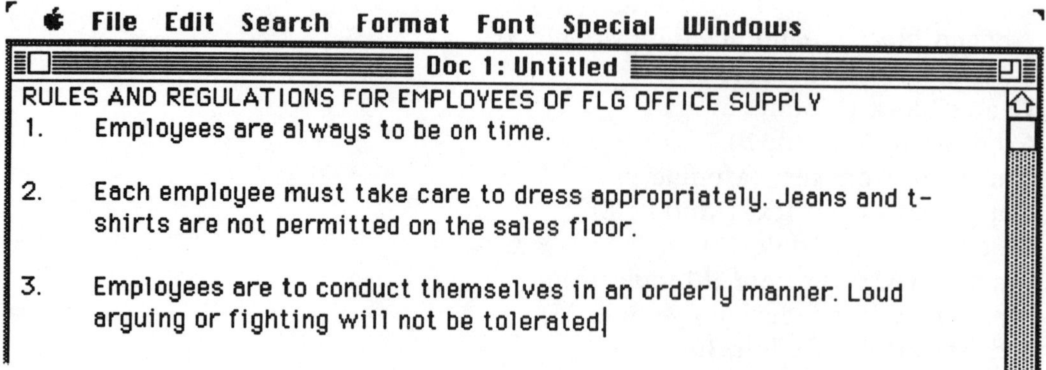

2. With the cursor on the number "2," click and hold the mouse and highlight rule number 1.

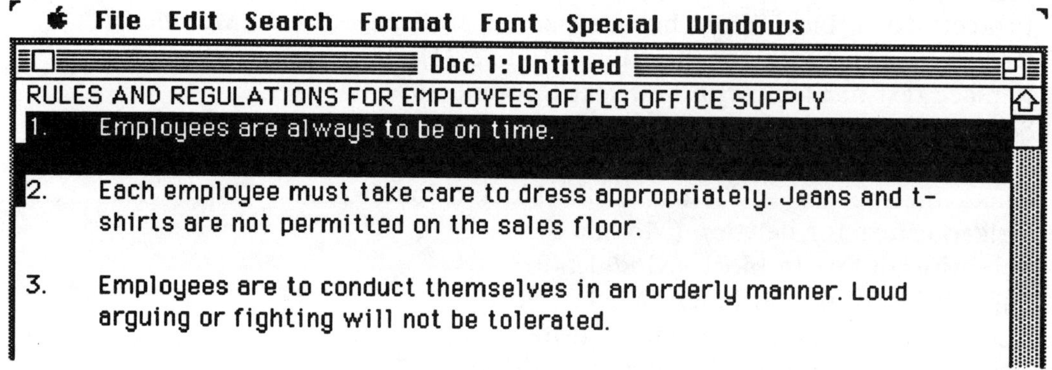

3. Now, click and hold the mouse until rule number 2 is highlighted. Since the original cursor location was at rule number 2, rule number 1 is no longer highlighted.

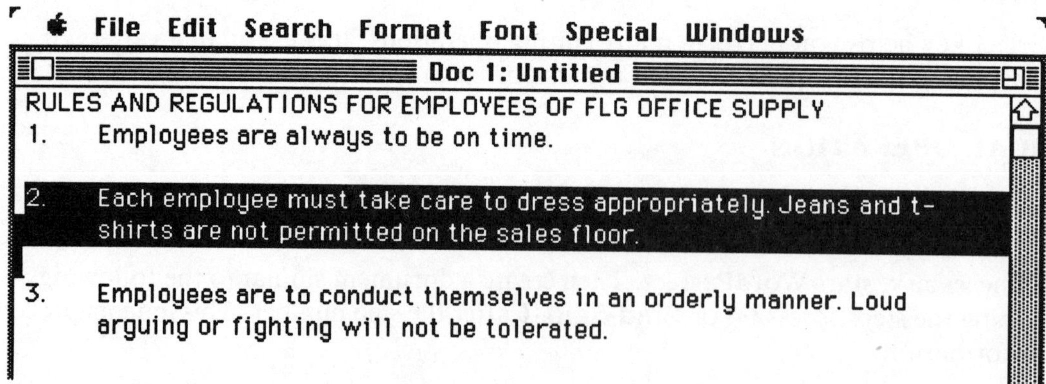

4. Press **Cmd-Shift-B** to boldface all text in the block. Then click the mouse to turn highlighting off.

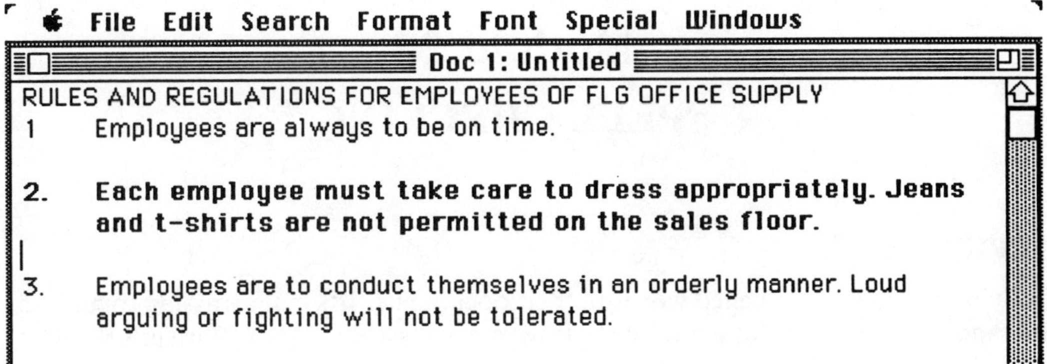

5. Move the cursor to the top of the screen. Using the mouse, highlight the text on the first line. Press **Cmd-Shift-C** to center the text, and then press **Cmd-Shift-B** to boldface it. Then pull down the Font menu and click on **18** to increase its font size. Click the mouse again to turn Select off.

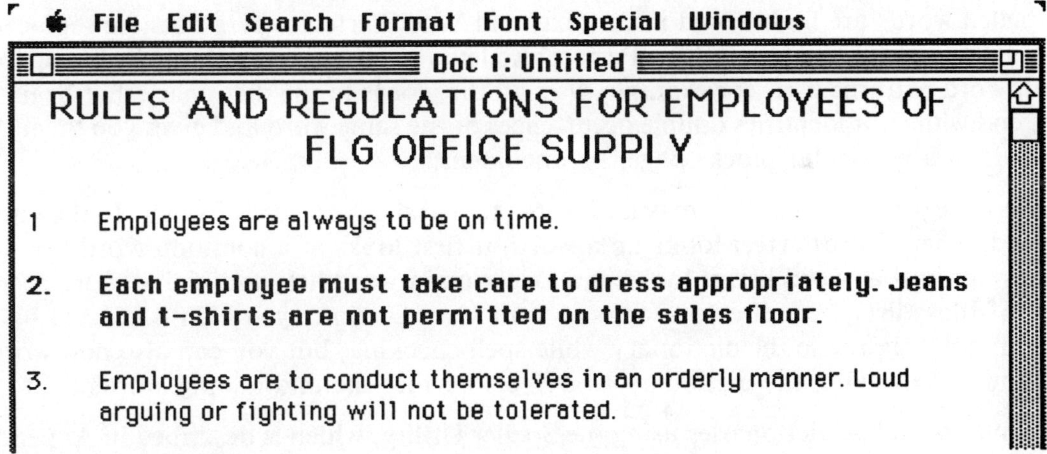

Notice how much more space the title takes up at the larger font size.

6. Press **Cmd-S** and type **Rules and Regulations**. Press **Return** to save the document.
7. Press **Cmd-K** to close the document. Then turn to Module 9 to continue the learning sequence.

Module 38

SPELL CHECKING

DESCRIPTION

Nobody likes to have misspelled words in their documents. It's embarrassing to mail someone a letter and later discover that words in the letter were misspelled. WordPerfect's Spell Checking feature gives you the opportunity to correct misspelled words before you submit a document to someone else.

The Spell Checker checks the spelling of words in your document by comparing each word to WordPerfect's 115,000-word dictionary. It lets you check words, pages, blocks, or entire documents. The Spell Checker checks words included both on-screen and in headers, footers, footnotes, and endnotes.

Misspelled words are highlighted in context, and WordPerfect offers possible replacement words for the misspelled word. WordPerfect also lets you check words phonetically (by sound) and in word patterns (a*t, for example, lists all the words in the dictionary that begin with a and end with t). It identifies double occurrences of the same word and gives you the number of words in a particular block, page, or document.

The dictionary is revisable. You may add words to it and delete words from it. In the interests of speed, when WordPerfect looks up a word, it first looks at a common word list. If the word is not in that word list, it looks at a larger main word list, and if that word is not in either of those lists, WordPerfect looks at your User Dictionary, which is created by you. You can not only revise the dictionary while spell checking, but you can also add words at any time by retrieving the dictionary as a WordPerfect file and adding words to it.

You can also change dictionaries using the Speller Utility, which is described in Appendix I.

SPELL CHECK If you have a hard disk, you loaded the Speller on it when you installed WordPerfect (described in Module 2). If you do not, you must keep the WP Dictionary diskette in any diskette drive at all times while performing spell checking procedures. Replace the System or Data diskette with the WP Dictionary diskette before proceeding.

To use the Speller, first make sure the document you want to spell check is on-screen. Then move the cursor to the word or page to check. If you are checking a document, the cursor need only be in that document.

CAUTION

As a safety measure against an unexpected system crash, always save a document before beginning spell checking.

Select Spell from the Special menu or press Cmd-E or Cmd-F2.

To spell check a document, either press Cmd-Shift-W or type or click on 1 from the Spell menu. To spell check a page, type or click on 2 from the Spell menu. To spell check a selection of text, highlight the text you want to spell check and type or click on 3 from the Spell menu. WordPerfect begins spell checking. When it gets to a misspelled word, it stops. For example, assume it finds a word spelled "compters."

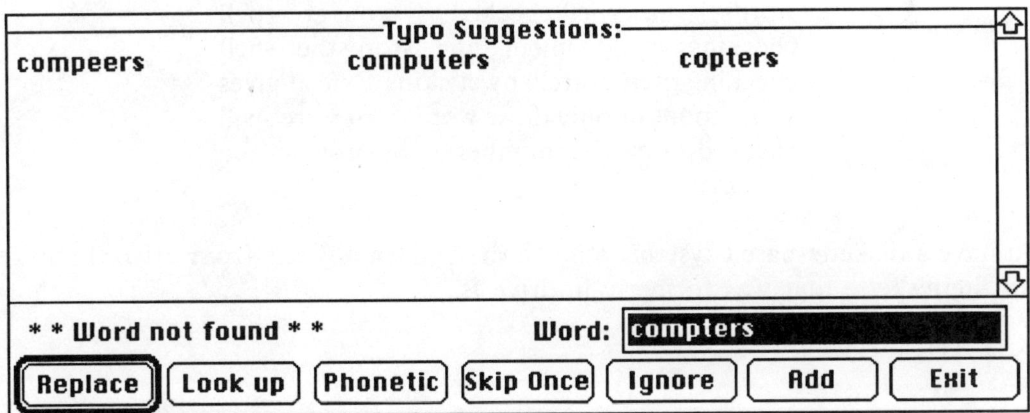

WordPerfect provides you with a list of suggested correct spellings, both typographical and phonetic. In this case, it could not make any phonetic suggestions. You have the choice of:

- Selecting one of the alternative choices to replace the word by clicking on that word and either pressing Return or clicking on Replace.
- Skipping this occurrence of the word and going on to the next misspelled word by clicking on Skip Once.
- Skipping all occurrences of this word by clicking on Ignore.
- Adding the word to the dictionary by clicking Add.
- Rejecting the choices offered and editing the word yourself. To do this, type the new word and click Replace or press Return to correct it and return to spell checking.
- Looking up words that match a pattern. For example, typing com*r at this selection and clicking Look Up would list all the words that begin with "com" and end with "r." Typing com?r lists all five-letter words beginning with "com" and ending with "r."
- Looking up words that match this word phonetically. This option gives you all the words that sound like the chosen word. You can find words that match "compter" phonetically by typing com*r and clicking on Phonetic.

Click on computers and click on Replace or press Return to correct the spelling of the word. WordPerfect continues to identify words not found in any part of its dictionary. When it is finished, WordPerfect tells you how many words are in the document. Click on Exit to resume normal editing.

NOTE

WordPerfect always gives you a count of the words it has spell checked. If you are spell checking a document and stop the spell checking prematurely by clicking Exit, it gives you a count of only those words that were spell checked, not the number of words in the document.

If you have a diskette-based system, remove the Speller diskette from drive B and replace it with the diskette that was formerly in drive B.

Double Occurrence Of A Word If WordPerfect finds that a word appears twice in a row, the following message appears on screen:

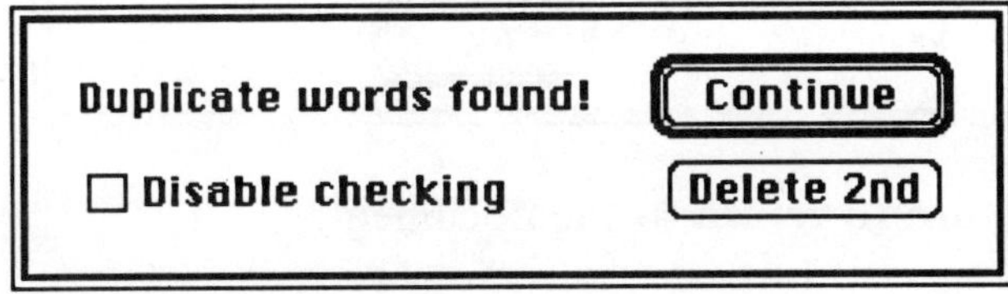

Clicking on Continue or pressing Return ignores the occurrence and continues spell checking. Clicking on Delete 2nd deletes the second occurrence of the word. Clicking on the Disable checking box and clicking Continue or pressing Return disables double word checking for the remainder of the document.

Word With Letters And Numbers WordPerfect gives you the option of skipping words with both letters and numbers in them during spell checking. If a word with letters and numbers is found, the following screen appears:

Clicking on Continue or pressing Return ignores the occurrence and continues spell checking. Clicking on Edit lets you edit the word. Clicking on the Disable checking box and clicking Continue or pressing Return makes WordPerfect ignore words with both letters and numbers for the remainder of the document.

WORD COUNT Anyone writing a report or an article likes to know how many words are in the document. WordPerfect automatically gives you a word count whenever you spell check a block, page, or document. That word count corresponds to either the block, page, or document. You can also count words without spell checking. To perform a word count, type or click on 4 from the Spell menu.

Click OK or press Return to return to the document.

LOOK UP Like the Look Up option during a spell check, this option gives you all the words in the dictionary that sound like the one you selected or all the words that match a certain word pattern. The advantage of this is that you can select the word or word pattern without doing a spell check first. To use the Look Up feature, type or click on 5 from the Spell menu. Then type the word pattern you want to look up and click Look Up.

Word patterns can be either full words or selections with wildcards. Question marks represent one letter while asterisks represent zero or more letters. For example, fo*d can be food, fooled, forearmed, etc. Fo?d can be food, fold, fond, or ford.

NEW DICTIONARY You do not have to use WordPerfect's dictionary when spell checking a document. You have the option of using a different dictionary, including third-party dictionaries from other vendors.

You can also change user dictionaries. For example, if you have a large dictionary you used with another word processing program, you can use it with WordPerfect. To change dictionaries, type or click on 6 from the Spell menu. WordPerfect prompts you to select a WP dictionary and a User dictionary. Select the appropriate dictionaries and press Return or click OK. Then begin spell checking.

APPLICATIONS

Spell checking is useful for reports, letters, memos, articles, term papers, theses, or any other document that someone else will read. It's always good practice to spell check a document.

Use the Look Up feature if you are unsure of the word you want to use. Use the Word Count feature to count words in reports and articles.

TYPICAL OPERATION

This example illustrates how to spell check a document.

1. If necessary, start WordPerfect. Then create a document similar to the following: You can type it without trying to make errors, or type it with errors. This example includes errors.

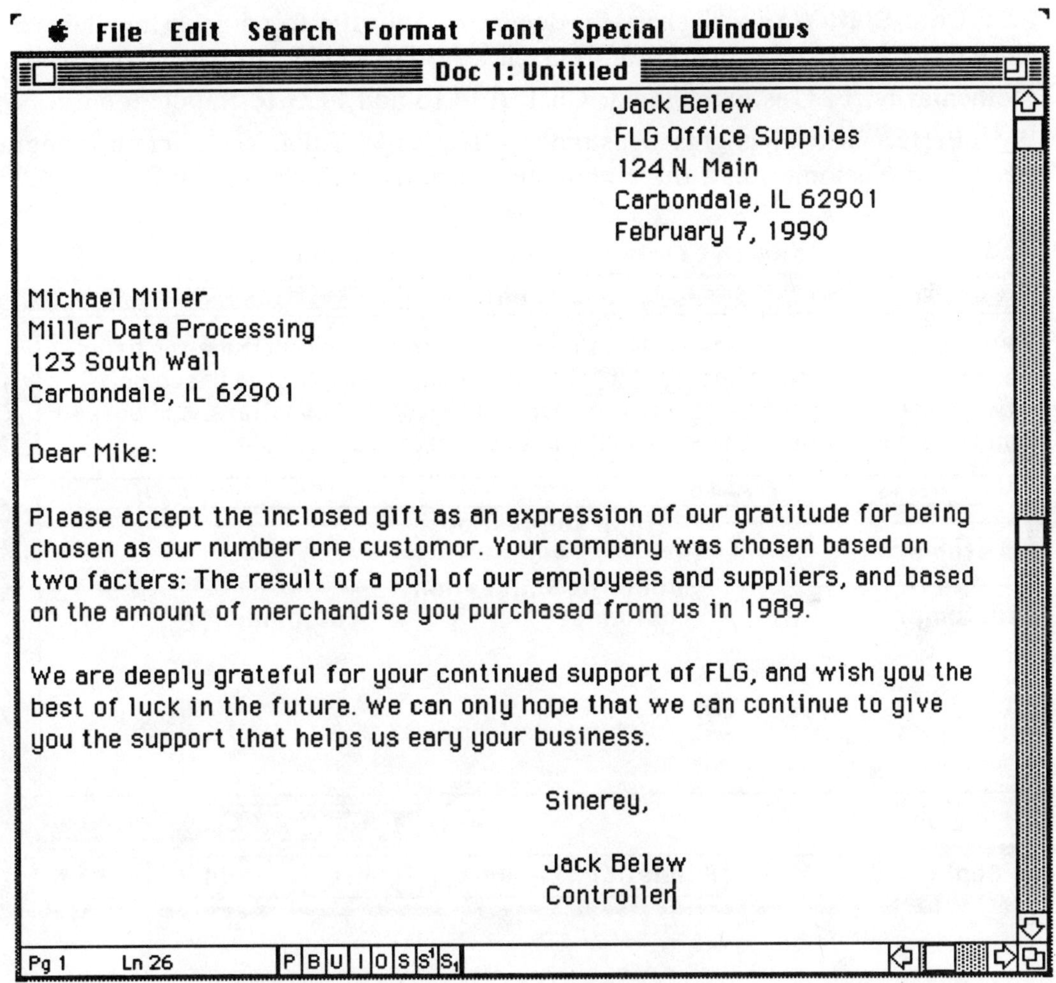

CAUTION

Do not remove the WP Dictionary diskette from drive B while performing spell-checking procedures.

2. If you have a diskette-based system, remove the diskette from drive B and replace it with the Speller diskette. If you have a hard disk system, proceed to step 3.
3. Press **Cmd-Shift-W** to spell check the document. WordPerfect quickly highlights Belew. Since Belew is one of the officers of FLG, click **Add** to add his last name to the dictionary.
4. Momentarily, FLG is highlighted. Click **Add** to add FLG to the dictionary.
5. WordPerfect next highlights "customor." Notice WordPerfect offers a typographic suggestion (customer) and three phonetic suggestions (including customer).

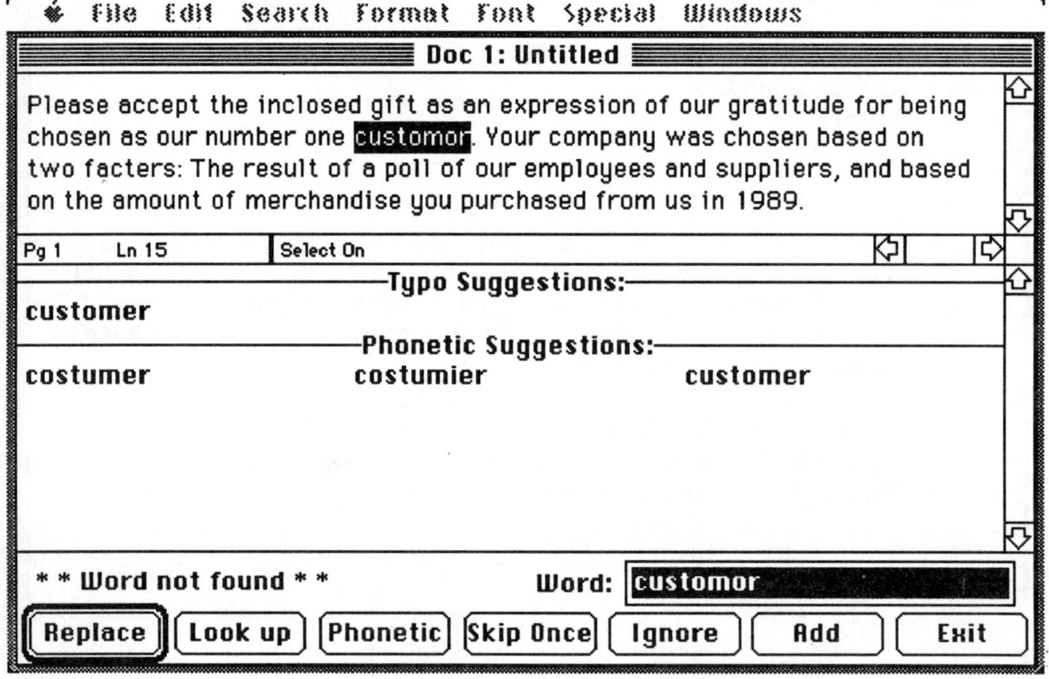

6. Click on **customer** and click **Replace** or press **Return**.
7. WordPerfect next highlights "facters." Click on **factors** and click **Replace** or press **Return**.

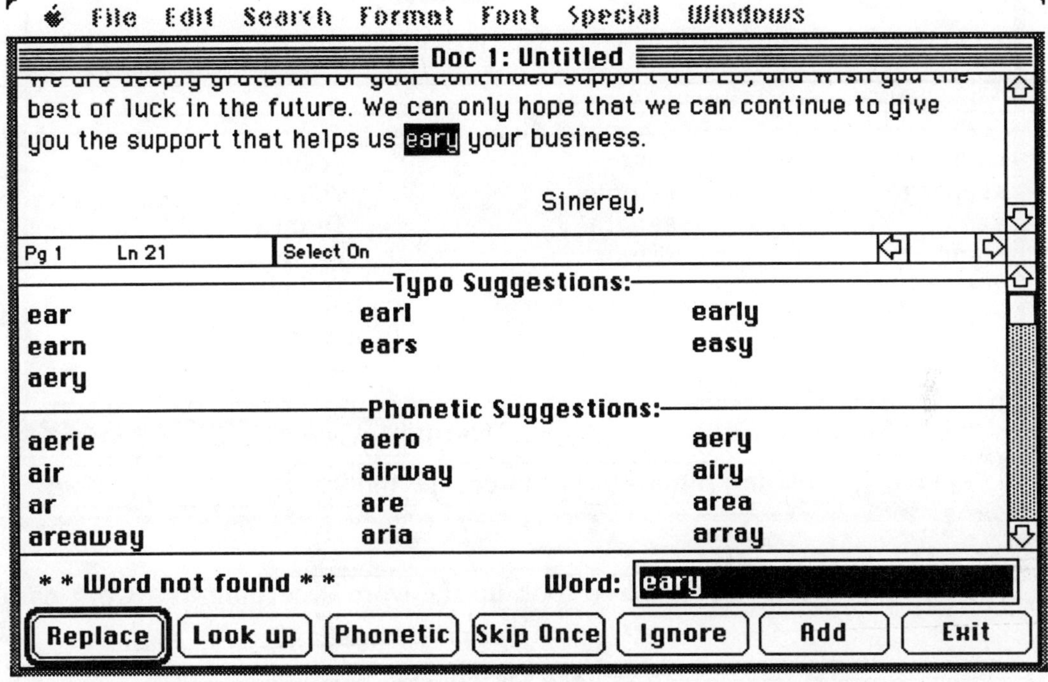

8. WordPerfect next highlights "eary." Click on **earn**, then click **Replace** or press **Return**.
9. WordPerfect next stops on "Sinerey." Notice WordPerfect does not offer the correct spelling.

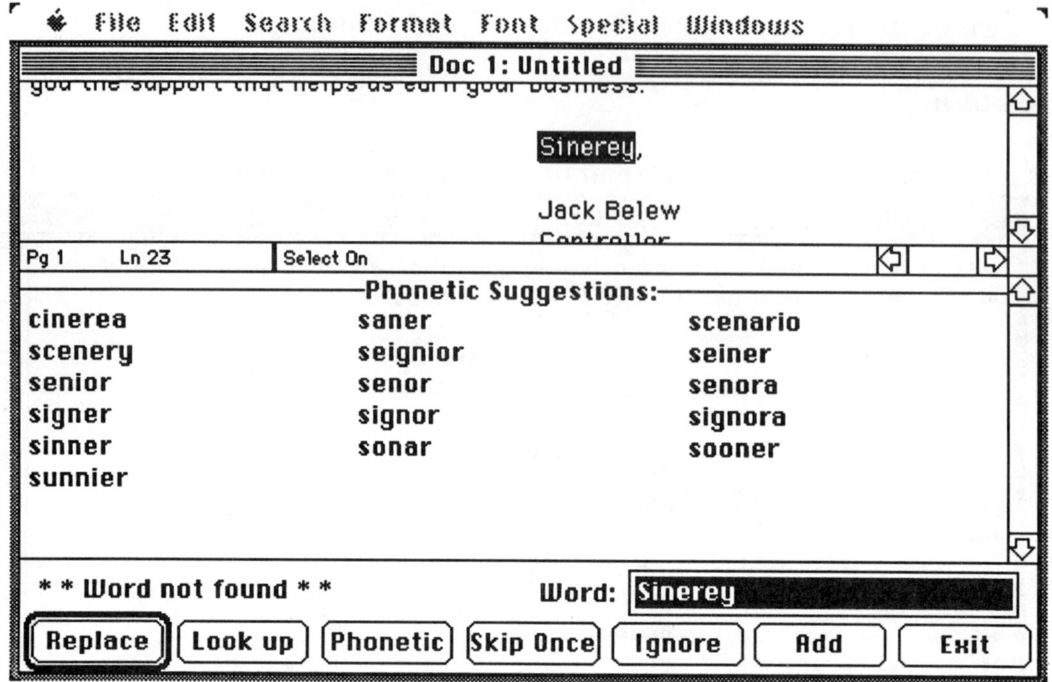

10. Type **sin*y** and click **Look Up** to look up the word according to a word pattern.

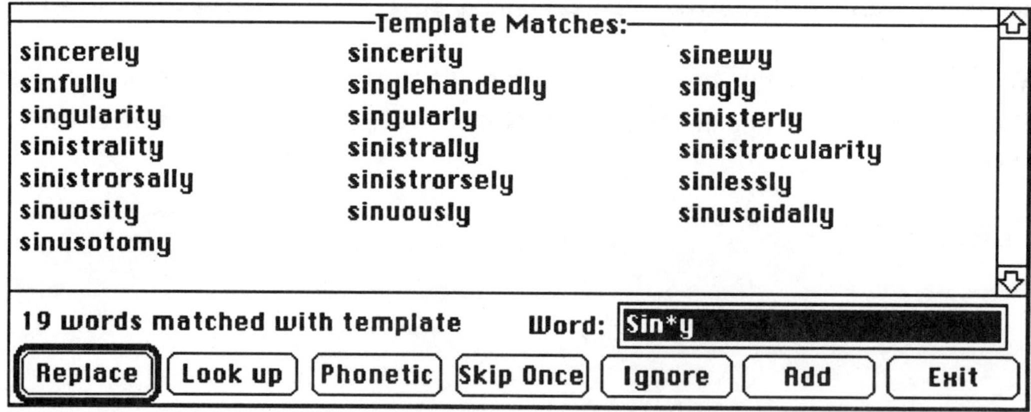

11. Click on **sincerely** and click **Replace** or press **Return**.

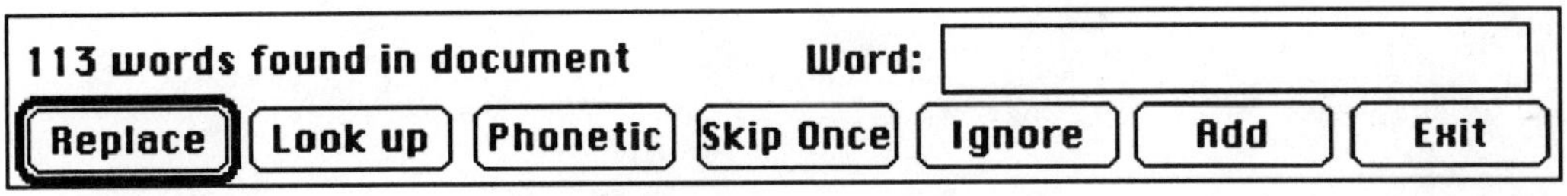

113 words found in document Word:

Replace | Look up | Phonetic | Skip Once | Ignore | Add | Exit

12. Click **Exit** to return to the document.
13. Click on **Yes** when the dialog box appears asking if you want to save changes to "User Dictionary." Then click on **Save** to save User Dictionary as "User Dictionary."
14. Press **Cmd-S** and type **Thank You Letter**. Then press **Return** to save the document.
15. Press **Cmd-K** to close the document. Then turn to Module 41 to continue the learning sequence.

Module 39

STYLE

DESCRIPTION

WordPerfect's Style feature offers you several different ways to emphasize text on-screen. You can boldface, underline, italicize, outline, shadow, and overstrike text. You can also subscript and superscript text, as described in Module 40, and redline and strikeout text, as described in Module 31. Text printed in an alternate style stands out in a document:

> **Boldfaced text looks like this.** Underlined text looks like this. *Italicized text looks like this.* Outlined text looks like this. Shadow text looks like this.

To change the style in a document, either type the command sequence associated with that style change, click on the appropriate letter in the Style Bar on the Status Line, or select Style from the Font menu and click on the style change from the Style menu.

Changing Styles With Keystrokes To change styles with keystrokes, press the appropriate keystroke, then type the text. You can also highlight the text you want to change to a certain style and then press the appropriate keystroke. You can use one or more of the following styles at one time:

Style Change	*Keystrokes*
Boldface	Cmd-Shift-B or F6
Underline	Cmd-Shift-U or F8
Italics	Cmd-Shift-I
Outline	Cmd-Shift-O
Shadow	Cmd-Shift-S

When you have finished typing the text in the style you want, press Cmd-Shift-P to return to plain text.

Changing Styles With The Style Bar To change styles with the Style Bar on the Status Line, click on the letter for the appropriate style, then type the appropriate text. You can also highlight the text you want to make a certain style and then click on the letter for the appropriate style.

P B U I O S S¹ S₁

From left to right, the letters correspond to plain, bold, underline, italics, outline, shadow, superscript, and subscript. When the style is selected, the designated letter in the Style Bar is highlighted in its appropriate style.

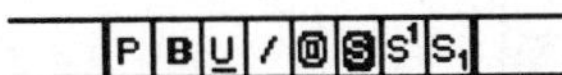

To return text to plain, click on P.

Changing Text With The Style Menu To change text with the Style menu, select Style from the Font menu.

Font

Style

✓1. Plain Text
2. **Bold** ⌘⇧B
3. Underline ⌘⇧U
4. *Italics* ⌘⇧I
5. Outline ⌘⇧O
6. Shadow ⌘⇧S

7. Superscript
8. Subscript
9. Options...

A. Overstrike ⌘⇧V
B. Strikeout
C. Redline

Click on the appropriate style change. If you select more than one style, each has a check mark next to it. Type the appropriate text, then return to the Style menu and click on Plain Text. You can also highlight the text you want to make a certain style and click on the appropriate style selection or selections.

Character Style The final way to select style is through the Characters dialog box. To do this, select Characters from the Format menu or press Cmd-5.

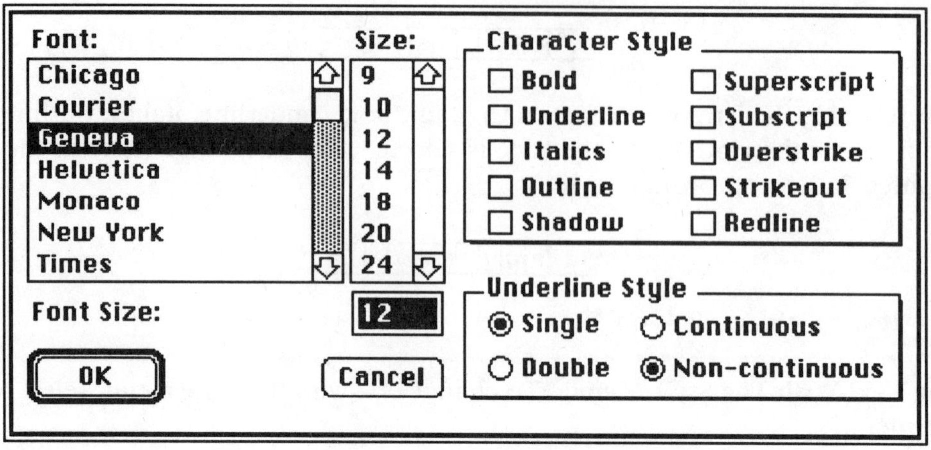

Font: Chicago Courier Geneva Helvetica Monaco New York Times
Size: 9 10 12 14 18 20 24
Font Size: 12
OK Cancel
Character Style
Bold Superscript
Underline Subscript
Italics Overstrike
Outline Strikeout
Shadow Redline
Underline Style
Single Continuous
Double Non-continuous

Click on the appropriate box or boxes, then click OK or press Return. Type the appropriate text, then select P from the Style Bar on the Status Line.

Underline Style Underlining is normally displayed as a single, non-continuous line, meaning tabs are not underlined, but spaces are. You can change the appearance of the underlining through the Characters dialog box. The options are:

- Single, non-continuous (tabs are not underlined)
- Single, continuous (tabs are underlined)
- Double non-continuous (double underlines, tabs are not underlined)
- Double continuous (double underlines, tabs are underlined).

To change the style for underlining, select Characters from the Format menu or press Cmd-5. The same dialog box that appears in the previous section appears. Click on the appropriate style for the underline, then click OK or press Return.

NOTE

You can change these settings throughout a document. If you want to underline tabular headings, for example, you can turn Tab Underline on at the beginning of the line you want to underline, and turn it off when you are finished. Alternatively, you can change the default settings through WP Defaults (Appendix B).

Changing Styles Back to Plain Text To change styles back to plain text, highlight the text and click on P from the Style Bar. Or, click on the appropriate style again to turn it off.

Overstrike The Overstrike feature lets you type letters over each other.

APPLICATIONS

Use Style changes for special emphasis. Italicized, underlined, outlined, shadow, and boldfaced text can be used interchangeably. Outlined or shadow text looks good for titles. Underlining should be used when adding columns of numbers. At the bottom of an accounting column, you might want to use a double underline. Continuous underlines are useful for titles.

Do not use these special effects indiscriminately, however. Using too many of them in a single document tends to make your document look busy and cluttered. The content of the document will lose out to the effects in the document.

TYPICAL OPERATION

Style is an important option for improving the appearance of text. This example illustrates this.

1. If necessary, start WordPerfect. Then create a document similar to the following:

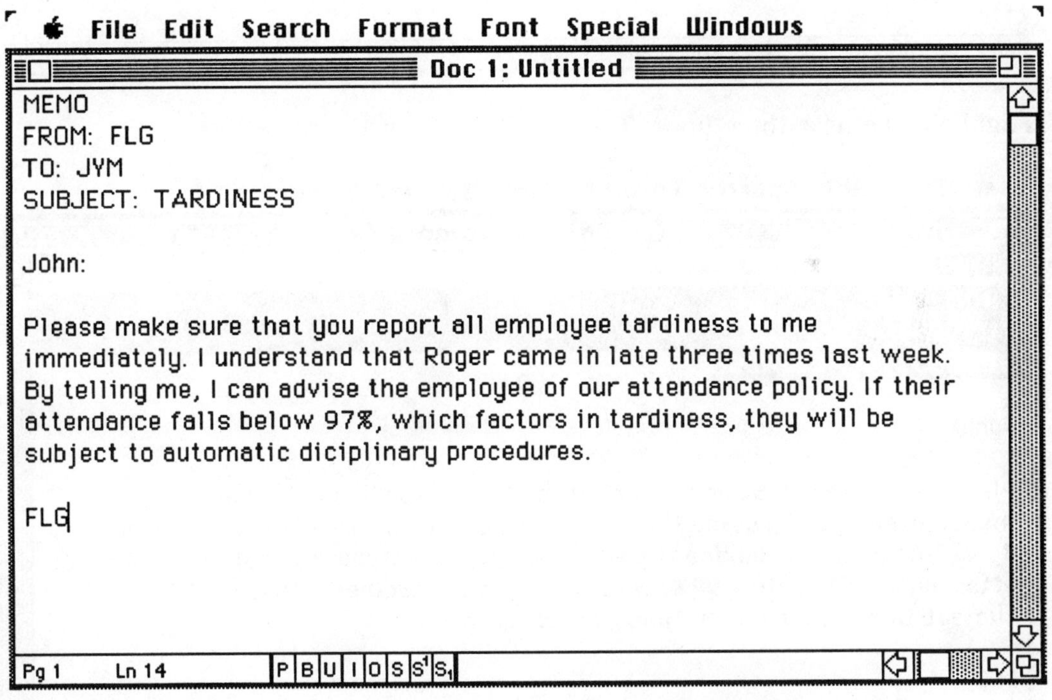

2. Highlight "MEMO." Then click on **S** on the Style Bar.

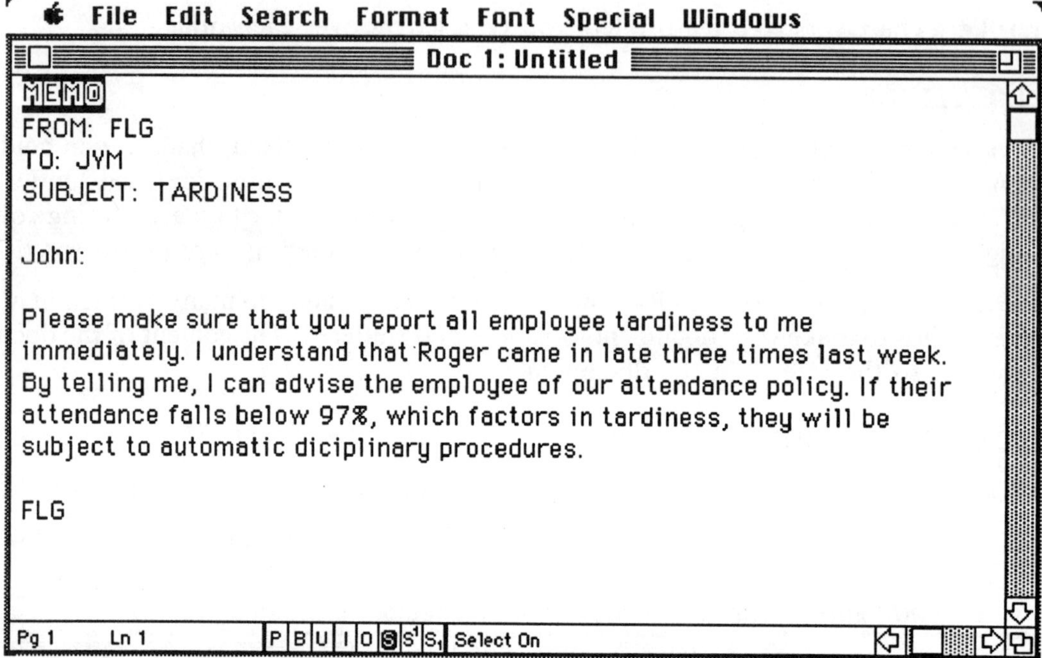

3. Highlight the next three lines. Then click on **B** on the Style Bar.

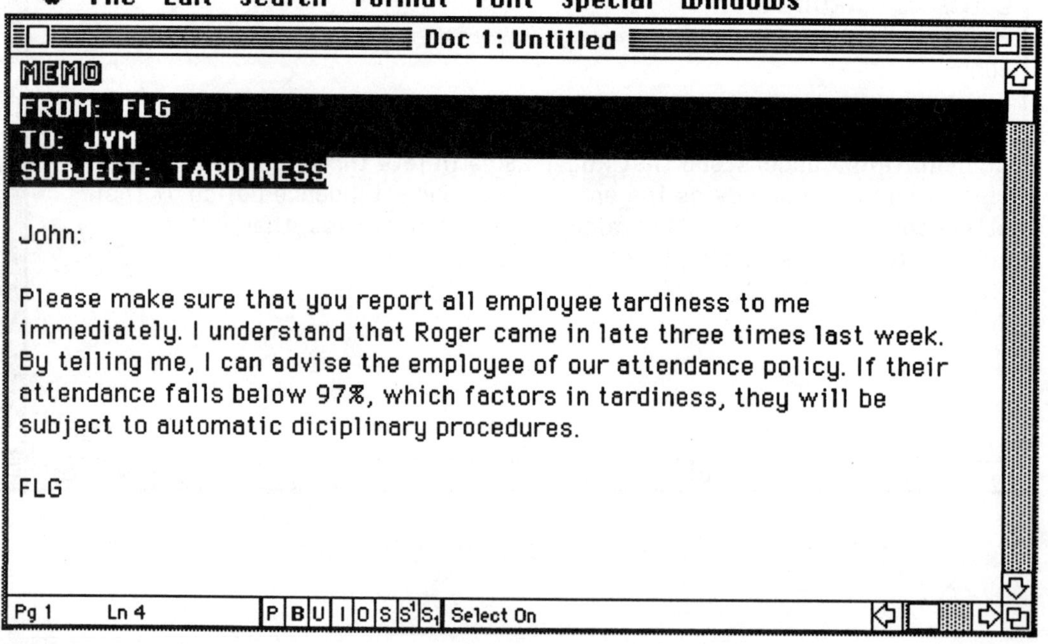

4. Highlight the first sentence in the memo. Then click on **U** on the Style Bar.
5. Highlight the initials "FLG" at the bottom of the document. Then click on **I** on the Style Bar.

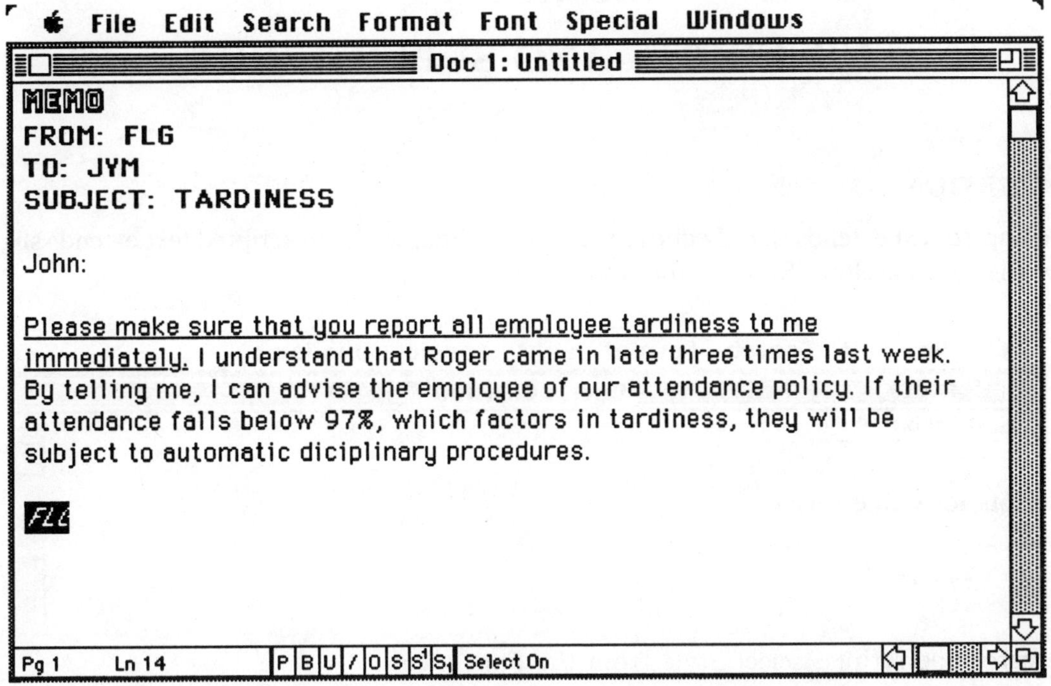

6. Press **Cmd-S**. Then type **Tardiness Memo** and press **Return** to save the document.
7. Press **Cmd-K** to close the document. Then turn to Module 6 to continue the learning sequence.

Module 40

SUBSCRIPTS AND SUPERSCRIPTS

DESCRIPTION

Superscripted text extends slightly above the text baseline, while subscripted text extends slightly below the text baseline. Superscripts look like this:

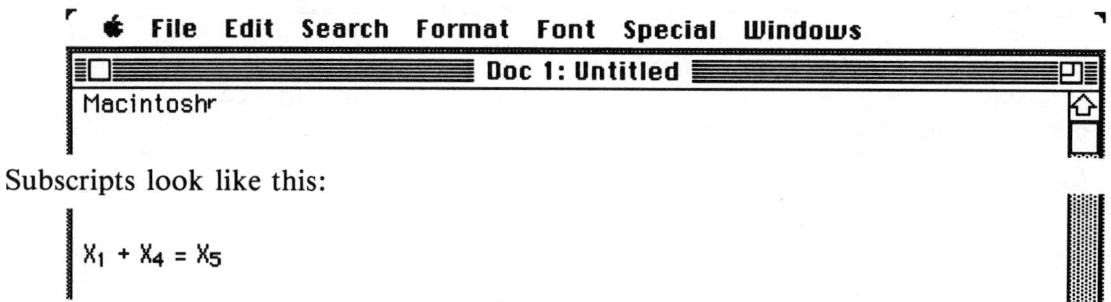

Subscripts look like this:

To create superscripts, select Style from the Font menu.

Font

Style

✓1. Plain Text
2. Bold ⌘⇧B
3. Underline ⌘⇧U
4. *Italics* ⌘⇧I
5. Outline ⌘⇧O
6. Shadow ⌘⇧S

7. Superscript
8. Subscript
9. Options...

A. Overstrike ⌘⇧V
B. Strikeout
C. Redline

Type or click on 7. Type the text you want superscripted, then select Superscript again from the Style menu to turn superscripting off. Alternatively, you can also turn on superscripting by clicking on its symbol (S^1) on the Status Line. To turn off superscripting, click on the symbol again.

To create subscripts, type or click on 8 from the Style menu. Type the text you want subscripted, then select subscript again from the Style menu to turn subscripting off. Alternatively, you can also turn on subscripting by clicking on its symbol (S_1) on the Status Line. To turn off subscripting, click on the symbol again.

NOTE

To delete a superscript or subscript, use the Codes key (Cmd-7) and follow the procedures in Module 7 for deleting codes.

You can also select text for subscripting or superscripting with the mouse, cursor keys, or Select command as described in Module 37.

SUBSCRIPT AND SUPERSCRIPT OPTIONS The way subscripts and superscripts are displayed on-screen and printed later on is determined by you. To choose the style of a subscript or superscript, select Options from the Style menu.

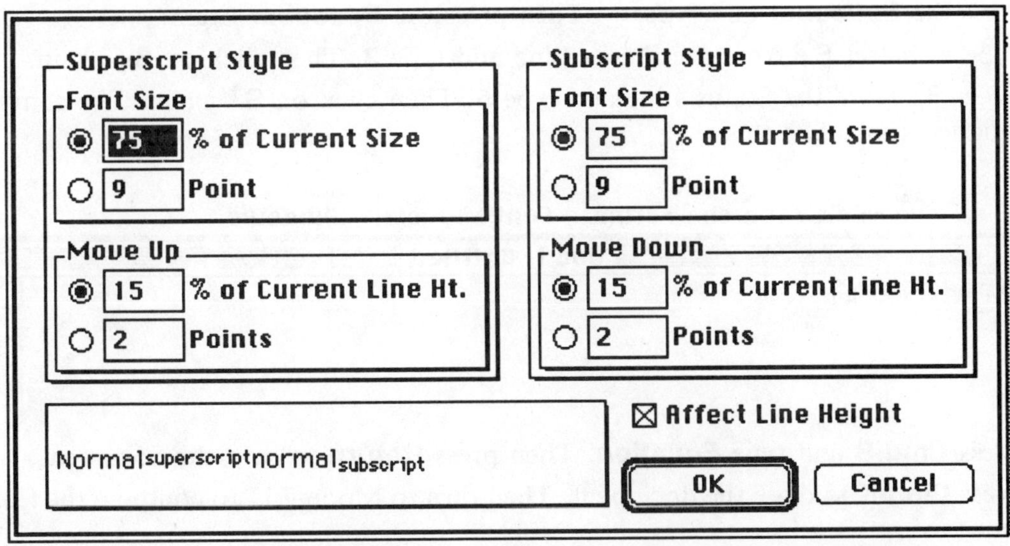

The screen shows the default settings for superscripts and subscripts. Both are 75 percent of current size (11 point in our case). Both are moved 15 percent from the current line height (3 points in our case). And both superscripts and subscripts affect line height.

To change these settings, click on the appropriate box and type a new value. If you type a new percentage, the point value below it changes automatically. And if you type a new point value, the percentage above it changes. When you have finished making changes, click OK or press Return.

APPLICATIONS

Subscripts are most commonly used in mathematical equations. Superscripts are used for trademarks, patent marks, and in mathematical equations.

TYPICAL OPERATION

This operation shows you how to subscript and superscript text in a document. Assume you are creating an equation.

1. If necessary, start WordPerfect. Then type **x**. Select $\mathbf{S_1}$ from the Status Line and type **1**. Then click on $\mathbf{S_1}$ again.
2. Select $\mathbf{S^1}$ from the Status Line and type **2**. Then click on $\mathbf{S^1}$ again.
3. Press the **Spacebar** and type **+**. Then press the **Spacebar** again.
4. Type **x**. Select $\mathbf{S_1}$ from the Status Line and type **2**. Then click on $\mathbf{S_1}$ again.
5. Select $\mathbf{S^1}$ from the Status Line and type **3**. Then click on $\mathbf{S^1}$ again.
6. Press the **Spacebar** and type **=**. Then press the **Spacebar** again.
7. Type **x**. Select $\mathbf{S_1}$ from the Status Line and type **3**. Then click on $\mathbf{S_1}$ again.
8. Select $\mathbf{S^1}$ from the Status Line and type **5**. Then click on $\mathbf{S^1}$ again. The completed equation looks like this:

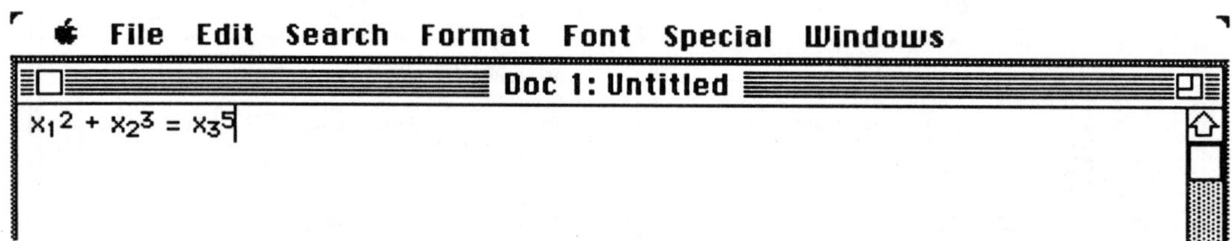

9. Press **Cmd-S** and type **Equation**. Then press **Return** to save the document.
10. Press **Cmd-K** to close the document. Then turn to Module 17 to continue the learning sequence.

Module 41

THESAURUS

DESCRIPTION

The Speller (Module 38) makes sure all the words in your document are spelled correctly. The Thesaurus helps make sure you use just the right word in all parts of your documents. The Thesaurus works just like a book version, but with the convenience of being electronic. WordPerfect does the searching for you; you do not have to thumb through a book.

The Thesaurus lets you select many of the words in your document. Words that can be selected are called *headwords*. WordPerfect includes synonym and antonym references for more than 10,000 such headwords. If a word cannot be selected, WordPerfect gives you a "Not a Headword" message.

The synonyms and antonyms WordPerfect retrieves are called *references* and are listed on the Reference menu. References are organized into *subgroups*. Subgroups are groups of references with the same connotation. The Thesaurus also separates references into nouns (n), verbs (v), adjectives (a), and antonyms (ant). There may be more than one subgroup in any of these classifications.

You can search among references that are headwords (identified by a •) to find even more references. Or you can find references for unrelated headwords. In this way, you can put up to three headwords and their references on-screen at any time.

All references are listed in columns. There is room for three columns of words. Use the cursor control keys to move between columns. Use the Elevator Button on the Scroll Bar to move down a column. You can also use Cmd-Enter or the Go To key to move between subgroups.

To use the Thesaurus, move the cursor to the word you want to find synonyms for. You can also type the word once you have started the Thesaurus. In this case, assume you are looking for synonyms for the word "better." If you have a diskette-based system, put the Thesaurus diskette in drive B. If you have a hard disk system, you should have already copied the Thesaurus onto your hard disk in Module 2. If the Thesaurus is not in the same folder as the WordPerfect file, you will be asked to tell WordPerfect what folder the Thesaurus is in.

CAUTION

Do not remove the Thesaurus diskette from drive B until you are through using it.

Select Thesaurus from the Special menu, or press Cmd-T or Alt-F1.

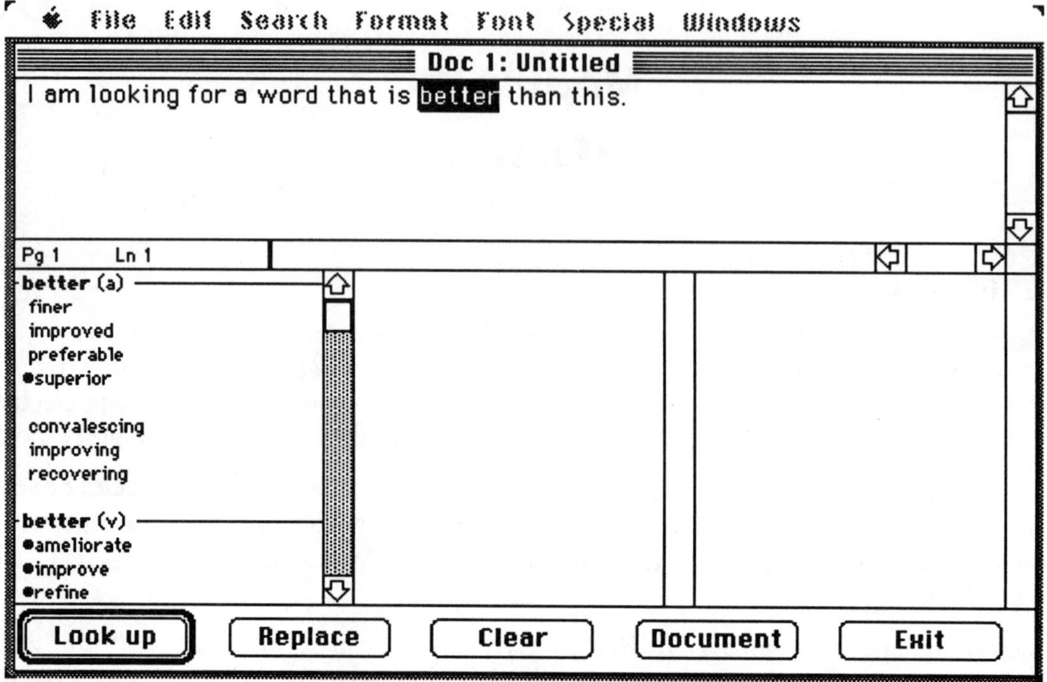

Use the Scroll Bar to locate other synonyms and antonyms for better. Notice there are six subgroups for "better," two adjective subgroups two verb subgroups, and two antonym subgroups.

Notice that all of the verb and antonym references have bullets next to them, making them headwords, while only one of the adjective references is a headword.

Highlight a headword and either double click on it or click Look Up or press Return twice to look up the synonyms and antonyms for that word. Or, highlight another word in the text and click Look Up to look up the synonyms and antonyms for that word.

If you select the Thesaurus when the cursor is not in a word, the following screen appears:

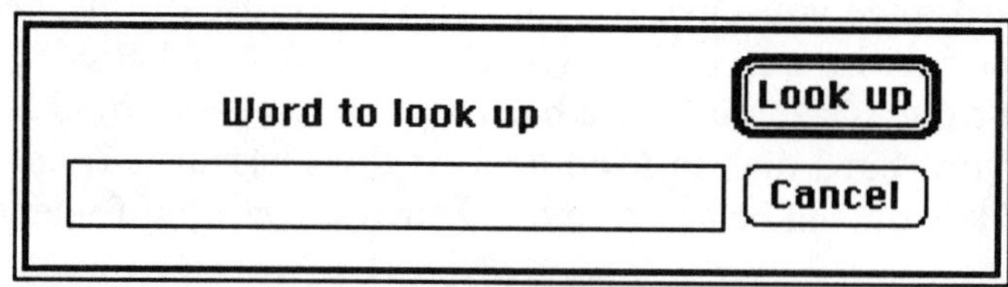

Type the word to look up and click Look up or press Return.

To replace one word with another, highlight the word in the Thesaurus and click Replace to replace the word in the document with the selected word from the Thesaurus.

If you want to select another word to reference, but there is not any room, you can clear a column. To clear a column, click Clear to clear all columns in the Thesaurus to make it ready to look up more words.

Click Document to move around your document while still using the Thesaurus.

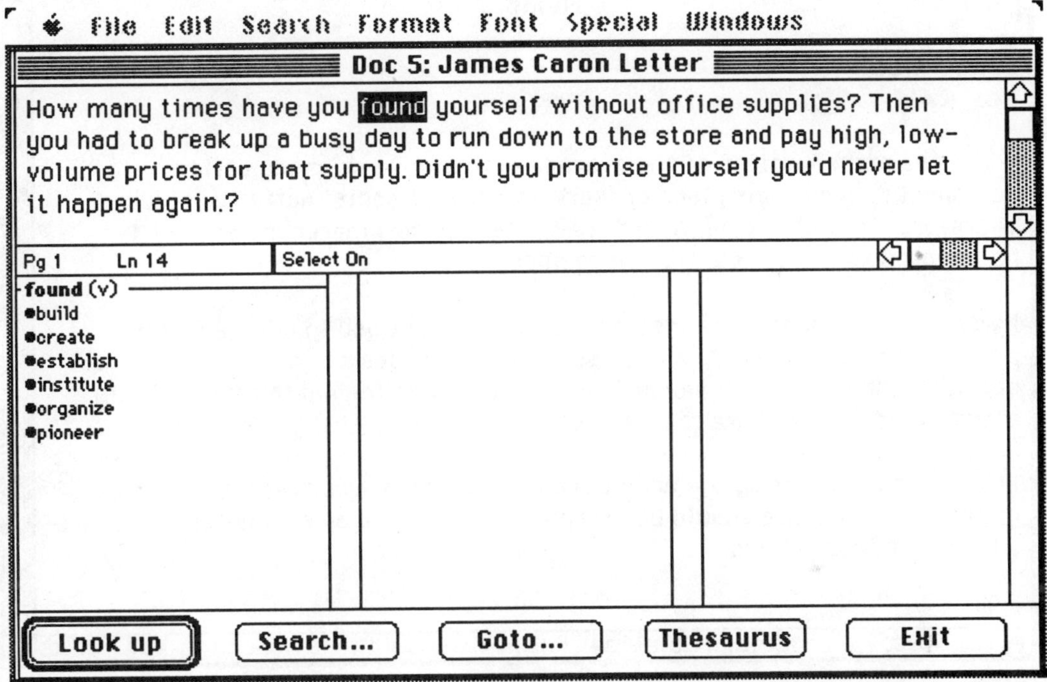

This is useful for seeing more of the text around a word. Use the Scroll Bar to scroll through a document. Use the Search or Goto buttons to quickly move through the document. You can edit an entire document with the Thesaurus active with the Document button. This is generally not practical, however, because only a few lines of text are visible at a time.

Moving Between Columns To move between columns, either click on the words in the next column, or use the Left and Right Arrow keys to move between columns. Use the Up and Down Arrow keys to move through a column. The active column has a Scroll Bar in it.

APPLICATIONS

A Thesaurus helps improve the quality of your writing. Use it whenever you want a better word than the one you have chosen. WordPerfect lets you choose synonyms, in the form of nouns, verbs, and adjectives, and antonyms (words that are the opposite of the selected word).

TYPICAL OPERATION

Use the Thesaurus in this example to improve the writing quality in a memo.

1. If necessary, start WordPerfect. Then create a document similar to the following:

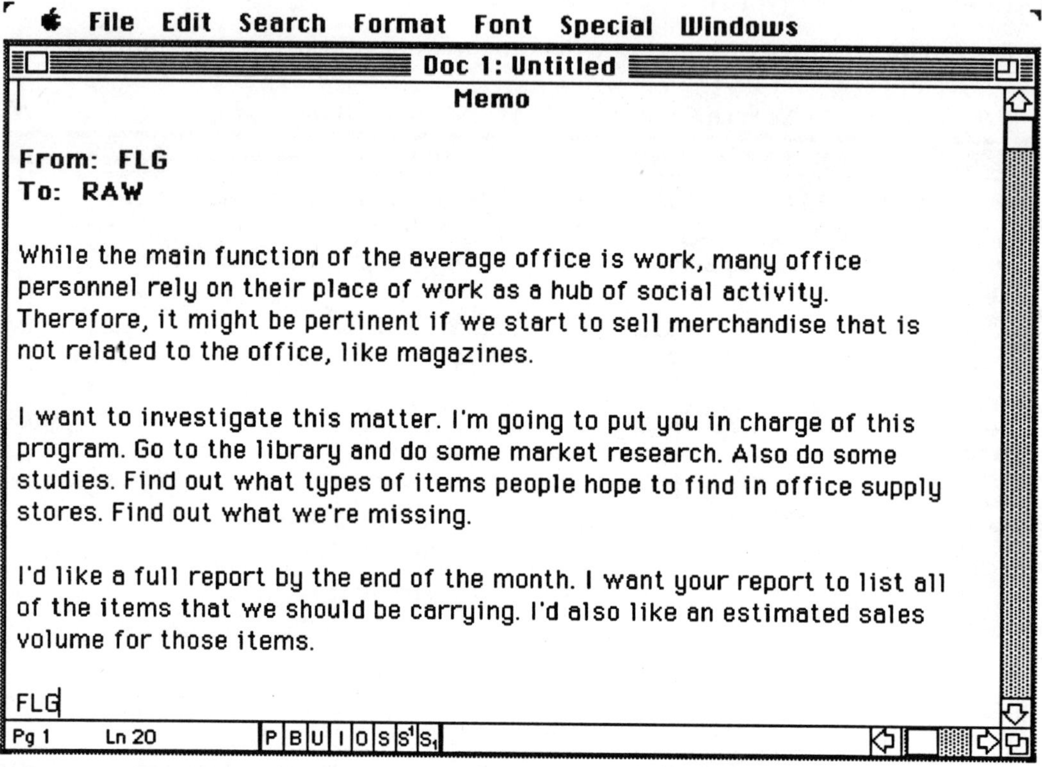

2. Move the cursor to the word "function" on line 5 and press **Cmd-T**.

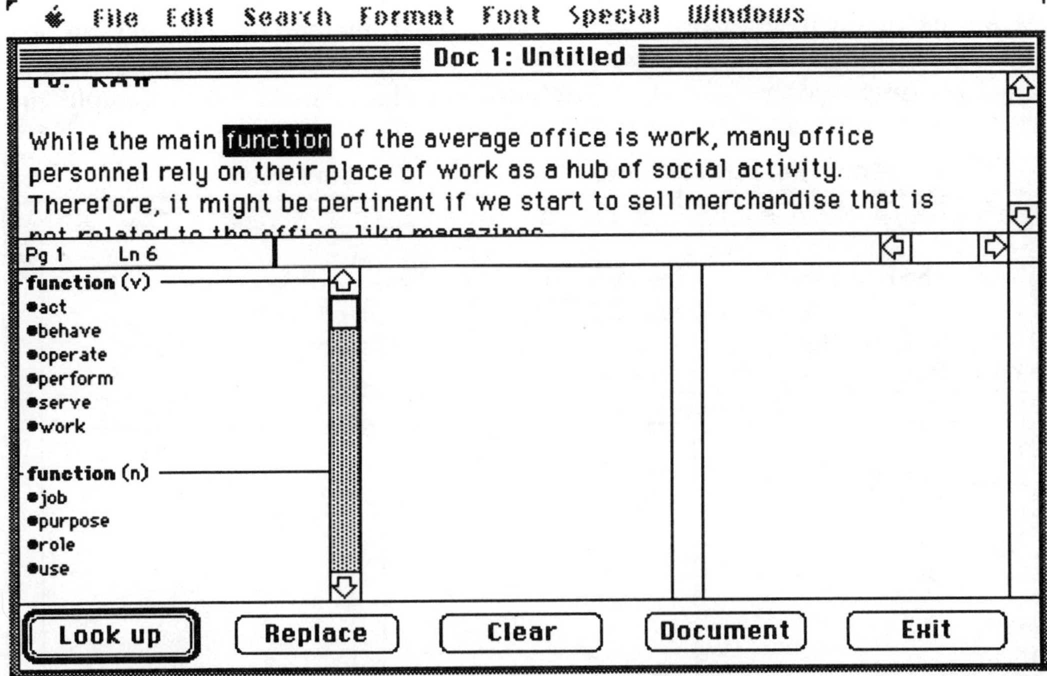

3. Click on **purpose**, then click **Replace**.

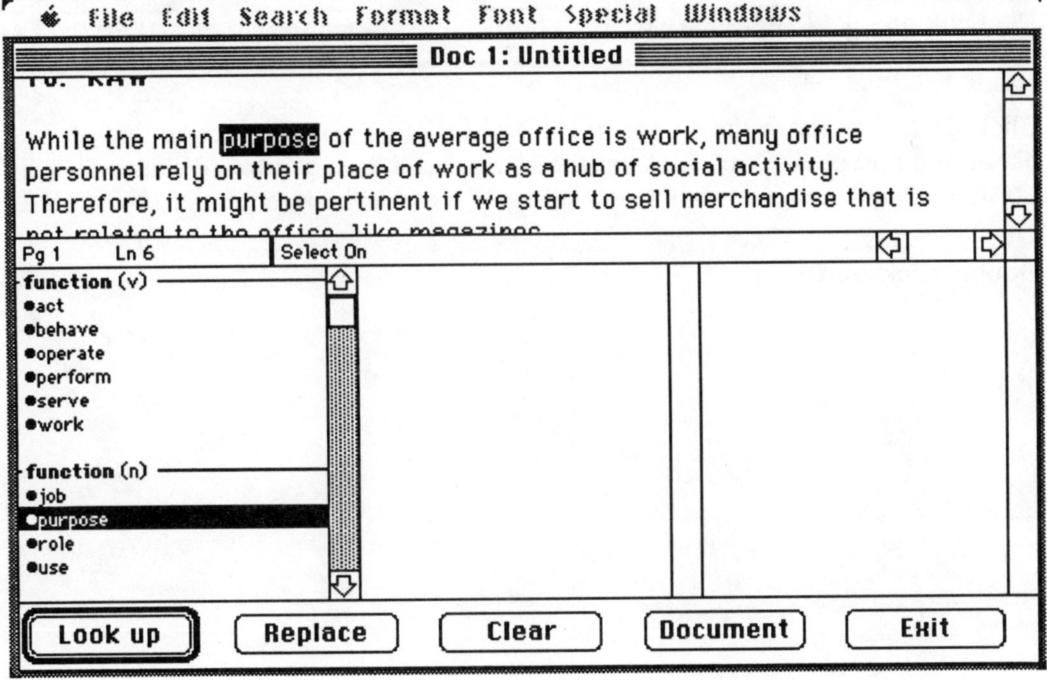

4. Move the cursor to the word "work" on the next line and double click on it. Click on **Thesaurus** and press the **Down Arrow** key to find the word "employment." Then highlight **employment** and click **Replace** to replace "work" with "employment."

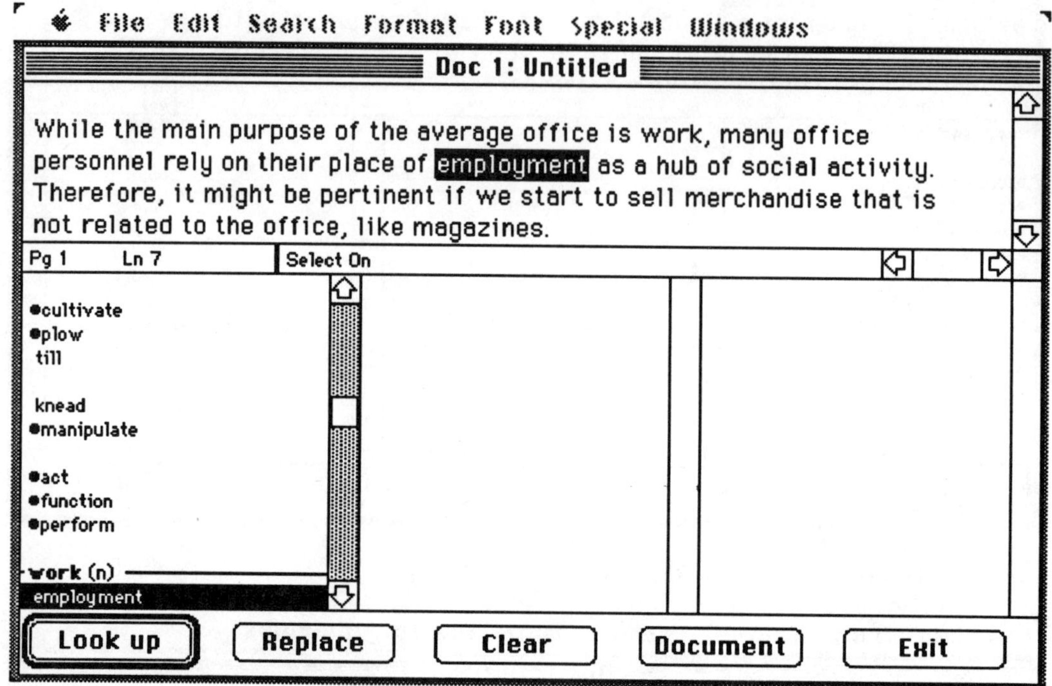

5. Click **Exit**, then move the cursor to the word "items" on the second line of the third paragraph and press **Cmd-T**. After the message, "Not a headword" appears, click on **Look up**, type **item**, and click **Look up** again. Notice the references for "item" appear on-screen.

6. Double click on **thing**.

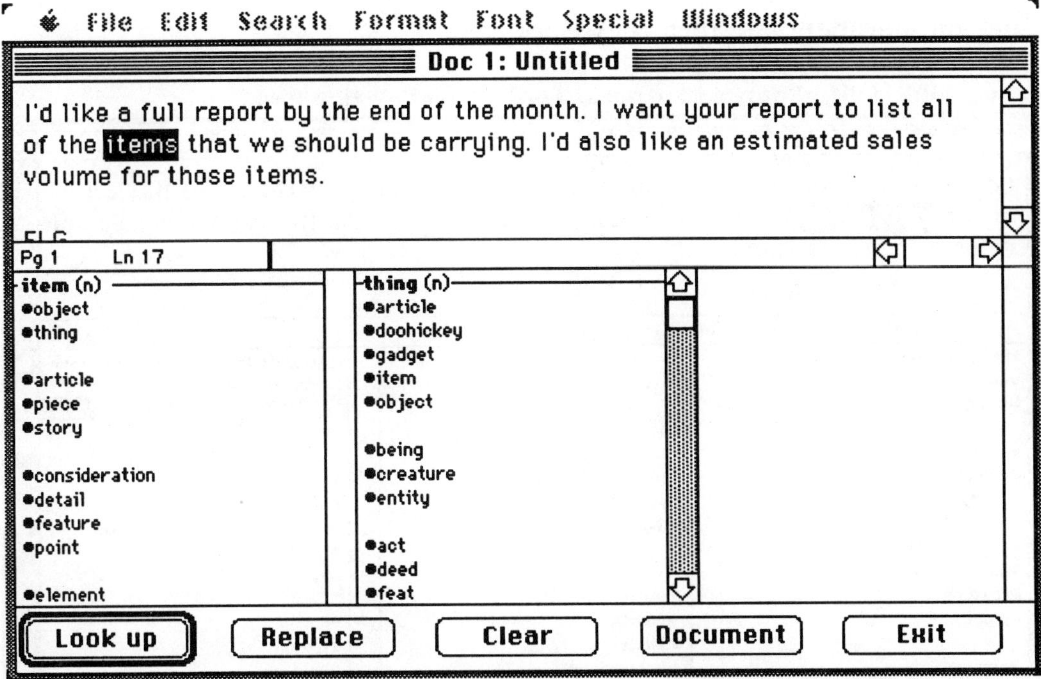

7. Scroll down through the listings under thing and double click on **goods**.

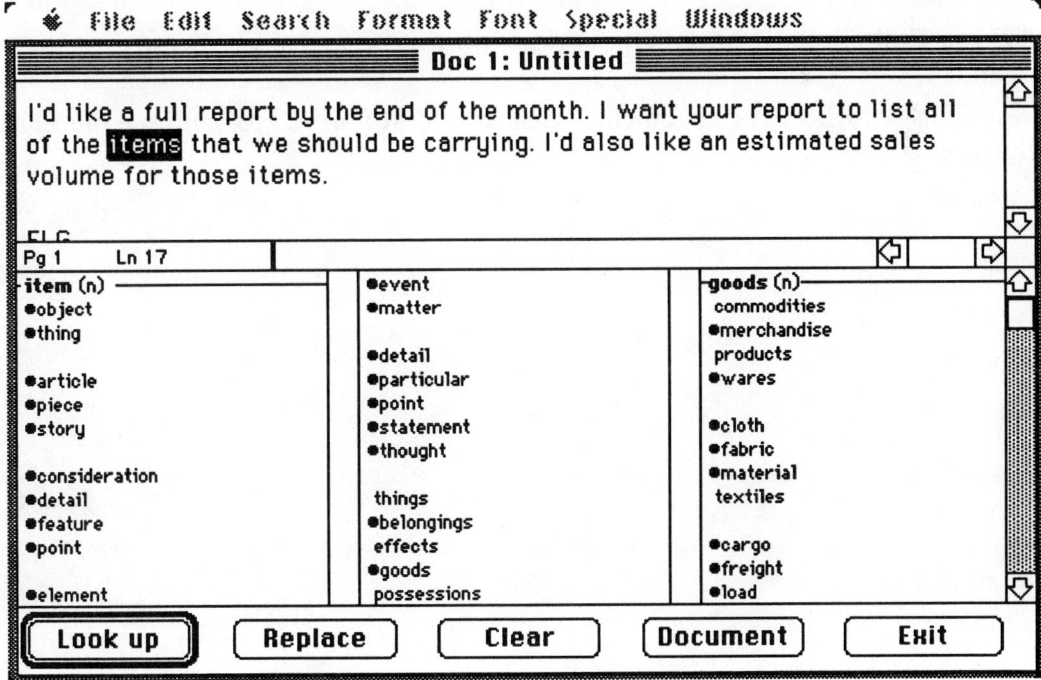

8. Click on **merchandise**, then click **Replace**.

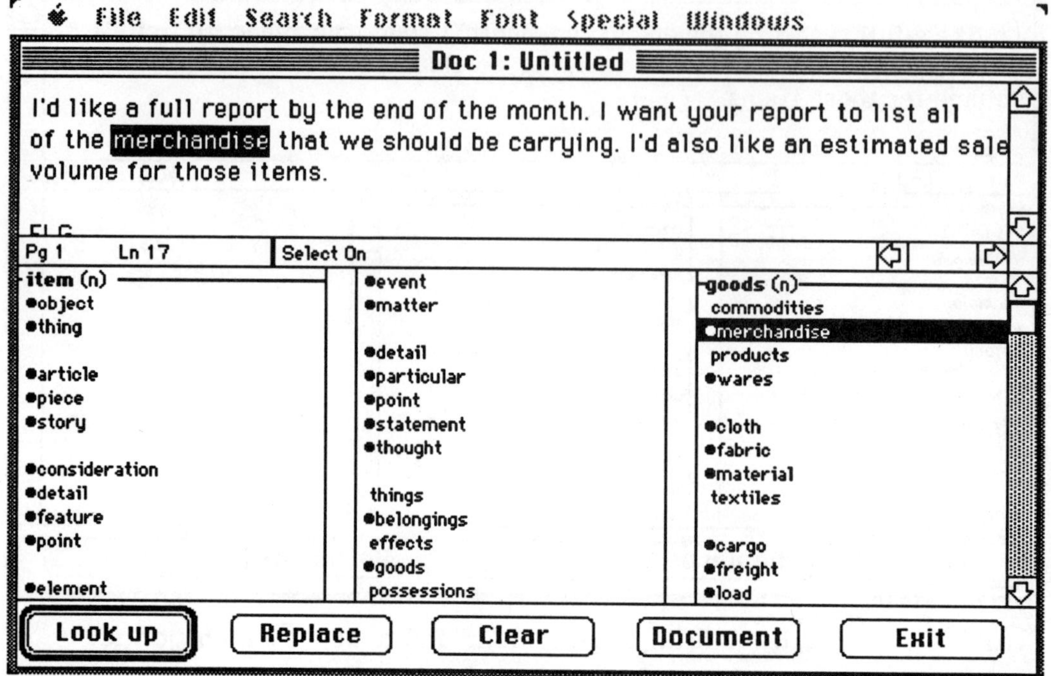

9. Click on **Exit**. Press **Cmd-S**, type **Magazine Sales**, and press **Return** to save the document.
10. Press **Cmd-K** to close the document. Then turn to Module 25 to continue the learning sequence.

Appendix A
TERMS AND DEFINITIONS

Term	*Definition*
Alignment Character	A certain character along which columns of numbers or text are aligned vertically. The typical alignment character is a decimal point.
Alphanumeric	Including both letters and number characters.
Application Program	Software that includes information for use. Typical application programs provide database management, word processing, spreadsheet, and communications aid.
Append	To add a selection of text to the end of a selected file.
ASCII	Acronym for American Standard Code for Information Interchange. It is the character set used in data communications. Also called text files.
Automatic Rewrite	Command that automatically rewrites (rewraps lines of text) to account for editing changes.
Backspace	A key that deletes characters and codes to the left of the cursor.
Backup Copy	An additional copy of a diskette or program that acts as insurance in case something happens to the original. The process of creating a backup copy is called "backing up" a diskette or file.
Binding Width	The width used to determine the available space for binding text or putting punch holes in a document.
Bit	A single binary digit used in combination with others to form characters that are usable by computers. In general, eight bits make a byte.
Block	A selected segment of a document. Blocks can be manipulated — copied, deleted, underlined, etc.
Block Protect	A WordPerfect function that keeps all of a designated block of text together on the same page.
Boldface	A means of darkening or highlighting text so that it stands out from the rest of a document.
Byte	A single computer character made up of eight binary digits called bits.
Cancel	WordPerfect's "oops" key that lets you undo or nullify a particular action.

Term	*Definition*
Case Conversion	A feature that changes a block of text to either all uppercase or all lowercase letters. In the case of all lowercase letters, the first word of each sentence retains initial capitalization, as do words like "I" and "I'm."
Center	An editing function that positions the designated text so that approximately the same number of characters appear to the right of center as to the left.
Character	A single letter, number, space, punctuation mark, or other symbol placed on the monitor by the computer keyboard.
Chooser	A Macintosh desk accessory that allows the user to tell WordPerfect what printer to use and where it is connected. The Chooser also allows the user to log on to a local area network, select an electronic mail system, or connect to a modem if any are available.
Clipboard	An area of memory that holds what was last cut or copied from the text, or from another program. Clipboard information can be textual, graphical, or both.
Close	To put a document back into its folder without leaving an application or to put a window back into its icon.
Codes	Symbols that tell the printer and computer where to insert a tab, change spacing or margins, and many other functions. WordPerfect hides these codes so you see them only when you use Codes.
Colors	Feature that allows the user to change the on-screen color of background, foreground, and highlighted text if you have a Macintosh that supports color.
Columns	The process of defining a group of columns. Columns may be parallel, where independent information is kept separately, or newspaper style, where information flows continuously.
Computers	A machine that facilitates manipulation of information like words, numbers, and pictures.
Copy	An editing function that duplicates a designated body of text. It "pastes" the copied text in another part of the document and leaves the original section intact.
Cursor	A screen indicator that shows where the next character typed will appear.
Cursor Control	Term referring to the activity of using the mouse and cursor keys to manipulate the position of the cursor on the screen.
Cut	Removing highlighted information from a document. The user can then move the cursor to another location and paste the information there.
Data	Information. Data can be in many forms including words, figures, and commands. Data is also the information used to create documents and the documents themselves.

Term	*Definition*
Date	A command that inserts today's date in various formats at the current cursor position.
Default	The value that the program automatically designates. The default remains in effect until the user changes it. The user can set the default repeat value to 16, for example. It remains 16 until changed. The user can also change the default folder or drive, so WordPerfect accesses a different directory on command.
Delete	The word processing function whereby text is erased from a document.
Desk Accessory	A program, accessible from the Apple menu at the left side of the screen. Once loaded into the system, these desk accessories are always available from the Apple menu. Some common desk accessories include the Chooser, the Find File, the Control Panel, and the Calculator.
Desktop	The Macintosh screen when no applications are open. The Macintosh desktop includes disk drive icons, the Trash, and the Menu Bar at the top of the screen. It also includes files and folders.
Dialog Box	A box on the screen that requests information or a decision from the user.
Diskette	A magnetic object that stores programs and data. Also called a disk.
Drive	A device that houses diskettes or a hard disk. It serves as the mechanism to record and retrieve data stored on the diskettes or hard disk.
Edit	A word processing function that permits creation of new files and modification of existing ones.
Endnote	Information, at the end of a document, that provides further details about a subject in the text.
Escape	A command that uses a repeat value to allow the user to perform the same activity (like deleting or typing a specific character) a set number of times.
File	A computer-generated document or program.
Filename	The name given to a file. It is usually up to 31 letters, characters, and spaces and identifies the contents of the file.
Finder	The Macintosh program that allows management of files and disks.
Flush Right	Term that describes text flush against the right margin.
Folder	A location on a disk (hard or floppy) designated to keep certain groups of files. A folder can be compared to a folder in a filing cabinet.
Font	A specific typeface, point size, and weight, such as 12-point Times italic.
Footer	A portion of text that is placed at the end of a page and repeated throughout the document.

Term	Definition
Format	The physical arrangement of a document, including margins and character and line spacing, that contributes to determining the appearance of a printed page. Also, the process of preparing diskettes so they can store data.
Go To	A word processing function used to send the cursor to a specific place in a document or a specific page.
Hard Copy	The printed version of a file.
Hard Disk	A rigid disk that is more rugged and stores more data than a floppy diskette. It can be inside the computer or in a separate drive.
Hard Page Break	A code that WordPerfect inserts when Cmd-Return is pressed to create a new page.
Hard Return	A code that WordPerfect inserts when the Return key is pressed to move to the next line.
Header	One or more standard lines of text, such as a chapter title, located at the top of a page within a document.
Help	A WordPerfect function that summarizes the functions and keys to help the user choose what action to take. It can be used while editing a document and serves as a first step before using the manual or this book.
Hyphenation	An option that separates a long word at the end of a line so that lines of text are more equal. This improves the appearance of the printed version of the document.
Indent	To align text along a tab stop. Pressing the Indent key moves the cursor to a tab stop. This temporarily changes the left margin so that all text typed until the user presses Return lines up along the tab stop.
Index	A WordPerfect function that lets a user automatically generate an index. The index can include the location of special terms used in a document.
Insert	An editing function that allows the introduction of characters, words, entire passages of text, figures, or other information at a designated point in an existing document.
Italics	A text treatment that slants letters to the right. It is a means of making text stand out from the rest of the document.
Justification	The creation of an even right margin by printing the last character on each line in the same right column. It is achieved by printing a document with extra space between words (and sometimes characters, depending on the printer used). Document justification is a printing, not an editing, function.
Kerning	Spacing between letters. WordPerfect sets letter spacing automatically to eliminate excessive white space.

Term	*Definition*
Leading	Pronounced "ledding." The spacing between lines. WordPerfect measures leading in terms of line height, which is the distance from the top of one line to the top of the next.
Line Format	A WordPerfect function that sets the format for each line of text in a document. It sets centering, flush right, tabs, margins, hyphenation, spacing, kerning, and other functions.
Lines Per Inch	The number of lines printed in a vertical inch. The standard line spacing is six lines per inch.
List Files	A WordPerfect function that lists all the files in a particular directory. It includes options for copying, deleting, renaming, retrieving, printing, searching for, and looking at a file. Options are also available for changing the default directory and retrieving DOS files.
Lists	A WordPerfect function that allows creation of up to five lists per document. The lists can be lists of tables or illustrations in a document, or used for any other purpose.
Macros	A feature that allows the "recording" of a series of keystrokes into a file for "playback" at a later time.
Mark Text	A WordPerfect function that marks text for use in index, list, and table of contents generation. This key also marks text for redlining and strikeout of text.
Menu	A list of options from which to select an activity. WordPerfect includes menus on-screen, pull-down menus from the top of the screen, and pull-out menus that pull out from pull-down menus.
Merge	The process of combining two documents to form a third. Printed merged documents are created from a "primary file," which contains boilerplate material, and a "secondary file," which lists the variable items, such as names and addresses.
Monitor	A device that attaches to a computer to display what is entered on the keyboard. The Macintosh Plus and SE have a built-in monitor.
Mouse	A device that connects to the computer to allow the user to point to cursor locations, pull-down menus, and click on options.
Move	An editing function used to identify an area of text (from a single character, up to entire pages) and position it at another point in a document.
Outline	A WordPerfect mode that acts as a "thought organizer." Each time the Return key is pressed, the next level of the outline is reached. Levels can be changed (i.e., from 11 to A) by pressing the Tab key.
Page	A designated number of lines that constitute a single page within a document. Pages are divided automatically by WordPerfect.

Term	*Definition*
Page Break	The boundary between two pages. Soft page breaks are created automatically by WordPerfect. Hard page breaks are created by the user.
Paragraph Numbering	A WordPerfect feature that automatically keeps track of paragraph numbers. This is useful for procedural steps. In the past, adding a step in the middle of a long procedure required renumbering the paragraphs by hand. WordPerfect automatically renumbers the paragraphs or steps.
Paste	The act of retrieving text or graphics from the Clipboard and putting it into a document.
Printing	The process of sending a document or part of a document to an attached printer so a hard copy of the document can be printed or distributed. WordPerfect allows printing of a document, a page, or a block of text.
Quit	To leave an application.
RAM	Acronym for Random Access Memory. It is temporary memory devoted to currently used computer information. RAM is erased when the power is turned off.
Redline	A mark that identifies text an editor recommends be added to a document.
Replace	A WordPerfect function that allows substitution of a character string in a document.
Required Space	A space positioned between two characters that prevents them from separating during editing or pagination.
Return	The key used to move the cursor to the next line (this is called a hard return). Pressing Return in a menu or dialog box generally accepts the default selection.
ROM	Acronym for Read Only Memory. It is permanent memory used by the computer to run. ROM is not erased when the power is turned off.
Scroll Bar	A bar displayed at the right of the screen that provides information as to the cursor's location in a document. Using the Elevator Button or the arrows in the Scroll Bar allows the user to move quickly through the document.
Search	A WordPerfect function that locates a character string in a document. The user can search forward or backward in a document at any time.
Search and Replace	A function similar to search, except once a character string is located, it is replaced. A confirm option offers the option of not replacing this occurrence of the character string.
Soft Return	When a user runs out of space on a line of text, WordPerfect automatically moves the cursor to the next line. It does this by inserting a Soft Return code into the document. This process is also known as word wrapping.

Term	*Definition*
Spell Check	The process of using the WordPerfect Speller utility to check the spelling of each word in a document.
Status Line	The last line on the screen. It shows the cursor location, the style of text being used, and messages.
Strikeout	A mark that identifies text an editor recommends be deleted from a document.
Style	A style of text, such as boldface, underline, italics, shadow, and outline.
System	A collection of programs that make the Macintosh work. This is generally the operating system and a series of other programs that determine the rules by which the Macintosh and application programs written for it operate.
Tab	A WordPerfect feature that places tabs and indents in specific locations in a document.
Table of Contents	A WordPerfect feature that automatically generates a table of contents based on information provided in a document.
Thesaurus	A WordPerfect feature that offers synonyms and antonyms for selected words in a document.
Title Bar	A bar at the top of the screen that identifies the filename of the document being edited. It also includes a Close Box to close a document quickly and a Zoom Box to change the size of the document.
Troubleshooting	The practice or technique of narrowing possibilities to discover how to correct a malfunction or problem.
Typeover	Opposite of insert. Types over text, deleting old letters and inserting new simultaneously.
Underline	The effect of putting a line underneath text to make it stand out from the rest.
Widow/Orphan	A widow is the last line of a paragraph appearing by itself on the first line of a page. An orphan is the first line of a paragraph appearing by itself as the last line of a page.
Window	A pocket of information into which disks, folders, and documents open.
Word Count	The number of words in a document. The Speller utility provides a word count.
Word Processing	The activity or computer program that allows the user to manipulate (edit) words in a document.
Word Wrap	A feature that automatically moves text that does not fit on one line down to the next.

Appendix B
WORDPERFECT DEFAULTS

WordPerfect defaults let you set up system defaults for initial settings of margins, tabs, folders, backup options, and other functions as illustrated in the following table:

Setting	*Default*
Alignment Character	Decimal Point
Date	Month, date, year
Endnote/Footnote	Note number is superscript
Font	Geneva
Hyphenation	On
Hyphenation Zone	6.75 inches to 7.5 inches
Lines Per Inch	6
Margins	1 inch from top, bottom, left, and right margins
On-Screen Justification	On
Page Number Column Position	Left-1 inch, Center-4.5 inches, Right-7.5 inches
Page Numbers	Off
Printed Justification	Off
Spacing	Single spacing
Tabs	Every .5 inches from the left side of the page
Text Style	Plain
Underlining	Non-continuous single
Widow/Orphan Protection	Off

All these settings are saved in a file in the System Folder called WP Defaults. After you change any of the settings, you can create a new WP Defaults folder to make these changes the new default settings for WordPerfect. To change defaults, change any of the settings, then select WP Defaults from the File menu.

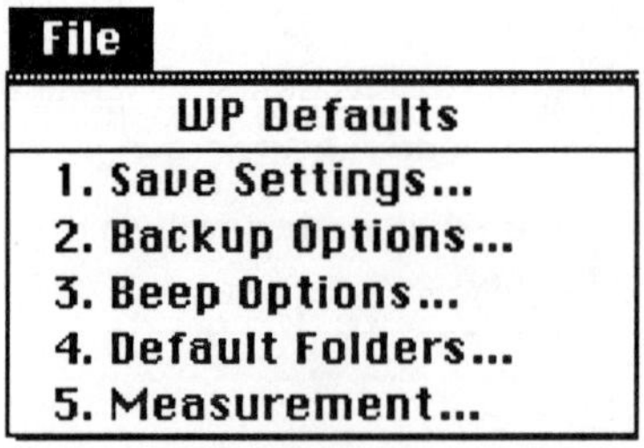

File

WP Defaults

1. Save Settings...
2. Backup Options...
3. Beep Options...
4. Default Folders...
5. Measurement...

Type or click on 1.

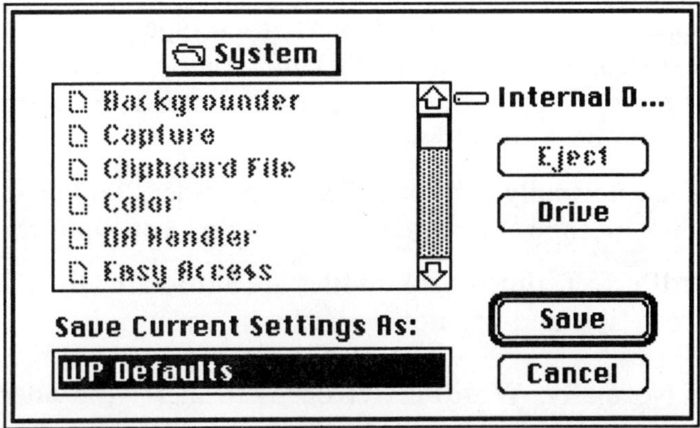

WordPerfect saves its defaults file in the System Folder. Whenever you change defaults, it asks you if you want to replace the WP Defaults file. To do this, click on Save or press Return. In response to the prompt asking you if you want to replace the existing file, click on Yes.

You can also type a new filename at this prompt to save custom default file. To use a custom default files, double click on the default file of your choice to start WordPerfect. The defaults in this file become the initial settings for this document.

A number of other default options are also available from the WP Defaults menu.

NOTE

After you change any of the default options in the WP Defaults menu, you must save a new defaults file by clicking or typing 1 from the WP Defaults menu.

BACKUP OPTIONS Normally, WordPerfect does not backup your files. But you can instruct WordPerfect to automatically backup your files every few minutes. You can also instruct it to automatically create a backup copy of an original document after you open it. That way, the original is always available should you choose to use it rather than the changed file. The original file is renamed Filename Backup. To set backup options, type or click on 2 from the WP Defaults menu.

Backup Options

Type
☐ Timed Backup Every [ ] Minutes
☐ Original File Backup

OK
Cancel

Timed Backup Folder
WORDWARE:System Folder:

Set

To select timed backup, click on Timed Backup, then type how often you want files to be backed up. To select Original File Backup, click on Original File Backup. You can click both options if you want them. Then click OK or press Return. Type or click on 1 from the WP Defaults file to save the backup settings.

Timed backup files are normally kept in the System folder. To keep them somewhere else, click on Set, then click on the folder and/or drive where you want the backup files stored.

When you quit WordPerfect, timed backup files are automatically deleted. Original backup files are stored as real files and are not deleted when you quit.

BEEP OPTIONS Normally, WordPerfect beeps to alert you when a word needs to be hyphenated, when an error occurs, and when a search fails. To change this, type or click on 3 from the WP Defaults menu.

Click on any of the boxes to turn off the beep option and click OK or press Return. Then type or click on 1 from the WP Defaults menu and save the new WP Defaults file.

DEFAULT FOLDERS This option lets you tell WordPerfect where to save documents and where a variety of files are located. These include the *work folder,* where documents are stored; the *temporary files folder,* where temporary files, such as backup files, are found; the *macro files folder,* where macro files are stored; and the *Speller/Thesaurus folder,* where the Speller and the Thesaurus are located.

The default locations for these files are:

Work Folder — Undefined
Temporary Files Folder — System Folder
Macro Files Folder — WordPerfect Folder
Speller/Thesaurus Folder — WordPerfect Folder

To change these settings, type or click on 4 from the WP Defaults menu.

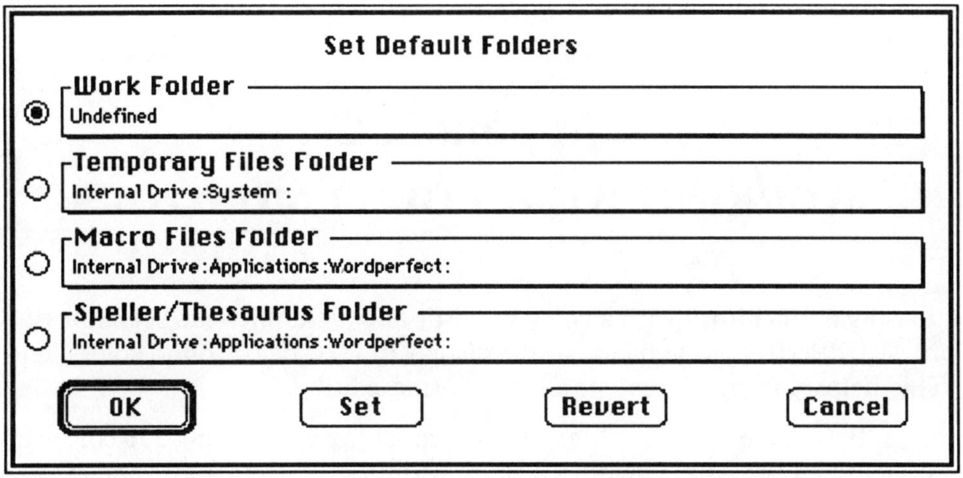

Set Default Folders

Work Folder
Undefined

Temporary Files Folder
Internal Drive :System :

Macro Files Folder
Internal Drive :Applications :Wordperfect :

Speller/Thesaurus Folder
Internal Drive :Applications :Wordperfect :

OK Set Revert Cancel

Type or click on the setting you want to change and click on Set.

WordPerfect then displays the Select Work Folder diaglog box. Click on the appropriate folder by opening folders, changing drives, and then clicking on the drive icon. Then click on Set to set the folder as the default folder. Then click on OK or press Return. Then type or click on 1 from the WP Defaults menu and save the new WP Defaults file.

MEASUREMENT The default setting for measurement options in WordPerfect is inches. But you can also choose centimeters or points. To do this, type or click on 5 from the WP Defaults menu.

Measurement Preference

Units
Inches
Centimeters
Points

OK Cancel

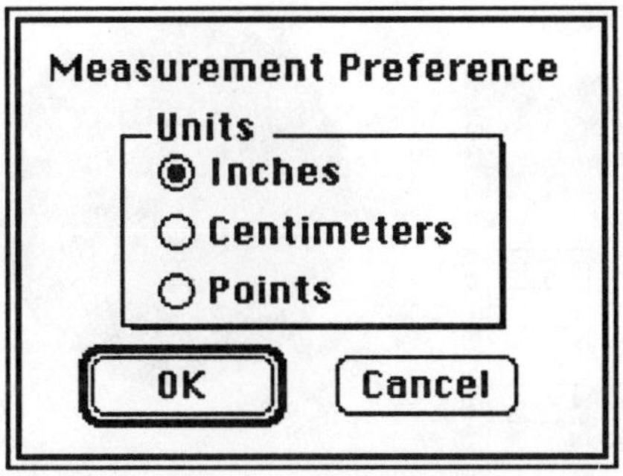

Type or click on the measurement option of your choice and click OK or press Return. Then type or click on 1 from the WP Defaults menu and save the new WP Defaults file.

Appendix C

WORKING WITH COLOR MONITORS

If you are using a Macintosh with a color monitor and a graphics card capable of displaying 256 colors, WordPerfect lets you change the display of text, background colors, and highlight colors. This helps you make text stand out during editing.

To set colors, first make sure your Macintosh is capable of displaying 256 colors by selecting Control Panel from the Apple menu. Click on Monitors, select Color, and click on 256 for the number of colors. Then close the Control Panel and select Screen from the Special menu.

Special

Screen

1. Full Window ⌘⇧Z
2. Show Position
✓3. Display Justification ⌘⇧J
4. Fractional Widths
5. Colors...

Type or click on 5.

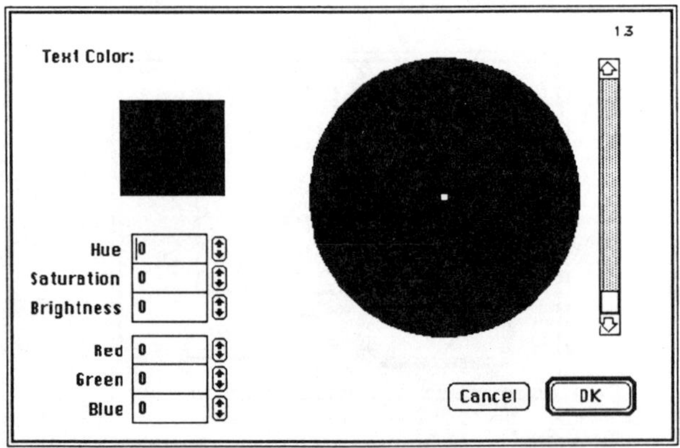

Using the arrow keys and Scroll Bar, adjust the hue, saturation, brightness, and red, green, and blue levels until you reach the desired color. Click OK or press Return. Then repeat the procedure for background and highlight colors. After you have finished, save the settings by selecting WP Defaults from the File menu and typing or clicking on 1. Then click on Save and click Yes to replace the old WP Defaults file.

Appendix D

WORKING WITH PC WORDPERFECT

While WordPerfect for the Macintosh has been available for only a short while, versions of WordPerfect for other computers abound. The most common version is WordPerfect for MS-DOS computers like the IBM PC. The current version of PC WordPerfect is 5.0.

Macintosh WordPerfect is directly file compatible with PC WordPerfect version 4.2. To use a PC WordPerfect 4.2 file, load it onto your Macintosh using a utility program. Many programs are available, including Apple File Exchange (included on your System Tools diskette) and MacLink Plus. Hardware devices like DaynaFile make the transfer process even easier, since you can load a diskette with PC WordPerfect files on it into a DaynaFile drive and directly read the data on it while using Macintosh WordPerfect. At this point, simply open the file you want to edit, either by pressing Cmd-O or Cmd-F5, or by selecting Open from the File menu. Select the file you want to open and either click on Open or press Return.

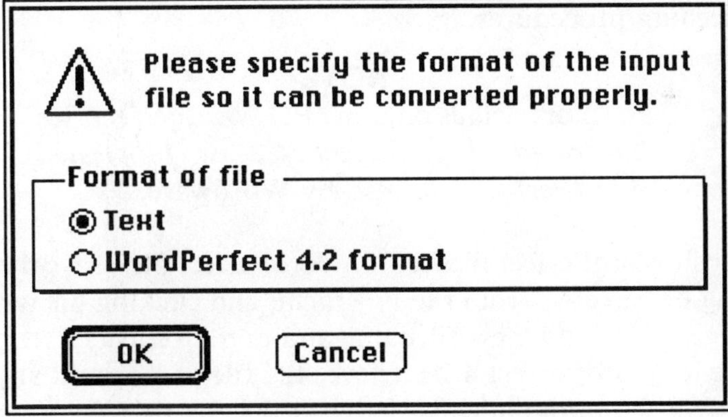

Click on WordPerfect 4.2 format and click OK or press Return. WordPerfect opens the file. It retains all formatting commands, such as boldface and underline.

To save the file as a WordPerfect Macintosh file, click on Save As from the File menu.

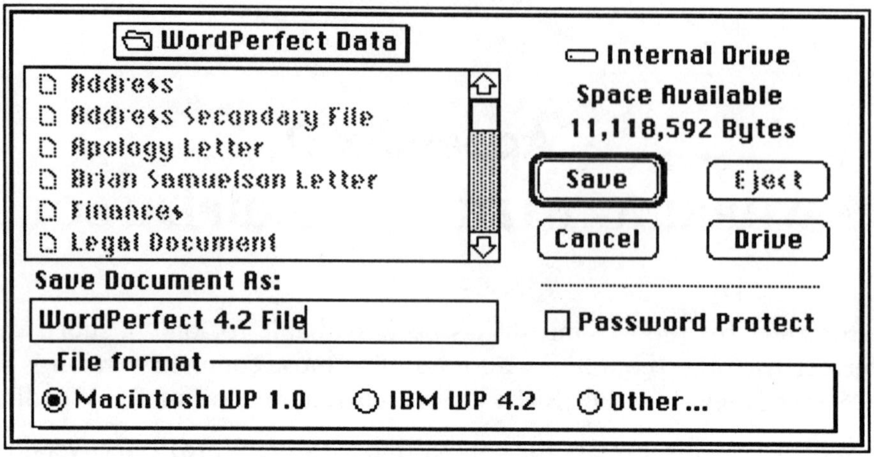

WordPerfect Data
Address
Address Secondary File
Apology Letter
Brian Samuelson Letter
Finances
Legal Document
Internal Drive
Space Available
11,118,592 Bytes
Save
Eject
Cancel
Drive
Save Document As:
WordPerfect 4.2 File
Password Protect
File format
Macintosh WP 1.0
IBM WP 4.2
Other...

Click on Macintosh WP 1.0, then rename the file if desired by typing a new filename. Then click on Save or press Return.

WordPerfect 5.0 files must be converted to WordPerfect 4.2 files before transferring them to the Macintosh, since Macintosh WordPerfect will not be able to read them otherwise. To do this, while in WordPerfect 5.0 with the file on the screen, press Ctrl-F5 and select WordPerfect 4.2 as the file format to save the file in. Then press Return to save the file. The file is now a WordPerfect 4.2 file and can be opened in WordPerfect Macintosh by following the preceding procedures.

NOTE

For more details on using PC WordPerfect, see *Illustrated WordPerfect 4.2* or *Illustrated WordPerfect 5.0,* also by Wordware.

To convert Macintosh WordPerfect files to PC WordPerfect files, save the files as WordPerfect 4.2 files by clicking on Save As from the File menu and clicking on WordPerfect 4.2 as the file option. Then give the file a new filename and press Return. After transferring the file to the PC, retrieve it. WordPerfect 4.2 retrieves the file as it would any other WordPerfect 4.2 file. WordPerfect 5.0 automatically converts the file to 5.0 format.

Appendix E

WORKING WITH OTHER MACINTOSH WORD PROCESSORS

WordPerfect may be the best word processor available for the Macintosh, but it was not the first and it will not be the last. As a result, WordPerfect works easily with other Macintosh word processors, particularly Microsoft Word 3.0 and MacWrite.

To save WordPerfect files with those of other word processors, open the file you want to save and either click on Save from the File menu or press Cmd-S or F7.

WordPerfect Data
Address
Address Secondary File
Apology Letter
Brian Samuelson Letter
Finances
Legal Document
Internal Drive
Space Available
11,112,448 Bytes
Save
Eject
Cancel
Drive
Save Document As:
Password Protect
File format
Macintosh WP 1.0
IBM WP 4.2
Other...

Click on Other for File Formats and press Return or click Save.

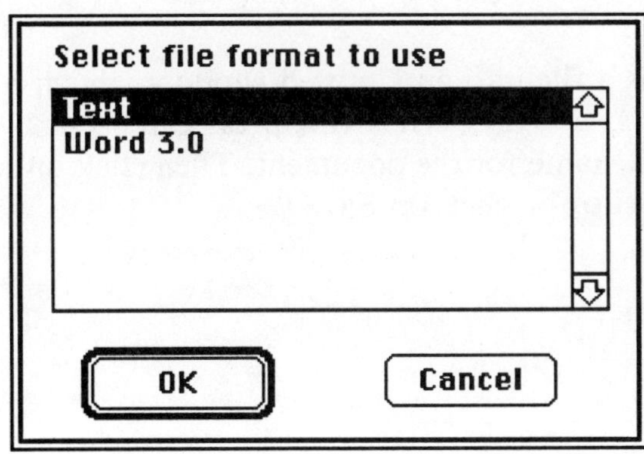

To use the file with Microsoft Word, click on Word 3.0, then press Return or click OK. To use the file with another Macintosh word processor, click on Text, then press Return or click OK.

Microsoft Word retrieves the file as it would any other Word file. The newest version of Word, version 4.0, retrieves the file as a Word 3.0 file.

Text files work with any Macintosh word processing packages including MacWrite, WriteNow, and FullWrite Professional.

Retrieving Word Processing Files WordPerfect retrieves any Word 3.0 file that is not saved in Word's Fast Save format into an Untitled window. To turn Fast Save format off, click on the Fast Save button in the Word File Save dialog box and press Return. If the box is not checked, Fast Save format is not selected. To retrieve a Word 4.0 file, first save it as a Word 3.0 file, then start WordPerfect and open the file.

WordPerfect also opens any MacWrite file without conversion into an Untitled window.

If you try to open a text file saved with another Macintosh word processor, the following screen appears:

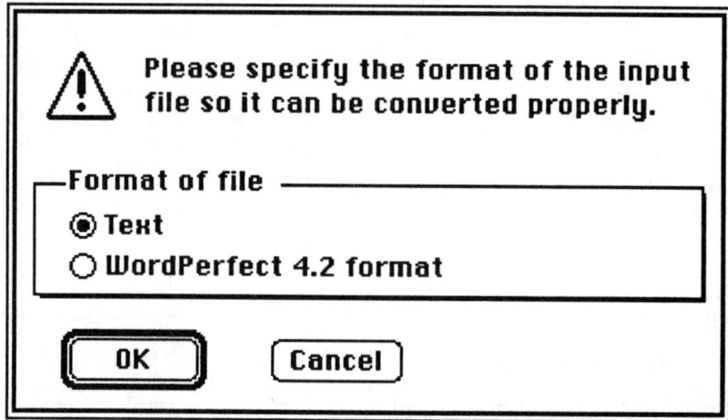

Click on Text, then press Return or click OK. WordPerfect opens the file into an Untitled window.

After WordPerfect opens a file into an Untitled window, give it a new filename by saving it. If you want to save it as a WordPerfect file, press Cmd-S or F7 or select Save from the File menu. Type a new filename for the document. Then click on Macintosh WP 1.0 as the file format and press Return or click on Save.

Appendix F

USING AN EXTENDED KEYBOARD

An Extended Keyboard is any keyboard that includes function keys, or F keys. The Apple Extended Keyboard and ones like it include 15 function keys across the top of the keyboard, numbered F1 through F15. Using the keyboard, you can quickly perform functions that otherwise would require multiple keystrokes or use of the mouse. The key sequences for these commands are listed throughout the book. If you are a user of PC WordPerfect, you may notice that many of the commands in PC WordPerfect are identical in the Macintosh version if you substitute the Control key on the PC for the Cmd key on the Mac and the Alt key on the PC for the Option key on the Mac.

The following table outlines WordPerfect's 60 function key commands.

Command	*Keystroke*
Append	Shift-F13
Bold	F6
Center	Shift-F6
Character Format	Shift-F1
Close	Cmd-F11
Columns	Option-F7
Columns On	Cmd-F12
Copy	F14
Cut	F13
Date	Shift-F5
Define Lists	Shift-F15
Footnote	Cmd-F7
Forward Search	F2
Flush Right	Option-F6
Go To	Cmd-F15
Help	F3
Indent	F4
Insert Literal	Option-F15
Left/Right Indent	Shift-F4

Command	*Keystroke*
Line Format	Shift-F8
List Files	F5
Macro Definition	Cmd-F10
Macro Invoke	Option-F10
Macro Options	Shift-F14
Mark Text	Option-F5
Merge	Cmd-F9
Merge Codes	Option-F9
Merge End of Field	F9
Merge End of Record	Shift-F9
Move	Cmd-F4
New	F11
Open	Cmd-F5
Outline	Option-F12
Page Format	Option-F8
Page Preview	Option-F14
Page Setup	Cmd-F8
Paragraph Format	Shift-F12
Paste	F15
Print	Shift-F7
Print Options	Cmd-F14
Quit	F7
Retrieve	Shift-F10
Reverse Search	Shift-F2
Show Clipboard	Cmd-F13
Show Ruler	F12
Save	F10
Save As	Shift-F11
Screen	Cmd-F3
Search and Replace	Option-F2
Select	Option-F4
Show Codes	Option-F3
Spell Check	Cmd-F2
Tab Align	Cmd-F6
Thesaurus	Option-F1
Transfer	Cmd-F1
Undelete	Option-F13
Underline	F8
Undo	F1
Windows	Shift-F3
WP Defaults	Option-F11

Appendix G
TROUBLESHOOTING TIPS

You may run into some problems from time to time when using WordPerfect. Many of these difficulties are discussed in the module pertaining to the subject. Others are discussed here, along with tips on how to solve the problem.

Problem	*Solution*
No picture	Check the screen controls. The brightness knob for the Macintosh Plus and SE is on the bottom left of the computer. If you have a Macintosh II with an external monitor, also check the cable connections between the computer and screen.
Cursor "locks" and will not move.	Make sure the cursor is locked by pressing the cursor keys repeatedly and by moving the mouse. If you are using the Macintosh in conjunction with electronic mail software, for example, the system might be temporarily hung up by an incoming message. If you are sure the system is hung up, turn the Macintosh off, then back on again. You can lose everything you have not saved, so it is recommended that you both save your data often and that you use the Backup feature discussed in Appendix A.
Text "jumps" unexpectedly and random characters appear on the screen.	Move the cursor keys repeatedly. Press Enter, Enter, Up Arrow, then Enter, Enter, Down Arrow to rewrite the screen.
When resaving a document, the message "Reference Number Error" appears on screen.	Use the Save As command to resave the document.
Printer does not operate.	Check to make sure cables are properly connected. Then make sure the printer is "on-line." Make sure the printer has paper. Make sure you have selected the printer from the Chooser. You can also turn the printer off and on again.

Appendix H
WORKING WITH GRAPHICS

It is very easy to import graphics into WordPerfect and to incorporate them into a document. WordPerfect lets you paste the graphic anywhere you want into a document and then to resize the graphic to fit your needs. To do this, create a graphic using a graphics program like Cricket Graph, a paint program like MacPaint, or a presentation graphics program like Microsoft PowerPoint. Use the Copy or Cut command to put a copy of the image into the Clipboard. If you have MultiFinder and enough memory to use it, click on the program icon to return to the Finder. If you do not, quit the program. Start WordPerfect and open the document you want to incorporate the graphic into. Move the cursor where you want the graphic to be and press Cmd-V to paste it into the document.

Resizing A Graphic To resize a graphic, move the mouse pointer anywhere in the graphic and click.

WordPerfect puts a box around the graphic and includes three *handles* on it. Using the mouse, drag any of the handles to change the size of the graphic. This may distort the graphic somewhat, so experiment with the size. Then click anywhere outside the graphic to remove the handles.

Appendix I

SPELLER UTILITY

The operation of WordPerfect's spell checking operation is described in Module 38. This appendix describes the Speller Utility, which lets you add or delete words from the Speller dictionary, create new dictionaries, check the location of a word (which dictionary it is in), and look up words. To use the Speller Utility, open the WordPerfect folder in the Applications folder and double click on the Speller Utility. Momentarily, the following screen appears:

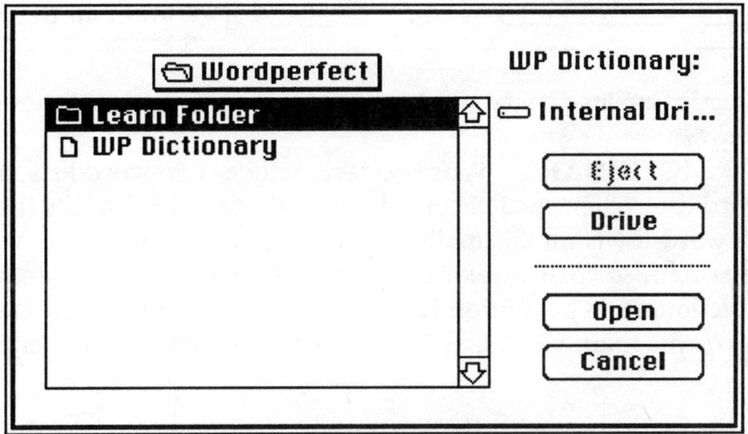

Double click on the dictionary of your choice. The default dictionary is WP Dictionary.

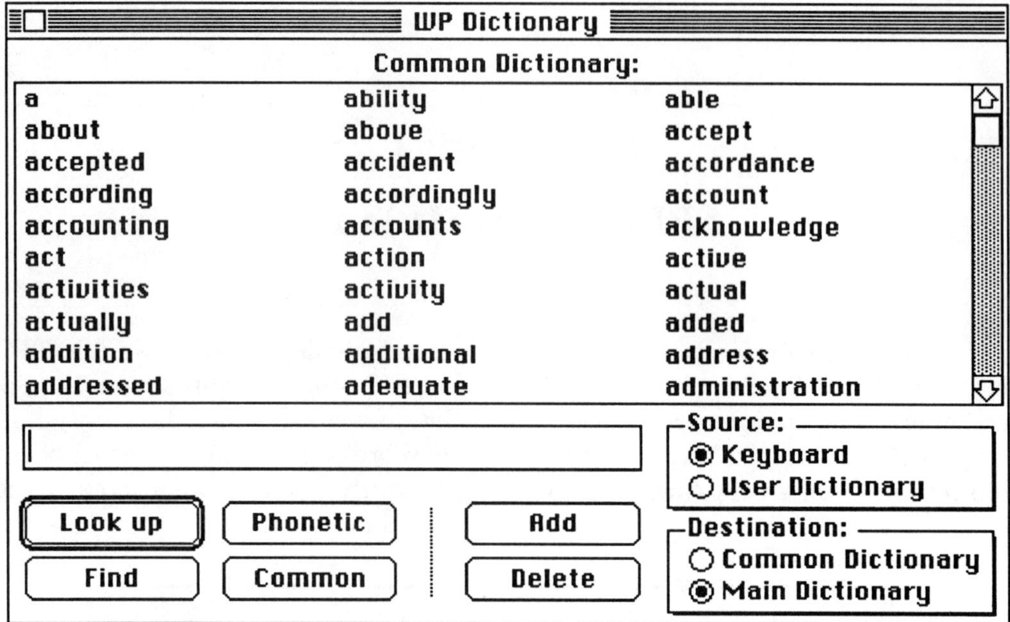

This is WordPerfect's Speller Utility. A description of each option follows.

ADD WORDS TO DICTIONARY WordPerfect includes two word lists, a common word list and a main word list. When spell checking, WordPerfect first checks the common word list. The common word list is much smaller than the main word list, but it includes words that are used more often, so spell checking is faster. If the word is not found, WordPerfect checks the main dictionary. This option lets you add words to the dictionary in either the common word list or the main word list. You can enter words from either the keyboard or a file.

To add words to the dictionary with the keyboard, make sure Keyboard is selected in the Source box. Click on the Destination box of your choice. Then type a word and click Add to add it to the dictionary. To add words to the dictionary from a previously created file, make sure User Dictionary is selected from the Source box. Click on the Destination box of your choice. Then click Add and double click on the file you want to add to the User Dictionary file.

When you have finished, click on Save from the File menu. Then press Return to save the changes you just made.

DELETE WORDS FROM DICTIONARY This option lets you delete words from either the common word list or the main word list. You can erase individual words or entire files from the dictionary.

To delete words from the dictionary with the keyboard, make sure Keyboard is selected in the Source box and the proper destination box is selected. Then type a word and click Delete to delete it from the dictionary. To delete words from the dictionary from a previously created file, make sure User Dictionary is selected from the Source box. Then click Delete and double click on the file you want to delete from the User Dictionary file.

To delete words with the mouse, highlight the word or words you want to delete by either clicking on them once or shift-clicking on them to delete multiple words. Then click Delete.

When you have finished, click on Save from the File menu. Then press Return to save the changes you just made.

LOOK UP This option works the same as the Look Up option described in Module 38. It lets you look up words that match a pattern. For example, typing re*l lists all the words beginning with "re" and ending with "l." Typing re?l lists all the four-letter words beginning with "re" and ending with "l."

To use the Look Up feature, type a word or word pattern from the Speller Utility dialog box. Then click on Look Up.

PHONETIC LOOK UP This feature is similar to the Phonetic Look Up feature described in Module 38. Like the Look Up feature, it lets you select words that match a word pattern. But it lets you find words that sound like other words. For example, to find which words sound like the word real, type real and click on Phonetic Look Up.

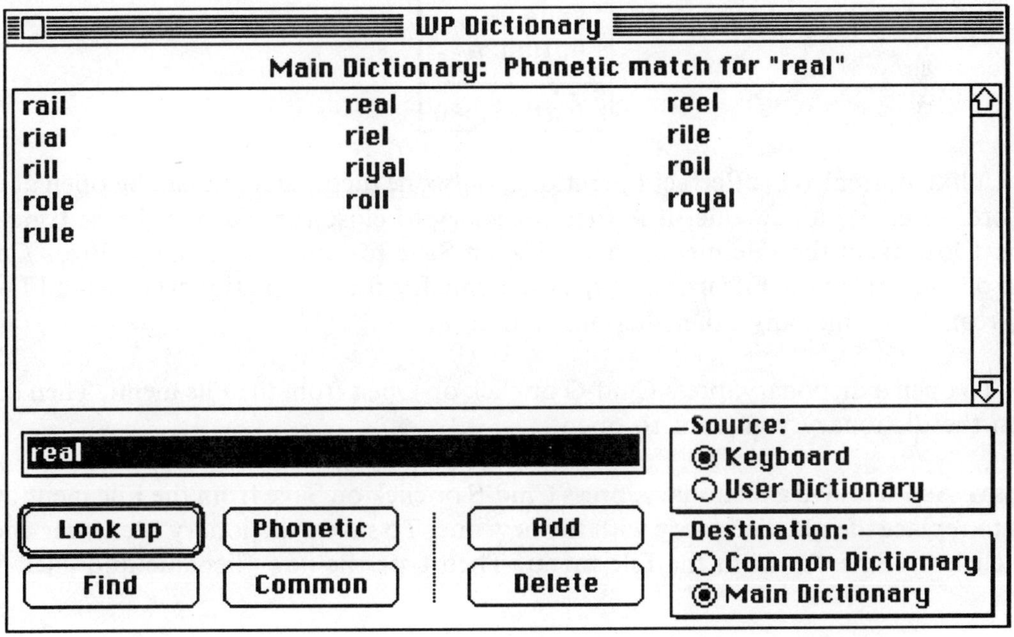

WP Dictionary

Main Dictionary: Phonetic match for "real"

rail	real	reel
rial	riel	rile
rill	riyal	roil
role	roll	royal
rule		

real

Look up | Phonetic | Add
Find | Common | Delete

Source: Keyboard / User Dictionary

Destination: Common Dictionary / Main Dictionary

FIND To see if a word is listed in the common or main word list, type the word and click Find.

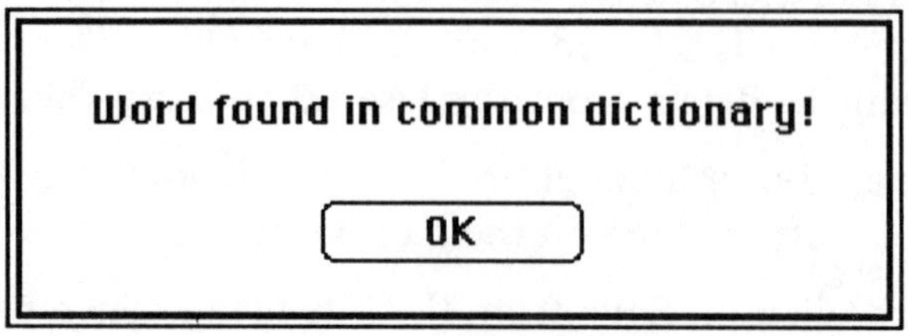

Click OK.

COMMON WordPerfect normally shows you the words in the main word list. To display the words in the common word list, click on Common.

USING THE FILE MENU The File menu works much like the File menu in other WordPerfect documents. You can open dictionaries, close them, save them, save them as new files, create new ones, and optimize them (make them run faster).

File
New ⌘N
Open... ⌘O
Close ⌘K
Save ⌘S
Save as...
Optimize
Quit ⌘Q

New Unlike normal WordPerfect operations, only one dictionary file can be open at once. Therefore, to create a new one, it is first necessary to close the old one. Press Cmd-K or click on Close from the File menu, then click on Save to save any changes. Press Cmd-N or click on New from the File menu. Type the name for the new dictionary, then add words to it. Treat it just like any other dictionary file.

Open To open a dictionary, press Cmd-O or click on Open from the File menu. Then double click on the dictionary you want to open.

Save/Save As To save a dictionary, press Cmd-S or click on Save from the File menu. Click on Yes to replace the old dictionary with the new one. To save a dictionary file under another name, click on Save As from the File menu. Then type the new filename and click Save.

Optimize Optimizing a dictionary makes it run faster. It is advisable to do this any time you make several changes to a dictionary file. To optimize a dictionary, click on Optimize or press Cmd-0.

Quit When you have finished using the dictionary, click on Quit from the File menu or press Cmd-Q. WordPerfect prompts you to save any necessary changes.

CONVERTING OTHER DICTIONARIES FOR USE IN WORDPERFECT If you have used a dictionary with another software program, it is relatively easy to convert it for use in WordPerfect. To do this, start WordPerfect, then press Cmd-L or F5 or click on File Management from the File menu. Select the dictionary file you want to use with WordPerfect and click on File/Folder Info or press Cmd-7.

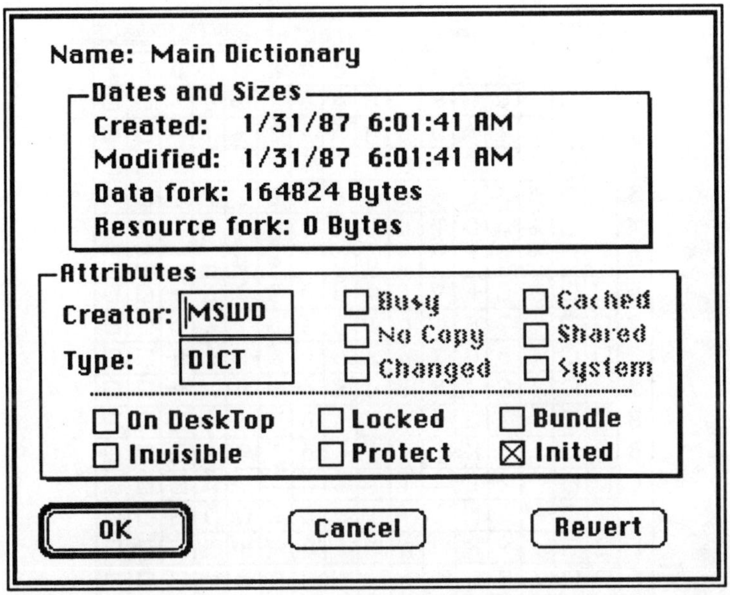

Name: Main Dictionary

Dates and Sizes
Created: 1/31/87 6:01:41 AM
Modified: 1/31/87 6:01:41 AM
Data fork: 164824 Bytes
Resource fork: 0 Bytes

Attributes
Creator: MSWD
Type: DICT
☐ Busy ☐ Cached
☐ No Copy ☐ Shared
☐ Changed ☐ System
☐ On DeskTop ☐ Locked ☐ Bundle
☐ Invisible ☐ Protect ☒ Inited

OK Cancel Revert

Highlight the contents of the Creator text box and type SSIU. Press Tab and type WPSP in the Type text box. Then click OK or press Return. Click Cancel to leave the File Management menu.

Appendix J

INSERT LITERAL

WordPerfect's Insert Literal command lets you insert any character that your font can produce into your document. To do this, press Cmd-I or Option-F15, or select Insert Literal from the Edit menu. With Geneva as the selected font, the following screen appears:

Select Character

	0	1	2	3	4	5	6	7	8	9	A	B	C	D	E	F
0		□		0	@	P	`	p	Ä	ê	†	∞	¿	–	□	□
1	□	□	!	1	A	Q	a	q	Å	ë	°	±	¡	—	□	□
2		□	"	2	B	R	b	r	Ç	í	¢	≤	¬	“	□	□
3		□	#	3	C	S	c	s	É	ì	£	≥	√	”	□	□
4		□	$	4	D	T	d	t	Ñ	î	§	¥	ƒ	‘	□	□
5		□	%	5	E	U	e	u	Ö	ï	•	µ	≈	’	□	□
6	□	□	&	6	F	V	f	v	Ü	ñ	¶	∂	∆	÷	□	□
7	□	□	'	7	G	W	g	w	á	ó	ß	Σ	«	◊	□	□
8	□	□	(	8	H	X	h	x	à	ò	®	Π	»	ÿ	□	□
9		□	)	9	I	Y	i	y	â	ô	©	π	…	[illegible]	□	□
A	⬚	□	*	:	J	Z	j	z	ä	ö	™	∫		□	□	□
B	⬚	□	+	;	K	[	k	{	ã	õ	´	ª	À	□	□	□
C	⬚	□	,	<	L	\	l	|	å	ú	¨	º	Ã	□	□	□
D		□	-	=	M	]	m	}	ç	ù	≠	Ω	Õ	□	□	□
E	□	□	.	>	N	^	n	~	é	û	Æ	æ	Œ	□	□	□
F	□	□	/	?	O	_	o		è	ü	Ø	ø	œ	□	□	□

With Times as the selected font, the following screen appears:

Select Character

	0	1	2	3	4	5	6	7	8	9	A	B	C	D	E	F
0		]		0	@	P	`	p	Ä	ê	†	∞	¿	–	‡	
1	]	]	!	1	A	Q	a	q	Å	ë	°	±	¡	—	·	Ò
2	]	]	"	2	B	R	b	r	Ç	í	¢	≤	¬	“	‚	Ú
3	]	]	#	3	C	S	c	s	É	ì	£	≥	√	”	„	Û
4	]	]	$	4	D	T	d	t	Ñ	î	§	¥	ƒ	‘	‰	Ù
5	]	]	%	5	E	U	e	u	Ö	ï	•	µ	≈	’	Â	ı
6	]	]	&	6	F	V	f	v	Ü	ñ	¶	∂	∆	÷	Ê	ˆ
7	]	]	'	7	G	W	g	w	á	ó	ß	∑	«	◊	Á	˜
8	]	]	(	8	H	X	h	x	à	ò	®	∏	»	ÿ	Ë	¯
9		]	)	9	I	Y	i	y	â	ô	©	π	…	Ÿ	È	˘
A	;	]	*	:	J	Z	j	z	ä	ö	™	∫		⁄	Í	˙
B	;	]	+	;	K	[	k	{	ã	õ	´	ª	À	¤	Î	˚
C	;	]	,	<	L	\	l	|	å	ú	¨	º	Ã	‹	Ï	¸
D		]	-	=	M	]	m	}	ç	ù	≠	Ω	Õ	›	Ì	˝
E	]	]	.	>	N	^	n	~	é	û	Æ	æ	Œ	ﬁ	Ó	˛
F	]	]	/	?	O	_	o	]	è	ü	Ø	ø	œ	ﬂ	Ô	ˇ

Click on the character you want to insert into the text. WordPerfect inserts it at the current cursor location. Change fonts to experiment with the variety of characters you can insert into your document.

Appendix K
WORDPERFECT COMMAND LIST

Function	*Menu Location/Keystroke*
Alignment Character	Format, Line Format/Cmd-4, 3
Append	Edit, Append/Shift-F13
Append to Clipboard (Select On)	Edit, Append/Cmd-A,1
Append to File (Select On)	Edit, Append/Cmd-A,2
Backup Options	File, WP Defaults
Backward Search	Search/Cmd-B
Binding Width	Format, Page Format/Cmd-2,1
Block Protect (Select On)	Format, Page Format/Cmd-2,6
Bold	Font, Style/Cmd-Shift-B/F6
Cancel	Cmd-Period
Hyphenation Cancellation	Cmd-Period
Printing Cancellation	Cmd-Period
Capitalization	Caps Lock
Case Conversion (Select On)	Edit, Mouse Only
Center	Format, Line Format/Cmd-Shift-C/Shift-F6
Center Page Top to Bottom	Format, Page Format/Cmd-2,1
Change Dictionary	Special, Spell/Cmd-E,5
Characters	Format/Cmd-5/Shift-F1
Close Document	File/Cmd-K/Cmd-F11
Clipboard, Show	Windows
Codes	Edit/Cmd-7
Codes, Show	Edit/Cmd-7/Option-F3
Codes, Hide	Edit/Cmd-7
Colors	Special, Screen
Column, Copy	Edit, Select/Cmd-6, 5, Cmd-C
Column, Cut	Edit, Select/Cmd-6, 5, Cmd-X
Column Options	Format, Columns/Cmd-1, 2/Option-F7
Columns On	Format, Columns/Cmd-Shift-K/Cmd-F12
Columns, Text	Format, Columns/Cmd-1, 2
Conditional End of Page	Format, Page/Cmd-2, 5
Copy (Select On)	File/Cmd-C/F14
Copy File	File, File Management/Cmd-L, Cmd-4
Cursor Movement (All cursor movement with numeric keypad)	
Beginning of Text	Enter, Left Arrow

Function	Menu Location/Keystroke
Beginning of Line (Codes)	Enter, Enter, Enter, Left Arrow
Beginning of Line (Text)	Enter, Left Arrow
End of Line	Enter, Right Arrow
End of Text	1
Go To	Search/Cmd-G
Page Down	3
Page Up	9
Screen Left	Enter, Left Arrow
Screen Right	Enter, Right Arrow
Screen Down	+
Screen Up	–
Word Left	Cmd-4
Word Right	Cmd-6
Cut	Edit/Cmd-X/F13
Cycle Windows	Windows/Cmd-W
Date/Time	Special/Cmd-D/Shift-F5
Date (Merge Codes)	Special, Merge Codes/Cmd-8, D
Date Format	Special, Date/Cmd-D, 3
Insert Function	Special, Date/Cmd-Shift-D
Insert Text	Special, Date/Cmd-D, 1
Delete	
Del, Backspace, decimal point	Cmd keys
Delete to End of Line	Cmd-1
Delete to End of Page	Cmd-3
Delete File	File, File Management/Cmd-L, Cmd-6
Delete Folder	File, File Management/Cmd-L, Cmd-6
Delete Left	Delete (Backspace)
Delete Right	Del, decimal point on numeric keypad
Delete Word	Cmd-Del
Endnote	Special, Footnote/Cmd-9
Endnote Creation	Special, Footnotes/Cmd-9, 5
Endnote Editing	Special, Footnotes/Cmd-9, 6
Endnote Options	Special, Footnotes/Cmd-9, 4
Endnote Renumbering	Special, Footnotes/Cmd-9, 3
Enter Key	Enter, 5 or 7 (on numeric keypad)
Enter Key Mapping	Apple Menu, WP Help/Cmd-?
File Management	File/Cmd-L
File Types	File, File Management/Cmd-L, Cmd-7
File Information	File, File Management/Cmd-L, Cmd-7
Folder Creation	File, File Management/Cmd-L, Cmd-8
Folder Information	File, File Management/Cmd-L, Cmd-7
Flush Right	Format, Line/Cmd-Shift-F/Option-F6
Fonts	Font
Footers	Format, Page/Cmd-Shift-H
Footnote	Special, Footnote/Cmd-9/Cmd-F7
Footnote Creation	Special, Footnotes/Cmd-9, 1
Footnote Editing	Special, Footnotes/Cmd-9, 2

Function	Menu Location/Keystroke
Footnote Options	Special, Footnotes/Cmd-9, 4
Footnote Renumbering	Special, Footnotes/Cmd-9, 3
Full Window	Cmd-Shift-Z
Generate	Special, Mark Text/Cmd-Shift-G
Generate Index	Special, Mark Text/Cmd-Shift-G
Generate List	Special, Mark Text/Cmd-Shift-G
Generate Table of Contents	Special, Mark Text/Cmd-Shift-G
Go To	Search/Cmd-G/Cmd-F15
Hard Page	Cmd-Return
Hard Return	Return
Headers	Format, Page Format/Cmd-Shift-H
Help	Apple Menu/Cmd-?/F3
Home	Home
Hyphen, Required	-
Hyphen, Soft	Cmd--
Hyphenation On/Off	Format, Line Format/Cmd-4, 4
Hyphenation, Auto Aided	Format, Line Format/Cmd-4, 4
Hyphenation, Automatic	Format, Line Format/Cmd-4, 4
Hyphenation Cancellation	Cmd-Period
H-Zone (Ruler)	Cmd-R
Indent	Format, Paragraph Format/Cmd-Shift-T/F4
Indent, Left and Right	Format, Paragraph Format/Cmd-Shift-L/Shift-F4
Index Generation	Special, Mark Text/Cmd-Shift-G
Index Marking (Select On)	Special, Mark Text/Cmd-J, 3
Insert	Ins
Insert Literal	Edit/Cmd-I/Option-F15
Italics	Font, Style/Cmd-Shift-I
Justification On/Off (Ruler)	Cmd-R
Display Justification	Special, Screen/Cmd-Shift-J
Kerning	Format, Line Format/Cmd-4, 6
Leading	Format, Line/Cmd-4, 5
Left Margin Release (Ruler)	Cmd-R
Line Format	Format/Cmd-4/Shift-F8
Line Height	Format, Line Format/Cmd-4, 5
Line Spacing	Format, Line Format/Cmd-4, 5
Lines Per Inch	Format, Line Format/Cmd-4, 5
List Files	File, File Management/F5
List Generation	Special, Mark Text, Cmd-Shift-G/Shift-F15
List Marking (Select on)	Special, Mark Text, Cmd-J, 1
Look at a File	File, File Management/Cmd-L, Cmd-3
Look at a Folder	File, File Management/Cmd-L, Cmd-3
Macro	Special/Cmd-M/Shift-F14
Macro Chaining	Special, Macro/Cmd-M,3
Macro Definition	Special, Macro/Cmd-Shift-M/Cmd-F10
Macro Delay	Special, Macro/Cmd-M, 4
Macro Execution	Special, Macro/Cmd-Shift-X/Option-F10
Macro Input	Special, Macro/Cmd-M, 5

Function	*Menu Location/Keystroke*
Pause Macro	Special, Macro/Cmd-M, 6
Margin Release	Shift-Tab
Margins (Page)	Format, Page Format/Cmd-2, 1
Margins (Ruler)	Cmd-R
Mark Text	Special/Cmd-J/Option-F5
Merge	Special/Cmd-F9
Merge Codes	Special/Cmd-8/Option-F9
Invoke Macro	Special, Merge Codes/Cmd-8, G
Merge Codes From Keyboard	Special, Merge Codes/Cmd-8, C
Merge End of Field	Special, Merge Codes/Cmd-Shift-R/F9
Merge End of Record	Special, Merge Codes/Cmd-Shift-E/Shift-F9
New Primary File	Special, Merge Codes/Cmd-8, P
New Secondary File	Special, Merge Codes/Cmd-8, S
Next Record	Special, Merge Codes/Cmd-8, Q
Retrieve Field	Special, Merge Codes/Cmd-8, F
Stop Merge	Cmd-.
Stop Merge	Special, Merge Codes/Cmd-Shift-Q
To Printer	Special, Merge Codes/Cmd-8, T
Transfer Codes	Special, Merge Codes/Cmd-8, V
Update Screen	Special, Merge Codes/Cmd-8, U
Minus Sign	Enter, –
New File	Edit/Cmd-N/F11
New Page Number	Format, Page Numbers/Cmd-2, 2
New Page	Cmd-Return
Number of Copies	Shift-F7
Open File	Edit/Cmd-O/Cmd-F5
Open File (File Management)	Edit, File Management/Cmd-L
Outline (Character Style)	Font, Style/Cmd-Shift-O
Outline (Organize Text)	Format, Paragraph/Cmd-Shift-Y/Option-F12
Overstrike	Font, Style/Cmd-Shift-V
Page Format	Format, Page/Cmd-2/Option-F8
Page Layout	Format, Page/Cmd-2, 1
Page Number Column Positions	Ruler/Cmd-R
Page Number Positions	Format, Page/Cmd-2,2
Page Preview	File, Print Options/Cmd-Shift-P/Option-F14
Page Size	File, Print Options
Page Setup	File, Print Options/Cmd-F8
Page Up	PgUp
Paragraph Format	Format/Cmd-3/Shift-F12
Paragraph Number Definition	Format, Paragraph/Cmd-3, 3
Paragraph Numbers	Format, Paragraph/Cmd-3, 2
Password Protection	File, Save As
Paste	Edit/Cmd-V/F15
Plain Text	Font, Style/Cmd-Y, 1
Postscript Commands	File, Print Options
Print	File/Cmd-P/Shift-F7
Print (File Management)	File, File Management/Cmd-L, Cmd-2

Function	*Menu Location/Keystroke*
Print Options	File/Cmd-F14
Print Preview	File, Print Options/Cmd-Shift-P/Option-F14
Print Selection (Select On)	File, Print/Cmd-P
Quit	Edit/Cmd-Q/F7
Redline Text	Font, Style/Cmd-Y, B
Remove Redline	Special, Mark Text/Cmd-J, 4
Rename File (File Management)	File, File Management/Cmd-L, Cmd-5
Rename Folder (File Management)	File, File Management/Cmd-L, Cmd-5
Replace	Search/Cmd-H
Required Space	Option-Space Bar
Retrieve	File/Shift-F10
Retrieve File (File Management)	File, File Management/Cmd-L, Cmd-1
Return	Return
Right Margin (Ruler)	Cmd-R
Ruler, Show	Cmd-R/F12
Ruler, Hide	Cmd-R
Save Document	File/Cmd-S/F10
Save As	File/Shift-F11
Save Copy As	File
Screen	Special, Screen/Cmd-F3
Screen Down	+ (Numeric Keypad)
Screen Up	– (Numeric Keypad)
Search Forward	Search/Cmd-F/F2
Search Backward	Search/Cmd-B/Shift-F2
Search & Replace	Search/Cmd-H/Option-F2
Select	Edit/Cmd-6/Option-F4
Select All	Edit, Select/Cmd-Shift-A
Select Column	Edit, Select/Cmd-6, 5
Select On	Edit, Select/Cmd-Shift-N
Select Page	Edit, Select/Cmd-6, 4
Select Paragraph	Edit, Select/Cmd-6, 3
Select Sentence	Edit, Select/Cmd-6, 2
Shadow	Font, Style/Cmd-Shift-S
Show Clipboard	Windows/Cmd-F13
Soft Hyphen	Cmd--
Spacing	Format, Line/Cmd-4, 5
Spell Checking	Special/Cmd-E/Cmd-F2
Spell Check Document	Special, Spell/Cmd-Shift-W
Spell Check Page	Special, Spell/Cmd-E, 3
Spell Check Selection (Select On)	Special, Spell/Cmd-E, 2
Strikeout Text (Select On)	Font, Style/Cmd-Y, A
Remove Strikeout	Special, Mark Text/Cmd-J, 4
Style	Font/Cmd-Y
Subscript	Font, Style/Cmd-Y, 8
Superscript	Font, Style/Cmd-Y, 7
Suppress Page Format	Format, Page/Cmd-2, 3
Tab	Tab

Function	*Menu Location/Keystroke*
Tab Align	Cmd-Tab/Cmd-F6
Tab Set	Format, Line/Cmd-4, 3
Tab Set (Ruler)	Format/Cmd-R
Table of Contents Definition	Special, Define Lists
Table of Contents Generation	Special, Mark Text/Cmd-J, 2
Table of Contents Marking (Select On)	Special, Mark Text/Cmd-J, 2
Tabs	Format, Line/Cmd-4, 3
Text Files	File, File Management/Cmd-L
Thesaurus	Special/Cmd-T/Option-F1
Time (Date)	Special, Date/Cmd-D
Transfer	File/Cmd-F1
Typeover Mode	0 (Number Pad)
Undelete	Edit/Cmd-U/Option-F13
Underline	Font, Style/Cmd-Shift-U/F8
Underline Style	Format, Characters/Cmd-5
Undo	File/Cmd-Z/F1
Widows and Orphans	Format, Page/Cmd-2, 7
Windows	Windows/Shift-F3
Cycle Windows	Windows/Cmd-W
Word Count	Special, Spell/Cmd-E, 6
Word Left	Ctrl-Left Arrow
Word Right	Ctrl-Right Arrow
Word Search (File Management)	File, File Management/Cmd-L, Cmd-9
WP Defaults	File/Option-F11

Appendix L
WORDPERFECT EXERCISES

1. About This Book
   a. What is word processing software and what do you think it will do for you?
   b. What is each module in this book centered around? Why do you think this structure was chosen?
   c. What is the logic behind the order of the modules presented in the Table of Contents?
   d. Who is the audience?

2. WordPerfect System Overview
   a. Why do you need to make working copies of diskettes? Backup copies?
   b. The WordPerfect program collection is made up of what individual diskettes?
   c. Can you identify the steps in loading the WordPerfect program into your computer?
   d. How does creating a new WordPerfect document differ from editing an existing document?

3. A Sample Session with WordPerfect Macintosh
   a. How are key sequences indicated in this book?
   b. What are function keys? How do they differ from standard typing keys in what they do for you?
   c. What is the function of the mouse? How does it help you?

4. Cancel, Undo, Undelete
   a. What are the two main functions of the Cancel key?
   b. Contrast Cancel, Undo, and Undelete.

5. Case Conversion
   a. When a block is converted to all lowercase text, is all text converted to lowercase or are some words or letters left uppercase? Is so, which ones?
   b. Name some applications where case conversion is useful.

6. Center
   a. How does the Center function compare with centering text on a typewriter?
   b. Name three uses for the Center command.

7. Codes
   a. Describe the Codes feature.
   b. How do you delete codes?

8. Columns
   a. What is the difference between newspaper style and parallel style columns? What are some applications for each style?
   b. How many columns can you fit on a page?
   c. Name three applications for columnar text.

9. Copy, Cut, and Paste
   a. What is the purpose of the Copy command? Contrast the use for Copy and Cut.
   b. Name two ways to copy text.
   c. How do you copy columns of text?

10. Cursor Movement
    a. How do you send the cursor to the top of a document? page?
    b. How do you send the cursor to the beginning of the current line?
    c. What role does the mouse play in cursor control?

11. Date/Time
    a. Name three applications for the Date function.
    b. What is the purpose of the Insert Tab option in the Date Format dialog box?

12. Delete
    a. Name three ways you can delete text.
    b. What is the chief purpose of deleting text?
    c. In what direction does the Delete key (or Backspace key) delete text? How many characters are deleted each time the key is pressed?

13. Escape
    a. What is the default repeat value?
    b. How do you change the default value temporarily? permanently?
    c. Name five uses for the repeat value.

14. File Management
    a. Contrast a computerized file and one kept in a filing cabinet.
    b. What is the difference between opening and retrieving a file?
    c. What is the purpose of the File/Folder Info feature?

15. Flush Right
    a. Name three uses for the Flush Right key.
    b. Name two ways to create text that is flush right.

16. Font
    a. Is 10-point New Century Schoolbook Bold a different font than 10-point New Century Schoolbook Italic? Why or why not?
    b. What is the purpose of the Font feature? When is it useful to change fonts?

17. Footnotes and Endnotes
    a. What is the difference between footnotes and endnotes?
    b. How do you edit footnotes?
    c. How do you delete footnotes?

18. Go To
    a. How is the Go To command used in regular text? columns? blocks of text?
    b. What is the difference between using the Go To command in regular text and using it in columns?

19. Headers and Footers
    a. What is the purpose of a header? footer?
    b. What kinds of information does a header or footer contain?
    c. How many headers and footers can you have per page?

20. Help
    a. How do you get help when editing a document?
    b. Why is the Help function called "on-line" help?
    c. What is Enter Key Mapping?

21. Indent
    a. What is the difference between Tab and Indent?
    b. How do you turn Indent off?
    c. What is Left/Right Indent?

22. Insert
    a. What is the chief purpose of the Insert mode?
    b. How do you turn on the Insert mode? Typeover mode?

23. Line Format
    a. What is kerning?
    b. What is the purpose of the Margin Release command?

24. Macros
    a. What are macros?
    b. How are macros used?
    c. What is macro chaining?

25. Mark Text: Index, List, Table of Contents
    a. How many lists can you create per document in WordPerfect?
    b. Where is the Table of Contents located in a document?
    c. What is the purpose of the Mark Text feature?

26. Merge Codes
    a. Describe the difference between merged documents and data files.
    b. Describe the difference between primary and secondary merge files.
    c. Describe the difference between a field and a record.

27. Outline
    a. What is the purpose of the Outline mode?
    b. How do you change the way outline numbers appear?
    c. How do you turn the Outline mode off?

28. Page Format
    a. Why would you want to center a page?
    b. What is the difference between a widow and an orphan? Why are these undesirable?

29. Paragraph Numbering
    a. What is the difference between the Paragraph Numbering feature and the Outline feature described in Module 27?
    b. How many levels of paragraph numbering are available?
    c. Name three applications for paragraph numbering.

30. Printing
    a. What three options are available for printing?
    b. What is the purpose of the Print Options feature?
    c. How does Print Preview help you?

31. Redline and Strikeout
    a. What is the difference between redline and strikeout?
    b. How do you remove the redline and strikeout markings from text?

32. Required Space
    a. What is the chief purpose of the Required Space feature?
    b. Name four applications for it.

33. Ruler
    a. Name six functions that can be changed through the Ruler.
    b. What icon do you click on to revert to original settings?

34. Save, Close, and Quit
    a. Why would you want to save text without quitting?
    b. What happens to unsaved text when you quit WordPerfect?

35. Screen/Windows
    a. Where is the Title Bar located on the screen?
    b. How does the Zoom Box work?
    c. What is the purpose of the Display Justification option?

36. Search and Replace
    a. What is the value of searching through text?
    b. How can you replace some instances of a word with a substitute but not others?

37. Select
    a. Name three ways to select text.
    b. How do you select all the text in a document?

38. Spell Checking
    a. Name the three types of Spell options available.
    b. What is the Look Up feature?
    c. What is the value of a word count?

39. Style
    a. What is a Style?
    b. How many fonts are available to you in WordPerfect?
    c. How do you change the appearance of text on the Status Line?

40. Subscripts and Superscripts
    a. What is the difference between a subscript and a superscript?
    b. How can you tell if on-screen text is superscripted? subscripted?

41. Thesaurus
    a. What is a headword?
    b. What is the value of an on-line thesaurus?

Index

Other Books from Wordware Publishing, Inc.

Artificial Intelligence
Artificial Ingelligence Programming Techniques in BASIC
Illustrated Turbo Prolog 2.0
Illustrated VP-Expert

Computer-Aided Drafting
Illustrated AutoCAD (Release 9)
Illustrated AutoCAD (Release 10)
Illustrated AutoSketch 1.04
Illustrated GenericCAD

Database Management
The DataFlex Developer's Handbook
Illustrated dBASE II (2nd Ed.)
Illustrated dBASE III Plus
Illustrated dBASE IV
Illustrated Paradox Volume I 1.2
Illustrated Paradox Volume II 1.2
Illustrated Paradox Volume II 2.0
Illustrated VP-Info 1.2
Illustrated VP-Info 1.4

Desktop Publishing
Desktop Publisher's Dictionary
Handbook of Desktop Publishing
Illustrated PageMaker 3.0
Illustrated Ready, Set, Go! 4.5 (Macintosh)
Illustrated Ventura 1.1
Illustrated Ventura 2.0

General Advanced Topics
The Complete Communications Handbook
Consulting Handbook for the High-Tech Professional
Illustrated Dac Easy Accounting 2.0
Illustrated Dac Easy Accounting 3.0
Illustrated Novell NetWare
Managing Your Megabytes

Programming Languages
Advanced Programming Techniques in Turbo Pascal
Illustrated C Programming (ANSI)
The FOCUS Developer's Handbook
From BASIC to 8086/8088 Assembly Language
Library of Turbo Pascal Programs
Illustrated PC/FOCUS
Illustrated QuickBASIC 4.0
Illustrated RM/COBOL
Illustrated Turbo Pascal 3.01

Programming Languages cont.
Illustrated Turbo Pascal 4.0
Illustrated Turbo Pascal 5.0

Spreadsheet/Integrated
Illustrated Framework II
Illustrated Framework III
Illustrated Lotus 1-2-3 2.01
Illustrated Microsoft Excel 2.01 (IBM)
Illustrated Microsoft Excel 1.5 (Macintosh)
Illustrated Multiplan 2.0
Illustrated Q & A
Illustrated Quattro
Illustrated Symphony 1.2

Systems and Operating Guides
Illustrated Microsoft Windows 2.0
Illustrated MS/PC-DOS 3.3
Illustrated MS/PC-DOS 4.0
Illustrated OS/2

Word Processing
Illustrated DisplayWrite 4
Illustrated Microsoft Word 5.0
Illustrated Sprint
Iiiustrated WordPerfect 1.0 (Macintosh)
Illustrated WordPerfect 4.2
Illustrated WordPerfect 5.0
Illustrated WordStar 3.3
Illustrated WordStar Professional (Rel. 4)
Illustrated WordStar Professional (Rel. 5)
The New WordStar Customizing Guide 4.0
WordPerfect: Advanced Applications Handbook
The WordStar Customizing Guide 3.3

Business-Professional Books
Business Emotions
How to Win Pageants
Innovation, Inc.
Investor Beware
MegaTraits
Occupying the Summit
Steps to Strategic Management

Regional
This Dog'll Hunt
100 Days in Texas — The Alamo Letters
Exploring the Alamo Legends
Wit and Wisdom
Forget the Alamo
Rainy Day Workbook, Texas Edition